FAMOUS SCOTS

BY THE SAME AUTHOR

Scots Proverbs and Rhymes

Moray Press (1948)
W & R Chambers (1962)
W & R Chambers (1970)
The Pinetree Press (1976)
Gordon Wright Publishing (1979)
Gordon Wright Publishing (1983)

Doric Spice

Blackford Press (1956)
The Pinetree Press (1960)

The Gowks of Moudieknowes
What is Education in Scotland
Macgregor's Mixture
Clan Gregor
Four Gates of Lothian
Greyfriars Bobby
Authenticated Facts relating
  to Greyfriars Bobby
Salt-sprayed Burgh
More Macgregor's Mixture

The Pinetree Press (1963)
Akros Publications (1970)
Gordon Wright Publishing (1976)
The Clan Gregor Society (1977)
Forbes Macgregor (1979)
The Ampersand (1980)

Forbes Macgregor (1980)
The Pinetree Press (1981)
Gordon Wright Publishing (1983)

Famous Scots

The Pride of a Small Nation

Forbes Macgregor

GORDON WRIGHT PUBLISHING
25 MAYFIELD ROAD, EDINBURGH EH9 2NQ
SCOTLAND

British Library Cataloguing in Publication Data

Macgregor, Forbes
  1. Scotland—Biography
  I. Title
  920'.0411   DA758

  ISBN 0-903065-47-9

Typeset by Jo Kennedy, Edinburgh
Printed and bound by Billing & Sons Ltd, Worcester

Contents

Introduction

Scotland is one of the smaller nations whose people have had an influence on the world out of all proportion to their numbers. In many fields of activity the lives of notable Scots, such as those we narrate in this book, should put the question of that influence beyond doubt. This is not to minimise the great contributions to human progress and happiness of the larger nations of the Old and New World, or of our partner England. But the phenomenon of a small nation's contributions of outstanding importance deserves notice and, if possible, some explanation.

Thomas Carlyle, as a young man, preached that 'the history of the world is but the biography of great men', and many philosophers have agreed with this. But the questions arise about the origins of these outstanding individuals, who their ancestors were, and what special qualities they had. Here we find that the most unlikely persons were progenitors of genius. For example, the great historian, Lord Macaulay, and a number of eminent Victorian relatives, were descended from Aulay MacAulay, a disreputable Highlander of the late sixteenth century. Many a famous son has achieved glory through the efforts of a father who got no credit for his work of love. History has shown that most of the splendid civilisations have been founded by barbarians whose sole virtues were in their stamina and aggressive energy.

Certain races of mankind have distinctive characters quite irrespective of morality. The most illustrious in the Classical World were the Greeks and Romans. Their racial origins were rather mixed, though allied in blood. Greek civilisation at its peak was famed for its grasp of the artistic and intellectual. Roman for order and organisation. But both originated in warring tribes.

We find the same pattern in the story of the Scots. The land now named Scotland was occupied at the end of the Dark Ages, about AD 800, by two totally different races, Celtic and Germanic. The Celts were in three small kingdoms; the Picts and Caledonians, a mixed confederacy, in the North-east; the Scots in the West Highlands and Islands; the Britons in the South-west and Cumbria. The Angles, a Germanic race, occupied the South-east of Scotland and North-east of England. Each spoke a different language. The Scots and Angles, and perhaps the Picts, were invaders, of the earlier centuries AD.

After about two centuries of countless inter-tribal battles, conquests and rebellions, these discordant elements were formed into one kingdom, taking its name from the dominant Scots, who imposed their language, Gaelic,

7

upon all except the Angles, who, in the region of Lothian, were allowed to keep their own language, laws and customs.

The Norman Conquest of England drove many Saxons into Scotland for safety. Amongst these was the princess Margaret, who married the Scots king, Malcolm Canmore. By him she bore six sons and set about the anglicising of Scotland. Weights, measures, money, style of church buildings and language were identical with England until the thirteenth century, except where Gaelic continued to be spoken, away from the influence of the court, where English and Norman French was used. Despite this, the Scots remained independent of England, by now under Anglo-Norman kings and queens.

The great crisis in Scottish history began with the death of Alexander III, one of the Scoto-Saxon Kings. On the death of the 'Maid of Norway' (the heiress) Edward I (nicknamed Longshanks, or *Malleus Scotorum*, the Hammer of the Scots), acted as regent of Scotland until a new ruler could be assigned. But he used his position to usurp the Scottish Kingdom and was opposed by the last native leader, William Wallace, a Strathclyde Briton. On Wallace's betrayal and execution as a 'traitor', the challenge to Edward was taken up by the Scoto-Norman, Robert Bruce, who successfully drove out the English.

The continued attempts of the English kings to add Scotland to the English Empire succeeded only in welding the racial elements into an indissoluble unit, though there were several attempts by traitors to undermine Scottish independence.

The four main races of Scotland, when finally united under one crown and parliament, each brought to the union its own inherent qualities. The aboriginal Scots of Dalriada, immigrants from Ireland, were reputed to be restless, pugnacious, fond of song and display. The Caledonians, the original tribes of Alba or Caledonia, who had defied the Romans, were shrewd, witty, athletic, able to endure hardship and much attached to land and family. The Picts who formed the alliance with the Caledonians were known as the practical Picts. The Britons were poetical, sociable, fond of drinking but inclined to be boastful and quarrelsome. The Angles were adventurous and hardy, rather taciturn and fond of solitude. These attributes are too general to be a sure guide and were often ascribed by prejudiced writers. Yet each tribe had a passion for liberty and strenuously resisted attempts to subdue them, never failing to give a good account of themselves on the battlefield. Once strongly united they adopted as their emblem the jagged Scotch thistle with the motto, *Nemo me impune lacessit*, freely translated, 'Wha daur meddle wi' me?'

During the Middle Ages and early modern times, the Scots travelled widely over Europe and were well-known in trade and in military and learned circles. Their reputed characteristic was expressed in a Latin phrase by a French Jesuit writer, André Rivet, of Poitou. We give the exact words because they are generally misquoted. *Scoticanae praesertim fervido ingenio ... et ad audendum prompto*. The particularly fiery Scottish nature ... eager for deeds of daring.

The French also had a vernacular proverb, based on their experience of the thousands of Scots, many of whom fought for France against the English invaders during the Hundred Years War. *Fier comme un Ecossais*, proud as a Scot.

However fiery was the original Scots character, it was not softened in the long wars waged by England to reduce Scotland to a province. The conflict lasted for three centuries with few respites, yet, despite domestic traitors and feuds between religious and partisan forces, it was as a proud and independent Kingdom that Scotland joined England under the Scots heir to Queen Elizabeth, James Stuart, VI and I. The Union of Crowns did not quite extinguish the old rivalry, nor was this ended by the Union of Parliaments a century later in 1707, but at least it lessened the old threat of mutual invasion and permitted both partners to pursue their wider destiny.

It could have been foreseen that the predominance of the larger partner would threaten the success of the Union and lead to the unremitting pressure by the English state to obliterate the Scottish identity. But it is a political curiosity that Scotland under three hundred years of such pressure still retains its own character and institutions, though regrettably deprived of any effective power over its own affairs.

Nevertheless a continual effort must be maintained to remind Scots and the world at large that Scotland has never given up the struggle for distinctive existence.

In recent years historians have been trying to explain the blaze of Scottish glory which astounded the world in the Age of Enlightenment; the Golden Age of the galaxy of philosophers, writers of all kinds, scientists, explorers, architects, engineers, inventors and statesmen, during the latter half of the eighteenth and early nineteenth centuries. It seemed like the last eruption of Scottish genius before the volcano became extinct.

Whatever may be agreed upon as the cause of that marvellous re-naissance, out-shining for half a century even the re-births of a like nature in England, Germany and France, it should not be considered alien to the known character of Scots. The elements had always been there from early mediaeval times, as can be exemplified from personal careers, and should not be attributed to the fruition of the political union with England.

Perhaps we could compare that brilliant eighteenth century outbreak to an actual fire where at first a single faggot, or even two or three, could only maintain a feeble flame, but when a score or more were combusted an intense conflagration would result. We may still witness an efflorescence of fireworks, intimating to the nations that modern Scotland, despite the present lethargy, can draw effectively upon its native intellectual and spiritual powers.

Although not despising physical prowess, the Scots above all prided themselves on intellectual strength which they fostered in a democratic educational system. During the Middle Ages the Church of Rome and its associated orders assumed responsibility for the education of able and ambitious youths up to their full capacity. A church career, entailing often a life of study and teaching, was usually aimed at. At the Reformation many such young men criticised the abuses within the Church and some of them helped to form the opposing body. The party of John Knox conceived an educational system which started, so to speak, at the grass-roots, by establishing parish and burgh schools, leading to courses at one of the universities already existing at St Andrews, Aberdeen and Glasgow (Edinburgh being founded in 1582). Students were much younger then, commencing at twelve to fourteen, for life was uncertain and usually short, and there was more urgency to begin a career. We need not be surprised at the eminence and responsibility attained by men in their early years.

For women in general in all countries there were few openings for careers other than marriage with its attendant hazards; none the less many Scots women were well educated in social arts and had command of several languages. A Spanish Ambassador to Scotland in 1497, Pedro de Ayala was surprised to find that the Scots ladies were undisputed mistresses in their own households. In a homely phrase 'they wore the breeks' and consequently ruled the roost, however powerful their husbands were in public life.

Arts and crafts had been fostered in the old church and monastic foundations and, as Christendom was one organised political unit (apart from the Byzantine and the Coptic Churches), skilled architects, gardeners, metallurgists and physicians and others had been introduced from the entire realm of the Church to instruct the natives. There was therefore no shortage of qualified workers to maintain the various guilds that controlled the metal workers, builders, carpenters, tanners, weavers, weaponry workers, ship-builders and multifarious mediaeval artificers.

If any activity lagged, it was probably farming, for 'John Up-a-land' was conservative, and unwilling to give up his time-honoured practices, which often produced famines. But by the efforts of several public-spirited men, agriculture underwent such a remarkable improvement, in common with England, in the eighteenth century that Scottish agriculture became world-famous.

Overseas the influence of Scots has been to a large extent responsible for the political and military establishment of powerful modern states, notably Germany, Russia, Sweden, Poland, and latterly the USA and South American countries. But to counteract these hawklike activities, Scots missionaries and administrators went as messengers of love and goodwill into so many benighted areas of the Old and New World that it was no exaggeration to state that they founded a Scottish Empire, for it was rediscovered, often redeemed from savagery, administered and improved by Scots, many of whom were of humble origin and were born in conditions little above those they encountered abroad.

In science and medicine the world owes many epoch-making discoveries to Scots, particularly of the Edinburgh School of Medicine, and to the scientific societies which were based in Edinburgh last century, especially in oceanography, geology and general biology.

In engineering, shipbuilding, commerce and all manner of industry, including pioneer work in motor-cars, Clydeside was for long pre-eminent in the world, both in invention and bulk of production.

In the graphic and plastic arts and in music, while the Scots cannot compete with Italy, Germany, the Netherlands and France, they have always been a musical nation, preferring melody to harmony and havé occasionally produced architects, painters, musicians and sculptors of first rank. But it is in literature and poetry that Scots share eminence with the supreme geniuses of other nations. Robert Burns is universally recognised as the poet of humanity, just as Sir Walter Scott is the novelist who inspired European and American romantic writers by being the first to bring the past to real flesh-and-blood existence.

Thomas Carlyle with his unusual and powerful prose provided a stimulus for nineteenth century English in Britain and America. David Hume, two centuries ago, undermined the philosophy of all the ages by his fresh approach to the study of the human intellect.

'Facts are chiels that winna ding', said Burns, meaning that they cannot be explained away. In this book, without being encyclopaedic, we present enough facts and interesting circumstances to convince any agnostic reader of the genius of that unique nation, the Scots. For those already converted to this opinion we present a goodly store of ammunition to maintain the battle. And for the enquiring stranger we trust this gallery of Scots will interest, inform and amuse for many a leisure hour.

Forbes Macgregor

War

In the Dark Ages of what is now Scotland, the tribes lived in a constant state of war, as the chronicles show. For example, the beginning of the record of one of the early Pictish kings, in the annals of AD 406 runs as follows: 'Drust, the son of Erp, lived a hundred years and fought a hundred battles. In the 29th year of his reign, Patrick, the holy bishop, came into Hibernia.'

That brief extract shows the peculiar nature of early mediaeval times in Scotland, as in most other parts of the disintegrating Europe, following the decay of the Roman power. Christian missionaries were trying to pacify the turbulent barbarians, but with mixed success. Even Columba, the Gaelic saint, had been personally responsible for a bloody battle in Ireland. As some kind of retribution he devoted the rest of his life to preaching Christianity amongst the Scots and Picts of Albany (i.e. Scotland). Another Irish saint, not nearly so well-known as Columba, was St Columban, who, a few years later than Columba, led a party of twelve monks to heathen Europe and founded two famous monasteries in Switzerland and Italy.

These men 'converted' whole tribes to Christianity, though this was often merely a political change, and the individuals remained in a state of savagery. The Catholic Church, to compel the warriors to observe a shorter working week, instituted a 'Truce of God'. This began each Friday, the day of the crucifixion, and ended on Monday, the day of the resurrection. But not all nominally Christian warriors kept to these limits. Alpin, the father of Kenneth MacAlpin, made his name odious to Christians because he attacked his Pictish enemies on Easter Friday, the holiest day in the calendar. Defeated not long after by his morally shocked enemies, he was beheaded as a mark of abhorrence, instead of being decently drowned, the usual form of Pictish execution.

The warlord of the Britons in the early sixth century was Arthur. The old Welsh records say he had the temper of an irritated bear. He ranged far and wide over Britain with his mounted commandos, and fought twelve battles, being himself slain in the last, at Camlan, in AD 537. Perhaps this was Camelon on the Forth near Stirling. Although his feats gave inspiration to the greatest poetic theme of the Middle Ages, the only historic basis for his existence is a brief entry in a monkish Easter chronicle of Strathclyde. In contemporary literature, he is only mentioned indirectly in a poem, *The Gododin*, by Aneirin, a British bard of the sixth century. Yet, for some strange reason, the English, who were his chief enemies, have claimed him, and tied his activities down to a corner of South-west England, despite the numerous place names in Southern Scotland bearing his name. For centuries historians have fought battles over Arthur's twelve battles, and no firm decision has been reached as to where they were fought, when they were fought, or against whom. Four of his battles have been traced with probability to the Loch Lomond area, where his only enemies could have been Scots or Picts, not Angles. We could claim Arthur as a 'Scottish' warrior, but of course, not as a Scot.

The Angles had many aggressive warrior kings which it would be tedious even to name, but when Northumbria was at the height of its power and had been converted by its native saint, Cuthbert, King Egfrith, son of Ossa, invaded Pictland and Strathclyde with a mighty host, penetrating as far north as Forfar in Strathmore. At Nectan's Mere or the Mire of Dunnichen he was met by the Pictish King Bruide MacBile in AD 685, and defeated much more completely than Edward II at Bannockburn six centuries later. The annals say, 'From that time the hope and valour of the English realm (Northumbria) began to decline and ever backward flow.' The Picts and Britons reclaimed much land earlier conquered by the Angles.

Mediaeval kings had to be warriors. If they were not, they usually earned a nickname for their lack of initiative. Every Scottish King worth his salt led his forces from the front, and quite a number died in conflict, and were buried in Iona, where a hundred assorted monarchs repose, including invaders. Macbeth, the last of the Scoto-Pictish kings, was a warrior. He did not assassinate Duncan, as Shakespeare makes out. He met Duncan in battle. Malcolm Canmore, despite his sanctified Saxon Queen Margaret, was a merciless enemy of the English, carrying off thousands of unhappy Anglian women and children to slavery in Scotland, so that 'not a house in the country was without an Anglian slave.'

It is only when mediaeval Scottish warriors take the field to defend their country that they begin to deserve individual notice.

Sir William Wallace (c. 1270-1305)

William Wallace was the son of an old established family of Strathclyde British origin. His father was Sir Malcolm Wallace of Elderslie in Renfrewshire. As we say in the chapter on Poets, we have to rely on the long epic *Wallace*, by Harry the Minstrel, for the events of his short career, and much of his poem, being traditional, is unreliable. The more veracious account, in Latin, by Wallace's friend John Blair, from which Harry got his story, perished long ago.

In his boyhood Wallace lived with his uncle, a parson in Stirlingshire. He was educated at Dundee where he and Blair were friends. While a student there, after the death of Alexander III, when many English officials were in Scotland, he killed a young Englishman named Selby, who had insulted him. For this he was outlawed.

Another popular account says that it was because of a tumult in Lanark that Wallace fell out with the English.

At any rate he was joined in rebellion by several patriots of rank similar to his own, Sir Andrew Moray, Sir John de Graham, Douglas le Hardi, and also Wishart, bishop of Glasgow. These, with an ever-increasing following, attacked the unpopular English judge Ormsby, who had the impudence to hold a court at Perth. Then followed such savage acts as the burning of the Barns of Ayr, in revenge for the slaughter of Sir Ranald Crawford, Wallace's uncle.

On Edward I sending a strong force into Scotland in 1297, Wallace's friends, all except Sir Andrew Moray, left him and signed a treaty of fealty to Edward, the text of which still exists, with the first mention of Wallace's name. Deserted by the noblemen, Wallace gathered a huge army of commoners in the Highlands and the North-east. Soon he had captured all the fortresses north of the Forth. When besieging Dundee Castle, news came of a large English force coming to meet him.

He marched rapidly to Stirling and from the Abbey Craig, where his monument now stands, he watched the English crossing the bridge. When half the army had crossed, Wallace attacked furiously. The English were routed and pursued by horse as far as Berwick. Sir Andrew Moray was slain here.

This victory was followed by a raid into England, and Wallace was elected Guardian of Scotland, in which he showed himself an efficient administrator, despite the opposition of the nobles.

Edward now left France and gathered a great army to suppress Wallace. The forces clashed near Falkirk where after a stern battle the Scots were defeated, Sir John Graham and Sir John Stewart being slain, to Wallace's great grief. A memorial to these heroes may be seen in Falkirk Churchyard.

Wallace retreated, resigned the guardianship, and carried on a guerilla war. His history is little known between 1298 and 1304, but several historical documents exist which reveal that Wallace was for some time at the court of Philip IV of France (the Fair), trying to obtain help against Edward, and also conducting embassies to other countries.

But traitors within Scotland were busy. In the winter of 1303-1304 the Scottish nobles made their peace with Edward and submitted to doing homage for their lands. A large reward was offered for Wallace, dead or alive, and unlike the Highlanders after Culloden, in a similar situation, the Lowlanders produced a scoundrel to earn the Judas silver. This was Sir John Menteith. Wallace was captured at Robroyston near Glasgow, detained in Dumbarton Castle and taken under strong guard to London. With indecent haste he was tried and condemned as a traitor, by a power to whom he had never owed fealty. Edward stayed away from the trial, the only trace of decency in a king whom Dante, of all people, regarded as 'the good King Edward who has done great things.' Wallace was hanged, drawn and quartered, at Smithfield, the meat market, with the usual barbarity, and his four quarters sent to be publicly exposed at Lanark, Perth, Stirling and Edinburgh as a warning to Scots who resisted Edward. Needless to say, what might have subdued a spiritless nation had the extremely opposite effect on the Scots, as the next several centuries were to prove.

Robert Bruce
(The Bruce, or Robert I, King of Scotland) *(1274-1329)*

This old Scottish family, like many others, is of French origin. The family name comes from a small town, Bruis, near Cherbourg. The first Robert de

Brus came over with William the Conqueror, who rewarded him with estates in Yorkshire. The Christian name of all these Bruces was Robert. The second Robert was granted estates in Annandale. By diplomatic marriages the family got themselves into the list of thirteen claimants to the Scottish throne, made vacant by the death of the Maid of Norway. The Bruces had previously a very strong hereditary claim to the throne. Indeed a Robert Bruce of Annandale had been recognised as heir presumptive in the days of Alexander II.

After the death of Wallace, Edward seems to have tried to pacify the Scots by offering them a measure of freedom, and he asked Bruce and other influential persons for advice. However, Edward had begun to suspect Bruce's loyalty to him, and Bruce, becoming aware of this, returned in 1306 to Scotland.

He made a disastrous start to his plans, by murdering his rival John Comyn in a church at Dumfries. He had burned his boats, for Comyn was a confidant of Edward. Bruce hastily got himself crowned at Scone, the old Pictish capital, and set off to win his kingdom. But he was defeated in two skirmishes and narrowly escaped with his life, so he crossed overseas to Rathlin, an island off the Ulster coast. His fortunes were at their lowest ebb. The myth of his encouragement by a spider in a cave at Rathlin was invented last century in a children's story.

But fortune smiled. Edward I died and Bruce, knowing the indecisive character of Edward's son, acted with speed. In true Norman fashion he ruthlessly devastated the estates of his rivals, the Comyns, in Buchan, Malise in Strathearn, and the Earls of Galloway. In Buchan for a space of fifty miles the prosperous region was reduced to an uninhabited desert.

Despite his excommunication for sacrilege, he induced Clement V, the Pope exiled at Avignon, to arrange a truce with England. Clement did this but would not recognise him as King. However, as Clement was a Frenchman and a tool of the French King, he was not averse to winking at excommunication to disoblige Edward II.

Now Bruce methodically set about the reduction of all the Scottish castles held by the English. By 1314 only Berwick, Bothwell and Stirling (the most strategically important) remained. Edward was forced to make the effort to relieve Stirling. He led a large army of mixed troops, English, Welsh and French, with other mercenaries, to Scotland. On Midsummer Day the Battle of Bannockburn was fought. Many minute descriptions of the battle have been published, so it is enough to say here that the English and their auxiliaries were routed and Edward pursued by the Scots as far as Berwick.

The Pope Clement V and his equally untrustworthy successor John XXII, still refused to recognise Bruce as King, or even to mediate with Edward II, so Bruce spent several years carrying war over the Border. 1320, the barons, much the same body as had deserted Wallace and had earlier refused to support Bruce by attending his coronation at Scone, now collected at Arbroath and enlisted Bernard de Linton, an erudite churchman, to write in classical Latin an address to the Pope, emphasising the determination of the Scots to be independent, even if their king did not support them. This may have influenced the Pope, though it was no great tribute to Bruce who had brought them out of Edward's power.

At last, in 1323, Bruce's claim was confirmed and in 1328, by treaty at Northampton and Edinburgh, Scotland's independence was recognised.

Bruce died of leprosy in his palace at Cardross on the Clyde. His body was buried in Dunfermline Abbey but his heart in a silver casket (which he had requested should be buried at Jerusalem, carried there by his friend Sir James Douglas), was brought back and buried in Melrose Abbey, as Douglas had been slain in an encounter with the Moors in Granada.

Agnes Randolph, Countess of Dunbar *(c. 1300-1360)*

She was the daughter of Bruce's companion, the celebrated Thomas Randolph, Earl of Moray, who daringly captured Edinburgh Castle for Bruce in 1313. She married the Earl of Dunbar and was known because of her raven locks as Black Agnes. The Earl's mother, the previous Countess of Dunbar, had been an amazon.

Dunbar Castle, which is built on the sea-cliffs and commands the harbour, had been in English hands, but the older countess handed it over to the Scots, though it was soon retaken.

Black Agnes, like her mother-in-law, was also an indomitable woman. In 1337 the Scots were still reeling under two great defeats in battle. Dunbar Castle had been strongly re-built when word came that the English, under the Earls of Salisbury and Arundel, were marching with a large army, well furnished with equipment of all kinds, to reduce the strong fortress. The Earl was away in the North with his forces, so his lady was put in charge of the defence.

The English set up their tents and erected their catapults, mangonels and trebuchets, and soon the air was thick with large stones which struck dust and splinters off the battlements. Agnes was here, there and everywhere, directing her archers and crossbowmen to pick off the men handling the siege machines. She mocked the English efforts by ordering one of her maids to flick her handkerchief across the points of impact, to dust off the damage.

The Earl of Salisbury, Sir William Montague, had Genoese sailors and artificers with him. Two Genoese ships lay in Dunbar Harbour. From these, material was assembled to make a siege engine, called a sow. This was a large wooden shed on wheels which covered a battering ram. It was run up to the main gate and about a score of hefty soldiers began to work the ram. The stout gate shuddered under the rain of blows.

But Agnes meantime had brought a huge boulder to the battlements immediately over the sow. Before launching her thunderbolt she addressed a very brief and witty warning to Montague:

> Beware, Montagow,
> For farrow shall thy sow.

The boulder tottered on the battlements and smashed down upon the roof of the sow, crushing it and sending such rammers as escaped death or injury, scuttling away like piglets from under their mother.

Montague raised the siege after wasting over three weeks in vain stratagems with a 'weak woman'. He had a grim humour too, for when one of

17

the defenders, Sir William de Spens, a powerful archer, drove a shaft through three coats of chain-mail and into the heart of one of his knights, he wise-cracked,

> This is one of my lady's pins;
> Her Cupid's darts into my heart runs.

And as he rode sadly away, leaving the field to Black Agnes, he is supposed to have said, in the language of a love lyric,

> Came I early, came I late,
> I found Agnes at the gate.

Agnes had her just reward. Nine years later, on the death of her brother, at the battle of Durham, she fell heir to the vast Moray estates, which included the Isle of Man and wide lands in the South-west of Scotland.

James Douglas, 2nd Earl *(c.1358-1388)*

Though not so formidable as his grandfather, the Good Sir James, friend of Bruce, after whom he was named, Douglas is noted in history and in poetry for his part in the Battle of Otterburn.

The Scottish policy was to raid the northern counties of England, in return for the English invasions of the Borders and Lothian. It was a vicious circle and led to endless misery for nearly three centuries, but it provided the matter for the heroic ballads, which, as one writer has said, 'thrill the heart like the sound of a trumpet'.

Douglas, in 1385, was assisted in the war against England by a large body of French troops under John de Vienne. The French found Scotland unlike their own land. Because of scarcity of provision and the sturdy independence of the ordinary people they were glad to return home.

In 1388 after a previous destructive raid on Carlisle, Douglas set off to do the same to Tynedale. His troops burned and robbed until they reached Newcastle, where Percy 'Hotspur', son of the Earl of Northumberland, accepted his challenge to single combat. Percy was worsted and Douglas carried off his pennon, saying he would fly it on his castle wall at Dalkeith in Lothian.

The Scots then withdrew slowly, 'trailing their coat' as if inviting the English to follow for a fight. They camped at Otterburn on 18 August and did not break camp on the following day. To their surprise Percy's force arrived at nightfall, more numerous than the Scots. The battle closed at once, 'close and bloody' and continued in the bright moonlight. Douglas hewed his way with a double-edged axe into the ranks of his enemies until he fell, impaled on three lances. Sir John Sinclair of Roslin asked how he was and was answered in the famous verse, or words like it,

> Last night I dreamed a dreary dream
> Beyond the Isle of Skye,
> I saw a dead man win a fight
> And I think that man was I.

Despite his expressed desire to be buried where he died, his body was carried to Melrose after the Scots had won. Percy's banner was hung in the Abbey while Percy and other English knights were held for ransom.

It was all magnificent, but not war, as the professional French military men said of The Charge of the Light Brigade.

As a grim factual note to the above heroic incident, a burial mound, assumed to cover the bones of those who fell in one of the many Border battles at that time, was opened by antiquarians early this century. Hundreds of skeletons, nationality not distinguishable, were examined by the medical men. Nearly all these were of youths below twenty years of age; a few exceptions were of veterans over thirty. As Hobbes, the English philosopher said, 'the life of man, solitary, poor, nasty, brutal and short' described those late mediaeval times in Scotland.

Hal o' the Wynd (*Gow Crom*) *(c.1390)*
(a wynd is a close or lane)

Only a year or two after Otterburn there took place a remarkable event on the great public meadow called the North Inch of Perth, on the banks of the Tay.

Two Highland clans from Speyside had fallen out, and their feuds were disturbing the country, so a wonderful solution suggested itself to the Earl of Dunbar and his peer the Earl of Crawford. Each clan should be represented by thirty warriors, armed with bows and arrows, daggers, swords and axes. Before King Robert III (wretched old pantaloon) and a vast crowd of spectators, including the Queen and her ladies, and ambassadors from the French, Spanish, and English and other courts, the Macphersons and Mackays, or Clan Chattan and Clan Quhele, should fight to a finish. Apparently the Highlanders were looked upon by the Lowlanders as a species of animal, to be hunted or slain for amusement.

When the Celts faced one another, a weakling of the Macpherson, either turned sick, or as some say took fright, and swimming across the Tay, pursued by the crowd, escaped to his native heath. The combat could not begin with unequal sides and no man of the Mackays would deign to withdraw. The King was about to break up the meeting when a crooked dwarf sprang over the barriers from the crowd. He was a well-known citizen, an armourer to trade, called Henry, the Bowed Smith, in Gaelic *Gow Crom*.

'Here I am. Will anyone hire me for half-a-mark (seven shillings) to play a part in this stage-play? If I come out alive will anyone board me for life?'

The King agreed to his request and a sickening slaughter began. Henry, or Hal, took first blood with a well-aimed arrow. With dirk and claymore the butchery went on until 29 of the Mackays and 19 Macphersons lay dead. The latter were declared the winners though all who survived were badly wounded. Hal o' the Wynd and the surviving Mackay were unhurt. History does not reveal whether or not he wore armour. This advantage sometimes balanced the berserk fury of the mountaineers.

Whole volumes would be needed to list the patriots who fought and died for Scotland against the aggressions of the English kings. Equally large tomes, sad to say, would be necessary to house the rolls of not such certain honour, naming those who were slain by their fellow-Scots in wars of religion and faction. We refer to one such instance in the next article, the Battle of Harlaw, or the 'Red Harlaw'.

Donald, Lord of the Isles *(1387-1422)*

In 1411, Donald, Lord of the Isles, jealous because he had not been granted the Earldom of Ross, collected a great army of Highlanders and marched on the town of Aberdeen, to loot and burn it to the ground. The Earl of Mar was the principal landlord in Aberdeenshire. When he heard of the outrages committed by the advancing Highlanders on his estates, he gathered all the men of war in the eastern counties, with their adherents. These mounted men were armour-clad and, though out-numbered ten to one, they advanced towards their hated foe.

The battle was fought with desperation for a whole July day, the Highlanders bringing down the horses by stabbing them and dirking the fallen knights. One by one the leaders on both sides fell, but neither side would give ground. At nightfall the Lowlanders were so exhausted that they lay on the battlefield powerless to leave, expecting to renew the struggle at dawn. But when morning came Donald had drawn off his men and retreated into the mountains leaving a thousand corpses including many chiefs and chieftains, for they usually were foremost in the charge. But the losses among the *Sassunach* (for that was the Gaelic name for their lowland countrymen), was a disaster, never paralleled until Flodden a century later.

Nearly all the notable Scottish Lowland families were wiped out, often a father and six sons. We read such names, famous later in Scots history, as Ogilvy, Murray, Abernethy. Among the dead was the Provost of Aberdeen and most of the burgesses of the town.

Admiral Sir Andrew Wood *(c.1450-1515)*

Although he was famous for his exploits in the reign of James III and IV, his name seems to have been obscured. He was a sea-captain and merchant in Leith. When James III was in danger, during a rebellion in favour of his son, the future James IV, Andrew Wood carried the King across the Forth to Fife where for a time he was safe. Andrew was rewarded for this by a gift of lands at Largo, which remained long in his family.

Shortly after the death of James III by assassination, after the Battle of Sauchieburn, there occurred a dramatic event in the Firth of Forth. Five armed English merchant-ships entered the Forth and, although the nations were temporarily at peace, they started attacks on the vessels sailing to and from Fife and the Lothian coasts. Andrew Wood was sent out from Leith with two armed vessels to confront the pirates. He attacked them with such vigour that they were forced to surrender. Wood brought his prizes back to Leith where, like many English and some Scottish pirates up to 1822 (the last hanging), they paid the full penalty.

Henry the English King was stung by the loss of his ships, so he sent his best sea-captain, Stephen Bull, with three ships of war to the Firth of Forth, to bring back Wood dead or alive. Sir Andrew was at that time in Flanders, so Bull had to anchor for some time to await his return.

Soon after dawn one morning the English saw Sir Andrew's two ships sailing past the Isle of May on their way to Leith. The ships were named the *Yellow Carvel* and the *Flower*. Without further ado the enemies closed and began a fierce cannonade which lasted a whole summer day, watched by excited groups of Scots from every village and point of vantage. Night brought a truce of a few hours and the contest was renewed off Fife Ness, clearly visible from Crail and St Andrews. Near the Bell, or Inchcape Rock, the Scots intensified their fire, and Bull and his captains had to strike the St George's Cross.

The prizes were taken into Dundee but James IV, perhaps with a weather eye on his future marriage with Margaret Tudor, sent the ships home and gave presents to Bull and his men.

Bull was knighted in 1512, but he thought twice about again crossing the bows of Sir Andrew Wood. As Sir Andrew Wood used his English prisoners to build fortifications to protect his Largo property against pirates, Bull and his men were very lucky to find a magnanimous monarch to keep them from several years' hard labour.

Several years after this sea-fight, Wood supervised the re-building of Dunbar Castle and the more spectacular construction at Newhaven, Edinburgh, of the largest ship constructed in that age, several times larger than the vaunted *Mary Rose*.

The *Great Michael* was the wonder of her times, her sides being ten feet thick. She is said to have wasted all the woods of Fife, save Falkland, which was a Royal preserve. She carried many guns of iron and bronze of heavy calibre. Sir Andrew was made her commander with Robert Barton skipper, but she achieved no warlike feats, probably being unwieldy, and was sunk in a storm a few years later.

A son of Sir Andrew took a leading part in the political intrigues concerning Mary, Queen of Scots; and a descendant, Sir James Wood (1756-1829) was a Rear-Admiral who did notable service in the French wars, under Admiral Cornwallis. He is chiefly famous for his unjust dismissal by a Captain Duckworth, which occasioned a corruption scandal. Wood was vindicated, restored in 1808 to his command, and knighted.

Maid Lilliard *(d.1544)*

Though two centuries had elapsed since the days of Black Agnes, the 'scorched earth' policy of English and Scots still went on, and now Henry VIII began his 'Rough Wooing' of Scotland in his anxiety to obtain Mary, Queen of Scots, then an infant, as a bride for his son. His armies burnt the Border abbeys and towns, massacred the inhabitants, and moved up the coast by sea, invading and burning Edinburgh and other towns. Nobody was spared, so the women felt it was just as safe to join the Scottish armies and fight alongside their men.

One of these amazons deserves a short notice. By the roadside on a ridge of the A58 from Edinburgh to Carter Bar, there stands, or stood sixty years ago, a small stone memorial with this rough verse:

Fair maiden Lilliard lies under this stane;
Little was her stature but muckle was her fame;
Upon the English loons she laid mony thumps,
And when her legs were cuttit off she fought upon her stumps.

The English army consisted of 3000 mercenaries, 1500 English borderers and 700 Scots from the Debateable Land or No-Man's Land near the Solway. The last were outlaws, Armstrongs, Turnbulls, Grahams etc. The Scots consisted of 1000 cavalry under the Earl of Angus, and a body of Fife footmen. They drew the English into an ambush, where they began to waver in the face of a fierce attack. The Scots outlaws, who had a greater love of loot than of country, changed sides. The slaughter of the English was merciless, and Lilliard took her full share of giving and receiving thumps.

Robert Monro *(c. 1600-1660)*

Sir Walter Scott in *A Legend of Montrose* introduces a tough old Scots mercenary named as Rittmaster Dugald Dalgetty, that is, captain of a troop of horse. Dalgetty was a pseudonym for a real character, Robert Monro, who was also in the Thirty Years War that made a desert of North Europe.

As a young man he joined Mackay's Regiment, when it was raised in 1626 by Lord Reay in Sutherland, for service abroad. Gustavus Adolphus had no less than thirteen regiments of Scots footsoldiers in his service, beside many troops of cavalry, all under Scots officers. Monro became a cavalry officer and eventually a Rittmaster. Out of the many heroic escapades in his career, perhaps one will show best the stuff he was made of, toughened in a hard school, where minor misdemeanours were punished by the offender being put on guard in full armour for eight hours under a blazing sun, 'till they were aweary of life', or worse still, during a long night of bitter frost, with the unlikely penalty of being shot for sleeping on duty.

With 700 Scots under his command Monro was on his way across the southern Baltic when the ships were wrecked. They had no horses, as these were to be supplied later, so the men managed to get ashore on the large island of Rugen off the Prussian coast. A line of forts, held by the Imperialist enemy, lay between them and the Swedish lines, eighty miles distant. They had brought their muskets and swords ashore but had no ammunition. The enemy pickets were near at hand. The position was desperate.

But Monro by pure luck and dogged search came upon an old and ruined castle which by chance was kept by a secret partisan of Gustavus, who supplied them with powder and shot. The Imperialists held the castle, but the owner let the Scots in by a secret door. They attacked the enemy, who panicked and scattered to tell the Imperialists in other parts of Rugen that a formidable force was on the island. Soon Rugen was in Adolphus' hands. Monro held the castle until he was relieved by a fellow-Scot, Sir John Hepburn, with a strong force.

With Hepburn, Monro blockaded the city of Colberg, and when a famous Italian commander approached to relieve the city, Monro, with a small force, opposed him and forced him to retreat. If Monro and his Scots had a fault, it was that they refused to act as pioneers and labourers. The French phrase *Fier comme un Ecossais*, Proud as a Scot, is based on this quality.

Gustavus Adolphus one night ordered Monro to drive a mine under the fortress of Frankfurt. In the morning not much progress had been made, so he burst out, 'You Scots, you are excellent in open warfare, but too lazy and proud to work.'

Robert Monro survived to return home and write a long-winded account of his 'Expeditions' which provided Scott with abundance of first hand material on the Scots warriors of the early seventeenth century.

David Leslie, Lord Newark *(1607-1682)*

He also, like Gordon and Keith, was of aristocratic origin, being the fifth son of Sir Patrick Leslie of Fife. When a young man he went to Europe and enlisted under the 'Lion of the North', the famous Gustavus Adolphus, the champion of the Protestant powers. In this hard service he met many Scots who, before the death of Adolphus in the battle of Lutzen in 1632, gained high rank in the Swedish army. To name only a few, these were, Ker, Drummond, Douglas, Lindsay, Forbes, Rutherford, Spence and Ruthven.

David Leslie rose to the rank of colonel of cavalry, and his kinsman Alexander Leslie was a field-marshal and governor of the Baltic ports. David returned to Scotland in 1640 at the beginning of the Great Civil War and was a major-general under Alexander Leslie at Marston Moor, where between them they shared with Cromwell the honour of this great Roundhead victory.

David was sent north to besiege Carlisle Castle held by the King's forces. He took it, though it was well fortified.

By this time, James Graham, Marquis of Montrose was sweeping all before him in King Charles' cause in Scotland, so Leslie was sent to oppose him. He surprised and defeated Montrose at Philiphaugh near Selkirk in 1645.

He returned to England to serve in the Cromwellian forces. The Scots of all parties now agreed to support Charles II, and Leslie was appointed commander of the new Scots army. Until his command was interfered with, at the Battle of Dunbar in 1650, by the Kirk party he outmanoeuvred Cromwell. At Dunbar he had Cromwell in a hopeless position, unable to retreat to England, and beginning to ship his famous cavalry from the harbour. Leslie proposed to starve him into surrender, but the fanatical ministers, quoting the Old Testament, persuaded him to act against all the principles he had learned the hard way under Gustavus. He ordered the Scots to leave their advantage point on the Doon Hill, to descend to the plain, where, after a desperate conflict, Cromwell broke through and slaughtered them, ill-using the prisoners barbarously and selling many into slavery overseas.

Even after Dunbar, Leslie continued to oppose Cromwell, and joined forces with King Charles at the battle of Worcester where he was lieutenant-general. After the Royalist defeat there, Charles escaped, but Leslie was imprisoned in the Tower of London.

On the restoration of Charles II in 1660 he was rewarded by being made Lord Newark and given a handsome pension by the Merry Monarch.

James Graham, Marquis of Montrose *(1612-1650)*

He was educated at St Andrews University and while still an undergraduate of seventeen, he married the daughter of Lord Carnegie. By this early romance he showed the poetical side of his character. Four lines from his poem 'To His Mistress' are immortal.

> He either fears his Fate too much
> Or his Deserts are small,
> That puts it not unto the Touch
> To win or lose it all.

When religious troubles broke in 1637, Montrose, a young enthusiast, signed the National Covenant, protesting against the attempts of Charles I to impose Episcopacy on Scotland. He helped to suppress the uprising in the Episcopalian area of Aberdeen, especially among the clan Gordon. He became one of the Covenanting leaders but fell out with the Earl of Argyll because he was manipulating the situation to his own advantage. James Graham had a strong Cavalier sense of honour and paradoxically this forced him to change sides eventually and support Charles.

The Great Civil War broke out, and Montrose, now a strong adherent of Charles, begged him to be allowed to raise the Royal Standard in Scotland. But Charles, who at first was successful in his battles with the rebels in England, did not give any encouragement to Montrose, and so lost his chance to win the war. Only when a Scottish force under David Leslie entered England to support Cromwell, was Montrose appointed Royalist Lieutenant-General in Scotland.

His first attack in the spring of 1644 was defeated by Argyll's forces so he went to the Highlands, and, with the help of a strong force of Irish-Gaelic troops under Sir Alastair MacDonald, he raised an army of great mobility and striking power. He conducted a brilliant campaign, never surpassed in military skill by any of the world's great commanders. In rapid succession he routed the Covenanters in six successive battles, of which the most spectacular was Inverlochy where, owing to their local knowledge of the mountain passes, his Highland guides evaded the forces of Argyll and did what no other army could have done. They waded through deep snowdrifts and lay exposed ill-clad and ill-fed on the bare mountains. They suddenly erupted down the mountainside upon the Campbells and in a few minutes slaughtered them or drove them into Loch Linnhe. Argyll escaped in his galley. Ian Lom (Bald John) MacDonald, who accompanied Montrose, composed a poem to celebrate the rout. But the severest blow, for which Montrose was never forgiven, was his overwhelming victory at Kilsyth when whole regiments of Fife and Lothian volunteers were exterminated without mercy.

David Leslie, the former mercenary soldier, was hastily called from England to check Montrose. He did this by a surprise attack at Philiphaugh, a victory which was stained by a massacre of innocent camp-followers, mainly Irish and Highland women and children, the Presbyterian clergymen applauding the slaughter. Montrose cut his way through his enemies and escaped. He failed to organise an army in the Highlands so he took ship to Norway, thence to Paris to seek help in vain for Charles. After the King's execution in 1649 he burned to avenge him and was re-appointed Lieutenant in Scotland. But the new king, on the promise by Argyll that the Scots would crown him, renounced Montrose, who in the meantime had lost practically all his small army by shipwreck, and after a defeat wandered about the Highlands friendless. At last, trusting his life to MacLeod of Assynt, not knowing him to be his enemy at heart, he was betrayed and taken to Edinburgh to be tried by his implacable foes. On the eve of his execution he composed these lines, also immortally famous, referring to the barbarous custom still unchanged from the days of Wallace, of quartering, and impaling the victim's head. Only, this time, the victim was to be executed by fellow-Scots.

> Let them bestow on every Airth a limb
> Open all my veins that I may swim
> To Thee my Saviour in that Crimson Lake
> Then place my par-boil'd Head upon a Stake.

Patrick Gordon *(1635-1699)*

He was born at Auchleuchries in Aberdeenshire of a famous Scottish family, one of whose early members was killed in such an ancient conflict as the Battle of the Standard in 1138. Like others of his family, including the notorious John Gordon (one of the murderers of Wallenstein the great Bohemian general), Patrick eventually became a mercenary soldier. This was very much an afterthought for, as a promising student, he had begun to train as a Jesuit priest in Prussia. He had been inveigled into this by the Scottish Jesuits whom he met at Konisberg. But he escaped from the college by night and, without much money or a knowledge of Dutch or German, he wandered about Northern Europe until he came to Hamburg, where Sweden was recruiting a large army. He was persuaded to join. He met many Scots all over North Europe. Having no particular allegiance he fought both on the Swedish and Polish sides, being taken prisoner by both.

At the age of twenty-six he took service with the Russians and was sent on a special mission to England. He campaigned for the Tsar Alexis against both the Turks and the Tartars, and rose steadily through the various ranks until he became Quartermaster-General. By a piece of good luck he was in charge of such a large body of men in Moscow that, when a revolution broke out in 1689, he was able to support the claims of the young Tsar Peter I, afterwards the Great.

Gordon was the confidant of the Tsar to the extent of being left in charge of Moscow when that progressive young giant went abroad to learn shipbuilding and other crafts. Gordon reorganised the Russian army on the lines of the foremost European powers, and was made General-in-Chief. The Tsar was deeply grieved at his death and gave him a magnificent funeral.

Hugh Mackay *(1640-1692)*

He was born at Scourie, Sutherland. At the age of twenty-two he enlisted as an ensign in Dumbarton's Regiment, later named 'The Royal Scots', who claim to be 'First of the Line'. The boastful claim to be 'Julius Caesar's Bodyguard' has also been made, and there is a humorous tale about a French regimental soldier who went one better and said that his company had been the identical one set to guard the tomb of Jesus in AD 29. The Scot agreed with this, but added, 'It was certainly not the Royal Scots, for none of us would have slept on duty.'

This story may originate in 1662, for Charles II lent Dumbarton's Regiment to Louis XIV at that time. The Scots Guard, like the Swiss Guard, had been long established round the French court, so Louis knew their reputation.

On return, Mackay got a personal Letter of Recommendation from Charles to be used on any occasion. Armed with this he enlisted with the Venetian republic and helped to drive the Ottoman Turks out of the seaport of Candia (now Iraklion) in Crete. With John Churchill (afterwards the famous Marlborough) as a fellow officer, Mackay now fought in a campaign against the Dutch. He repented of this soon after, and, realising that the Netherlanders were fighting for freedom against the Spaniards, he switched over and became a captain in the Scots Dutch Brigade, composed entirely of his countrymen.

When Monmouth landed in England in 1685 to oust James II, Mackay was appointed commander to oppose him. The sudden collapse of the invasion made Mackay's help unnecessary. His service in Holland had made him a confidant of William of Orange and when William landed at Torbay, Mackay was one of the first to come ashore.

The Dutch rule of William and Mary was opposed in Scotland by James Claverhouse, who raised a strong force to support the Jacobites, (followers of James or Jacobus). Claverhouse was able to raise the Highland clans, except the Campbells, who were always on the Whig side as opposed to the Stuarts. Mackay had an army of about 3000, half of them raw recruits, but, as he realised that speed was essential to prevent a general rising, he pushed on to face Claverhouse.

The Government forces passed safely through the narrow Pass of Killiecrankie only to find the clans poised to charge them. Mackay said himself that, a few moments after the wild charge of the Gaels, he looked about him and to his amazement 'both his army and the enemy had vanished.' Claverhouse was shot dead in the moment of victory and Mackay with a small party managed to escape over the hills to safety. Mackay attributed his defeat to the slowness his troops showed in fixing bayonets, so he invented a new type of bayonet which clipped on to the muzzle of the musket enabling it to be fired with bayonet attached.

Mackay did not give up the campaign. He pursued Claverhouse's successor Cannon, an Irishman, and forced him to give up the struggle. Fort William, named after the new king, was planned and built under Mackay's direction. He resigned, but could not resist taking over a command to fight the forces of James in Ireland, the Battle of the Boyne being one of the conflicts. He then commanded the army in Flanders against the French and their allies. He died in much the same glorious way as his opponent Scot, Claverhouse. At Steinkirk he attacked (at the head of his men) and drove back the enemy, but on taking the fortifications and requesting reinforcements, he was denied help. His last words were, 'The will of God be done.' He was killed with most of his army.

John Graham of Claverhouse, Viscount Dundee
(1649-1689)

He was educated at St Andrews University and served as a volunteer abroad. In France and Holland he gained military experience, returning to Britain as a captain of a troop of cavalry to suppress the Covenanter rebellion.

The murder of Archbishop Sharp by a band of extreme Covenanters, including the veteran continental soldier, Balfour of Burleigh, brought the unrest to a head, and Claverhouse was sent to Ayrshire to suppress it. Even though at the head of professional soldiers, Claverhouse was routed by the ill-equipped hill folk, because they were so advantageously placed by Balfour. The rebellion gathered strength. At Bothwell Brig a few weeks later a large body of Covenanters, not under good discipline, were scattered, many killed or taken prisoner, to be harshly treated in Edinburgh. Claverhouse was present at this battle but the commander was the ill-fated Duke of Monmouth, executed in 1685 for treason.

For the next eight years, known as the 'Killing Times', hard measures were used against those whose only crime was that they worshipped God in their own way. Unfortunately for Claverhouse, he was associated with a clique of violent and cruel men such as Grierson of Lag, Bonshaw and Lauderdale, but although hated bitterly by the Covenanters and reviled to this day, associated with the devil and credited with magical powers, the gravest crime ever laid to his door was robbery. He was, however, accused by Woodrow, the author of *A Cloud of Witnesses*, of the personal murder of John Brown of Priestfield, or Priesthill, in the parish of Muirkirk. Another writer on the Covenanters, Patrick Walker, guilty himself of helping to murder a trooper, and a hunted man, compiled *Memoirs of the Covenanters*. He described Woodrow's statements as 'lies and groundless stories'.

John Brown was certainly killed in Claverhouse's presence and with his authority, but Brown was alleged to be an outlaw with a price on his head. The truth is hard to find, but Claverhouse has been cursed heartily for three centuries. The old proverb says, 'There's aye some water where the stirkie droons' so, without doubt, 'Bonnie Dundee' as Scott calls him in his song, did not appear in that light to South-west Scotland.

However his end made some sort of cancellation of his debt to humanity. When James II fled and William took over, Claverhouse was in England with an army trying to support the Stuart cause. He had been created Viscount Dundee by James, one of the King's last acts. The new Viscount now returned quickly to hold Edinburgh castle for the Jacobites, but the Governor of the Castle would not co-operate. The story is told dramatically in Scott's famous poem, *Bonnie Dundee*.

£20,000 was placed on Dundee's head as a traitor, but he could ignore that, for he was soon leading a large army of clansmen. As we have said in the note on Mackay, the Battle of Killiecrankie was over in a few minutes, but Dundee was slain. An eye-witness, describing the carnage after the action, said that never, in all the wars in Europe, had he seen such incredible dismembering as that done by the Highland broadsword at Killiecrankie.

As Burns wrote in grim humour:

I've focht on land, I've focht on sea,
At hame I focht wi' my auntie, O,
But I met the Devil and Dundee
On the braes o' Killicrankie, O.

An ardent defender of the Jacobites, William E. Aytoun, describes the death of Dundee.

And the evening star was shining
On Schiehallion's distant head
When we wiped our bloody broadswords
And returned to count the dead.
There we found him gashed and gory
Stretched upon the cumbered plain
As he told us where to seek him
In the thickest of the slain.

Robert MacGregor (Rob Roy) *(1671-1734)*

He was born at Glengyle and christened in the parish of Buchanan, son of Donald Glas (Grey) MacGregor and Margaret Campbell. He was the third son. He earned his nickname Rob Roy (Red Robert) because he was covered by a strong growth of red hair. His arms were long, almost to the point of being grotesque and he was extremely muscular and active, especially with the broadsword.

His father had led a hundred MacGregors to help Dundee at Killie-crankie. These included Rob's eldest brother, John, but Rob may not have been present, for only his father and brother were imprisoned as rebels with other Jacobites in Edinburgh. The bad treatment he received there may have caused the early death of Donald MacGregor in 1695.

But all MacGregors were under a severe proscription, renewed by William of Orange in the year after the massacre of the MacDonalds in Glencoe in 1692. They were forced on pain of death, to adopt other surnames, so Robert signed his documents as a member of the clan Campbell, which he was, on the maternal side.

At an early age he took part in a cattle-raid known as the Herschip, or harrying, of Kippen. In 1690 when still a youth he led an expedition to Speyside to help a friendly blood-related chief of the Grants against the MacIntoshes.

He now started the respectable business of a dealer in black or store cattle. These were driven from rough pasture in the glens to the big markets in the Lowlands and in England, to be fattened for the butchers. A thorough knowledge of all the drove roads was essential, as was an ability to sleep rough in all seasons. However, a rogue of a partner absconded with the cash, and left Rob to face his irate creditors, notably Graham, Duke of Montrose.

Unable to lay hands on Rob, Montrose sent out a party under his factor to impound MacGregor's household goods in the depths of winter. His wife, Mary, a peaceful cultured woman (not the virago misrepresented by Scott in *Rob Roy*) was insulted and turned out with her young family of four sons to face the elements. Rob's nature was not one to submit to such high-handed cruelty.

For the term of his life he waged a personal war on Montrose. In this conflict, marked by many daring and amusing exploits, he was aided and abetted by his kinsman, the Duke of Argyll, who carried on a perennial family feud with Montrose. Argyll gave Rob and his family a house and croft near Inveraray, and when charged with supplying such a desperado with 'wood, water and a roof' he replied that Montrose was even kinder as he supplied Rob with beef and mutton, *gratis*, on the hoof.

Rob carried on the very dubious trade of blackmail, which at that time meant drawing a fee for guaranteeing safety against theft of cattle. This was open to abuse but there was no option in a lawless country like the Highland border.

Now occurred the Jacobite risings of 1715 and 1719. In the first, Rob was uncertain whom to support with his clan, for his chief, Bolhaldie, left Rob to lead the warriors. The Government forces, only 3000, were led by Argyll, Rob's protector; the Earl of Mar, with a much larger force of Highland and other Jacobites, was nearer Rob's political colour. The battle was claimed by both sides as a victory: for the right wing of one army, the Jacobites, defeated the left arm of the government with heavy losses, while the right wing of Argyll's forces defeated the rebels.

Rob Roy earned the animosity and ridicule of both sides by refusing to help either. With a strong party of mountaineers, he sat and watched the mixed fortunes of war. Perhaps he was wise, for either way he would have been the loser.

After a skirmish with Government forces at Dunkeld, where he was repulsed, he took illegal possession of Falkland Palace. No power was strong enough to eject him, and his clansmen raided far and wide for provisions.

He balanced his robberies by his charities, like Robin Hood; and left an ever-growing tradition which found its way into many books, of his exploits, and even a ballad by Wordsworth.

He died in peace in his cottage near Balquhidder in his sixty-fourth year and was buried in Balquhidder Churchyard where his gravestone is the object of thousands of pilgrimages each year.

Of the three sons, who survived him to take an active part in the 1745 Rising, one was hanged in 1752 with dubious justice in Edinburgh for abduction; another fled to Paris where he died in poverty; a third was still living in Balquhidder when Walter Scott visited the district as a legal apprentice in 1786.

The great peculiarity about Rob Roy was his being an anachronism, living the unprincipled life of a free-booter only a day's journey away from two Scottish cities, where commerce and literature and the arts were being conducted in a polished and sophisticated society.

Sir Andrew Agnew *(1687-1771)*

He was born at Lochnaw in Wigtownshire, eldest of the family of twenty-one children of one of the Lairds of Lochnaw. As a youth he enlisted in the Royal Scottish Dragoons, (latterly the Scots Greys). The Wars of Marlborough were in progress against the ambitious Louis XIV. Agnew fought at Ramillies, Oudenarde and Malplaquet. Marlborough had glorified his own name, and British arms, by winning the hard fought conflict of Blenheim in 1704, but the French had rebuilt their armies. The campaigns ending in the three battles above mentioned were hard and bitter. In the Battle of Malplaquet the British losses were very severe and Agnew was lucky to come out alive. The remaining years of the war dragged on with minor campaigning, and, at the age of twenty-five, Andrew Agnew found himself bored with barrack life after the thrills and perils of fighting with the Scottish Dragoons.

He caught the eye of a pretty girl, a distant cousin of his own, daughter of Thomas Agnew his superior officer in the 'Greys'. A penniless officer, on half-pay after the peace of Utrecht, his only chance of success in love was to elope, which he did. It was a long and fruitful union. They did not let the family tradition down, having eighteen children. The lady outlived him by a few years, dying at eighty-seven, no doubt surrounded by troops of little Scots Dragoons.

Agnew, doubtless, as a result of this moonlight flitting, was transferred to the Royal Scots Fusiliers, which are recruited from the West coast of Scotland. With them he fought at Dettingen in 1740, as their Lieutenant-Colonel. This was the last battle where a British monarch (George II) was on the field taking a personal risk.

Still in Flanders with the R.S.F., Agnew was commanded by the notorious Duke of Cumberland when at Fontenoy, after terrible casualties, especially among the newly-enrolled Highland troops, the combined British, Hanoverian and Dutch had to retreat before the French. On the outbreak of the Jacobite rising, troops were slow to go to Scotland, so rapid was the advance of the Highlanders. In 1746, Agnew was sent to face his own countrymen. He held Blair Castle for a month and was thanked by Cumberland. He retired in 1746, as Colonel of the R.S.F. and enjoyed a very long retirement in Wigtownshire.

To show the extent that personal spite can go in these matters, when an official *Historical Record of the Royal Scots Fusiliers* was published by the Adjutant-General of the Horse Guards, Agnew's name was not once mentioned.

Francis Edward James Keith (1696-1758)

Like Gordon he came of an ancient line of soldiers and statesmen. He was born near Peterhead, second son of William, 9th Earl Marischal of Scotland. His family were Episcopalians and Jacobites, so with his friends and relatives he took part in the 1715 Rising. On its failure he exiled himself to Paris but came back to share in the equally ill-fated 1719 Rising. He became a mercenary soldier in the Spanish and Russian armies, successively, having a high reputation for both military and civil administration.

At the age of fifty-one he approached Frederick the Great of Prussia, who was glad to accept him with the rank of field-marshall. At this time Keith's brother was living in Prussia, having fled from Scotland after Culloden; otherwise he would have ended on Tower Hill with other followers of Prince Charles. Both brothers were great friends of Frederick, and it is said that through this powerful advocacy George Keith was allowed to return to Scotland and be pardoned in 1759.

Meantime the Seven Years War broke out and Britain supplied Frederick with money to engage France and her allies. Frances commanded the Prussians with distinction in several campaigns, though not all were successful.

He was killed by a cannon-ball in the great battle of Hochkirche, fought two years after the war started. A memorial was placed in the village church near the battlefield, by his cousin, not long after. It is in Latin, as was the fashion then, and tells how Keith died, when he was in the act of encouraging his men by personal example, waving them on and shouting slogans in the face of the enemy gunfire.

Charles Edward Louis Philip Casimir Stuart *(1720-1788)*

Son of James III, 'the Old Pretender' (1688-1766) by whom he was entitled Prince of Wales, he is best known as 'the Young Pretender', 'the Young Chevalier' or 'Bonnie Prince Charlie'.

His campaign of 1745-6, leading a forlorn hope to recover the throne of his ancestors, has made him the hero of innumerable songs and romances. His ancestress (great-great-great grandmother) Mary, Queen of Scots, is the romantic counterpart of Charles. But on the maternal side he was descended through only two generations from the Polish hero-king Jan Sobieski, so he had a double share of military inheritance.

James III, the Old Pretender, exiled from Britain, held a miniature court in Rome. There Charles was educated in Jacobite principles and taught English, French and Italian. His English spelling and speech were always that of a European, though in his campaigns in Britain he learned to speak some Gaelic idiomatically.

When he was only thirteen he accompanied an expedition under his cousin (later Duke of Berwick) in the successful siege of Gaeta. A mixed force of Spaniards, Italians and Sardinians besieged this fortified seaport between Rome and Naples for four months before taking it from the invading Austrians. Charles saw active service all that time and was often in personal danger.

Ten years later, when he was twenty-three, Charles was secretly sent to Paris to accompany an invasion of Britain, aided by a squadron and transports for 7000 French troops. But stormy weather and a strong British fleet prevented this attempt. Nevertheless, not long after, Charles told Murray of Broughton, a Jacobite agent in Paris, that even if he (Charles) had to invade Britain single-handed, he would do so in the summer of 1745. But the messengers from Scotland, warning him not to embark on this mad venture, failed to contact him, and on 13 July 1745 he set out from Nantes on a small brig, *La Doutelle* accompanied by a war frigate, the *Elisabeth*. The frigate was chased home by an English man-of-war, but Charles arrived at Eriskay in the Hebrides on 3 August.

Macdonald of Boisdale received him drily, so he sailed to the mainland of Scotland. Once again the Macdonalds and others tried to dissuade him, but Cameron of Lochiel decided to send round the fiery cross and raise the clans. On 19 August at Glenfinnan the royal standard of James III of Scotland and VIII of England was raised. In a week 2000 men, mainly Macdonalds, assembled. As he marched towards Edinburgh many other clans joined, despite the fact that it was harvest time and inconvenient for most of the clansmen, who depended on the oat and barley harvest. Edinburgh was captured by a ruse of the Camerons, and on 18 September James III and VIII was proclaimed at the Market Cross of the capital.

Two days later the Highland army routed General Cope's government force at Prestonpans, a few miles east of Edinburgh. Everything seemed to favour the prince but he wasted nearly six weeks in Holyrood, holding levées and balls as if he had already succeeded.

He was advised to restrict his ambitions by claiming the Scottish throne for his father. Had he done so he would have perhaps secured the full support of the Scots. But in November, at a very bad season for campaigning, he set off south by several routes, with 5000 men. Many of these deserted on realising where they were going, but he captured Carlisle Castle in mid-November and two weeks later reached Derby, only a week's march from London, where the government was in a panic.

Here Charles' officers refused to back him up and advised a retreat, despite his angry tears and remonstrances. The golden opportunity was lost. The French had failed to keep their promises, the English Jacobites were faint-hearted, so the dreary retreat began, but in good military order, with no desertions or looting, though the armies of Cumberland and Wade were following closely.

At Falkirk, General Hawley challenged the Prince's forces and was completely routed, but Charles kept moving towards Inverness, reaching it at the end of March. He sent out hundreds of clansmen to procure supplies and to intimidate the northern clans who were antagonistic to him. He was in the worst strategic state to face the well-equipped British army under Cumberland, which was supported by the powerful Campbell clan and several Scottish regiments, as well as with cannon and a new method of opposing the dreaded Highland charge with broadswords. A night march to surprise Cumberland was unsuccessful, and a weary, hungry army faced the foe on the morning of 16 April. There was hesitancy in their ranks over some points of precedency. The Macdonalds were dissatisfied with their position and refused to attack although their ranks were shot to pieces by the British cannon. When the clans did attack they failed to break through the lines of bayonets. Finally the order for retreat was given and Charles was dragged reluctantly from the field of Culloden by his officers.

The Duke of Cumberland issued an order that no quarter was to be given and prisoners were to be put to death. He based this inhuman order on a document falsely attributed to Lord George Murray, Charles' commanding officer. No such document was ever written. Cumberland earned his title, 'The Butcher' for his subsequent barbarism upon military and civilian Highlanders. Lord George Murray has been criticised but if his advice had been taken by Charles, Culloden would never have been fought, and the war continued perhaps to a Jacobite victory, as a guerilla campaign.

Charles, despite the price of £30,000 on his head, after a series of hair'sbreadth escapes and privations, escaped, and boarded a French ship at Loch-na-nuagh, the place where he had landed a year before. Flora Macdonald, though not a Jacobite, disguised him as her serving-maid and got him safely through the Isle of Skye, though it was occupied by Hanoverian troops.

His subsequent history of expulsion from France, of intrigues and gradual dissolution, and quarrels with his aged father, does not concern his military career. He was undoubtedly brave to the point of foolhardiness, not averse to sharing the hardships of his tough Highland clansmen, and merciful in victory. He would have made a much more admirable soldier than his brutal cousin William the Butcher, had fortune been more favourable. But even in defeat his glorious adventure shall always illuminate the dull pages of eighteenth-century British history.

Always associated with Charles both in history and in song, is Flora Macdonald. She was born on the Island of South Uist, in the Hebrides. Her father owned a small estate. He died when she was two. At thirteen she was adopted by Lady Clanranald, wife of the chief, in whose household and at school in Edinburgh she received a good upbringing and education. She returned to Uist just before 1745 and, as is well known, after a price was placed on the head of Prince Charles, she conducted him from Benbecula to Skye, disguising him as her maid, under the name of Betty Burke.

She was not a Jacobite, but she protected the Prince out of humanity, for three days, when his life was in extreme danger. It is certain that he would have been executed on Tower Hill, like others of noble and humble blood, had he been taken.

Flora was arrested and spent twelve months in captivity on a troop-ship off Leith, then at London. But she was fêted as a heroine by everyone, whether Jacobite or Hanoverian, whereas the Duke of Cumberland was execrated as the 'Butcher' all over Britain.

In 1750, after returning to the Hebrides, Flora married the son of Macdonald of Kingsburgh. Many years later, in 1773, she entertained the Tory Doctor, Samuel Johnson, when he made his Highland tour. He was favourably impressed by her and describes her as 'of middle stature, soft features, gentle manners and elegant presence.'

She emigrated, as did many of her people, in 1774, to North Carolina. Her husband, a loyalist to the British, despite his wife's imprisonment earlier, was a brigadier in the American War of Independence. He was captured but released later to join his wife who had returned home. She died at Kingsburgh, Skye, much loved by her friends of all parties.

Hugh Mercer *(1721-1777)*

Born in Aberdeen and educated as a doctor at the university there. He attended the Jacobite army as an assistant surgeon and was present at Culloden. As a result, like hundreds of others, he was forced to emigrate. He went to Pennsylvania and settled as a surgeon. In the Indian wars he became a captain and friend of Washington. He was wounded in General Braddock's expedition, separated from his men and, suffering great hardships made his way alone through a hundred miles of forest to safety.

He joined the Revolutionary army in 1776, first as a Colonel, then rose to be a Brigadier. At the head of his battalion he led the attack at the engagement at Trenton. Then he put forward the plan for a night attack on Princeton where he was fatally wounded by the British, surviving only a few days.

A monument to Hugh Mercer stands on Laurel Hill, Philadelphia, and Congress provided for his family, a much better recognition than he would have got in his native land.

Adam Duncan, Viscount Camperdown *(1731-1804)*

He was born at Lundie, Forfarshire, entered the navy at fifteen, and took part in many engagements in the Atlantic and European coastal waters. He was appointed Admiral of the North Sea Fleet in 1797, when sixty-six. The mutinies at the Nore and Spithead in that year, because of justified grievances, kept many of the vessels out of action, and when Duncan was ordered to confront De Winter, the Dutch admiral, whose fleet of fifteen large men-of-war lay off the Texel, he could only sail with two ships, the *Adamant* (fifty guns) and the *Venerable* (seventy-four guns).

Had the Dutch known of the mutiny they would have attacked Duncan and proceeded to the British naval bases. But Duncan, at intervals, sent signals to an imaginary fleet which De Winter thought must be approaching beyond the Western horizon. In this way Duncan procrastinated for a month, until the mutiny was ended by a mixture of concessions and punishments. When reinforcements came, the British retired, only to approach the Dutch coast in October when De Winter's fleet was seen about nine miles off-shore between the villages of Egmont and Camperdown.

The British broke through the Dutch line and engaged heavily at close quarters with enormous casualties on both sides. Eleven of the Dutch vessels were captured. Duncan was created Viscount Camperdown, with a generous pension. His son was made the Earl of Camperdown.

Sir Ralph Abercromby *(1734-1801)*

Born at Tullibody, Clackmannanshire, and educated at Rugby and Edinburgh University, he was intended for the legal profession and went to Leipzig to study for this. But he was commissioned in the Dragoon Guards, aged twenty-two, and served in the Seven Years War where he had a chance to study the military genius of Frederick the Great of Prussia. In 1781, until the end of the war, he served as a colonel of an Irish regiment.

His personal sympathies were with the American revolution and he retired because of his disagreement with the Government. But when the war against revolutionary France began he re-enlisted and was appointed brigadier under the Duke of York in the unlucky Dutch expedition. He had the difficult job of protecting the retreat of the British, and for this was made a Knight of the Bath. He was in service in the West Indies, where Sir John Moore was under his command.

In the Irish rebellion he restrained the army and refused to allow troops to be called upon to suppress any minor disturbances. But all his efforts to create an atmosphere of confidence were ruined by the harsh measures of the English government, so he resigned.

After a spell as a commander in Scotland, he went on a second disastrous expedition to Holland. In 1801 he was sent to Egypt to turn out the French. His conduct of the landing at Aboukir Bay in the face of stiff opposition was one of the finest achievements of the whole war. But in a surprise attack by the French on the British camp, soon after the landing, he was struck by a spent bullet and died aboard the flagship a week later.

A monument was erected in St Paul's, and his widow and successors were generously provided for.

Sir Samuel Greig *(1735-1788)*

During the sixteenth and seventeenth centuries innumerable Scots helped to establish the military power of France, Prussia, Sweden and Russia. Some of these we have noted were in key positions. It is a very sobering reflection that most of these eminent soldiers were driven out of Scotland to serve foreign masters, often for a bare subsistence. An even more grim fact emerges. Britain had to struggle through long wars with France and Germany, which drained her of men and money and ultimately reduced her to a second-rate power. She is now antagonistic to Russia, the last power to owe much of its military and naval growth to Scots at a time when Scotland was still being humiliated by England in myopic domestic policies.

Samuel Greig opens a new phase of these Scottish activities in Russia, which has developed into the present ubiquity of Russian sea-power.

Greig was born in Inverkeithing on the Firth of Forth near the old ferry passage, now spanned by two bridges. His father was a shipowner; his craft mainly small coasting vessels. Samuel, after a village-school education, served as a merchant for several years. He then enlisted in the Royal Navy as a master's mate, or second officer, in a small ship named the *Firedrake Bomb*, whose function was to bombard with small cannon. He took part in the capture, off the west coast of Africa, of the fortified island of Goree, held by the French who had taken it a century before from the Dutch. In the blockade of Brest he was an officer in the famous *Royal George* in the great 'Annus Mirabilis', 1759, when Britain had one victory after another in the Seven Years War. (The *Royal George* sank with all hands, including Admiral Kempenfelt, during repairs, in 1782.).

Greig saw service, still only as master's mate, at Quiberon Bay and Havana, and at the end of the war as he was not urgently required, he was lent to help the Russians in their efforts to compete with European navies.

He was made captain, commanding a Russian flotilla in the Eastern Mediterranean, where the Turks were at war with Russia. Co-operating with Admiral Elphinstone of the British Navy, Greig destroyed the Turkish fleet in 1770, and returned after a series of voyages to St Petersburg where he was promoted to vice-admiral.

His advance was meteoric. After another Mediterranean campaign, he returned once again to be appointed by the grateful Tsarina to be governor of Cronstadt, the naval base founded by Peter the Great. He was made a Knight of the Orders of St Andrew, St George, St Vladimir and St Anne.

His success induced many British naval men, principally Scots, to enlist in the Russian service. This proved a source of much embarrassment to Britain, for the Empress, or Tsarina, Catherine had initiated a move entitled 'Armed Neutrality' in 1780, whereby all neutral nations such as Holland and Russia resisted the attempts of Britain to impose a blockade of Europe. The British Navy did not worry about attacking and destroying Dutch vessels, but they could not with good conscience declare war on Russian vessels commanded by Scots, so the blockade in Baltic water was ineffective.

In 1788 Sweden, which had been a formidable naval power for much of the century, clashed with the growing power of Russia. The Swedes had a traditional contempt for Russian naval pretensions, so Greig decided to teach them some respect.

Near Hogeland in the Gulf of Finland, the Russian and Swedish fleets met on a stormy summer's day. A fierce gale whipped up the normally calm channel, strewn with rocky islands. Even to handle a man-of-war, without swamping her, seemed a feat of superb seamanship. Some of the Russian captains were not capable, or their courage failed when the cannonade intensified, and the decks were covered with dead and wounded. But Greig fought on until evening, when both fleets sheered off. The fiery Scot clapped no less than seventeen senior Russian officers into irons and sailed east to St Petersburg where Catherine had them sentenced to the hulks, or floating prisons, which lay at Cronstadt.

The Swedes were not defeated, but they did not tell the world about Hogeland. In fact it is difficult to get a true account of it, for the only record, by a German, is obviously biased in favour of Sweden. But the Swedes never again took the offensive, and indeed Greig shut them up in Svenborg. It must have consoled his last illness to look through the porthole and think that a humble master's mate from Inverkeithing had sent a proud fleet into hiding. The Battle of Hogeland had left its effects on him and he died off Svenborg.

Catherine sent the court into mourning and in St Petersburg mounted one of the most magnificent state obsequies, in barbaric style, to mark her gratitude.

Greig's son, Alexis Samuilovich Greig (1775-1845) was born at Cronstadt. He became a rear-admiral and served in the Russo-Turkish wars of 1807 and 1828-29, as full admiral in the latter. Reorganisation of the Russian navy was continued by Alexis and to him Russia owes the creation and early development of the Black Sea Fleet. He died at St Petersburg, decorated with many orders of merit, and his monument was erected at Nicolaev.

In the third generation of adopted Scots, a son of Alexis, Woronzow, distinguished himself fighting against the British and French in the Crimean War at the siege of Sebastopol. He was aide-de-camp to General Menschikoff and was killed at Inkermann in 1854.

Alexander MacGillivray *(1739-1793)*

He was born near Wetumpka, Alabama. His father was a Scottish merchant and his mother the daughter of a French officer and an Indian Chief's daughter.

He received a good education, but at seventeen he returned to the Muscogee Indians who elected him chief. He held the rank of colonel in the War of American Liberation and led attacks on the frontiersmen of Georgia and North and South Carolina.

At the peace in 1783 the state of Georgia confiscated some of his property so he remained in arms. His aim was to stop the spread of American settlements westward. He was recognised as an important figure and was invited to visit New York to make a settlement on his loss of property. He was made a brigadier-general and given compensation but he remained hostile. He had an army of about 10,000 warriors, armed with guns.

Towards the end of his life he changed his policy and trained his followers in the white man's way.

He was intelligent, cultured, a good businessman. On the reverse side he was also noted for treachery and love of display. However, time has shown that he was outdone in the first by the white man. Though he was of mixed blood, his exploits indicate his Highland character.

John Paul (John Paul Jones) *(1747-1792)*

He was born on St Mary's Isle, off the coast of Kirkcudbrightshire. His father was a landscape gardener to the eccentric Douglas, Earl of Selkirk, who was a very exacting employer. His craze was for symmetry, the garden being laid out in parterres after the Dutch and French style. An amusing anecdote tells that John Paul's father caught a boy stealing apples and locked him in the sunhouse. But when the old Earl made his rounds of inspection he saw two boys looking tearfully from the windows of the sunhouse. The gardener explained that one boy was there for pilfering apples and the other, the future father of the American Navy, had been locked in for symmetry. No wonder that at the age of twelve he was glad to serve as a cabin-boy in a merchant-ship to Virginia where he visited his older brother, a tailor in Fredericksburg. He next was warranted as a midshipman in the British Navy, but he may not have served long, if at all, for he was chief mate at the age of twenty-four for two years on a Jamaican slave-ship.

He quit this disgraceful trade and was on board a vessel bound for Scotland when the captain and mate died of fever. He brought the brig safely to port and was made master.

Now began the critical period of his career, He had flogged a ship's carpenter for laziness. The man deserted and died months later on another vessel. Paul was arrested in Scotland on a charge of murder, broke his bail and went off to the West Indies, seeking witnesses to acquit him. Not able to find any satisfaction, he bought a ship and traded in the West Indies. Then happened his 'great misfortune'. In 1773 he killed the head of a mutinous crew. Fearing a prejudiced trial in a British Admiralty court, he fled and changed his name from John Paul to John Paul Jones.

The revolution was stirring in America and in the autumn of the outbreak, in 1775, Jones got a commission as a senior lieutenant in the 'Continental Navy' of the new Union. He commanded a small fleet and under the Grand Union flag he commenced a long series of engagements with the British in which he captured or destroyed much shipping up and down the Atlantic coast of America from Bermuda to Nova Scotia.

His successes did not apparently influence Congress, for, to his bitter annoyance, he was placed far below a number of newcomers to the navy.

The day when the Stars and Stripes was first adopted, Jones was given command of the new *Ranger*, of 18 six-pounder guns. Burgoyne had surrendered at Yorktown and the freedom of the United States was assured. Jones now began to cruise daringly in British waters, taking prizes in the Irish Sea, and even landed at Whitehaven, Cumberland, and disabled the battery. He returned to his birthplace the same day, intending to capture Lord Selkirk, the son of the eccentric gardener, but finding him from home, took the silver plate, which he later returned with apologies. His greatest achievement on this privateering voyage was the capture of the British warship *Drake*.

He was put in charge of an expedition of French and American ships to harry the British coasts. His arrival in the Forth, meaning to attack Leith, caused a panic in all coastal towns. But a gale saved Leith from an attack, and off Scarborough the squadron fought one of the most famous minor battles of the time. The Baltic merchant fleet, convoyed by men-of-war heavily armed, was attacked by moonlight on 23 September 1779. It was a close bloody battle and the *Serapis*, a 54-gun ship, surrendered to Jones. Hundreds were killed or wounded on both sides. Jones' ship sank, so he took over the British warship and with his prizes sailed for the friendly Dutch port of Texel. Louis XVI honoured him for his great victory. He received a gold medal from Congress.

In 1788 he joined the Russian navy, perhaps encouraged to do this by the presence of Samuel Greig and many other Scots. But Greig died in the same year, and Paul Jones found that the Russian service was disappointing. He was made Rear-Admiral in the Black Sea Fleet and promised full command, but his victories were credited to others, and as a last straw a trumped-up charge of criminal assault made him leave St Petersburg for Paris where he died broken-hearted at the ingratitude of his two adopted countries. His grave in a Protestant cemetery was unmarked for a century, until a US ambassador, early this century, found it, and brought back Paul Jones' remains to Annapolis, the naval base, where his grave is a national shrine.

Sir John Moore *(1761-1809)*

Born in Glasgow, he became an ensign in the 51st Regiment when fifteen and trained in Minorca. In 1778 he was appointed an officer in a new Scottish regiment raised to fight the American rebels. He served in America until the new state was recognised. At the early age of twenty-three he was an MP for several combined lowland Scottish burghs.

He was commissioned with the 51st for service in the Mediterranean against the French, where he was wounded. He made friends with the Corsican patriots and so drew down the anger of Lord Minto, who expelled him from the island. Luckily, the Prime Minister, Pitt the younger, took a good view of Moore's ability and he was promoted to brigadier-general, where he was under Sir Ralph Abercromby.

In 1798 he was engaged in putting down the Irish rebellion, being at the Battle of Vinegar Hill. The next year he was wounded in the disastrous Dutch campaign but was appointed Colonel to the 52nd, whom he trained to be the finest regiment in Europe.

He took part in the Battle of Alexandria, Egypt, with great distinction, being wounded for the fifth time. After the short peace of Amiens, he commanded the force on the Channel coast, assembled to face the threatened invasion by Napoleon. Here he trained troops to such perfection that he left a long tradition of military efficiency.

In 1808 he was sent to Sweden to help Gustavus IV against the Russians, French and Danes, but this arrogant monarch misconducted himself and even put Moore under arrest for daring to advise him on military matters. Moore had to escape in disguise.

Moore now had a European reputation as a general, and his anger can be imagined when he was posted to the Iberian Peninsula to be under two undistinguished officers, Sir Hew Dalrymple and Sir Henry Burrand. However, both were shortly sent home and Moore was in sole charge of the largest British force of the Napoleonic war.

At this point the great Napoleon himself led an enormous army of seasoned troops for the conquest of Spain. Moore now made the bold plan to march north and cut off Napoleon's supplies and line of retreat. This move, when discovered by French spies, paralysed Napoleon's movements so he turned from his conquest of Spain to destroy the British.

The inevitable retreat to Corunna, where a fleet of British transports lay, was fought gallantly at every step against the Napoleonic army. Finally, on the heights above Corunna the last battle was fought and the French repulsed, ensuring the safe embarkation of the British. But Moore received his sixth and fatal wound, surviving only long enough to hear the cheers of victory. His last words were to ask that his friends who had so distinguished themselves, should be recommended to the Government. He had been in love for years with Lady Hester Stanhope, and he murmured her name as he died.

The memorable poem by the Revd James Wolfe *The Burial of Sir John Moore* became one of the most popular in the English language. The retreat to Corunna was highly controversial but there is general agreement that, but for Moore, Wellington's work would have been in vain. Moore's approach to training, showing sympathy and interest, was totally different from the general policy of that time and later, which relied upon the gallows and the lash. Wellington for all his reputation, complained bitterly about the quality of his officers and men, but made no effort to train them, as Moore did. The list of distinguished commanders, trained under Moore, contains such notable Scottish names as Graham, Crawford and the Napiers.

General Sir David Baird *(1765-1829)*

He was born at Newbyth, East Lothian, and entered the army as an ensign at sixteen, and in 1779 went out to India with a Highland division. When the Indian leader Hyder Ali burst into the Carnatic province in 1780, with a French-led army, Baird was captured and imprisoned for four years. When his mother was informed that the prisoners were chained in pairs by the Indians, she made the famous remark, 'I'm sorry for the poor fellow that's chained to our Davie.'

On his release he served in South Africa, then returned to India to storm Tippoo's fortress of Seringapatam, where he had been a prisoner. On taking it he was bitterly disappointed that Sir Arthur Wellesley (afterwards Wellington) was given command of the town, so he resigned. After campaigns in Europe and Africa, he was with Moore at Corunna and would have taken over had not his left arm been amputated.

He was repeatedly passed over for promotion because of the enmity of the 'Wellington clique', but given honours by Parliament.

Thomas Cochrane, Earl of Dundonald *(1775-1860)*

An aristocrat by birth, he was the son of Archibald Cochrane, an inventive genius who was well before his time in applied science. But he lost money by his schemes and Thomas went to sea in his uncle's ship when eighteen. With such family influence he was promoted rapidly and when twenty-five commanded the brig *Speedy*. He captured a Spanish ship and was promoted. He was also a Member of Parliament, being very outspoken, especially on naval abuses. Trouble was brewing. In a brilliant attack on the French in Biscay he was hampered by the incompetence of the admiral, Lord Gambier, whom he publicly accused. This led to Gambier's court-martial, where he was acquitted by his peers. But Cochrane, for the time, was dismissed from the Navy.

He was now the victim of an unlucky circumstance. His uncle and others were found guilty of a Stock Exchange swindle and Cochrane, although innocent, was condemned with his associates. He lost his decoration and seat in the House, so he was glad to leave Britain at the invitation of Chile, in 1817, to help in the revolt against Spain, as admiral of their navy. After five successful years, during which he brilliantly captured a Spanish frigate in Callas harbour, he switched over to Brazil to help the Emperor Pedro I to shake off the Portugese domination. However, his temper was such that he fell out with Brazil and went to help Greece in their war of liberation against the Turks. But he found no chance to help them and returned to Britain where, in the Reform year 1832, he found the Radicals more helpful. He resumed his career in the navy and took command of the Atlantic fleet for some years.

His inherited inventive faculty began to produce many improvements on the propulsion of ships, on mining, on rotary steam-engines and screw-propellers on ships. His merits were at length recognised, and after a tempestuous career he found haven in Westminster Abbey.

Sir Charles Napier *(1786-1860)*

Born at Merchiston Hall, Stirlingshire, of a celebrated and talented Scottish family of several branches, he was educated at Edinburgh High School and joined the navy at thirteen. After service in the Mediterranean and the West Indies his thigh was broken in a naval battle. He took part under Wellington in the Peninsular War and saved his cousin from death on the field of battle. In 1814 he was present in the British attack on Washington, DC. He commanded the Portugese fleet, and attacked the fortress of Acre while serving with the British. He gained many honours both civil and military.

Colin Campbell, Lord Clyde *(1792-1863)*

Born in Glasgow, his baptised name was Colin MacLiver, a sept of the Clan Gregor, but on his uncle, Campbell, presenting him for an ensign in the 8th Regiment, by a misunderstanding he was entered under his uncle's name. He was perhaps the most experienced of all nineteenth century warriors of rank. At an early age he fought under Wellesley (later Wellington) on the Peninsula, retreated with Moore to Corunna, and later returned to take part in the whole campaign, being severely wounded at St Sebastian while leading an assault. At the crossing of the Bidassoa, an operation which exposed the British to heavy casualties, he was again wounded and forced to recover at home. He took part in the American campaign of 1814 and for some years studied military tactics. He was sent to suppress an insurrection of slaves in Jamaica in 1823, and in 1842 took part in the Opium War in China where he helped to enforce the debauching of the Chinese. He was in the Sikh war of 1848-49 in India, where he was again wounded after contributing to the British success. He was awarded a KCB on returning home.

He commanded the Highland Division in the Crimean War and, at the Soldiers' Battle, the Alma, where confusion reigned, his troops distinguished themselves. A famous painting *The Thin Red Line* commemorates the heroic stand his kilted men made at Balaclava.

Though over sixty he was recalled on the outbreak of the Indian Mutiny in 1857. He left eagerly, so anxious was he to avenge the massacre of the British women and children. His campaign is presented in dramatic form by J.G. Whittier, the American poet in *The Relief of Lucknow*, where 'the tartan clove the turban as the Goomtee cleaves the plain.'

For his services he was created Lord Clyde and received the thanks of the nation.

Robert Napier of Magdala *(1810-1890)*

He was another of that famous family of military and naval achievements. He was born in Ceylon (Sri Lanka) son of Major Charles F. Napier. At sixteen he entered the Bengal Engineers and after a course at Chatham went to India. Among other civil engineering works he laid out the new hill-station at Darjeeling. He invented a new system of barracks, named after him, and commanded the Engineers, who were also a fighting unit, at the battle of Mudki where his horse was shot under him. He took part in several small wars, being wounded. After the outbreak of the mutiny he was appointed to assist Outram in the first relief of Lucknow. The rebels continued the siege and Napier supervised the defence until the second relief by Sir Colin Campbell. Here, as he went to meet Campbell, he was severely wounded. On recovering he began a series of campaigns to defeat rebel leaders, ending the war in 1859.

He now was sent on an expedition to China, entering Peking after several engagements. For the next four years he was military member for the governing of India, and commanded the Bombay army. But his greatest exploit was still to come. In 1868 he was sent to relieve a large number of European prisoners held far inland in the Abyssinian mountains in the fortress of Magdaia. In a strenuous march his force covered the 420 miles from the coast, stormed Magdala, set the captives free and razed the place to the ground.

Honours were heaped upon him but he remained in India for six years, working on army training and organisation. For some years he was governor of Gibraltar, and ended his days as Constable of the Tower of London.

His career is perhaps the epitome of a Victorian military empire-builder, an Empire which, to a large extent, was a Scottish one.

Sir Hector Archibald MacDonald *(1852-1903)*

He was born at Muir-of-Allen Grange, Ross-shire, son of a crofter. He enlisted as a private in the 92nd (Gordon) Highlanders when he was eighteen. He was conspicuous for his bravery and attention to duty in the Afghan War of 1879 and in the first Boer War of 1880-81. After the death of General Gordon of Khartoum he was engaged in the long campaigns against the fanatical followers of the Mahdi. During his service he was steadily promoted from the ranks, being made a sergeant and then, almost uniquely, being commissioned, owing to his outstanding qualities. He rose to be Major and was transferred to the Royal Fusiliers.

He commanded a brigade of Egyptian native troops or fellahin, and led them at the battle of Toski and other engagements. He received the DSO for his conduct at Toski. The final battle of the war was Omdurman where Kitchener was in command. Omdurman was the headquarters of the Mahdi and his successor, and was the centre of the rebellion. A number of European prisoners were held here under guard by a host of Sudanese tribesmen.

Preparations were made to capture Omdurman. A railway was laid to Atbara, some distance off, and 26,000 troops were concentrated. Kitchener's force marched up the west bank of the Nile to within four miles of the enemy and were not opposed. They built a zariba, or fortification of trees, luckily, for they were attacked next morning by 40,000 tribesmen. Kitchener repulsed them and advanced but was fiercely attacked on two sides, MacDonald's brigade taking the worst of it. MacDonald himself, by his brilliant tactics, repulsed the enemy.

Soon the Khalifa and the dervishes were in a rout, and the British cavalry went in pursuit. Omdurman was occupied, the prisoners released and the war at an end. But, although Hector MacDonald had saved the day, it was Kitchener who was created Kitchener of Khartoum (K. of K.). But 'Fighting Mac' was made colonel and aide-de-camp to Queen Victoria. In the South African War he was called to command the Highland Brigade after it had been nearly annihilated, by the Boers at Spion Kop, under General Wauchope.

In the last year of Victoria's reign he was made a Knight Commander of the Order of the Bath and in 1902 commanded the troops in Ceylon. What happened on 25 March 1903 caused the biggest scandal of the age. He shot himself in a Paris hotel, and after a great deal of speculation and the mysterious appearance of a wife and son that few knew about, he was buried in the Dean Cemetery Edinburgh, mourned by every rank of Scots. Speculation about MacDonald's suicide still goes on. This however is not relevant to his brilliance as a warrior in the ancient Highland tradition.

Sir Ian S.M. Hamilton *(1853-1947)*

He joined the army at nineteen and served for over sixty years. As he had taken part in the Afghan War and the Boer War of 1881 with the 92nd Highlanders, and had been severely wounded and permanently disabled in an arm at Majuba Hill, he may be said to represent the traditional British frontline warrior. In modern war everybody is in the front line, whether they choose it or not, and during the 1914-18 War few, if any, leaders were anywhere near it. But we can say that Hamilton, and to some extent Douglas Haig, were warriors because of their early soldiering days.

Hamilton served in the Nile Expedition of 1884-85 when General Charles Gordon of Khartoum was involved. He was in the Burmese War and commanded a brigade on the North-west Frontier. He was Kitchener's deputy during the end of the South African War.

After a spell in the War Office, he accompanied the Japanese armies in 1904 on the battlefields of the Russo-Japanese War, and published a book on his experiences. This literary gift was not appreciated by the old-fashioned barrack-square soldiers.

In March 1915 he was chosen to lead the ill-planned Dardanelles campaign. He had the impossible task of landing an invading force on a terrain that the Turks, being fore-warned, had had plenty of time to prepare for defence. After disease and heavy casualties had reduced his forces, a stalemate developed. Sir Ian, bred in a grim school, refused to countenance a withdrawal, so he was personally withdrawn and a more amenable commander appointed to supervise the evacuation.

Hamilton published his own account and faded away slowly to the age of ninety-four.

Sir Douglas Haig *(1861-1928)*

He was born in Edinburgh and educated at Clifton and Oxford, joining the 7th Hussars at twenty-four. He was with the Egyptian Army during the Omdurman campaign (1898). In the South African War he was in action at Ladysmith. He was chief staff-officer in the cavalry division during Lord Robert's victorious advance into the Transvaal. At the end of the war in 1902 he was made aide-de-camp to King Edward VII. Until 1914 he held various important staff posts. When hostilities began in August 1914 he commanded the First Army Corps at Mons, the Marne, the Aisne and the first battle of Ypres, when the war was mobile. As full general he took charge of half of the expeditionary force and fought the battles of Neuve Chapelle,

Festubert and Loos, as a result of which he was given full command when Sir John French retired.

The conduct of the entrenched war is still a controversial subject in which no general escapes censure. The circumstances were unprecedented in world history and should have led to an immediate political situation, for there was no military one. Haig had to work with the French and this led to friction. It was the discontent and the mass mutiny of French units in the horrific Verdun conflict which directly caused Haig to entangle the British in the morass of Passchendale from which they could not extricate themselves. Only the arrival of American forces balanced the massive German reinforcements released from the Russian front after the Revolution. Haig will be best remembered for his 'backs to the wall' appeal to the troops in March 1918. He conceded full command to General Foch and in the autumn of 1918 he was rewarded for his patience by a general breakthrough which, on his advice, was directed at the Hindenburg line.

He devoted his retirement to organising Poppy Day sales for the benefit of ex-service men, and to promoting the British Legion.

Philosophy

Every race of man from the earliest times has formed some philosophy or other to reduce the universe to order and to explain existence. Only a few individual men have had the time, inclination or ability to put forward theories that seemed at all satisfactory, and invariably these have led to arguments without end.

In the Western World the Greeks had several eminent philosophers, of whom Plato, Aristotle and Socrates are widely known, though there are dozens of others. Even in the glorious freedom of Greece, where thought was unrestricted, these philosophers were subjected to persecution from the powers of state, and in the notorious case of Socrates this ended in his condemnation to death for his ideas.

From the early Middle Ages until the ninth century, lumped together under the misleading name of the Dark Ages, Western Europe was completely subjected to the authority of the Roman Catholic Church, and free thinking was a dangerous pastime which became suicidal if published. Some liberty of thought, nevertheless, was exercised by philosophers, within the permitted limits.

The most influential of these was John Scotus (815-877) claimed by both Scotland and Ireland. At that time there was no Scotland as such, but the Scots of Dalriada had territory in Argyll and Ulster. Centuries later John Scotus was further entitled Erigena (i.e. born in Eire) to distinguish him from another eminent philosopher also named John Scotus, born in Duns, Berwickshire and commonly called John Duns Scotus.

The many published works of Erigena, in Latin, sought to show the compatibility of the best Greek philosophy with Church dogma. Duns Scotus, on the other hand, engaged in a dispute with Thomas Aquinas of Naples on subtle differences of doctrine which the modern world rarely tries to comprehend.

The reign of these Church disputants, or Schoolmen, came to an end when Erasmus of Rotterdam expounded the philosophy of humanism, in which he was supported by the Frenchman Montaigne.

The mental upheaval of the Renaissance and the Reformation marked the beginning of Modern times and a revival of unrestrained thought equal in freedom to Greek philosophy.

Beginning in the middle of the seventeenth century, but not attaining their full power until a century later, there arose a school of Scottish philosophers whose works took rank with the most original thinkers of England, Germany and France, and in the case of David Hume completely shattered the assumptions of earlier writers in this abstract science.

The term philosophy was originally used to comprehend all branches, natural, moral, metaphysical; mathematics, astronomy, physics, religion. Latterly a philosopher came to be regarded as someone who accepted life without complaining, but the men we now notice are not selected on that personality basis.

John Scotus Erigena *(815-877)*

All we can guess of his birthplace is, that it was on the coasts of the Irish Sea, some think Ulster, some Ayrshire. He was educated for the Church and was perhaps connected with the great monastery of Bangor on Belfast Lough, which originally was the centre of the Celtic Church, sending thousands of missionaries to Europe as well as Britain. In the eighth century it was Romanised. In AD 822 it was devastated by the heathen Vikings and its inhabitants massacred or scattered. At this terrible time of martyrdom it is probable that John fled to Europe for safety with his friends and parents.

It is known for certain that when he was thirty-five he was invited by Charles the Bald of France to be head of the Court School. He was a master of Latin as well, of course, as of Celtic. His Greek was also well written and he probably knew Old French, as it was emerging from Latin at that time.

His chief work was to insist upon reason as the principal method of establishing truth, though he bowed to the authority of the fathers of the Church. He taught that the universe, all nature, and God are a unity, a doctrine which could have been called pantheism. He was bold enough to say that religion was only a step towards man's complete realisation of his possibilities and ultimate evolution.

This was highly revolutionary, but perhaps more so, as a churchman, was his affirmation that the ceremony of the Lord's Supper was merely symbolic or commemorative. This led to a great argument. Even Charles the Bald wanted to know the truth, but he was mystified by the arguments. The controversy raged for a thousand years and it is not settled yet.

Erigena's great work, *The Divisions of Nature*, which regarded God as the beginning and end of all things, was surpisingly condemned by Popes as late as the thirteenth and sixteenth centuries. His doctrines had a wide and long influence on European thought and are to be recognised in works published until modern times.

Michael Scot *(1214-1290)*

He was born at Balwearie, Fife, and educated at home until he could go to Oxford (St Andrews University was founded two centuries later). From Oxford he went to Paris and held several church posts in Italy. He was offered the archbishopric of Cashel in Ireland but refused it. He aimed at more exotic places and began to study Arabic at Toledo, which was now in Christian hands, after four centuries as the centre of Moorish and Jewish culture. The expulsion of these people had not yet been contemplated, and Scot was able to study physics, arithmetic and many other sciences unknown to non-Arabic scholars.

He joined the Court of Frederick II, the Holy Roman Emperor, known as 'Stupor Mundi' or the 'Amazement of the World'. At this royal centre, Frederick gathered Christian, Mohammedan and Jewish scholars without any bigotry of race or religion. Scot translated Aristotle and Averroes, the Greek and Arabic savants, at Frederick's request. Scot's own writings were on astrology, alchemy and occult sciences. He is said to have had the second sight and to have foretold the time and manner of the Holy Roman Emperor's death, an event which the world would not believe for a long time, thinking him immortal.

Scot was generally regarded throughout Europe as a magician. Dante included him among wizards in his *Inferno*, describing his spirit in Hell as 'so slender of shape round his loins was Michael Scot, practised in every sleight of magic wiles'. Boccaccio writes, 'Not lòng ago there was in Florence a great master of necromancy who was called Michele Scotto, because he was from Scotland.'

Although his books of magic were said by Dempster in his *History of the Church* to be still in existence at the end of the sixteenth century, the common tradition is that they were buried with him, either in Italy, or in Cumberland, or in Melrose Abbey. The latter place is most likely, as he is known to have been one of the ambassadors sent to bring the Maid of Norway to Scotland after the death of Alexander III in 1286. His death was recorded in a chronicle of the age of Dante himself.

A great deal of incredible rubbish surrounds Scot's name in his native land. He is supposed, for example, to have split the Eildon Hills in three. But these hills were named Trimontium by the Romans over a thousand years before Scot's birth. The truth is that he was a brilliant philosopher, translator, mathematician and chemist in the most distinguished company of the High Middle Ages.

John Duns Scotus *(1265-1308)*

A great gathering of churchmen of all persuasions was held in Duns in 1965 to pay tribute to the quiet Berwickshire town's most famous son.

He was educated at the local Franciscan church school and went to Oxford, probably to Balliol College, to complete his education. While there he lectured on the 'Sentences', that is, passages from Scripture. He spent four years in Paris, returned to Oxford, then back to Paris. There he was fully licensed as a preacher and went to Cologne where he died aged forty-three.

Perhaps, by his Scottish origin in the old Anglian province of Lothian, he was always inclined to 'hae his doots' about any argument that convinced others too easily. At any rate he was not convinced by the various theories of Thomas Aquinas, but remained a supporter of the schoolmen of tradition founded by his namesake Scotus Erigena. He had many supporters among the Franciscans, in Oxford, as in Paris and elsewhere. As Thomas was a Dominican, this division of opinion split the friars into acrimonious septs and developed into all sorts of accusations which were not justified. The Dominicans nicknamed Scotus' supporters as Dunses, whence came the word dunce.

But John Scotus stuck to his guns, holding to the scientific principle that philosophy can only advance by a close examination of other persons' theories. We find the same kind of scepticism in David Hume five centuries later; strangely enough, or perhaps understandably, also belonging to the Duns region.

Duns Scotus was accused of all sorts of heresies, especially of being an obsolete defender of pantheism, scepticism and other 'isms' without number.

A startlingly modern theory of Duns Scotus was his contention that matter is not passive but has a nature of its own quite apart from its form. This we know now to be only too true. His theories were specific in insisting that all matter was reducible to an ultimate entity. This supported the age-long search for the Philosopher's Stone.

In psychology he would not grant the separation of the body and soul, and thought that will, intellect and memory were inseparate from the soul. He claimed that the will predominated over the intellect. It is little wonder that he was nicknamed 'The Subtle Doctor'. Even after eight centuries our modern philosophers have their work cut out to keep in touch with this 'brisk young lad from the country.' The motto of Duns is 'Duns dings a'".

Sir Robert Murray or Moray *(1600-1673)*

Son of Sir Robert Murray of Craigie near Perth. He was educated at St Andrews, then in Paris, and entered the French Army, where he was favourably noticed by Cardinal Richelieu. He returned to Britain to support Charles I in the Civil War. He planned to help Charles to escape from the Cromwellian troops but the King hesitated and was captured and finally condemned and beheaded. Murray returned to Scotland and was made Lord Justice Clerk, or head of the judiciary. On the Restoration of Charles II, Murray was reinstated in his appointments.

One of the first acts of Charles II was to encourage the formation of the Royal Society of London for Improving Natural Knowledge, now called simply The Royal Society.

At the first meeting after the Restoration a group of learned men were present, including Boyle, Sir Robert Murray, and Christopher Wren. Many of these had been meeting for the previous fifteen years to discuss scientific problems, but a properly constituted society was now started. The first president was Sir Robert Murray. The King himself was a member.

From the start, the Society kept up a correspondence with European philosophers, and published *Philosophical Transactions* as a result. One of the early publications, in Latin, was Isaac Newton's *Mathematical Principles of Natural Philosophy*. But this was some years after Sir Robert's death. Besides framing the regulations of their society, the oldest in Great Britain and one of the oldest in the world, Murray read several philosophical papers. Though perhaps not an original philosopher of note, he was a promoter of scientific research at its very beginning.

Thomas Reid *(1710-1796)*

Born at Strachan, Kincardineshire, son of the parish minister. He matriculated at the Marischal College Aberdeen at the age of twelve, taking a course in Divinity. With one of his professors he went to London, Oxford and Cambridge where he met many eminent men of learning. At twenty-seven he became minister of New Machar, Aberdeen. He was appointed professor of Moral Philosophy at King's College, Aberdeen, where he founded a society of literary persons.

In middle life he took on the role of champion to confute what he considered the agnostic and atheistic philosophy of the English thinker Berkeley and the even more destructive David Hume.

Hume had published his *Philosophical Essays* in 1749, which denied the possibility of miracles, and indeed all supernatural religious events. In 1764 Reid published his *Inquiry into the Human Mind on the Principles of Common Sense*. He naturally had a great following amongst religious people. He was made a Doctor of Divinity of Aberdeen and succeeded the famous Adam Smith in the professorship of Moral Philosophy in Glasgow.

Reid founded the 'Common Sense' school of philosophy which held sway for generations in Britain, France and America.

David Hume *(1711-1776)*

Although his father had a small estate named Ninewells in Berwickshire, he had also a town house in Edinburgh, where David was born. He entered Edinburgh University at twelve. This was early, but not uncommon, as student classes were taught on the same elementary lines as secondary schools. After graduation Hume spent some time with a business firm in Bristol. He was afflicted with the same disease as troubled the young Robert Burns, hypochondria. To cure himself he went to France where he spent several years studying philosopy and reflecting on it. At the age of twenty-six he returned to London and published his *Treatise of Human Nature*, which, however, in his own words, 'fell dead-born from the press'. Yet this is a book which has never yet been properly answered, which shows the value to be placed on human judgement. Vastly disappointed, Hume brought out a further treatise in explanation of his first book. He then went into the country on his father's estate at Ninewells and studied political economy. He was more successful here, and his essays attracted favourable notices. He was for some years secretary to General St Clair, and travelled abroad. His *Philosophical Essays* came out in 1748, dealing with such controversial subjects as miracles, providence and immortality. This was a success also and he gained £1000 by its publication.

After a year or two at Ninewells he returned to Edinburgh, moving about to different apartments. These twelve years in the capital were productive. His *Political Discourses* were well received in England and abroad. He was a strong Tory and that party became well disposed towards him for obvious reasons. His rewriting of part of his famous *Treatise*, he considered incomparably the best of his writings.

But he did not publish a book, written at this time, on his scepticism regarding religion, *Dialogues Concerning Natural Religion* as he was unwilling to arouse popular antagonism.

As it was, his views were responsible for his being refused a professorship and he had to be content with the librarianship of the Advocates' Library in Edinburgh at a salary of £40 per annum. It gave him access to one of the best reference libraries in Europe, however, despite the poor salary.

He now turned to History and wrote on the period from the Union of the Crowns under James VI and I until his own lifetime. Although he was scrupulously fair and objective, his first volume received such a hostile criticism in London that he, from that day on, entertained a virulent hatred of all things English, of London society, and especially of the Whig party and the public in general. This affected the latter volumes of his *History of England*, which he used to beat the Whigs and boost the Tories. But with all its faults it introduced a new social approach to history and it also brought Hume more money than he had thought possible.

In 1763 he went as secretary to the British Embassy in Paris where he was received with honour. He spent the happiest years of his life here, being 'feasted on ambrosia and nectar and sleeping on beds of scented roseleaves.' He finally settled in Edinburgh in a house in St David Street, not, however, ironically named after him, but planned in honour of the patron saint of Wales. He was rich, had many friends, and was of an even temper and of cheerful and hospitable disposition. He bore no animosity to Thomas Reid for his attack on his philosophy. His last year was spent uncomplainingly, though he was afflicted by an embarrassing bowel complaint.

It is impossible in a short notice to give an account of Hume's theories and opinions. His chief characteristic in philosophy was his agnosticism, a negative attitude. So-called cause and effect, he repeated often, had no logical relationship. They were merely associated by our impressions and experience. Because stones had fallen from a height for ages, there was no guarantee that they would always do so. Mankind apparently was always betting on the main chance.

James Burnett, Lord Monboddo *(1714-1799)*

Born at Monboddo, Kincardineshire. He was educated at Aberdeen and Edinburgh Universities. He became an advocate at twenty-three. He met Thomson, the poet of the 'Seasons' and other literary men. One of his most famous court cases was the 'Douglas Cause', a very involved business which attracted universal interest.

In 1767 he was made a Lord of Session as Lord Monboddo. But even this elevation did not tone down his eccentricity. He was hated and condemned by his associates in law, yet his judgements were scrupulously fair and his legal knowledge was deep and wide. Speaking in an unaffected Scots voice he astounded the court by his eloquence, peppering his learned discourse with classical quotations from Latin and Greek.

He lived in St John's Street off the Canongate and always kept a hospitable table, to which the best society in the country were attracted, not the least of the attractions being his youngest daughter Elizabeth, amiable and extremely beautiful. She was made the subject of one of Burns' poems.

She received many offers of marriage but vowed never to leave her father, for all his peculiar habits. Her vow was accomplished in a tragic way, for she died of consumption in her twenty-third year. Monboddo kept her draped portrait before him all his remaining nine years.

Monboddo's philosophy was unique because it dealt in speculations on the origins of language and the remote ancestry of mankind. He anticipated Darwin in his theory of man's elevation from the state of an ape to that of an intelligent human being. In his linguistic studies he considered man to be of the same species as the orang-outang, the Bornean 'Man of the Woods', and thought that language was the result of man living in a community, with the necessity of communicating his needs and feelings. Monboddo employed Professor John Hunter, one of the best scholars of his time, as his secretary.

On the dreadful night of the Porteous Riots in Edinburgh, in 1736, Monboddo, then the young James Burnett aged 22, and a student, was inadvertently drawn into the mob through curiosity and forced to witness the 'kangaroo trial' and mob execution of Captain Porteous. He was so terrified that he resolved to flee from Edinburgh for ever, as a place unfit for a civilised being to live in.

Adam Smith *(1723-1790)*

He was born at Kirkcaldy, the posthumous son of Adam Smith, controller of customs. At the age of three he was kidnapped by a band of tinkers but rescued not long after, in Leslie Woods, by his uncle. After an education at Kirkcaldy, he studied at Glasgow, attending the lectures in moral philosophy of Dr Francis Hutcheson. He won a Snell exhibition in 1740 and went to Oxford. For four years he studied moral and political science and modern languages. He then returned to live with his widowed mother in Kirkcaldy, studying at home.

At the age of twenty-five he was invited by Lord Kames to give lectures on literature. He met David Hume and formed a close friendship. For the years 1751-64 he was a professor in Glasgow and during that time published a book on moral philosophy, *The Theory of Moral Sentiments*, which did not gain him many adherents as it was, if anything, a shallow treatment of the subject. He also published his theories on the first formation of languages, a matter which Monboddo was later to tackle.

But at the beginning of his professorship in Glasgow, as he later divulged, the first ideas of his great book on the wealth of the nations were being put together. This was not to be published for some years. In the meantime he travelled much in France as tutor to the young Duke of Buccleuch, and met many eminent intellectuals, including the writer of epigrams, the Duke of Rochefoucauld.

He lived in Kirkcaldy with his mother for ten years and laboured on his *Inquiry into the Nature and Causes of the Wealth of Nations*. This, on publication in 1776, was well received, the first to congratulate Smith being David Hume, then only a few months from death. The obvious place to go next was London, where he was enthusiastically welcomed by the political leaders and authors of that age. On the strength of the *Wealth of Nations*, Smith was appointed Commissioner of Customs for Scotland and lived with his aged mother and his cousin Jane Douglas in Panmure House off the Canongate in Edinburgh. Here he kept open hospitality to such famous men as Robert Adam, the architect, and Dr Black the chemist. He also belonged to one of the many Edinburgh convivial clubs. A few days before his death in 1790 he ordered that all his manuscripts, consisting chiefly of his lecture notes, on moral philosophy and law, were to be destroyed. A history of astronomy was a book he had projected but only a part had been written. This was to be spared from the flames and may still be seen. Adam Smith's grave is in an obscure corner of the nearby Canongate Churchyard.

Although the *Wealth of Nations* is a philosophical work, its abstractions have proved of greater advantage to economists than the theories of any other writer on economics, and still form a guide to what has been called 'the dismal science', i.e. political economy.

Adam Fergusson *(1724-1816)*

Born at Logierait, Perthshire, a son of the manse. Educated at Perth and the Universities of St Andrews and Edinburgh.

He was appointed deputy chaplain to the Black Watch regiment, but, like the Revd Howell Forgy, American chaplain at Pearl Harbour, his cry was 'Praise the Lord and pass the ammunition.' Fergusson fought shoulder to shoulder with his Black Watch congregation at the bloody battle of Fontenoy in 1745. He afterwards abandoned his military career as a chaplain and became successor to David Hume as Librarian of the Advocates' Library in Edinburgh. He was also tutor to Lord Bute's family.

He was appointed professor of natural philosophy at Edinburgh and later of the strange sounding science of 'pneumatics' which dealt with mental philosophy, perhaps including swelled heads.

He published an *Essay on the History of Civil Society*, and, on the outbreak of the American Revolution, brought out a pamphlet on the subject, which suggests that he did not support the British Government's point of view. In 1783 he published a book on the Roman Republic which had passed through several editions before Gibbon's great work on the *Decline and Fall of the Roman Empire* appeared in 1788.

Fergusson's last philosophical work was his *Principles of Moral and Political Science*. A French critic of eminence considered that Fergusson's principle of 'perfection', rather than 'benevolence and sympathy' in morals placed him above all his predecessors. He is certainly a philosopher to be admired, for most persons of that kidney never ventured into battles other than on words and ideas, whereas Adam got down to primitive emotions at Fontenoy.

Dugald Stewart *(1753-1828)*

Son of the brilliant mathematician Matthew Stewart, he was born in the Old College, Edinburgh, where his father was Professor of Mathematics. He attended the High School nearby until thirteen, then matriculated at the College. He went to Glasgow to sit under Thomas Reid, Professor of Moral Philosophy. In 1774 he took over the Professorship of Mathematics at

Edinburgh from his father and in 1783 visited Paris with the Marquess of Lothian.

In the year of British political unrest, 1793, he took no active part, being busy preparing an *Account of the Life and Writing of Dr Adam Smith* who had died three years before. He also published *The Outlines of Moral Philosophy* for the use of his students and to provide an argument for the young against David Hume's agnosticism.

He wrote biographies of the historian William Robertson and of Thomas Reid the philosopher, shortly after their deaths. He was the centre of a large circle of the supporters of the 'Common Sense' philosophy which, in the political atmosphere of that time, was ardently opposed to the liberating principles of the French Revolution. He contributed to the *Encyclopaedia Britannica* in the form of a 'review of philosophy in Modern European times.'

His conspicuous monument, copied from classical Greece, is in a less elaborate style than that erected to Burns lower down the Calton Hill, Edinburgh. A more permanent memorial exists in the fact that his writings inspired the Revd Henry Duncan to found the first savings bank in Britain in Ruthwell, Dumfriesshire in 1810.

Thomas Brown *(1778-1820)*

He was born in Wigtown, son of the parish minister. At fourteen he matriculated at Edinburgh University where he got to know Dugald Stewart and took his degree in 1803. He wrote articles to the *Edinburgh Review* and published several books of poems. He could be expected to join the 'Common Sense School', but he appears to have read widely in philosophy of different ages and schools, and to have decided to oppose the theories of the large Scottish school. He wrote for his students in Moral Philosophy a series of lectures on the *Philosophy of the Human Mind* in which he opposed Stewart and Reid.

Sir William Hamilton *(1788-1856)*

He was born in Glasgow and educated at the University there and at Balliol, Oxford, as an exhibitioner. He was a brilliant student and passed as an advocate at twenty-five. He was Professor of History, then of Logics and Metaphysics in Edinburgh. He wrote for the Edinburgh Review on certain aspects of philosophy in which he attacked Thomas Brown (above, then deceased). He also attacked the famous French philosopher and education pioneer Victor Cousin (1792-1878) although, like Brown, Cousin had made a long study of every system of philosophy, ancient, mediaeval and modern, and his reorganisation of French primary education, based on sound philosophical ground, was foremost in Europe.

Cousin's philosophy was tolerant and broadminded, but Hamilton was another disciple of the Common Sense School, as he showed by editing the works of Reid and Dugald Stewart.

As the reader will have realised, philosophy in Scotland was a battlefield, as elsewhere, and demonstrates only one thing for certain. John Duns

Scotus spoke the truth, six hundred years before, when he said that the will predominated over the intellect. None of the minds of these conflicting philosophers started as a blank sheet; they were all prejudiced.

Henry Calderwood *(1830-1897)*

He was born at Peebles and educated at the Royal High School (Edinburgh) and University there. At twenty-six he was appointed to the Greyfriars Church, Glasgow. He taught Moral Philosophy in Glasgow and then in Edinburgh. He achieved fame early, when at twenty-four he published *The Philosophy of the Infinite* in which he attacked the philosophy of Sir William Hamilton who had argued that man can have no knowledge of the Infinite. By this term neither protagonist was speaking of infinity as astronomers, but as theological philosophers.

In his day Darwinism was driving many theologians frantic in their condemnation of evolution. Calderwood took up the cudgels on the side of the angels with *Science and Religion* and *Evolution and Man's Place in Nature*. His books were very popular in their day but now gather dust.

Edward Caird *(1835-1908)*

He was born at Greenock and educated at Glasgow University and Balliol, Oxford. He was a brilliant classical and theological student. At thirty-one he became Professor of Moral Philosophy at Glasgow and in 1893 succeeded the famous Jowett as Master of Balliol College. Along with Thomas Hill Green (1836-82) his colleague at Balliol, he founded a school of English philosophy and theology which had a wide influence on national life. One of its main principles was that it may occasionally be a moral duty to rebel against the state in the interest of the state itself. Their motto was, 'Will, not force, is the basis of the state'. This will be seen as the philosophical principle opposed to the idea of a police state, detested by democratic people, but unfortunately now becoming more evident in modern Britain.

Caird and Green did not wholly approve Hume's philosophy, as it made nonsense of any principle of man's responsibility for his actions. But compared with Hume's clear thought and logic they both seem rather vague.

John Henry Muirhead *(1855-1940)*

He was born in Glasgow, educated at Glasgow Academy and University, and Oxford. His classical learning enabled him to make many excellent translations. His philosophical books include *Philosophy and Life* (1902), *German Philosophy in Relation to the War* (1915), *Coleridge as a Philosopher* (1930), *Rule and End in Morals* (1932). He was a quiet studious man, almost the type of a philosophic hermit, much perturbed by the sudden decline of civilised life.

Richard Burdon Haldane, Viscount *(1856-1928)*

Born in Perthshire, son of a Writer to the Signet, he was educated at Edinburgh Academy, Edinburgh and Gottingen Universities. He was one of the very eminent students of his time in philosophy.

Before entering Parliament as a Liberal Member for Haddingtonshire he practised law. In 1905 Campbell-Bannerman made him Secretary for War and he carried out a complete re-organisation of the British Army. This was appreciated in 1914 when the British Expeditionary Force, though small in number, surprised the German Command by its discipline and fire power, though armed only with rifles against machine-guns. Obvious later, this lack of modern equipment could be put down to the usual reluctance of the War Office to accept new inventions. This was not Haldane's fault. He had to face fierce opposition from the Colonel Blimps of his day, amongst them generals who later took commands on the Western Front. Haldane created the Officers' Training Corps as early as 1909. Sad though it seems now, this secured a steady supply of junior officers from schools and universities to the trenches, where their average survival time was about a fortnight. The Territorial Army was another of Haldane's efforts.

Haldane also implemented the formation of the Imperial General Staff but, most important, recognised the place of science in war. He set up the National Physics Laboratory at Teddington, and the aeronautics centre at Farnborough. After the opposition to his ideas had died down, he was recognised as a great war minister.

In addition, he had already, before 1914, done great service as chairman of a committee on university education. Its funding took a long time to be implemented. He had also done his best, by visiting Germany and trying to solve political problems, to avert war. His reward for this was to be accused of pro-German sympathies and to be excluded from the first Coalition Cabinet.

He now felt justly aggrieved and turned back to his first love, philosophy. In 1921 he published *The Reign of Relativity* a considered work of reconciliation between scientific fact and metaphysics. *The Philosophy of Humanism* followed in 1922, in which he summed up all the principles of the continental philosophers from Erasmus, the father of humanistic philosophy.

He continued to demonstrate that philosophy was not a handicap to practical men, but that it is necessary as a basis for any substantial advances. He spent much time on the Workers' Educational Association and on arranging the organisation of knowledge in the national interest.

John Scott Haldane *(1860-1936)*

He was born in Edinburgh and also attended Edinburgh Academy and Edinburgh University, but favoured Jena University in Germany. Like Viscount Haldane, above, philosophy was a minor interest, taking a back seat to practical activity. J.S. Haldane from an early age took an interest in science and particularly in mining research, being President of the Institute of Mining Engineers. His judgement was employed as chairman of Committees on Public Health and other commissions.

He published *Essays on Philosophical Criticism* when only twenty-three, in collaboration with another philosopher. The last of his numerous books was in his seventieth year when he brought out *The Sciences and*

Philosophy. There seems to have been a hereditary disposition in the Haldanes towards a combination of abstract speculation and practical application. A sister of R.B. Haldane was a student of philosophy and at one time a nurse and ultimately manager of the Royal Infirmary of Edinburgh. Two earlier brothers Haldane, born in London, carried their philosophy so far as to initiate a plan for training African children in England, to be sent as Christian missionaries to their own countrymen. The world owes much to the Haldanes, philosophical and practical.

Mathematics

Most of the philosophers, especially the natural philosophers, had to study mathematics to a very advanced level. Some eminent men, such as Adam Smith and David Hume, were also well-versed in mathematics. It should therefore be assumed, in nearly all cases of eminent engineers of all branches, in physicists and chemists and students of other sciences, that mathematics was a *sine qua non*.

For centuries, up to the present, mathematics was regarded as the purest presentation of truth, and the axioms that formed the basis of, for example, geometry, were thought to be logically unassailable. But this solid foundation has now been undermined and mathematics has joined other philosophies as a study which is indispensable to progress but unsupportable by logic. The weakest link in the mathematical chain is in the enormous assumption that is made in accepting that results obtained in calculations of finite quantities are also compatible into infinity. Einstein and many others have shown that time and space can make nonsense of Euclid. But, as Hume said, while we can never pursue an inquiry to an absolute conclusion, it is a source of satisfaction to go as far as we can.

Scottish mathematicians have contributed a fair share to mathematical advances. Perhaps the most important was John Napier's invention of logarithms which was an epoch-making breakthrough in aiding calculations relative to astronomy, and other sciences involving either minute or vast calculations. We note him in the chapter on inventors, because his mathematical genius was eclipsed by his ability in other sciences.

Robert Balfour *(1550-1625)*

He was born in the same year as Napier. He was educated at St Andrews and at Paris. Most of his life was spent on the Continent, which prevented his being drawn into the civil and religious struggle in Scotland. He was appointed principal of Guienne College, Bordeaux, which was at the height of its reputation as the University of the Arts and Theology for the ancient French province of Guienne. The famous essayist and humanist Montaigne, whose chateau was only a few miles from Bordeaux, had been educated here, and was still living nearby during Balfour's principalship. The English had been expelled from Guienne in 1453, to the great benefit of the province. Balfour, on account of being a Scot, was acceptable in Bordeaux. He was one of the foremost propagandists for the fiery image of the Scots character.

Besides being an eminent mathematician he translated Aristotle's works from Greek into Latin. A copy of his book, printed in Bordeaux in 1618, is in the British Museum, along with many poems praising him as 'the Phoenix of his Age, a scholar worthy to be compared with the ancients.'

Colin MacLaurin *(1698-1746)*

He was the son of the Revd John MacLaurin of Glendaruel. He was born at Kilmadan, a wild picturesque part of Argyll near Dunoon. From the start he was brilliant, proceeding to Glasgow at a tender age and graduating MA when only fifteen. He was elected to the Chair of Mathematics in the Marischal College, Aberdeen, when nineteen. At twenty-one he was made Fellow of the Royal Society in London and met Sir Isaac Newton, then seventy-seven. In his first year as an FRS he published his notable work on geometry, describing the general rules for lines and curves. It was, of course, in Latin. He carried Newton's work further, in this book, but also advanced a theorem which bears his name.

He travelled on the continent and obtained a prize from the French Academy for an essay on the percussion of bodies. At twenty-seven, he was recommended by Newton as Professor at Edinburgh. He published a book on ocean tides in which he expounded his theory known as MacLaurin's Ellipsoids. Strange to say, no workman up till then had worried about scientifically correct level surfaces. MacLaurin defined this. At his suggestion the Philosophical Society (later the Royal Society) of Edinburgh was set up.

Despite his Highland origin and name, he opposed the Jacobites in 1745 by helping to make trenches and barricades to protect Edinburgh against Prince Charles. Then he wisely fled to England when Cameron of Lochiel entered the city by the Netherbow Port. He returned, however, after Culloden and died at Edinburgh in June 1746.

John Playfair *(1748-1819)*

Also son of a parish minister, he was born at Benvie, Forfarshire, and educated at home. He matriculated when fourteen at St Andrews to take a divinity course. He was inducted to his father's vacancy and intended to support his parents as a minister but science called strongly. He wrote a paper on *The Arithmetic of Impossible Quantities* for the Royal Society, London. He succeeded Dugald Stewart as Professor of Mathematics in Edinburgh and taught there for many years. His *Elements of Geometry*, a textbook, went through many editions. His life was fully occupied in looking after the affairs of the Edinburgh Royal Society and taking up the cudgels on behalf of John Leslie, the physicist, who had antagonised the clergy because of his friendship with David Hume. Playfair was Professor of Moral as well as Natural Philosophy at Edinburgh. He wrote on these subjects and also contributed an article on the progress of Mathematics and Physics for the *Encyclopaedia Britannica*. He had an axiom named after him. His monument, with a classic Latin inscription, stands at the corner of the Old Observatory on the Calton Hill, Edinburgh.

Sir James Ivory *(1765-1842)*

He rose by his own efforts to great eminence. His father was a watchmaker in Dundee and James attended the local school before entering St Andrews College to study divinity. But like MacLaurin he turned away from the ministry to mathematics, a subject in which he had distinguished himself at St Andrews. With his friend John Leslie he went to Edinburgh but afterwards took up school-teaching in Dundee. This was an ill-paid profession so he left it for flax-spinning which was perhaps less wearisome. He was now approaching forty with little hope of recognition in his study. But he sent several papers on mathematics to the Royal Society in Edinburgh.

He gave up expectations in his native land and was appointed Professor of Mathematics at the Military College, Great Marlow (later moved to Sandhurst). Now he got recognition in his profession, being knighted and awarded a pension. He was made a Fellow of the Royal Society and received a rather belated honour (LLD) from his own Alma Mater, St Andrews. His interest in astronomy found expression in many essays. He also, like MacLaurin, had immortality conferred on him by reason of his theorem on ellipsoids being named after him.

Sir John Leslie *(1766-1832)*

Like Ivory he had a struggle and realised how hard it was to overcome the burden of a humble parentage. He was born in Alexander Selkirk's (Crusoe's) town of Largo in Fife, and received a very scrappy schooling. But he showed such ability that his parents saved all they had, to send him to St Andrews University at the age of thirteen. He studied theology and met Adam Smith, who was a fellow Fifer and at this time was living at Kirkcaldy and probably often at St Andrews reading for his *Wealth of Nations*. With Ivory, Leslie went to Edinburgh, where their ways parted, Leslie going to Virginia as tutor to two American students. He returned to London and did hackwork for several booksellers. He then travelled in Europe with others, studying briefly at various colleges. He met Hume and was befriended by that genial and urbane philosopher, but, as stated above, he found his application for the Chair of Mathematics in Edinburgh opposed by the clergy. In 1819 he was Professor of Physics and Natural Philosophy in Edinburgh. He also, like Playfair, wrote a text-book on *The Elements of Geometry* and a *Philosophy of Arithmetic*. Perhaps his work as a physicist showed more practical results, for he invented a differential thermometer which had as a testing bulb the 'Leslie Cube'. He used this instrument in many and varied experiments including the measurement of light and the temperature of high altitudes by means of space balloons. Recognition, when it came, was unanimous, apart from a few growls arising from theological bile, due to Hume's association of half-a-century before. Nevertheless his famous experiment of boiling ice-cold water survived him for generations to astound students in Edinburgh University.

Andrew Russell Forsyth *(1858-1942)*

Born in Glasgow, he studied at Liverpool and at Cambridge. At twenty-four he was professor of Mathematics at University College, Liverpool. Two years later he moved to Cambridge as lecturer, then was Professor for fifteen years before being appointed as Professor of Mathematics at the Imperial College, London.

His chief work was in the abstract field of pure mathematics where he produced many original and ingenious theories on such themes as differential equations and problems of space measurement.

He was very conversant with the works of many European and American mathematicians and wrote appreciations and explanations of their works. He edited the *Journal of Mathematics* at the end of last century and was awarded the Gold Medal of the Royal Society. When seventy-seven he published *The Intrinsic Geometry of Ideal Space* incorporating many of the new discoveries by physicists and astronomers.

The Church

The earliest native saint was St Ninian, a Briton of Strathclyde, who died in AD 432 after having founded the church of Candida Casa, or White House, at Whithorn in Galloway about AD 400. He carried out missionary work and founded churches in Ayrshire, Lanark, Stirling and Forfar and right up the east coast of Pictland as far as St Ninian's Isle, Shetland, where an ancient stone was found bearing this inscription 'The enclosure of the disciple of Ninian'.

Christianity had been introduced to Britain when it was under Roman rule, and when they left there were many Christian churches all over southern Britain and Ireland. They sent missionaries northwards amongst their fellow-Britons in Strathclyde and among the Picts who spoke a language similar to Brythonic, the British language.

St Kentigern, whose familiar name was Mungo, was a Briton also, born early in the sixth century. His church was on the site of a former foundation of Ninian at Glasgow. For a time he was forced to retire to Wales because of the oppression of a heathen British king, but he returned to his seat in Glasgow.

St Columba was a Scot of Ireland who fled from that country because of his part in a sanguinary battle at Culdrevny. With twelve companions he landed on Iona and obtained permission from the Pictish king Brude to build a church there, about the middle of the sixth century. From this centre missionaries were sent out to many parts of Britain and Europe. St Columba met St Kentigern some years after landing in Alba (now Scotland).

St Cuthbert was an Angle of Lothian who became Abbot of Melrose about AD 661. The Anglian kings, notably Edwin and Egbert, were waging war on their neighbours, despite the fact that all were fellow-Christians. Even Cuthbert founded a church in Galloway at Kirkcudbright to oppose the Pictish church at Whithorn. He tried to dissuade Egbert from campaigning into Pictland, an expedition which ended in Egbert's death and the ruination of Northumbria. Shortly after Cuthbert's death the Roman Catholic Church, headed by the Pope and organised under bishops, took over from the Celtic Church, and the subsequent history of churchmen is therefore under central discipline, and devoted to the cultivation of knowledge and the arts of peace until the end of the Middle Ages. In Scotland, in common with other lands, the Church was openly criticised for abuses which had crept in. These criticisms had come to a head in Scotland in the middle of the sixteenth century, which marked the start of a period of bitter religious strife whose repercussions have not yet died away.

We propose to note some of the outstanding figures, whether leaders or humble protagonists, irrespective of creed.

Bernard de Linton *(c.1270-1331)*

Little is known of his early life but he was well educated in Latin, having studied all the available classic writers, including Sallust and Cicero. This points to a monastic schooling. He was parson of Mordington, near Berwick in 1296 and must have been horrified in that year (as the whole of Europe was) by the massacre of the entire population of Berwick by Edward I, the first act of war between Scotland and England for a century.

When Bruce became King after 1306 de Linton was made Chancellor during the whole of his reign. He was elected Abbot of Arbroath in 1311. He was responsible for writing many important documents, both diplomatic and legal, but the most far-reaching was probably the famous *Declaration of Arbroath* of 1320, addressed to Pope John XXII at Avignon. The style was based on Sallust, a fine example of the best mediaeval religious prose and the subject was the determination of the Scots to remain independent of England. For the last year of his life de Linton was awarded a pension and made Bishop of the Isles, resident in the Isle of Man.

James Kennedy *(1408-1465)*

He was a grandson of King Robert III, educated at the new University of St Andrews, then studying at Louvain, in Brabant, now part of Belgium. He was a favourite nephew of James I who made him Bishop of Dunkeld when he was barely thirty.

He went on a mission to Rome in 1439, two years after the murder of his royal uncle. The Pope was so much impressed by Kennedy that he made him Abbot of Scone and Bishop of St Andrews. Naturally he supported the papacy in the troubled time that lay ahead. He is said to have given James II much wise counsel, one legend being that he took up a sheaf of arrows and showed how, by breaking them one by one, the King's enemies could be likewise overcome.

He was a munificent endower of St Andrews, founding the College of St Salvador, which had a bell named after his niece Katherine who inspired the annual Kate Kennedy festivities still held in St Andrews.

William Elphinstone *(c.1431-1514)*

He was the grandson of the Laird of Pittendreich, Stirlingshire, and graduated MA at Glasgow. After being a parson in Perthshire he studied law at Paris and at Orleans. On his return to Scotland he became deputy Bishop at Glasgow, then Lothian. He became Chancellor to James III and on the latter's death he was ambassador to Europe for James IV. As Bishop of Aberdeen he laid the foundations of King's College and was responsible for the Papal sanctioning of the new University in 1495.

He prepared the Aberdeen Breviary, which was one of the first books to be printed in Scotland, to take the place of the English (Sarum) Breviary. The end of his long life was saddened by the disaster of Flodden. He had warned the King against the invasion of England but James thought he knew better.

Patrick Hamilton *(1504-1528)*

He was the great-grandson of James II and the son of Sir Patrick Hamilton. Being of such noble rank he was made titular Abbot of Ferne, Ross-shire, when only thirteen. At sixteen he graduated from the University of Paris, and then studied at Louvain, where the great humanist Erasmus was a lecturer.

He returned to Scotland and became a member of the newly formed University of St Andrews. He composed a musical mass and conducted it himself in the cathedral. But his heretical teaching had annoyed James Beaton, the Archbishop of St Andrews, so the young priest took flight back to the continent. He met Martin Luther and Melancthon the reformers at Wittenburg and enrolled as a student at the new University of Marburg.

He was now totally won over to the new doctrines and, probably trusting to his royal blood and powerful Hamilton following, he returned to Scotland. He was invited by Archbishop Beaton to a conference at St Andrews and, trusting to a safe conduct, he attended and preached and argued for a whole month. He was then summoned before a court of bishops and clergy presided over by Beaton where evidence, cunningly obtained by a Dominican friar, Campbell, was brought against him.

He was condemned to be burned alive on 29 February 1528 and, knowing that the Hamiltons would mount a powerful force to rescue him, his accusers carried out the sentence without delay. But, as was said later, 'the reek of Patrick Hamilton infected all it blew upon'. His exposition of Lutheran principles, *Loci communes*, was immediately translated into English and spread through both Scotland and England.

George Wishart *(1513-1546)*

He was born at Pitarrow, Aberdeenshire, son of James Wishart. He attended the University of Aberdeen, recently founded, and then travelled in Europe, which was stirring with religious unrest following Luther's defiance of the Church. Already in France and Germany heretics were being condemned to the flames. John Calvin had published his *Institutes*, containing the text of a reformed religion. From within the Roman Church, popes and theologians had attempted for centuries to bring about reform, but this did not make the new rebellion any more acceptable.

Wishart came back to Scotland and began teaching in Montrose where he soon aroused opposition from the Church. He was accused of heresy and fled to England in 1538. Henry VIII had just been excommunicated by the Pope so, for the time, Wishart thought himself safe. But in 1539 he was accused of heresy at Bristol and fled to Germany and Switzerland where he lived and studied with the Calvinists. He returned to England and joined the Corpus Christi College at Cambridge for some years, unmolested.

Mary, Queen of Scots, was born in 1542 and a scheme was set afoot to marry her, as a child, to Edward, son of Henry VIII. Wishart was a member of the Commission sent to Scotland to arrange this. But the Scots leaders of Church and State suspected Henry's motives and refused to consider the proposal.

Wishart began to preach through the towns to enthusiastic gatherings. His success in Edinburgh, Perth, Leith and Haddington was alarming to the Church. He was arrested by the Earl of Bothwell at Ormiston in East Lothian, and carried for trial to St Andrews. He was condemned by a clerical court presided over by David Beaton, Cardinal of St Andrews. As an obstinate heretic he was burned at the stake on the Castle Green.

John Knox *(1514?-1572)*

He was born in the Gifford-gate, Haddington, the son of a well-to-do countryman. He was educated at Haddington and at St Andrews University, for the church, one of his professors being John Major, a very erudite Latin scholar and author of tales of Scottish traditions. There is no record of Knox's life for some years after his college days, but when George Wishart, the martyr, was arrested in 1546, Knox sprang to his defence carrying a two-handed sword, which Wishart told him to return to its sheath.

Archbishop Beaton was murdered the following year and Knox was openly preaching Protestantism in Fife. He had renounced his priesthood, but it is not known why. He joined the Archbishop's murderers in St Andrews Castle. The French Fleet, in support of the Catholic queen mother, Mary of Guise, attacked the defenders in the Castle and they surrendered. Knox and his associates were condemned to the French galleys for nineteen months, and no doubt this cruel experience hardened Knox's heart. He was released at the request of the young son of Henry VIII, Edward, and became first a licensed preacher in England, then a royal chaplain and was even offered a bishopric, which he refused.

Unluckily the Protestant Edward died young and was succeeded by the Catholic Mary, known for the persecution of heretics as Bloody Mary. Knox escaped to Europe where he travelled until he settled in Geneva for a peaceful few years with his English wife and her mother. He prepared an English Bible.

His heart was in Scotland and he returned to brave the opposition of Mary of Guise, but his life was immediately in danger. He was declared an outlaw in Edinburgh but fled to Dundee. He now inspired the multitude to destroy the monasteries.

He made a truce with the Queen Regent and the French, and continued to preach the reformed faith. But civil war broke out and battles were fought around Edinburgh and Leith until, on appeal for help to the Protestant Elizabeth, English troops arrived and the French Catholic armies were expelled by ship.

Mary, Queen of Scots, now a young widow of nineteen, returned to Scotland to find that Knox's party, the Lords of the Congregation, had passed acts virtually condemning Catholicism and making the celebration of mass a penal offence. She was not a woman to be intimidated. She immediately celebrated mass in her household at Holyrood House, her palace in Edinburgh.

Knox had several stormy interviews with her but she gave as good as she got. Both spoke French. Mary's was courtly, Knox's the rude tongue of the galleys.

Mary now married her Catholic cousin Henry Darnley. The two rulers were represented on the coinage as Mary and Henry. Darnley attended Knox's sermons but was immediately offended by Knox comparing him to Ahab who could not control his wife. Knox was forbidden to preach in the capital so he went to the west country.

While he was absent, Darnley and his friends murdered the Queen's Italian favourite David Rizzio, through jealousy. But, shortly after, Mary took a dislike to her husband, the father of her child the future James VI and I. She fell in love with the ruffian Bothwell and Darnley was conveniently assassinated.

During the subsequent scandal which led to the Queen's imprisonment, Knox was in England seeing to the education of his two sons. He returned in time to see Mary's escape and defeat and flight to the tender mercies of Elizabeth, who finally beheaded her.

Civil war broke out in Scotland, Knox took a paralytic stroke and retired to St Andrews but came back, a dying man, to preach a powerful sermon in St Giles, Edinburgh, denouncing the Catholic French King to his ambassador, for the Massacre of St Bartholomew which had shocked Europe. He died in his house in the High Street.

The English ambassador wrote to Elizabeth at the time, 'This one man was able in one hour to put more life in us than five hundred trumpets continually blustering in our ears.' Yet, even at the present day, Knox is generally disliked by Scottish writers and readers alike, though, for all his preaching of intolerance, he did not descend to practising it, as many religious bigots did out of Scotland.

Andrew Melville (1545-1622)

He was born at Baldovy, Montrose. His father, Richard, was killed by English invaders, at the battle of Pinkie, east of Edinburgh, when Andrew was two. He was educated at Montrose and learned Greek from a French scholar in Montrose. His unique knowledge of Greek surprised the professors at St Andrews, to whom it was unknown. He went to Paris and there added Oriental languages to his repertoire. He studied law at Poitiers then had to leave for Switzerland because of civil war. He was made Professor of Latin and Greek at Geneva.

At twenty-nine he returned to Scotland as Principal of Glasgow University. The Scottish Universities had fallen into ruin, so Melville set about the tremendous task of reviving them. He collected scholars and students in all subjects to Glasgow, and made it once more renowned. He did the same with Aberdeen and St Andrews but his new doctrines and his attack on age-long philosophical beliefs were opposed by other teachers.

He was elected Moderator of the General Assembly of the Presbyterian Churches and opposed James VI's attempts to enforce a system of Episcopacy in Scotland. He was summoned before the Privy Council, a body by which James carried out his personal likes and dislikes. To escape imprisonment in Blackness Castle Melville wisely fled to England where his reputation for learning was recognised by his reception at Oxford and Cambridge.

Defiantly he returned to Scotland and resumed his teaching as Rector of St Andrews. He maintained that Scotland was a theocracy and not subject to the ruler in spiritual matters. The King deprived him of his rectorship, but he remained dean of the theological faculty.

James was made monarch of Great Britian in 1603 and conducted all business from London. He summoned Melville and seven other clergymen, including James Melville, Andrew's nephew, to a conference in London to settle the religious differences. Andrew delivered his opinion freely in two long speeches, adding in private a sarcastic epigram in Latin, which, on being told of it, James well understood, because it was aimed at the Royal Courts' religious ritual. Furious at this freedom, he committed Melville to the Tower for four years. He would have had him to the block but he feared the Scots reaction. On his release Melville went to Sedan where he was a professor for the rest of his life, a voluntary exile from despotism.

St John Ogilvy (1580-1615)

He was born in Scotland of a famous family of which the Earl of Airlie is chief. They were all supporters of royalty in the civil wars and suffered for it at the hands of the Whigs. The Ogilvys rose in the Jacobite Rebellions of 1715 and 1745 and of course were punished for their loyalty to the losing side.

Many young men of Catholic faith fled from England and Scotland during the persecutions that followed the Protestant ascendancy, for both sides of the religious conflict resorted to execution of their opponents. Even Jean Calvin in Geneva, opposed over certain doctrinal questions which were considered mere quibbles by other theologians, condemned and executed Michael Servetus, bringing discredit upon himself and his followers.

In Scotland after 1560, the celebration of mass was penal and for deliberate repetition, death was the sentence. John Ogilvy was educated in Germany where he came in contact with the colleges under the teaching of the Society of Jesus, or Jesuits, formed by Loyola earlier in the sixteenth century. Knowing very well that martyrdom awaited them in England, Scotland and Ireland, if discovered, many young priests of the Society went back during the reigns of Elizabeth, the Stuarts and the Commonwealth. John Ogilvy, disguised as a soldier, crossed into Scotland and was arrested in Glasgow in October 1614. He was taken to Edinburgh and tried on the Act of 1560. Despite his able defence he was condemned to death by hanging, which was carried out on 28 February 1615.

At the time of his death Archbishop Spottiswoode, who was sympathetic to a policy of tolerance, published in Edinburgh *A True Relation of the Proceedings against John Ogilvy, a Jesuit*. And in Paris, in 1885, James Forbes brought out in French an account of the Catholic Church in Scotland, alluding to the martyrdom of John Ogilvy. Ogilvy was canonised in 1976.

Robert Leighton *(1611-1684)*

He was the son of Dr Alexander Leighton, a religious author and minister. Opinions differ as to his birthplace, whether at London or in Edinburgh or at Ulysseshaven or Usan, or on the coast of Forfar. But his family belonged to the latter place. When he was a student at Edinburgh, the year before taking his MA, his father was summoned to the infamous Court of Star Chamber in England, where Archbishop Laud sat in secret to pass sentence quite arbitrarily on civil or religious offenders. Alexander had written against Episcopacy, after studying medicine at Leyden. His sentence was atrocious, even in an age of cruelty. He was fined £10,000, forced to stand in the pillory, have his ears cut off, his nose slit and his face branded. He escaped, but was recaptured, and his sentence carried out with inhuman exactness. Laud over-reached himself in time and was beheaded, and Leighton was recompensed by the Commonwealth by being made Keeper of Lambeth Palace for a short time before his death.

The effect of this intolerance upon his son can well be imagined. During his entire life he was noted for learning, benevolence and tolerance. As a young minister he was inducted to Newbattle parish, Midlothian, in 1641, after spending several years in France, where he met many shades of religious faith. He signed the National Covenant, but took a dislike to the Covenanters and gave up the ministry in favour of university life. He was made Principal of Edinburgh, and taught divinity.

When Charles II was restored after the fall of the Commonwealth, he resolved to avenge his father's betrayal by the Scottish covenanting party. He tried to impose bishops upon the Presbyterians and fixed on Leighton as a likely candidate. The chosen bishops met in London and a form of Episcopacy was agreed on, so off they set to Scotland to face the Covenanting party. Leighton discovered that his colleagues looked upon their return to Scotland as a kind of triumphal tour, so he left them. Eventually he chose the poorest of the bishoprics, that of Dunblane, and did his best to persuade his fellow-bishops to come to terms with Presbyterians.

After trying in vain to stop the persecution of the Covenanters he went to London to resign his seat at Dunblane but was persuaded to keep it. After the Battle of Rullion Green and the cruelties that followed, he again protested to the King with little success. He was appointed Archbishop of Glasgow where he tried more earnestly to get reconciliation. Seeing the persecution renewed and no hope of either side relenting, he retired to Sussex where he spent his remaining years happily. He left his library to the diocese of Dunblane and his money to educational charities in Scotland.

Alexander Peden *(1626-1686)*

He was born at Auchincloich, Sorn, Ayrshire, and after village schooling took a degree in divinity at Glasgow University. He was ordained as minister of New Luce, Galloway, in 1660, where he remained for three years. Unluckily on the restoration of Charles II strong measures were enforced against the Presbyterians and by the Ejectment Act of 1663 he was put out of his ministry as were many others, and forbidden to preach anywhere.

A rebellion broke out in 1666, in which Peden was probably involved. This was crushed in a skirmish on the Pentland Hills near Edinburgh where fifty Covenanters were slain and many prisoners taken and punished. Those who escaped were branded as rebels with a price on their heads.

Peden escaped to Ireland but was caught in the south of Ayrshire and brought to Edinburgh. With many others he was imprisoned on the Bass Rock, a dreary and uncomfortable spot off the Lothian coast. Several prisoners lost their reason, others died of privation, but Peden survived, only to be ordered to be sent to Virginia with sixty others as a slave. But the captain refused to handle such a crew of enthusiasts and they were set free at London.

Peden made his way back to the west country where he was chased about by the dragoons, sheltering in woods, caves and cottages, and preaching to the hillmen, or Covenanters, in conventicles on the moors. One of his congregation was the young James Renwick, fated to be the last of the covenanting martyrs. Peden died peacefully in hiding in his brother's house in Ayrshire.

Gilbert Burnet *(1643-1715)*

He was born in Edinburgh, son of Robert Burnet, afterwards Lord Crimond. Following his father's example he took the middle road in politics, siding neither with the Covenanters nor with the Royalists. He was educated at Marischal College, Aberdeen, and became a probation minister in the year when his father died. He would not accept a benefice as the state was very unsettled, following Charles II's return. He studied for some time at Oxford and Cambridge and then in Holland and France, learning Hebrew in Amsterdam and meeting Protestants of all septs.

He became a member of the new Royal Society when in London, and met the future Duke of Lauderdale, at that time inclined to treat the Covenanters leniently. He became minister of Saltoun, East Lothian, then was appointed Professor of Divinity in Glasgow. He worked with Robert Leighton in trying to make a compromise between the extreme religious bodies, but his efforts met with Lauderdale's disapproval so he thought it wise to go to England. But Lauderdale's spite denounced him to Charles II and he lost his chaplainship at court. He fell out of favour with the Duke of York, once again due to Lauderdale. Even when preparing his *History of the Reformation in England* he was denied access to the famous Cottonian Library, through Lauderdale.

He could do nothing right in such an atmosphere of bigotry and personal malice. Even his efforts to save those noblemen condemned to the block in the Popish Plot of 1678, was used to deprive him of his appointments, and his sermon against Catholics on Guy Fawkes Day, 5 November, preached by every clergyman in England as a routine, made him an enemy of James II, a secret Catholic. Burnet fled to Holland and became a Dutch subject, marrying a Dutch heiress of Scots descent, Mary Scott.

He rendered William of Orange great service, and when the Revolution occurred and William and Mary reigned over Britain and Ireland, he drew up the English text of their declaration to the nation. He was rewarded with the see of Salisbury but once again the theological bile was in evidence. The Archbishop of Canterbury refused to consecrate him. The provision known as Queen Anne's Bounty, which benefits the poorer livings of the Anglican Church, was Burnet's original idea, though his influence disappeared on her accession.

His most valuable book is *History of his own Times* where he was so frank that his famous sons had to omit certain passages for their own well-being. One of his last acts of tolerance was his effort to have the Non-Conformists admitted to the Church of England, but it only gave mighty offence to the High Church clergy.

He met with the normal fate of the man of peace who attempts to reconcile the quarrelsome fiddler and his wife. They both turn and rend him.

James Renwick *(1662-1688)*

He was a native of Moniaive, Dumfriesshire, son of a poor weaver. By scraping and saving, his father educated him, and he enrolled at Edinburgh University where he maintained himself by teaching until the end of his divinity course. Students were required to take an oath of allegiance to the Crown but Renwick refused. He was capped, nevertheless, and became an adherent of Richard Cameron's party of extreme Covenanters, named the Cameronians after their leader, who had been killed by the dragoons at Aird's Moss in 1660.

Renwick's preaching soon made him prominent. When in Edinburgh in 1681 he was a witness of the execution of the Covenanter Donald Cargill, aged seventy-one, on the gallows in the Grassmarket. This unlawful event merely confirmed him in his course.

He was persuaded for his own safety to go to Holland where he studied theology at Groningen and was ordained a minister. He returned to Scotland, more enthusiastic than ever, determined to fight religious oppression to the death. He became a field-preacher and was declared a rebel. The South-west of Scotland was a scene of unrest; assassinations of government supporters were followed by arbitrary executions, finings and imprisonments. At Sanquhar, on the coronation of James II, Renwick and his friends renounced the king, but refused to join the ill-fated rebellion under the Earl of Argyll against James. Even when some concessions were made to the Covenanters, Renwick's followers continued to hold the illegal field-preachings.

A reward was offered for his capture and to protest against the Indulgence Act he was foolhardy enough to visit Edinburgh where he was recognised and seized. At his trial he maintained his right to worship God as he chose, refused to accept a pardon on condition of acknowledging the King's authority, and was condemned to death. He met his unjust end with resolution. He was the last covenanting martyr, for the tyrannical regime ended shortly after.

John Glas *(1695-1773)*

He was born in Auchtermuchty, Fife, son of the parish minister. He was educated at Perth Grammar School and at St Andrews and Edinburgh Universities. He was ordained minister at Tealing, near Dundee.

He soon began to show a marked hostility to organised religion. The National Covenant was declared to be of little value to Christians. He would have nothing to do with the established church and drew his very select congregation from any parishioners who cared to follow him. He was the sole authority apart from Christ, whom he called the King of Martyrs. But he renounced his position as minister, calling himself merely an elder.

The Glasite churches aimed at a literal primitive Christianity as practised by the early believers. The church was ruled by a band of officials who held equal authority. No education or training was thought necessary. If any church member differed from the majority he had either to conform or leave the community. The Sacrament was observed weekly, and between the morning and afternoon services, a love feast was practised where everyone had to attend. Anyone who had, or fancied they had, the gift of tongues was allowed to address the congregation. For a number of years the members washed one another's feet and received new adherents with a love-kiss. As at that time the act of kissing was forbidden on any occasion, in or out of church, and even husbands and wives were condemned for breaking this regulation, the scandal attending the Glasite or Sandemanian Church (named after Glas's son-in-law) can well be imagined. Worse was to follow, for money was considered unscriptural and immoral if hoarded up. Each member's savings were liable to be requested to help poorer brothers and sisters or for church purposes.

The Glasites spread to all large Scottish towns and even to London and Liverpool and to America. The famous chemist Michael Faraday was for years an elder of the Sandemanian Church in London. There is no doubt that it represented a form of Christian communism similar to that practised in the original church and in many more modern churches in various parts of the world.

Glas was, of course, deposed by the General Assembly in 1730, but they revoked the sentence nine years later, to a modified extent. He was acknowledged to be a minister of the gospel of Christ but not of the Established Church of Scotland, a subtle distinction which did not unduly worry John Glas. His name, by the way, is Gaelic for grey.

In 1851, there were still six churches and over 1000 members in Scotland.

William Robertson (1721-1793)

He was born at Borthwick, Midlothian, son of the parish minister. He was educated at Dalkeith school and the University of Edinburgh. His father was appointed minister of Old Greyfriars Church when William was a student. At the age of twenty-two he was ordained to Gladsmuir in East Lothian. Here, on a stipend of £60 per annum he supported his six sisters and brother after their mother died.

At this time, the Church of Scotland was split by the question of patronage, which had arisen in connection with the political change of the English Revolution. The Stuarts had been generally opposed to a democratic church so, when William and Mary, Queen Anne and the Hanoverians reigned, the church felt that it should support the government which had released them from tyranny. Livings, that is, ministerial appointments, were made by church patrons and it frequently happened that a minister so placed was not liked by his parishioners, but they had to put up with him or go elsewhere. The Moderate party of the Church supported the patronage system, which at least made for peace, if accepted. But the Popular party wanted the minister to be 'called' by a majority vote of the people. As can be imagined, this clash of principles led to law-suits, in which the verdict usually supported the Moderates. More and more people left the Established Church and set up meeting-houses.

Robertson's place in church history is as a placator, supporting the Moderates and trying to secure the assent of the Populars to the system of patronage. He was not very successful in this.

But he is notable for being at the head of affairs when the church influence was most illustrious. His associates were a galaxy of brilliant men, noted in our chapter on philosophers, such as Reid, Fergusson and Home. The latter, John Home, a dramatist and poet, had his play *Douglas*, performed in Edinburgh to an enthusiastic reception. But the General Assembly was so bigoted against theatrical art that Home was reprimanded and had to resign his living. Robertson sprang to his defence and through his powerful influence Home was granted a pension and appointed to a government post.

In every way possible Robertson supported the Establishment. As a young man he had joined the volunteers against the Jacobites in 1745 and he continued to support patronage all his life. His histories were very popular and even though David Hume was philosophically opposed to the Moderates he had the highest praise for Robertson's *History of Scotland during the reigns of Queen Mary and James VI*, which showed a commendable impartiality.

Robertson was King's Chaplain for Scotland and Principal of Edinburgh University. He was a member of many European academies.

Alexander Carlyle *(1722-1805)*

A son of Cummertrees Manse, Dumfriesshire, not many miles away from Ecclefechan, the birthplace of Thomas Carlyle, the most influential Victorian writer. No doubt there was a family relationship. Alexander's family came north to Prestonpans, East Lothian, where he spent his youth. He was educated at Edinburgh where he passed MA when twenty-one. Then he went to Glasgow College and to Leyden to make advanced studies in classics and theology.

As a lad of fourteen he was a witness of the Porteous Riots in Edinburgh and, like Robertson and all Whig supporters, he volunteered to defend Edinburgh against the Highlanders in 1745, with marked lack of success. But he was witness of the extraordinary victory of Prince Charles at Prestonpans in the same month of September. He saw the battle from the safe position of the steeple of the Parish Church.

He was appointed to Inveresk when twenty-six and remained there as minister until he died at the age of eighty-six, the same age as Thomas

71

Carlyle attained much later in history.

Carlyle was a very handsome man, described by Walter Scott as, 'the greatest demi-god I ever saw.' He was, for this reason, nicknamed 'Jupiter Carlyle'. He supported Robertson and the Moderates, being for a time the leader of that 'Broad' party, encouraging the arts and liberal views generally, except on the question of patronage. He left the manuscript of a record of his own times, published by the historian J.H. Burton.

John Brown *(1722-1787)*

He was born at Carpow in the parish of Abernethy, Perthshire. His father was a poor weaver, almost uneducated, but a man of superior intelligence and character who brought his family up in religious faith. John could only attend school long enough to get the elements of reading, writing and arithmetic, though, unknown to his parents, he spent a whole month learning the basics of Latin. He had a good memory and, being inclined to theology, he learned three complete books of catechism off by heart.

When he was eleven his parents died of a fever and he barely escaped with his life, but an old shepherd, John Ogilvy, quite illiterate, looked after him. In return he taught the venerable man to read, for at that period of civil disturbance in the seventeenth century when the old shepherd should have attended school as a boy, the schools had fallen into ruin.

Brown taught himself to read Greek and set off to walk the twenty-four miles to St Andrews to buy a Greek testament. His request was overheard by some professors who, amazed at hearing the rough country lad reading Greek, paid for the volume. His unusual skill in classical tongues made the superstitious think he was in league with Satan, so he travelled about the country as a pedlar.

When the Jacobite army descended on the Lothians, Brown joined the volunteers until after Culloden. He was now a member of the Secession Church, which objected to patronage. He took up school-teaching, studying philosophy and divinity, until in 1751 he was licensed to preach in the Associate Synod at Dalkeith.

He soon received a simultaneous 'call' to two churches, at Stow, Midlothian, and Haddington. He chose the latter, but periodically preached at Stow until another preacher was appointed.

His ministry at Haddington was uneventful, except for one strange incident in 1773 when he met the poet Robert Fergusson in the churchyard. Fergusson was walking back from some election work near Dunbar. Brown was struck by his pensive appearance and 'offered him certain serious advices which deeply affected him at the time and doubtless had their share in exciting and promoting those terrible convictions which latterly overwhelmed the poet's mind.' Fergusson died not long after in Edinburgh's Bedlam. No one will ever know how far Brown's 'advices' were responsible.

Brown published several works, the most popular being his *Self-Interpreting Bible*. But he is more famed for his descendants, a line of John Browns running to three generations, the first two being noted Secession churchmen, and the last a physician and famous author mentioned in the chapter on writers.

John Strachan *(1778-1867)*

Born in Aberdeen in an Episcopalian household, he took his degree at the University there. He was schoolmaster at Dunino and Kettle in East Fife for two years before emigrating to Canada in 1799. He was ordained there in 1803 and appointed in turn to Cornwall Parish and York Parish in Ontario on the St Lawrence River.

He was appointed to the executive council of Upper Canada in 1815 and was the chief mover in a political group known as the Family Compact. In 1820 he was appointed to the legislature. He was sent to Britain in 1824 to talk over colonial questions. Two years later he went to London to get a Royal Charter for King's College.

He was a strong advocate of the claims of the Episcopalians to independent use of funds for their own colleges and schools, and when he was made Bishop of Toronto on the division of the see of Canada, following the death of Bishop Stewart, he made strong representations on the disposal of the Clergy Reserve Funds.

He was first president of King's College, of which the name was changed to the University of Toronto in 1849. Before that time, as in Oxford and Cambridge, in former days, students were subjected to religious tests before matriculation. Strachan had this abolished. Not yet satisfied he broke away and established the Episcopalian Trinity College and returned to the vexed question of Clergy Reserve Funds, which were later secularised. Strachan was a devoted bishop and put the Episcopal Church in Canada under democratic government.

Thomas Chalmers *(1780-1847)*

He was born at Anstruther Easter, Fife, and educated there and at St Andrews University. At nineteen he was licensed to preach, by the Presbytery of St Andrews. He studied mathematics at Edinburgh and returned to St Andrews as assistant to the professor of mathematics. He was then made parish minister of Kilmany, Fife.

He contributed an article on Christianity to the *Edinburgh Encyclopaedia* and was recognised as a promising author. He went to the very populous and wretched parish of the Tron in Glasgow, where he laboured hard to help his parishioners. His preaching was becoming famous not so much for oratory as for persuasive argument. In 1817 he published his sermons relating Christianity to the latest amazing discoveries in astronomy. Their success was phenomenal. Wilberforce, the social reformer, said, 'All the world is wild about Dr Chalmers.'

He moved to the Glasgow parish of St John to continue his work among the poor. His methods of relief have been questioned, the emphasis being on self-help and practiced economy, which no doubt raised the moral tone of the parish, but not always without accusations of intrusions into family life. The phrase 'deserving poor' was coined at this time. After eight years he was glad to quit this sea of troubles and find haven in the Chair of Theology in Edinburgh.

In 1834 he became leader of the Popular or Evangelical Party of the

Church. The century-old argument on patronage was still going on, but in the Reform atmosphere of the times, it was rapidly drawing to a crisis. Chalmer's party enunciated this principle 'No minister shall be appointed against the will of the congregation.' But in three parishes where law-suits were fought the courts refused to support the Evangelicals so they appealed to the Government who gave a peremptory 'No'.

On 18 May 1843, when the General Assembly met in St Andrews Church in Edinburgh, Chalmers led out 470 clergymen and disrupted the church to form a Free Church of Scotland. Funds had been raised to provide the new stipends, but a struggle lay ahead, for the Scottish landowners refused to sell land for the building of the new Free Churches. Chalmers returned to Edinburgh on 30 May 1847, from giving evidence to the House of Commons on this refusal. The following morning he was found dead in bed.

The Disruption was a notable fight for liberty of choice and a triumph for democracy, but it weakened the ranks of Scotland when it came to national causes where England sought to impose conformity in Education, Law, Banking and Commerce. However, the churches ultimately re-united, and old wounds were healed, although there were smaller septs who refused to be reconciled.

Edward Irving *(1792-1834)*

Born at Annan, Dumfriesshire, he was educated at Annan Grammar School and entered Edinburgh University at thirteen. He graduated MA when seventeen and in 1810, at eighteen, was chosen master of the new academy at Haddington. There he became the tutor of Jane Welsh (later Mrs Carlyle) who was then a vivacious nine-year old, only child of the town doctor. He became engaged to Isabella Martin in 1812, which made his tutorship of Jane Welsh rather dangerous, for that headstrong miss of eleven summers had fallen in love with him and he with her. The Martins would not release him, so he left Haddington for Kirkcaldy. After a long engagement he married Miss Martin in 1823. He introduced his friend Thomas Carlyle to Jane Welsh and after years of hesitation she married him in 1826.

After the completion of his divinity studies he taught for several years, then was appointed assistant to Thomas Chalmers in St John's Parish, Glasgow. His preaching was too fine for the congregation of St John's, but his sympathetic visits to homes made him a universal favourite. In 1822 he was appointed to the Caledonian Church, Hatton Garden, London, where his preaching combined with his handsome appearance drew crowds of fashionable folk. The second coming of Christ had been confidently preached at irregular intervals through history and it was expected again in the nineteenth century, 1866 being the favourite date. Irving had been studying a work by a Jesuit priest, under a pseudonym. He published a translation of it in 1827. He associated with the mystic poet Coleridge and was now convinced of the imminence of the Millennium. He went to Edinburgh in 1828 and drew full churches early on Sunday mornings with his lectures on the coming end of the world.

His friends, including Carlyle, tried to bring him to his senses. Some gave up the effort and deserted him. He was excommunicated by the London Presbytery for his heresies on Christ's nature. His own congregation were disturbed by his wild utterances and he was declared unfit to be their minister. At this crisis he formed the Holy Catholic Apostolic Church in a new building in Newman Street, London. Other churches of this order were built in Edinburgh and elsewhere. The presbytery of his native town, Annan, deposed him from the Church of Scotland because of heresy, in March 1833, but he was consoled by being made chief pastor of the church in Newman Street, dying shortly after.

Had he lived in the Middle Ages he would perhaps have led a crusade, or been canonised. But in the prosaic Britain of the early nineteenth century he was looked upon as a religious fanatic.

Robert Moffat *(1795-1883)*

He was born of humble parents at Ormiston, East Lothian. Until he was nineteen he worked as a gardener on various estates. When employed at an estate in Cheshire he wrote to the London Missionary Society and was sent out to South Africa in 1816.

He spent a year in South West Africa in Namaqualand, converting many of the people. On returning to Cape Town he married and set off for Bechuanaland with his wife, where he formed a mission station west of the Vaal River. Here he worked for half a century, often making journeys northwards, into the territories of the warlike Matabele. He found, on arriving in Bechuanaland in 1820, that the inhabitants were bloodthirsty savages. Gradually, by his courage and example, he built up a civilised community, taught them horticulture, carpentry, the elements of hygiene and medicine, and how to work iron and make ploughs and other peaceful tools.

He translated the entire Bible, the Psalms and *Pilgrim's Progress* into Sechwana, the dominant language which up to that time had been spoken but never committed to script. This gave the natives a literature of their own upon which to build.

Reluctantly he returned to Britain where he published an account of his lifework in Africa. One of Moffat's daughters married David Livingstone and after accompanying him on many hazardous expeditions, died during his long journey to the Zambezi region, a true heroine worthy of her father.

Alexander Duff *(1808-1878)*

Born in Pitlochry, Perthshire, he was educated at Kirkmichael, then St Andrews University where he met Dr Thomas Chalmers and was sent out by the foreign mission committee as the first missionary to India. He was ordained as a preacher in 1829 and set off immediately. His start was unlucky as he was twice shipwrecked and lost all his books and papers before reaching Calcutta. Then he was faced with a vast problem. The Mohammedan communities were antagonistic to Christianity. The Hindu people already had an ancient system of plural gods which they were unwilling to replace with a monotheistic system resembling the Mohammedan. The only people accessible to conversion were the low-caste Hindus and the pariah or untouchable outcasts. These had already been approached by missionaries of various faiths.

Duff realised that to convert the educated classes who were most influential, he would require to appeal to the intellect. The best way to do this was to conduct an educational mission and, starting with the teaching of the English version of the Bible, proceed to all kinds of general science and art. His school was graded from early primary classes to a university standard.

His school was staffed by teachers from Britain as well as by Indians. It soon developed into a missionary college, training young men and women as Christian teachers. The British Government supported his movement to the extent of defining that the aim of higher education in India should be the advancement of western science and literature.

Duff returned after several years of success to encourage the Scottish Church to support the Indian missions. He was made a Doctor of Divinity.

He returned to India in 1840 to find that the Government had made a compromise over the aim of education and had introduced the study of Oriental languages and studies. Leaving his college in capable hands he returned again to his native land.

The storm over patronage was brewing and Dr Duff remained in Scotland long enough to take part in the historic walk-out led by Chalmers.

He of course had to give up his college building in India and start afresh. Luckily he had a devoted band of several young high-caste Indians. The Government threw open appointments to all young men trained in colleges similar to Duff's, which naturally made his work easier.

From 1845 to 1849 he was editor of the *Calcutta Review*, a paper in English, which had a wide circulation of mixed readers. Once again he returned to Scotland and was elected Moderator of the Free Church Assembly.

In India again he helped to found the University of Calcutta. This was the period of the Indian Mutiny and the end of the reign of the East India Company. Duff's influence on the India under British rule was far-reaching and perhaps still has some effect on maintaining good relations between Britain and an independent India and Pakistan.

Archibald Campbell Tait *(1811-1882)*

Born at Edinburgh and educated at Edinburgh Academy and the High School, he won a bursary from Glasgow to Balliol College, Oxford, where he became a fellow and tutor. He was ordained priest in 1836 and became a curate of the Church of England which all through his life was undergoing a series of controversies.

The Tractarian Movement was the first of these. This is also known as the Oxford Movement, which swept England in the early mid-century. It was an evangelical revival of mediaeval thought and was initiated by the conversion of Cardinal Newman to Catholicism. Tait was an opponent of it, to the extent of publishing a protest against it.

But, as he succeeded the famous Dr Arnold as headmaster of Rugby, he was forced to subscribe to his campaign to purify the English public schools of their notorious immorality and abuses. But he was not the man to promote 'Muscular Christianity' so, after a serious illness, he was appointed Dean of Carlisle where he restored the cathedral and was much respected by his people. But Heaven did not shower blessings on him in Carlisle. In the spring of 1856 five of his children died of scarlet fever, which was at that time, and for generations after, a deadly disease.

Later that year he was made Bishop of London, a hollow triumph in his sorrow. Twelve years later he became Archbishop of Canterbury but this eminence was dimmed by illness and the death of his wife and only son.

In Parliament as Archbishop he dealt with many church improvements. He had a hard time trying to ensure peace in matters of church ritual and in the question which still haunts the Church of England, relations with Rome.

James Chalmers *(1841-1901)*

He was born at Ardrishaig, Argyll, and prepared for missionary work by the Glasgow City Mission. In 1865 he went as a Congregational Missionary to Rarotonga in the Cook Archipelago in the Pacific.

In 1876 he went to the dangerous land of New Guinea where white men had rarely been seen. He explored parts of Papua and realised the delicacy of dealing with the cannibalistic communities, hoping that the area would come under British protection, rather than Australian. On leave, Chalmers visited fellow-Scot R.L. Stevenson in Samoa.

In 1892 he returned to New Guinea to seek out and reform the cannibals of the mangrove swamps. Nine years later, when attempting to pacify some aggressive tribesmen, he and his friend Tomkins were murdered and eaten.

Mary Slessor *(1848-1915)*

She was born in Aberdeen, her parents moving to Dundee to seek work in the jute-mills, where Mary and her brothers Robert and John were employed for twelve hours a day. At that time the fame of David Livingstone was thrilling all Britain to a missionary zeal. Mary made up her mind to go to Africa as a missionary, despite her handicaps of poverty and lack of training. The Calabar Mission had been founded by Dr Ferguson in 1843 and Mary applied to the Foreign Missions Board of the Church of Scotland for service there. She was sent out on the *Ethiopia* to take up work at Old Town and Duke Town.

Conditions on the Calabar Coast were primitive, as she had expected, but she was not deterred either by the savagery and degradation of the Africans or by the prim behaviour of the Scottish Mission staff. Her style of dress, trousers and cropped hair, shocked everyone, but her aggressive manner astounded blacks and whites alike. She was athletic and scrambled through the jungle, climbed trees and carried loads. When confronted by sexual orgies in African villages she attacked the warriors with her umbrella and routed them. They assumed that she had a very powerful *ju-ju* to support her, and reformed without protest.

She was put in charge of Old Town and effected great changes in hygiene and general observation of Christian morals. She was told by letter of the deaths of her mother and sister but she carried on with her plans to go up country to convert the tribes of Okoyong.

At forty-three romance entered her life. A young missionary, Mr Morrison, aged twenty-five, proposed marriage but he was not given permission to accompany her to Okoyong, and she left alone. He pined and died soon after in North Carolina. But Mary civilised the Okoyong at the cost of a crippling arthritis, and died, adored by her people.

Cosmo Gordon Lang *(1864-1945)*

He was born at Aberdeen of an Episcopalian family and educated there and at Glasgow and Balliol College, Oxford. Like Tait he was elected a fellow and was ordained a curate in the Church of England, at Leeds. For three years he was a fellow and Dean of Divinity at Magdalen College, Oxford, and vicar of the University Church of St Mary's. Then he became vicar of Portsea and in 1901 Bishop of Stepney and Canon of St Paul's Cathedral.

As Archbishop of York he was noted for his logical arguments and eloquence in the House of Lords. He was a member of the Royal Commission on Divorce.

In 1928 he became Archbishop of Canterbury. This was a critical year for the church as the revised Prayer Book had been twice rejected by Parliament. Lang argued convincingly in its favour.

But apart from these doctrinal matters he was a keen social worker. His experiences in Stepney had given him an insight into the wretchedness of the English slums.

He retired from the primateship in 1942 and died just after the end of the Second World War, wherein he had seen the greater part of his first see at Stepney demolished by German bombs.

Donald C. Caskie *(1902-1983)*

He was a native of Bowmore, Islay. After studying for the ministry he was appointed to Gretna Church, Dumfriesshire, for five years. Then he took charge of the Scots Kirk in the Rue Bayard, Paris, which had been a focus for religious Scots for a century, like Scots Kirks in other European capitals.

Donald Caskie did not anticipate the heroic role he was now about to play. In 1940 the Nazi *blitzkreig* swept across Europe, both East and West. Paris fell within weeks and France capitulated. The French government, centred now on Vichy, collaborated with the Germans, but Caskie decided to help his own countrymen, whatever the cost to his own life.

After a perilous journey with other refugees, during which he was almost shot as a fifth columnist, he reached Marseilles, where he was allowed to use the British Seaman's Mission as a headquarters to help British civilians only. But he found it impossible to refuse British troops who had escaped from Dunkirk and other battles and had been directed to Caskie's headquarters to get help.

Eventually the 'Tartan Pimpernel', as he was called, was arrested, brutally treated in Italian prisons and finally sentenced to death by the

Nazis. Through the intercession of a German clergyman he was freed and after D-day came home to Scotland. The Scots Kirk in Paris was rebuilt, Queen Elizabeth laying the foundation stone, and Caskie resumed his work unmolested. His autobiography, *The Tartan Pimpernel*, reveals a true Highlandman.

Medicine

Throughout the Middle Ages medicine was governed by rigid rules set out by Galen, a doctor of the second century AD. The human body was assumed to be controlled by natural, vital and animal spirits, the first formed in the liver, the second in the heart and the third in the brain. Equally simple ideas governed men's idea of the universe. It was composed of four elements, earth, water, air and fire. It followed quite naturally that the human body was composed of four humours, blood, phlegm, black bile and yellow bile. There was little progress to be made as long as these ideas were tyrannically supported by powers of church and state.

Of the cause of diseases by infections, of the nature of gases and chemical compounds, of the functions of the blood or the organs of the body, nobody had the least idea. Even to dissect the human body was to incur excommunication. When King Robert the Bruce requested that his heart be taken out after his death and buried in the Holy Land, this was looked on with horror, for the mediaevals, and generations of moderns too, believed in the actual corporeal resurrection.

Scotland, like the rest of Christendom, was subjected to charlatans until the end of the seventeenth century, when modern rational medicine began. Yet for two centuries previously there had been great schools in Europe, the principal one being in Padua, Italy, where a study of anatomy led to a transformation of surgery.

The periodic plagues which decimated Europe, including Britain, induced doctors to examine epidemic disease. New drugs from America, including tobacco, used first as a narcotic, also helped in controlling disease. All through the Middle Ages the puzzling disease called lepra had remained endemic throughout Christendom. It was classed with leprosy, but was at last found to be a venereal disease, which was of course seized on by the theologians to point the moral, but not a medical one, that love-making was a mortal sin.

The discovery by the English doctor, William Harvey, of the circulation of the blood, was a direct result of his contact with the great professor Fabricius of Padua who had investigated the valves of the veins but had failed to follow up his discoveries. The English chemist Robert Boyle, a little later than Harvey, contributed a vast amount by his discoveries.

But it is to Dutch physicians that Scotland owes its world pre-eminence in modern medicine. Students came from all over the world, from as far as China and Russia, to study at Leyden. Even Peter the Great, Czar of Russia later, attended classes under Boerhaave (1668-1739) who had introduced a novelty in medicine. He actually went to see the patients and conversed by the sickbed, thus finding out the symptoms at the source, instead of speculating from theory. Leyden also had a large collection of growing herbs, from all parts of the world, especially from the Dutch Empire in the East and West Indies.

Many Scots had previously studied all manner of sciences and arts at Leyden, Utrecht and other Netherlands colleges, but the popularity of the predecessors of Boerhaave attracted several Scots who were the initiators of the Edinburgh School of Medicine, which was to be a worldwide source of supply of teachers and practices for the next three centuries.

Sir Andrew Balfour *(1630-1694)*

Born at Denmylne, near Newburgh, Fife, on the estate of his father, Sir James Balfour, Lord Lyon King-of-arms. He studied at St Andrews in natural philosophy and medicine, then at Oxford where he became acquainted with William Harvey, his professor, discoverer of the circulation of the blood. Balfour then went to Paris, Montpellier, Padua and Caen in Normandy, where he took his MD. He returned to St Andrews for a time but settled in Edinburgh where his interests were chiefly in botanical medicine. These will be noted in the chapter on naturalists.

Sir Thomas Burnet *(1632-1715)*

He was born in Edinburgh, son of an advocate, and brother of Bishop Gilbert Burnet. After studying in Scotland and in Europe, he took his medical degree at Montpellier. He was appointed physician to Charles II in Scotland, and in his old age to Queen Anne (1702-1714). His two books on medicine were highly popular everywhere in Europe, the most useful being his *Medical Treasury (Thesaurus Medicinae)*. The other was a concise presentation of the teachings of Hypocrates or Hippocrates, the author of the Hypocratic Oath, administered still to all doctors.

The very fact that Burnet was intimate with all the writings connected with Hippocrates indicates his attitude to medicine, for the actual cases described are so honestly written that in most of them it is admitted that they ended fatally. He, too, like his fellow-founders of the College of Surgeons, had a respect for truth, reinforced by their studies under great doctors in France, Italy and Holland.

Sir Archibald Stevenson *(c.1640-1700)*

He was an Edinburgh physician who is associated with the foundation of the Royal College of Surgeons. It was through the Duke of York that Charles II gave the royal assent to the project, for it was bitterly opposed by the University, and the Bishops, who at that time of enforced Episcopacy, had a powerful voice with the King.

Sir Robert Sibbald *(1641-1722)*

Younger son of the Sibbalds connected with Balgonie in Fife, he was born in Edinburgh and educated at the High School and University. He had studied theology at Edinburgh but when nineteen went to Leyden to study medicine. Boerhaave had not yet been born, but Sibbald studied anatomy and surgery under Van Horne, botany under Vorstius, and the practice of medicine under Sylvius. He wrote an account of his life at Leyden, giving full details of a student's experiences in the mid-seventeenth century.

He afterwards studied botany in Paris, then won his diploma as Doctor of Medicine at Angers.

He returned to his native city in 1672 and along with Sir Andrew Balfour, a Fifer, he established a Botanical Garden, the first in the city, in the eastern bed of the old North Loch. He had a large and prosperous practice in and around Edinburgh, and with his fellow doctors founded the Royal College of Physicians. He was first president and was also knighted by the Duke of York, afterwards James II of England. In addition he was first professor of Medicine in Edinburgh.

His genius was not confined to medicine. He also wrote a descriptive geography of Scotland on his experiences as Geographer-Royal, and books on the topography of Fife and Stirling.

Archibald Pitcairne (1652-1713)

He was not only the most celebrated doctor of his age but the most colourful. Son of a merchant and magistrate in Edinburgh, he was born at Dalkeith and educated at the town school there, before going to Edinburgh University, then to Paris to study medicine. The most curious authentic ghost story known, is about this period of his life, which is worth telling as it throws light on his character.

Pitcairne had a bosom companion in Edinburgh University named Robert Lindsay, a great grandson of the famous poet, Sir David Lindsay, author of the *Thrie Estates*. Before Pitcairne left for Paris, a dangerous journey at that time, he and Lindsay had sworn an oath that whoever died first should let the other know. In 1675 Pitcairne had a vivid dream in his Paris lodgings. Lindsay appeared to him and this dialogue took place.

Lindsay: Archie, perhaps you heard I'm dead?
Pitcairne: No, Robin.
Lindsay: Ay, but they bury my body in the Greyfriars. I am alive, though in a place whereof the pleasures cannot be expressed in Scotch, Greek or Latin. I have come with a well-sailing small ship to Leith Road to carry you thither.
Pitcairne: Robin, I'll go with you, but wait till I go to Fife and East Lothian to take leave of my parents.

Every night of Pitcairne's life thereafter (and he lived another thirty-eight years) he was visited by Lindsay's ghost, telling him he was alive. When Pitcairne had a dangerous illness in 1694 in Edinburgh, Lindsay's ghost assured him that their meeting was not yet due.

One of the founders of the College of Physicians, he was not thereby assured of honour in his own country, for he was a keen Jacobite, which prevented his promotion. But he had the singular honour of being asked to accept an appointment as Professor of Medicine in Leyden. This arose in rather an unusual way. His friend David Gregory, Professor of Mathematics in Edinburgh, persuaded Pitcairne to take up mathematics. He did this so enthusiastically that he made himself the founder of a medico-mathematical philosophy which was believed in for a century. Simply stated, it tried to maintain that, as the blood circulated, therefore all bodily functions were mere mechanical exercises. It was for his part in this that he went to Leyden.

There, he had many pupils who later attained great eminence. Amongst them was Boerhaave, already mentioned, and Richard Mead, head of the English medical profession, who attended Queen Anne on her death-bed and was physician to George II.

Pitcairne was a great controversialist and made many enemies, but he was more than a match for them. One of his satirical poems, unluckily for those satirised, was in English instead of his normal Latin. It was entitled *The Assembly* and was described by a notable Churchman as personal, sarcastic and profane, unfit to be acted in public. But his merits were so appreciated by Czar Peter the Great that on Pitcairne's death he purchased his whole library and transferred it to St Petersburg.

The Edinburgh School of Medicine was famed for the family groups of doctors who dominated it. The most numerous of these were the Gregorys of whom no less than nineteen, all related, occupied Chairs of Medicine and allied subjects. There were also the Bells of two separate families, the Munros, the Duncans, the Combes, the Cleghorns, the Rutherfords, the Hunters, etc. Because of this we present many doctors in family groups.

Alexander Munro *(1697-1767)*

He was the second in a line of six, though his title is *Primus*, his father John Munro not having achieved fame, being only an old Army surgeon and member of the new College of Surgeons. Alexander was educated by his father with a view to taking up the teaching of anatomy in Edinburgh. He studied this subject in London, then went to Paris and Leyden. In the latter he had Boerhaave as a teacher which helped him to a professorship in Edinburgh at the age of twenty-three.

Collaborating with Lord Provost Drummond he founded the Royal Infirmary, opened in 1729. Here he followed the 'bedside' doctoring he had learned in Leyden, and the giving of clinical lectures to his students. He was the chief influence for many years in the development of the new medical school. His main work was a book on osteology, or study of bones.

Alexander Munro (Secundus) *(1733-1817)*

A son of the above, he excelled his father as a lecturer and in the excellence of his published works. His father deliberately educated him to succeed to his Chair of Anatomy. Born in Edinburgh, he was educated at the High School, and assisted his father in the dissecting room, after studying at the University. He worked in London under William Hunter, physician to Queen Charlotte. He also studied at Paris, Leyden and Berlin. His achievements in medicine were, notably, his discovery of the order of the lymphatic system, and the structure and function of the nervous system. His other important observations on bodily functions, hitherto unsuspected, were supplemented by his papers on the action of drugs. He published a work on the comparative anatomy of fishes and animals and man, surely a forerunner of the evolutionary theories of the century following. His elder brother was also a distinguished physician in London and senior physician to the Army.

Alexander Munro (Tertius) *(1773-1859)*

He occupied the Chair of Anatomy in succession to his father and grandfather. He taught many distinguished men though he was not noted for any important discovery. This dynasty of anatomists occupied the Professorship for 126 years.

The line of the Munros did not end there, for in 1859 Sir David Munro, the sixth in line from the old Army surgeon who had set the ball rolling, presented to the University a large collection of anatomical specimens, prepared by his father.

William Cullen *(1710-1790)*

Born and educated at Hamilton, he was apprenticed to an apothecary in Glasgow. He was appointed ship's surgeon and voyaged several times to the West Indies. Leaving the sea, he practised as a doctor at Shotts, Lanarkshire. The Duke of Hamilton and other notables helped him and he qualified at Glasgow as an MD. He lectured there on chemistry and later became professor. He was appointed to the Chair of Chemistry at Edinburgh in 1756, agriculture being also included. There he did all his notable work on chemistry, receiving many honours.

Cullen did for Edinburgh what Boerhaave had done for Leyden. Two of his most famous pupils were William Hunter and Joseph Black. He was very successful in clinical teaching. He helped to prepare that monumental work, the *Edinburgh Pharmacoepia*, published in 1774.

He was noted for the effect he had in educating the public on the new medicine, in attracting students from foreign lands (modern politicians take note), and for his sound common sense and judgement. He spoke clearly, brightly and with ease. His publications aimed at a greater clarification and classification of diseases, on the same extensive lines as those introduced by the Swede Linnaeus in classifying plants, some years earlier. His arrangements were later discarded, but he served to simplify medicine for two generations after his death.

Robert Whytt *(1714-1766)*

He was born at Benochy, Aberdeenshire, son of an advocate. He studied extensively at St Andrews, Edinburgh, London, Paris and Leyden. In his day and for long before and after, stone in the bladder was a prevalent disease, for which cures were many and often illusory. When a young man, Whytt published a treatise on the cure of this painful trouble. His controversial book on vital motions of animals drew him into argument with Haller, the leading European authority on physiology. Whytt's greatest work was on nervous diseases. It was translated into French. His was the first account of tuberculous meningitis, commonly known as 'water on the brain'.

George Cleghorn *(1716-1789)*

He was born on a small farm at Granton near Edinburgh, of poor hard-working parents. He attended Cramond village school and at twelve was sent to Edinburgh University to study Latin, Greek, French and mathematics. After three years he began to study physics and surgery under Alexander Munro (Primus). He was with him for five years and, with others, while still a student, founded the Royal Medical Society of Edinburgh.

When twenty he was appointed surgeon in the 22nd Regiment of Foot, (then Moyle's Regiment) which was stationed in Minorca. This was an Irish Regiment, and thirteen years later, he accompanied it on return to Ireland. In 1750 he published *Diseases of Minorca*, with which he was all too well acquainted.

He settled in Dublin and, in the style of his professor Munro, and of the famous Hunters, he gave lectures on anatomy, on his own. A year or two later he was appointed lecturer and then professor of anatomy. In 1774 his only brother died in Scotland so he brought the widow and her nine children across to Ireland. This kind act was not rewarded by Fate, for, a few years later, his own eldest son, on whom he placed great hope, died after graduating as a physician. However he turned his attentions to one of his nephews, also William, and between them they established the first School of Anatomy in Ireland. He was made a fellow of the newly-established Royal Medical Society of Paris and also of the College of Physicians in Dublin. At this time scurvy was prevalent among the population and especially so among sailors on long sea voyages. After Cleghorn's death the *Edinburgh Magazine* said of him, 'We are indebted to him for the use of acescent (slightly acidic) vegetables in low, remittent and putrid fever, and early and copious use of bark (quinine)'. A large proportion of the rural population of Great Britain suffered from a malaria, called tertian or quartan fever, due to the many undrained marshes where mosquitoes bred. Cleghorn's diet and prescription of quinine was effective in reducing this disease, but only the draining of the swamps eliminated the endemic fevers.

James Lind *(1716-1794)*

He was almost a contemporary of Cleghorn and took his MD at Edinburgh under the same teachers. He was appointed physician to the Royal Naval Hospital at Haslar where he worked for twenty-five years. Scurvy was rampant. The records show that, after only a ten weeks' voyage, Lind had 350 cases in his hands. The cure had been known since the days of Sir Richard Hawkins in Elizabethan times, but never systematically applied. Lind rediscovered it, and the juice of citrus fruits was prescribed by the Admiralty on Lind's recommendation, though this was not very popular among the Jack Tars. British ships, after being compelled to adopt Lind's formula in 1865, were scoffingly named 'lime-juicers'. But scorbutic disease was eliminated.

Lind also attacked typhus, called jail-fever, responsible for a death-rate of 4.5 per cent per annum in the slums of Edinburgh and other crowded towns. Lind's remedy was the use of wood-smoke, not a scientific method, though it may have deloused the population to a small extent, for typhus was caused, like bubonic plague, by carriers of viruses. In typhus, these were lice; in plague, fleas preying on rats and humans alike.

Lind also compelled the use of hospital ships in tropical ports, arranged for distillation of drinking-water in ocean-going ships, and in many ways made sea-faring less of a hazard.

William Hunter *(1718-1783)*

He was born at Long Calderwood, Lanarkshire, and educated at Glasgow University, where he practised medicine under William Cullen. He went to London as a physician where he soon won a great reputation for his lecturing. He began to concentrate on midwifery, where he excelled, and was appointed to Middlesex and the British Maternity hospitals. In a house in Great Windmill Street he made a large collection of anatomical specimens, as well as of coins, medals, minerals and shells. This, with a fine library, he left to the Hunterian Museum in Glasgow.

He was fond of controversy, like Pitcairne and other brilliant doctors, but his work on surgery was outstanding. His most famous book concerning obstetrics, is *The Anatomy of the Gravid Uterus*. He was made physician-extraordinary to Queen Charlotte in 1764.

John Hunter *(1728-1793)*

He was younger brother of the above, and the youngest of ten. For some time as a youth he was a cabinet-maker, but his brother got permission from his professor to allow him to work in his celebrated anatomy department in London, but he was not certain of success there, and had plans to join the army if necessary.

Luckily for humanity, he persevered at dissection and was soon in charge of the practical class. After experience in Chelsea and St Bartholomew's he was appointed house-surgeon in St George's Hospital. With his brother's collaboration he solved many medical problems on nerves and glands.

When he was thirty-one he was threatened with pulmonary tuberculosis, so he went as surgeon on an expedition to Belleisle on the NE coast of Canada. He served with the army on the Portugese campaign of 1762 where he gained knowledge of gun-shot wounds, luckily not at first-hand. He made a large collection of natural and diseased parts of the body.

He returned to London and set up a practice. His hobby was comparative anatomy, and he made a large collection of animal skeletons. He was made a Fellow of the Royal Society. The range of subjects covered by his papers to the Society is extraordinarily wide. For example, he wrote on *The Torpedo; Resuscitation of the apparently Drowned*; smallpox infection; hearing in fishes, whales and bees. For the last twenty-nine years of his life he lived at Brompton, where he kept many tame birds and animals from all over the world, including leopards for which he had no fear.

It is impossible in a short notice to mention all Hunter's achievements. One alone of his innovations (in an operation for an aneurism) was a triumph of applied observation, and his method has saved hundreds of lives. The arterial sheath involved has since been christened 'Hunter's Canal'. He raised surgery to a scientific profession, from having been the 'mystery of barbers' in former ages.

His vast collections which he left to the nation were eventually, after much hesitation, properly housed and opened to the public.

John Gregory *(1724-1773)*

He was the grandson of James Gregory, the inventor of the reflecting telescope, and son of Dr James Gregory, Professor of Medicine in King's College, Aberdeen. Sir Walter Scott tells of a very strange incident in John's early life. Rob Roy Macgregor, on a visit to Aberdeen, called on Professor Gregory, who was by descent a Macgregor but was under a proscription of that name. Rob thought highly of his son, then a boy of eight or nine, and offered to take him away to the Highlands to educate him in many exercises, including the knack of 'Driving a dirk through a two-inch board'. The professor, with great tact, dissuaded Rob from carrying out his promise.

John Gregory was educated for medicine at Aberdeen and Edinburgh, then studied at Leyden in 1745-1747. He was then elected to the Chair of Philosophy at Aberdeen and later to professorship of Medicine. When forty-three he went to Edinburgh where he was Professor of Physic. His publications were principally these; a comparison of the human faculties with those of animals, and a book on the duties of a physician.

James Gregory *(1753-1821)*

Mentioned later as the 'starving doctor', he was the son of John Gregory. He was born and educated at Aberdeen like his father and also proceeded to Edinburgh and Leyden. At the age of twenty-three he was made the Professor of the Theory of Physic at Edinburgh, and succeeded Cullen in 1790 in the 'Practical' Chair. He was a man of many parts and contributed to literary and philosophical magazines. His works in Latin, on medical matters, dealt with the stages of certain diseases and with a summary of medical theories. He was brilliant and witty as a lecturer but not inventive. A very funny dialogue, too long to print here, described a characteristic consultation with a wealthy Glasgow business man. After a close inquiry by Gregory into the merchant's diet, he is offered a wad of banknotes for his services, but indignantly refuses to take a fee, and tells the surprised Glaswegian that he is a confessed drunkard and glutton and that, if he does not mend his ways, he will be dead within the year.

Gregory's regime attracted many students from all parts of the English-speaking world, who propagated his doctrines of blood-letting, cold affusions, purging, blistering and vomiting and other self-tortures, reminiscent of mediaeval penitents.

William Gregory *(c.1800-1850)*

One of the descendants of James Gregory, he discovered in 1831 a method of preparing morphia very inexpensively. Up to this date it had been far too dear for common use. The importance of Gregory's discovery is in its subsequent expansion of the manufacture of alkaloids from various plants, in Edinburgh, and also in the impetus it gave to Sir Robert Christison in his pharmacological discoveries.

Joseph Black *(1728-1799)*

Though born in France he was Scottish by extraction and residence. He went to school in Belfast, then attended Glasgow University, where he was a pupil of William Cullen. Later Cullen adopted him as assistant, recognising his ability. At twenty-six, in the thesis he presented for his doctor's degree, in Latin, he described his chemical experiments which anticipated modern chemistry by indicating the presence of gases distinct from air.

He succeeded Cullen as Chemistry lecturer in Glasgow and also taught anatomy, which he gave up for the chair of medicine. He discovered the principle of latent heat and taught this, though he never published a treatise on it, so others were able to claim the credit. His discoveries were fundamental to James Watt and others.

John Brown *(1735-1788)*

He was born at Lintlaws, near the village of Preston, by Duns, Berwick-shire. After attending the local school he matriculated at Edinburgh and took his MD. He was not above arguing, even as a young man. He had been a member of the Duns dissenting Church but he, in turn dissented from them and joined the Established Church.

At Edinburgh he attracted the attention of William Cullen, and assisted him in experiments, but fell out with Cullen's theories and set up a system of his own. He gave lectures and published many treatises, attacking not only Cullen but all other professors. He proceeded to condemn all previous theories of medicine, and in his *Elementa Medicinae* he put forward his system known as the 'Brunonian theory'.

He went to London two years before his death and attracted many supporters, but he died in poverty.

Andrew Duncan *(1744-1828)*

He was born at St Andrews and educated there and at Edinburgh, in medicine. He became a ship's doctor for a time and voyaged to India. For some years he lectured in Edinburgh University on medicine, then gave independent lectures. He founded a dispensary for the poor, who had no other means of medical help at that time. This dispensary was later merged with the Royal Public Dispensary. He published a quarterly journal of medicine, later to develop into the *Edinburgh Medical and Surgical Journal*, under his son's management. This publication survived for well over a century.

The incident which caused Duncan to devote much of his life to the alleviation of mental illness was the miserable end of the poet Robert Fergusson in 1774 in Darien House, then used as a paupers' asylum. When Duncan became the Professor of the Institutes of Medicine, in 1782, he proposed that a public asylum be built in Edinburgh. It has often been claimed that the Frenchman Pinel proposed this in his treatise published in 1801. But by that time Duncan was well advanced in his schemes, despite much opposition of all kinds to his idea. He obtained a Royal Charter in 1807 and a grant of £2000 from the Highland Estates forfeited after the '45 Rebellion. In this way Craighouse Asylum was built. It is of personal interest that a lock of Robert Fergusson's hair, taken by Duncan after his death, is preserved in the parlour at Craighouse.

His son, also Andrew Duncan, published the *Edinburgh New Dispensatory* which was translated into German and French, went into ten editions, and was widely used in the USA. He was professor of Medical Jurisprudence, a subject taught 'in every reputable university in Europe.'

Benjamin Bell *(1749-1806)*

He was the first of a long line of Bells who practised surgery in Edinburgh with great distinction. He was the 'Father of the Surgical School'. He was born in Dumfries and, after schooling there, attended Edinburgh University. He then studied in Paris and returned to Edinburgh, where in 1770 he was elected to the Professorship.

He had a very observant eye and alert mind, and was well in advance of his age. He saw the danger inherent in surgery, but of course could not anticipate the discoveries of antiseptic and chloroform. Nevertheless he advocated measures to lessen the pain of operations, and realised the danger of admitting air into septic wounds. He advocated massage for stiffness in muscles. His most important advance in the science of medicine was his clear distinction, by demonstration, that those scourges of civil and military hygiene, gonorrhea and syphilis, were separate diseases. He met with opposition from John Hunter, also an established authority on venereal diseases.

The dynasty of Bells continued in the surgical line until 1911, even beating the Munros. In that year Joseph Bell, a great-grandson, died.

John Bell *(1763-1820)*

John was born in Edinburgh and studied medicine at the University. He travelled in Russia and, on return to Edinburgh, lectured in surgery and anatomy. He seems to have had an independent mind, as he set up a school of anatomy of his own, and fell out with Dr James Gregory, the 'Starving Doctor' and inventor of 'Gregory's Stomach Mixture', a nauseous preparation of rhubarb, ginger and magnesia. He also quarrelled with Dr Benjamin Bell, not related, on the question of surgical attendance at the University.

Sir Charles Bell *(1778-1842)*

Charles, the younger brother of the above, was born in Edinburgh, educated in the usual style and studied under his brother who was fifteen years his senior. He went early to London and lectured at the school set up by William Hunter. He is famous for having attended some of the wounded after the terrible carnage of Waterloo. He became Professor of Surgery at Edinburgh. His notable books were on *Nervous System* and *Animal Mechanics*. The two brothers created the subject of surgical anatomy. Charles' fame rests on his researches into physiology.

Sir William Beatty *(1770-1842)*

He was born near Langholm, Dumfriesshire. He studied medicine at Edinburgh and joined the navy as a ship's physician, a rough job in that age of sanguinary naval battles, where 'surgery' below decks was awash with blood and strewn with amputated limbs. He was surgeon in the *Victory* at Trafalgar and had the personal anguish of attending to his friend and commander Horatio Nelson when he was mortally wounded in the middle of the battle, living long enough to hear of the famous victory. *The Death of Nelson* is a well-known painting of which many thousands of copper-plates were made. It shows Nelson attended by Beatty and Captain Hardy.

Beatty published *An Authenticated Narrative of the Death of Lord Nelson* in 1807, with many illustrations, including one of the souvenir which he valued all his life. This was the French sniper's bullet which shattered Nelson's spine. In it were embedded pieces of blue cloth, gold lace and silk pad. Beatty had it enclosed in crystal and mounted in gold.

From 1806 till his death, thirty-six years later, he was head physician in Greenwich Naval Hospital. St Andrews honoured him with an MD in 1817, and in the same year he was made a licentiate of the Royal College of Surgeons. He was created a Fellow of the Royal Society in 1818 and, to sum up, was knighted by William IV in 1831. But of course his hour of splendour was on 21 October 1805, about five o'clock on a smoky bloody afternoon.

Sir James McGrigor *(1771-1868)*

Born at Cromdale, Strathspey, he was educated at Aberdeen Grammar School and Marischal College. He studied medicine at Aberdeen and Edinburgh. He purchased the post of surgeon in De Burgh's corps, later known as the Connaught Rangers. He first spelt his name MacGregor. As the proscription of that name was lifted in 1775 there seems no reason for the slight change. He served in Flanders and in the retreat from Bremen, though he was very ill from typhus. He then saw service in the West Indies, Bombay and Ceylon. At Rosetta in Egypt he was called upon to deal with a fatal epidemic of plague. On the way home he was nearly captured by a French frigate. To aid him in his poor circumstances Lord Melville used his influence to place him in charge of the Medical Division in England.

When the British Peninsular Army returned from Corunna they were heavily infected with fever and the situation was declared quite unsurmountable. But James McGrigor took such stringent measures with the sanitation that the outbreak was gradually confined to the military hospitals and eventually suppressed.

McGrigor was now ordered out to Walcheren, where the expedition to oppose the French occupation of Holland had met with an unexpected enemy. This was a small black fly from the marshes, carrying malaria. 3000 British troops were prostrated by it. On the way to Walcheren McGrigor was wrecked off the mouth of the Scheldt. He was rescued exhausted, but carried on, stricken with fever, until he had treated the outbreak and the army had been evacuated.

The Peninsular Army under Wellington was now heavily engaged for two years and McGrigor was put in charge of the medical corps there. He was at the Siege of Badajos, where British casualties were enormous, as they also were at the battles of Burgos and Vittoria. In ten months McGrigor's staff treated 95,348 cases of wounds and sickness and kept the gaps in the fighting ranks filled up with convalescents. Even the French paid McGrigor a high compliment. One of the chief officers said, 'The British forces are under sanitary discipline. The French army is a perambulating brothel.' Wellington was less enthusiastic, but he called McGrigor 'One of the most industrious, able and successful public servants I have ever met.' He did not mention the others he had met, or had not met, so we are left guessing.

On retiral he had plenty of time on his hands, as he lived to eighty-seven. He founded a Museum of Natural History and Pathological Anatomy, and inaugurated a system of regular reports on the health of the Army. He was in fact the father of the British Army Medical Corps.

Sir William Putney Allison *(1790-1859)*

He succeeded the Duncans and later became Professor of Medicine. He studied at Edinburgh and is chiefly noted for his contributions to knowledge of fevers.

Smallpox, which at that time was being alleviated by the new idea of vaccination, was the subject of his observation. His most important work was with social conditions in Scottish cities, where disease and poverty seemed to present a hopeless problem. His publication of a report on this, in 1840, aroused the public conscience. A Royal Commission of Inquiry started in 1844, followed by an Act containing all Allison's suggested reforms. His initiative led ultimately to the provisions of a universal Health Service.

Robert Knox *(1791-1862)*

He is notorious for his connection with the Burke and Hare murders of 1827-28. He and his laboratory assistants bought several of the murdered persons' corpses for dissection. When the public riots started, after the revelations of this extraordinary series of crimes, the mob attacked Knox's house and he was condemned on all sides. A typical verse against him, published in December 1828, is entitled 'An Expostulation', with the sub-title 'Thou canst not say I did it'. It starts,

Ah, can'st thou, with cold indifference, see
The hand of execration point to thee?
Can'st thou, unmoved, bear a whole nation's cry
To cleanse thyself from the polluted sty
Of Burke and Hare, and all that fiendish crew,
Who, for mere gain, their fellow-mortals slew.

Burke, in an interview after his condemnation, confessed to all his crimes and also replied to the question, 'To whom were the bodies so murdered sold?'

'To Doctor Knox. We took the bodies to his rooms and then went to his house to receive the money. Sometimes he paid us himself. No questions were ever asked as to the mode in which we had come by the bodies.'

Admittedly Knox seemed guilty of being an accessory, and was ruined by his laxness in dealing with 'subjects' for dissection. Yet on the credit side he was a very popular lecturer, his classes in anatomy often having 500 students. He also published several books with these titles. *The Edinburgh Dissector; The Races of Men*, an ethnological study, and two manuals of anatomy. He built up an enormous collection of anatomical specimens ranging from tropical fish to human beings. His notebooks reveal him to have been a highly gifted observer and a brilliant student of biology. The paradox, which emerges from a true knowledge of his life, is that he had no need to purchase 'subjects' from Burke and Hare. He already had, preserved in his laboratory, over a hundred human corpses, obtained from various sources after dying natural deaths. Many of these came from Ireland, some from pauper institutions, and perhaps a number were robbed from local graves, a method which Burke and Hare denied ever having stooped to.

Robert Liston *(1794-1847)*

He was born at Ecclesmachan, West Lothian, son of the parish minister. He graduated at the Royal College of Surgeons after being taught first by his father. One of his first teachers was the noted anatomist John Barclay (1760-1826). For a time he was a house-surgeon in the Royal Infirmary of Edinburgh, then went to London for further experience. Despite his frank criticism of the policies of the Infirmary in Edinburgh, he was made a surgeon there. After seven years he went to University College, London, as professor of clinical surgery and surgeon of the North London Hospitals.

He had a wide reputation in Europe and the USA as a surgeon. He was very skilful and swift and successfully carried out operations that had never been attempted before. In doing this he invented many procedures and devices, one of which, the thigh splint, bears his name.

He published the *Principles of Surgery*, and *Practical Surgery*.

He made history in Edinburgh surgery by performing the major operation of amputation through the thigh, using an ether anaesthetic.

An expert on fractures, bone disease and aneurisms, he was paradoxically fated to die at the height of his powers with an aneurism of the heart. A year before his death he had the future Lord Lister as a witness of one of his operations conducted under the new anaesthetics.

Sir Robert Christison *(1797-1882)*

Born in Edinburgh, son of Alexander Christison, Professor of Latin and Greek, he studied in Edinburgh and took his MD when twenty-one. He became Professor of Medical Jurisprudence when twenty-five and was twice President of the College of Surgeons, and physician to Queen

Victoria.

He was called upon in 1828 to give evidence in the Burke and Hare trials relating to the bruises found on the bodies of the murdered persons, and corroborated that these could not have been caused after death. This was damning evidence which led to Burke's conviction.

Christison's work in toxicology, or the study of poisons, was of immense value in subsequent investigations. He was notable for his interest in oxalic acid, arsenical and lead poisoning. He was Chairman of the Committee which prepared the first *Pharmacopoeia of Great Britain and Ireland* in 1864. He isolated the poison conine (the active part of hemlock), the poison in the Calabar bean, and digitaline, the agent in foxgloves. He also investigated the properties of opium and various sorts of wine.

James Syme *(1799-1870)*

He was born in Edinburgh with Fife connections. He studied anatomy under Liston, assisting him in the laboratory. He was resident surgeon in the Infirmary and fever hospital for a time, then started a surgical hospital on his own as a charity. This was one of the first schools of clinical teaching. He accepted the Chair of Clinical Surgery at London but returned to Edinburgh to work, for the rest of his career, winning a European reputation. His pressure on the Government forced through some much-needed medical legislation.

He was one of the greatest surgeons of all time, noted especially for his new methods in amputation, as well as in treatment of inflammation and intestinal operation. Many of his methods were adhered to for nearly a century. He was the first to take advantage of anaesthetics. He could also have been said to have revolutionised surgery. Syme was really the inventor of the 'macintosh' for it was he who, early in his career, discovered the solvent for rubber. Charles Macintosh patented his 'discovery' a few months later.

Alexander Wood *(1808-1877)*

He merits mention as being the first in Britain to use a hypodermic syringe for the administration of morphia, atropine and other substances. Although this method had been used in Europe two years before, Wood did not know about it. Wood published a *New Method of treating Neuralgia by Subcutaneous Injection.*

Sir William Fergusson *(1808-1877)*

He was born at Prestonpans and educated at Lochmaben and Edinburgh. He studied anatomy and surgery under Robert Knox, later rising to be Professor of Surgery at King's College. He was named 'the greatest practical surgeon of his time', being most anxious to save limbs rather than to amputate. He suggested, though he did not venture to perform, the delicate operations of excision of the prostate glands, and operations on the brain and heart.

Sir James Young Simpson *(1811-1870)*

He was born of humble parents in Bathgate, West Lothian. It is of unusual interest to know that the village doctor, called to deliver Mrs Simpson, made a note in his casebook that he 'arrived too late'. Despite this precarious entry into the world, Simpson survived to render infinite blessings to mankind, and in particular womankind.

After his education at the local school he graduated from the Medical College in Edinburgh, a difficult task for a boy who was ill-provided with the world's goods. But this brilliant young man of only twenty-nine was appointed Professor of Medicine and Midwifery at the University of Edinburgh.

Although renowned universally for his discovery of the use of chloroform he was also a very skilled gynaecologist and invented a device to aid in childbirth. His discovery of chloroform has a rather comic side to it. On 28 November 1847 he set about satisfying himself as to the safety of using chloroform. With his two medical friends, Dr Keith and Dr Duncan, he sat in his room. Each was provided with a napkin and a tumbler of chloroform. At a signal each poured some chloroform on to the napkin and inhaled. Simpson became drowsy but was aroused by Duncan snoring and by Keith kicking about in a far from graceful manner. The great discovery had been made which was to free humanity from the terrors of the surgery.

Simpson also invented acupressure, instead of ligatures, for preventing haemorrhages, and instituted hospital reform, advocating isolation of each patient in the hospital as far as possible. This was suggested many years before Lister's invention of antiseptics rendered it to some degree unnecessary.

Simpson was noted for the equal treatment he gave to rich or poor patients and for his help to the latter. In his spare time his hobbies were archaeology and literature.

John Goodsir *(1814-1867)*

He was first employed as Curator of the Museum of the College of Surgeons of Edinburgh, then Curator of the University Museum. He became Professor of Anatomy from 1846 to the year of his death.

His scientific work was at first in the study of parasites. At the time of the disastrous potato blight that indirectly led to the devastation of Ireland, he identified the fungus responsible for the blight. He then studied, by microscope, the vital cell, and discovered the function and organisation of human cells.

The celebrated German anatomist Virchow acknowledged his debt to Goodsir by dedicating his *Cellular Pathologie* to him, and calling him 'one of the most acute observers of cell-life'. Goodsir's publications deal with nutrition, diseases of glands, and also with natural history subjects and the mechanism of the limbs.

Sir Henry Littlejohn *(1828-1914)*

He was a native of Perthshire and received his first schooling at Perth

Academy. He completed his schooldays at the High School of Edinburgh and graduated from the University there as a doctor. He then studied medicine at Paris.

He was appointed police surgeon in Edinburgh shortly after the Police Act of 1856. He was then a young man and had a very responsible job. Attended by only two constables he had to deal with all cases of murder, suicide, sudden death. Edinburgh was a very crowded, dirty, unhealthy city, that is to say in the old town, where it was impossible to control disease and crime owing to the density of the population. The police surgeon had also to inspect nuisances and to ensure that butchers complied with the sanitary regulations. As if that were not enough Littlejohn had to attend sick constables to ensure that they were cared for and their sick pay was earned. One of his patients whom he visited on 7 February for the last time (for he died the following evening) was John Gray, the constable who owned Greyfriars Bobby, whose fidelity to his master is one of the great animal stories of the world.

From 1856 to 1862 Littlejohn held the police surgeon's onerous position. He was then appointed first Medical Officer of Health for Edinburgh, a post he filled with distinction for forty-six years. Almost from the beginning he stirred up trouble by issuing a sensational report (1865) on the incredibly unhygienic state of Central Edinburgh. The nation was shocked and despite the protests of interested proprietors, large areas of slums were demolished and new houses built.

Littlejohn's ability and energy were at last recognised. He was called the Napoleon of the Health Service, pushing aside all opposition and of course making countless enemies. But he saved thousands of lives from the endemic disease of typhus, and other infectious fevers as well as tuberculosis, simply by his drastic measures.

He was President of the Royal College of Surgeons, Professor of Forensic Medicine (1897-1906) and a public figure active in all enlightened movements. For example, his signature is to be seen on a Remonstrance to Nicholas II, Czar of Russia, against his annexation of Finland in 1899. Florence Nightingale's signature is also on the document.

Sir Patrick Manson (1844-1922)

It was Manson's theory that biting insects were responsible for the introduction of the nematode parasite into human blood, which caused the breakthrough in the fight against the dreadful diseases, malaria, plague and yellow fever. Inspired by Manson, Ronald Ross, faced by disheartening obstacles, was able to prove Manson's hypothesis correct. Between them, these two Scottish doctors saved mankind from an age-long scourge.

Sir Ronald Ross (1857-1932)

Of Scottish descent, he was born in India in the year of the Mutiny. He studied medicine at St Bartholomew's London, and proceeded to India in the medical service. The prevalence of malaria made him carry out special investigation, and after many years he began the scientific study to find the micro-organisms said to be responsible for the disease. He was not first in the field. In 1880 malarial parasites had been found in the blood-stream, by Laveran, at Constantinople. Italian doctors in the 1880s had demonstrated the life-cycles of tertian and quartan parasites. But Ross discovered the complex chain of circumstances whereby the disease spread. In this he was helped by Patrick Manson and other doctors.

After Ross retired from the Indian Service he went to West Africa to continue his malarial studies. He became Professor of Tropical Diseases at Liverpool and, later, Director of the Ross Institute and Hospital for Tropical Diseases. He received the Nobel Prize in 1902.

After Fleming, of penicillin fame, Ross has probably saved more human lives than any other, for malaria caused more sickness and death than any other single disease.

Sir Robert Philip (1857-1939)

He was the son of a Glasgow minister, educated at Edinburgh High School and University, reading medicine. He undertook post-graduate study in Vienna where he was taught by Robert Koch who had recently discovered the tubercle bacillus which causes phthisis in all its forms.

On his return to Edinburgh, he was opposed by established physicians who did not believe in microscopic discoveries. He was, however, awarded a Gold Medal in 1887 for his work on tuberculosis. He then started his long campaign against the disease, establishing finally the Royal Victoria Hospital. His 'Edinburgh System' became world famous.

He was rewarded by being knighted, and elected President of the Royal College of Surgeons from 1917 to 1922. But his greater reward was in the saving of millions from what was regarded as an inevitable death.

John Brownlee (1868-1927)

His fame rests on his work as a medical statistician, particularly on his very important publication on the rise and fall of epidemics of phthisis (pulmonary tuberculosis), measles and influenza.

John James Rickard MacLeod (1876-1935)

He was born near Dunkeld, Perthshire, educated at Aberdeen Grammar School, Marischal College and Leipzig University. He was demonstrator in physiology in London Hospital and later Professor in Cleveland, Ohio in the same subject.

His most important work was in the control of carbo-hydrates in animal bodies, and in collaboration with two other doctors he isolated the hormone insulin, for which he shared the Nobel Prize for Medicine in 1923 with Dr Banting. He published several books on physiology.

Sir Alexander Fleming (1881-1955)

He was born at Lochfield, Ayrshire, and studied at Kilmarnock Academy before proceeding to St Mary's Hospital School, London, where he was given awards of Merit. As a post-graduate he worked under Sir Almroth

Wright, pioneer in vaccine therapy. During the First World War Fleming was a captain in the RAMC, being mentioned in dispatches. As professor in the Royal College of Surgeons he continued research on anti-bacterial substances and his first reward was the discovery of the anti-biotic lysozyme. His epoch-making discovery of the mould from which penicillin is made he described as a 'triumph of accident and shrewd observation'.

The 'accident' was some mould having been allowed to develop on a plate where bacteria were being cultured. The 'observation' was that the mould was so destructive of the bacteria that even when diluted 800 times it still destroyed them. It is hard to estimate how many lives have been saved by that rare coincidence of accident and observation.

Fleming was knighted and received the Nobel Prize in 1944.

Sir James Learmonth *(1895-1967)*

A native of Girthon, Galloway, he attended the parish school, then Kilmarnock Academy, and Glasgow University, where he graduated as a doctor. He was made a Fellow of the Royal College of Surgeons in Edinburgh in 1928. Numerous distinctions followed, an MD of Oslo and a Doctorate of Paris and Strasbourg. He attended King George V during his last illnesses and was appointed Surgeon in Scotland to Queen Elizabeth in 1960. He received the Award for Outstanding Achievement from Minnesota in 1964, having already been recognised in France by being made a Chevalier of the Legion of Honour.

Norman McOmish Dott *(1897-1973)*

He was educated at George Heriot's School, apprenticed as a joiner, then as an engineer. An accident to his hip in 1913 forced him to leave engineering and he began a medical course at Edinburgh in 1914, graduating as a doctor in 1919. He was made assistant surgeon in hospitals in Edinburgh for a time, then appointed Neurological Assistant in Boston, USA. He returned to Edinburgh and held various posts from 1925 to 1931.

His professorship of Neurology extended from 1947 to 1962 during which time he performed many daring and successful brain operations. He was president of various associations and was acknowledged throughout the world as a leading authority on brain damage, paraplegia and spina bifida.

William Ritchie Russell *(1903-1980)*

He was born in Edinburgh, son of Professor William Russell, one of six children who all became doctors. He was educated at Edinburgh Academy and Edinburgh University. He was appointed Assistant Physician in the Edinburgh Royal Infirmary in 1934, Lecturer in Neurology in Edinburgh in 1938, and held a similar post in Oxford from 1949 to 1966.

During the war of 1939-45 he served in the RAMC, being made Consultant Neurologist to the British Army in 1943. He edited the *Journal of Neurology* and devoted the years 1948 to 1969 to his work as a neurosurgeon and psychiatrist. He published three books on the human brain; *Brain Memory Training, Traumatic Aphasia* and *Traumatic Amnesia*.

Exploration

The early Celtic missionaries, in the age of Columba, ventured on frail curraghs, or coracles of wicker and hide, as far afield as Iceland, but, apart from trading with Europe, mediaeval Scots did little exploration by sea, though it was a common enough thing for Scots students to travel through Europe to various universities. The great ocean explorers were the Spaniards and Portugese, later rivalled by the Dutch, British and French.

Early in the seventeenth century William Lithgow, an extraordinary traveller from Scotland, made a peregrination, by foot mostly, through Europe, the Near East, Egypt and North Africa. He covered 36,000 miles in nineteen years and was nearly condemned by the Spanish Inquisition. The reason for his voluntary exile was that, having been caught in an illicit love-affair and punished by having his ears cut off, he was ashamed to show his face in Lanark, his native town, where he was known as Lugless Willie Lithgow. His book of travels may still be read. He was recently described as the first representative of self-catering abroad.

At the end of the seventeenth century from much the same domestic scandal, not involving sex, but a family quarrel, Alexander Selkirk, or Selcraig, of Largo, Fife, went to sea to seek relief. He took his quarrelsome character with him and off the coast of South America he fell out with his captain who put him ashore with a few necessities on the desert island of Juan Fernandez, where he could quarrel with his shadow. He was rescued after four years, came home, and by chance recited his tale to Daniel Defoe who glorified and magnified it into the immortal *Robinson Crusoe*. Some of the articles belonging to him may still be seen.

These were more or less accidental explorations. Deliberate scientific exploration began with attempts to know more about the interiors of the great land masses only touched on by navigation.

AFRICA

The nearest land mass, but strangely the least known, was Africa, the Dark Continent of which Jonathan Swift in the early eighteenth century wrote,

Geographers, in Afric maps
With savage pictures filled their gaps
And o'er unhabitable downs
Placed elephants for want of towns.

The scandal of the slave trade, in which Britain had a large share, was the initial reason for inquiries and with this aim the African Association was formed in London in 1788. But a Scot was much earlier in the field.

James Bruce *(1730-1794)*

James Bruce was born of well-to-do parents at Kinnaird House, Stirlingshire. He was educated at Harrow and Edinburgh University. He studied law but left it, going into business with his father-in-law. His young wife died after nine months; Bruce, broken-hearted, set off to travel in Spain. There he began to study Arabic. Although he inherited his father's estate he worked for the War Office and was made Consul at Algiers.

From this point begins his exploration of the ruins of ancient civilisations in Africa which led him to try to discover the source of the Nile. In disguise after many adventures he reached Abyssinia and in 1770 discovered the source of the Blue Nile which, with the White Nile, forms the main river. He traced the Blue Nile to its junction with the White Nile and after great hardships got back to Cairo and Europe where he was received with great congratulations by French scientists.

In London no one would believe him, though he published five magnificent volumes of his travels at his own expense, dying not long after, still bitterly and justly offended by his English traducers.

Mungo Park *(1771-1806)*

Mungo Park was born in a wayside cottage in Yarrow, a few miles from Selkirk. The house is still there. He studied as a surgeon in Edinburgh and when qualified was appointed assistant surgeon on board an East Indiaman. He studied new fishes and wrote for a biological journal.

The African Association, now six years old, appointed him to explore the Niger. The Gambia, by African standards, is a small river but he sailed up it for 200 miles before travelling overland to reach what he guessed might be the Upper Niger. Nearly a year later, after a long humiliating imprisonment by a Moorish chief, he reached the Niger alone. For another year, full of adventure, he mapped the Upper Niger, reaching home safely where his book of travels was very popular.

He intended to settle for life in Peebles, as a doctor, but unluckily for his schemes, he accepted the offer to lead another Niger Expedition along with his brother-in-law Alexander Anderson. The expedition was a disaster. Fever and hostile savages accounted for all the members. Mungo Park's body was never found, nor his journals. His second son, thinking his father a prisoner, set off to find him but died of fever in the jungle.

Hugh Clapperton *(1788-1827)*

Hugh Clapperton was born in Annan in Dumfriesshire. He was a merchant seaman until press-ganged into the navy where he became a lieutenant. He was sent on a government expedition in 1820 with Walter Oudney and Denham to explore the Niger. For two years they travelled visiting the large towns of Kano and Sokoto. Oudney, an Edinburgh native and medical graduate died of pneumonia in the Sudan, because of the intense cold the expedition suffered at night.

Clapperton was made a commander and sent again to the Niger. Before long two of the party's leaders died of fever but Clapperton carried on to reach the Niger at the point where Mungo Park had died, twenty years before. Not long afterwards he himself died of dysentery at Sokoto. Records of his expedition were published soon after, being brought home by his devoted servant and friend Lander, a Cornishman.

Alexander Gordon Laing *(1792-1826)*

Alexander Laing was born in Edinburgh and educated at Edinburgh University. He served in the army, being given a commission in the Royal African Corps. While he was at Sierra Leone (the White Man's Grave), the governor dispatched him to put down slavery and establish trade up-country. He tried to find the source of the Niger but was prevented by the tribesmen, though he located it by mapping. He fought in the Ashanti war.

The government requested him to go by Timbuktu to the Niger so he set off from Tripoli to cross the Sahara, leaving his bride of two days. The Tuareg tribesmen attacked him treacherously and he arrived in Timbuktu severely wounded, leaving in two days to be murdered not far into the desert. His journal was never found.

Sir Andrew Smith *(1797-1872)*

Sir Andrew Smith was born in Roxburghshire and took his medical degree at Edinburgh University. In an African Expedition of 1834-5, he reached as far north as the Tropic of Capricorn and brought back the first reports on the upper reaches of the Limpopo River. Those were early days in Africa and it was still known as the Dark Continent.

Macgregor Laird *(1808-1861)*

Macgregor Laird was born at Greenock, the younger son of William Laird founder of the famous shipbuilding firm. He with certain Liverpool merchants formed a company to develop the Niger region. In 1832 two small ships, one being the first ocean-going iron-hulled vessel, were sent to Africa. Macgregor Laird with a large party of Europeans led by Richard Lander (mentioned above), set off up river. Lander died of wounds, forty others of fever, but Laird took the expedition up to the confluence of the Niger and Benue Rivers, returning to Liverpool to publish the story. Laird spent the rest of his life in developing West African trade and transatlantic shipping.

David Livingstone *(1813-1873)*

David Livingstone was born at Blantyre, Lanarkshire. He worked in a cotton-mill from the age of ten and, after great efforts, began a college education at twenty-three, studying medicine, Greek and theology at Anderson's College, Glasgow. He took a medical degree at Glasgow after joining the London Missionary Society and wanted to go to China but was disappointed to be sent to Africa.

He went to Robert Moffat's mission in Bechuanaland, and commenced to find native agents to convert the heathen. Here he was mauled by a lion which left him troubled for life. He built a house for himself and married

Mary, daughter of Moffat. He explored the Zambezi, nearly died of fever at Loanda, and sent observations back to the Royal Geographical Society for which he was awarded a medal.

In 1855 he discovered the Victoria Falls on the Zambezi. His discoveries filled the hitherto blank map of Africa. The Zambezi Expedition followed. Lake Nyasa was discovered. The deaths of a missionary bishop C.F. Mackenzie and of Livingstone's wife was a double blow. The Portuguese slave trade was devastating the whole area and rendering Livingstone's explorations difficult.

Against all kinds of misfortunes he discovered Tanganyika and arrived back at Ujiji to be met by Stanley with ample supplies sent by the *New York Herald*, Gordon Bennett being the editor.

He died in Ilala and his body and possessions were carried faithfully across Africa to Zanzibar and to eventual burial in Westminster Abbey. Stanley said, 'We look in vain among other nationalities for a name such as Livingstone's.'

His example gave the death-blow to the slave-trade. Unfortunately his gentlemanly attitude to the native tribes has not been adopted by other Europeans in Africa.

William Balfour Baikie *(1824-1864)*

William Baikie was born at Kirkwall, Orkney. He took his doctor's degree at Edinburgh and joined the navy. He was appointed surgeon and naturalist in 1854 on a Niger expedition sent out by Macgregor Laird. The party went up the Benue tributary in a small steamer for 250 miles and returned without loss of life. In 1857 he led another expedition exploring the Niger for two years, when the vessel was wrecked on rapids. All but Baikie returned home. He purchased a site and founded a city, acting as ruler, teacher, doctor and priest. He opened up Niger navigation and established a market. The vocabularies of fifty African dialects were collected by him and parts of the Bible translated into Hausa.

James Augustus Grant *(1827-1892)*

Grant was born at Nairn, son of the parish minister. He was educated at Marischal College, Aberdeen and joined the Indian Army at nineteen. He served in the Sikh War and in the Indian Mutiny, being wounded at the Relief of Lucknow. In 1860 he joined Speke in the expedition to solve the mystery of the sources of the Nile. He was in the Abyssinian Expedition of 1868, under the command of Field-Marshal Robert Napier, sent to relieve prisoners from Magdala.

H.B. Cotterill *(c.1840-1900)*

He was the son of the Bishop of Edinburgh and in 1877 made a safari from Lake Nyasa to Ugogo in the highlands of Tanganyika, a journey into the unknown a century ago.

Verney Lovatt Cameron (1844-1894)

Cameron was born of a Scottish family near Weymouth, entered the navy at thirteen and served in the Abyssinian campaign along with Grant. He helped to suppress the East African slave trade. When sent out from Zanzibar to succour Livingstone he had the strange experience of meeting Livingstone's servants bearing their master's mummified body. While his companions accompanied the corpse to Zanzibar, Cameron went on to Ujiji where he recovered Livingstone's valuable papers. He explored the area where the Congo and Zambezi rise and was the first European to cross Central Africa from coast to coast. His book of travels *Across Africa* was published in 1877. He was killed in Bedfordshire by a fall from horseback.

Joseph Thomson (1856-1894)

He was born at Penpont, Dumfriesshire in a house built by his father. He was attracted to geology and studied at Edinburgh under Balfour, Huxley and Geikie. He was appointed geologist to Alexander Keith Johnston's African Expedition of 1879. They started from Dar-es-Salaam with 150 men and marched SW. At Behobeho, several days out, Johnston died of fever and Thomson, aged twenty-one, took command.

He knew Johnston's plan, which was to explore between Lakes Nyasa and Tanganyika. He managed this without losing more than one carrier and without firing one shot in anger, though much of the expedition lay through the land of the warlike Masai. His tactics were to make great circuits to deceive any possible enemy. As he approached the source of the Congo his carriers mutinied as they feared entering the territory of a cannibalistic tribe. Thomson had to lead them back but as a consolation he discovered Lake Leopold, being the first white man to see it.

Instead of returning to base he explored the foothills of the great mountains of Kenya and Kilimanjaro, then ascended to heights over three miles. He was also able to solve the problem that had baffled V.L. Cameron and Stanley (the discoverer of Livingstone). This was, in which direction did the overflow of Lake Tanganyika go? He said, 'I got a new lease of life as I watched the mighty Lukuga River flow from the lake to the west, to the Congo and the Atlantic.' But his life was not to be a long one. He died, aged thirty-six, partly due to his African hardships.

ASIA

The great land mass of Eurasia, limitless, where whole armies could be swallowed up, as Hitler and Napoleon discovered, has usually defeated travellers and explorers. But a lone Scot from a quiet country district traversed these great steppes and deserts before most of Europe had even heard of them.

John Bell (1691-1780)

John Bell was born at Antermony, Aberdeenshire, and studied medicine, probably at Aberdeen. At the age of twenty-five he set off for St Petersburg, now Leningrad, which had been founded only a few years before and where

Peter the Great had put the new shipyard in charge of Farquharson, a Scots mathematician. Perhaps this was the fellow-countryman who introduced the unknown John Bell to Valensky, the ambassador to Persia. Bell was appointed Valensky's medical attendant. He travelled in Persia and the Middle East with him for three years. From 1718-22 Bell accompanied an embassy to China through Siberia and the great Mongolian deserts. When he got back to St Petersburg the Tsar requested his attendance in his dangerous campaign to the Caspian. After Peter's death Bell was sent on a mission to Constantinople. In 1747 he returned to Scotland where he wrote a book about his travels which was published in Glasgow in 1763, going through many editions.

George Bogle *(1746-1781)*

George Bogle had graduated at Edinburgh. He was born at Bothwell, Lanarkshire and commenced his education at Haddington and Glasgow. He joined the East India Company in 1769 and was appointed by Warren Hastings (later made notorious for his impeachment), to be an envoy to Tibet, where he was to approach the Tashi Lama in Lhasa, the capital, with a view to furthering trade.

Bogle was the first Briton to cross the difficult passes of the Tsan-pu range. Several other Europeans had visited Lhasa. The Jesuits and other religious orders had founded missions there, but Bogle was on a trade quest. He was well received by the Tibetans and for years after his return to India he kept up a correspondence with the Lama.

Hastings arranged to send Bogle on a second expedition but the Scot died. The manuscript of the first journey had been sent to Alexander Dalrymple, the geographer of the East India Company, for publication, but this was not done, although the manuscript was safely delivered to the British Museum.

James Baillie Fraser *(1783-1856)*

Fraser was born at Reelick, Inverness. Early in life he went to India and explored the Himalayas. He was made guardian of two Persian exiled princes in England and returned with them to Constantinople. He went to Persia on a diplomatic mission, going on horseback through Asia Minor. He made many useful astronomical observations later used by map-makers of Asia. Several accounts of his travels and stories of eastern life were published.

Basil Hall *(1788-1844)*

Hall was born in Edinburgh, son of Sir James Hall, chemist and geologist. He entered the Royal Navy at fourteen, travelled over the island of Java and accompanied Lord Amherst on the mission to China of which he wrote an account. He then commanded a ship, visited the coasts of South America and Mexico and later travelled in Syria. He was a friend of Sir Walter Scott and suggested that the government provide a ship to convey Scott abroad for his health during his last illness.

Sir George Adam Smith *(1856-1942)*

Smith was educated at the Royal High School, University of Edinburgh, and New College. He travelled extensively in the Middle East and wrote the classical *Historical Geography of the Holy Land,* published in 1894.

ARCTICA AND ANTARCTICA

Many attempts were made to explore the Arctic regions from as early as Columbus's discovery of America. Large fleets from Britain, Holland and other European countries set off regularly to exploit the rich fishing and whaling grounds off the Labrador and Greenland coasts. Intrepid explorers like Frobisher and Davis attempted to realise the long-pursued dream of the North-West Passage, which would enable Western Europeans to reach the fabulous wealth of China and the East Indies by a shorter route. The English explorer of Jacobean times, Henry Hudson, after many discoveries and hardships in three voyages, was deserted by his crew and perished with his young son. Many another adventurer died trying to find a passage that, when found at last by the Irishman Robert McClure, was of no practical use for shipping.

It was not until after the Napoleonic Wars that scientific expeditions set out in earnest to explore the Poles.

Sir John Ross *(1777-1856)*

Ross joined the Navy at nine. At thirty-one he captained the Swedish Fleet, being promoted commander when he was thirty-five. In 1818 he led an Arctic expedition which found nothing new, but from 1829-33 his second expedition was frozen in, and from his base he made many discoveries, geographical and scientific. Four years in the Arctic without help tested his powers as a commander of men, but he never gave up hope of escaping from the ice. In 1835, without aid, he freed his ship and to everyone's amazement sailed safely into the North Sea. In 1850 he went searching for Franklin but unsuccessfully. He was appointed Admiral of the Fleet in 1851.

Sir James Clark Ross *(1800-1862)*

Nephew of Sir John Ross, born in London, he entered the Navy at twelve. He accompanied his uncle on his first Arctic voyage in search of the North-West Passage when he was eighteen. Between 1819 and 1827 he made four Arctic expeditions under Parry and was with his uncle from 1829-33 when iced up. From their headquarters he set off and discovered the exact position of the North Magnetic Pole in 1831. He worked on the magnetic survey of Great Britain. From 1839-43 he commanded the Antarctic expedition of the *Erebus* and the *Terror*. He was captain of the *Enterprise* in the first Franklin expedition.

His first Antarctic voyage when he took possession of the continent in the name of Queen Victoria (1841) and when he named the twin volcanoes after his ships, was the most remarkable antarctic voyage ever made, because of its dangers and the extent of discoveries.

The following year the expedition reached 78° S, the highest latitude reached for sixty years. Ross wintered in the Falkland Islands. He made a third attempt but found the pack-ice impenetrable so returned to New Zealand.

No more Antarctic expeditions were made for thirty years.

Sir John Richardson *(1787-1865)*

Richardson was born in Dumfries. He accompanied Franklin in 1819 on his expedition to the Great Slave Lake and in 1820 helped to survey 550 miles of the North Coast.

In 1825-6 he discovered the shore between the mouths of the Mackenzie and Coppermine Rivers.

In 1848 with John Rae he searched the coast of these rivers for any trace of the Franklin Expedition which had been lost for over two years.

John Rae *(1813-1893)*

John Rae was born in the Orkneys. He took his medical degree in Edinburgh and made a voyage as surgeon in a Hudson Bay ship. He was resident surgeon at Moose Factory, James Bay. He surveyed 790 miles of coastline. Next he joined in the search for Franklin under Sir John Richardson. In 1851 he travelled over 500 miles, mostly on foot, surveying new coast. This gained him the Gold Medal of the Royal Geographical Society. Latterly he travelled over Iceland, Greenland and Canada surveying telegraph routes.

His finest achievements were, first, in 1846 completing the survey of the North American coast, when he and his Orkney men wintered in a stone hut living on deer which they shot; second, in 1854 when, after a winter of hardship, he brought back the first positive evidence of Franklin's fate which he obtained from the Eskimos. For this news the Admiralty awarded him the £10,000 prize that had been put up for that purpose.

William Spiers Bruce *(c.1867-1921)*

He is noted in our chapter on Naturalists, but he is also well known for being the leader of the Scottish expedition to Antarctica in 1903-4 which confined itself chiefly to oceanography.

Alastair Forbes-Mackay *(1878-1914)*

He was born in Argyll and served as a soldier with Baden-Powell in South Africa, then as a surgeon in the Navy. He was given a well-merited place in Shackleton's South Polar Expedition of 1908-9. His job was, first, to handle the Manchurian ponies used to carry baggage and second, to perform surgical operations on the personnel. On this expedition he ascended Mount Erebus, over 13,000ft. With two others he reached the South Magnetic Pole early in 1909, three years before Amundsen and Scott reached the geographical South Pole.

He died in 1914 on Stefansson's Arctic Expedition.

Henry Bowers *(1883-1912)*

Although not the leader of a Polar expedition, Bowers was by chance drawn into the great dramatic tragedy of the Scott Antarctic exploration.

He was born at Greenock, son of Captain Alexander Bowers of the Royal Naval Reserve, who had experience in the old tea-clippers. On his father's death, Henry was only four. With his mother he went to Kent where he was educated at Sidcup. He then enrolled as a sea-cadet in HMS *Worcester*, where his small stature (5ft. 4in) and remarkable agility won him the nickname of 'Birdie'. Captain R.F. Scott, already an experienced Antarctic explorer, asked Bowers to join the new expedition, as he was struck by Bowers' resourcefulness, optimism and toughness.

The tragic tale is universally known. On 3 January 1912, only 150 miles from the South Pole, Scott selected a team which was to make a final dash to the objective. They consisted of Oates, Scott, Wilson and Bowers – a party of five but with rations for only four. They reached the Pole on 18 January only to find Amundsen's tent had been pitched there on 14 December. Sick at heart, Scott's party returned, but were unable to reach the supply depot only eleven miles distant, owing to blizzards. Evans had broken down and died, and Oates sacrificed himself in vain, for the three survivors died in their tent, their frozen bodies being recovered nearly a year later by Dr Atkinson, base commander.

Bowers had been in charge of navigation and despite frostbite and exhaustion had guided the party accurately to the Pole, never relinquishing his instruments or neglecting his records, faithful unto death.

NORTH AMERICA

Sir Alexander Mackenzie *(1764-1820)*

Born in Stornoway, Lewis, he emigrated at an early age to America and worked as a fur trapper and trader at Lake Athabasca. With his brother and several companions he made a long journey by canoe, in 1789, down river from the Great Slave Lake reaching to the Arctic Ocean. The river bears his name. The journey home was very wearisome and winter had begun before the party returned to camp. His two journeys of 1792 and 1793 were more hazardous, crossing the Rockies and descending to the Pacific by canoe.

John Muir *(1838-1914)*

He was born in Dunbar where he early acquired a great love of nature. His family emigrated to Wisconsin where he continued to be a naturalist but also enjoyed factory and city life. He attended the University of Wisconsin and shortly afterwards suffered an accident to one eye. To recover from this he set off wandering through the States. He visited the Yosemite, California and Alaska. After his marriage he settled to horticulture. He published the story of his wandering in several volumes. Through his efforts several national parks, including the Yosemite, were established.

Sir James Hector *(c.1840-1900)*

A native of Edinburgh, he discovered a feasible passage through the Rocky Mountains. It was named picturesquely Kicking Horse Pass and was the first crossing of that formidable barrier to the Pacific Coast by the Canadian

Pacific Railway. Hector was later the Director of the Geological Survey of
New Zealand.

Robert Brown *(1842-1895)*
He was born in Caithness and graduated in Edinburgh. At twenty-one he led
an expedition to the interior of Vancouver Island and mapped a part of it,
previously unexplored.

AUSTRALIA
The first settlement in Australia was made in 1788 in Botany Bay. The new
land did not raise much enthusiasm. It was called by an English
parliamentarian 'a sterile dumping-ground for convicts.' The coast of New
South Wales on either side of Botany Bay appeared very constricted and
several attempts were made unsuccessfully to cross the Blue Mountains. At
last a road was constructed and the town of Bathurst was planned in 1815 by
MacQuarie, and named after the Secretary of State for the Colonies. The
Scottish botanist Alan Cunningham made several explorations, along with
others, to trace the courses of the west-flowing Lachlan and MacQuarie
rivers which, to their disappointment, ended in swamps. Cunningham spent
two years exploring the Liverpool Range and made many discoveries of
great value. But the nature of the interior had still to be explored. Stuart was
sent out and discovered the river system of Eastern Australia.

Sir Thomas Macdougall Brisbane *(1773-1860)*
He was born at Brisbane House, Largs, Ayrshire, and after serving in the
army in Flanders and the Peninsular War and in the North American
campaign of 1814, he missed Waterloo. He was appointed Governor of
New South Wales in 1821. Although he introduced vines, sugar-cane and
tobacco plants and encouraged horse-breeding and land-reclamation he was
a failure with finance. He sent out exploring parties, one of which discovered
the river which bears his name. He also took advantage of the clear skies
under the Southern Cross to set up an observatory from which he discovered
over 7000 stars which also entitles him to fame as an astronomer.

Sir Thomas Livingstone Mitchell *(1792-1855)*
He was born at Craigend, Stirlingshire and joined the navy as a surveyor. He
was engaged in the Peninsular War surveying the later battle-fields and was
appointed Surveyor-General of New South Wales. He made four explorations between 1831 and 1846, establishing much of the geography of
the south-east of the continent, tracing the course of several rivers, including
the Darling. He was the first to penetrate into what he called *Australia
Felix*, the more fertile parts of Australia, quite different from the central
Sparseland. He reported on the Bathurst goldfields in 1851, which led to the
great gold-rush of that time. His strangest invention, perhaps his only one,
was a boomerang propeller for steamers, a prototype of the reversible
turbine.

John MacDouall Stuart *(1815-1866)*

Stuart was born at Dysart, Fife. He emigrated to Australia in 1839 and accompanied Captain Sturt as draughtsman on his expedition of 1844-5. In 1858 and again in 1859 he explored the Lake Eyre district. He then put this experience to good use by competing for the prize of £10,000 offered to the first man to cross Australia from south to north. He started at Adelaide, passed the Lake Eyre region and discovered good pasture land before crossing the Macdonnell Mountains. He reached the centre of the continent where Mount Stuart is named after him. Owing to illness he abandoned his journey at latitude 18° S, but returned the following year to reach 17° S when he once again had to confess that lack of water and dense scrub had defeated him. He persevered and by the same route in the next year he completed the crossing, reaching the Indian Ocean by way of the River Adelaide.

Natural Philosophy

Philosophy is concerned with the nature of the whole of existence. The philosopher weighs up the evidence of the senses, or even disagrees with such evidence, preferring some less subjective evidence. He then pronounces judgement on the basis of the evidence and in this way decides on a solution to the problem of existence.

Scots have always tended to be of an inquiring mind from the early Middle Ages, as we have witness in Erigena, Duns Scotus and Michael Scot. But they were under the discipline of the Middle Ages where little free thought or honest experiment was encouraged. It was only in modern historical times, from the middle of the sixteenth century, that students felt free to provide the evidence on all branches of science from which general philosophers could base a true verdict on the universe.

The nature of such investigation seems to fall logically into two main sections, the physical basis of existence and the superimposed structure of living things.

The physical basis starts with astronomy, although in the distant past this did not provide much solid evidence to observers, for the reason that they had few instruments to measure the heavenly bodies, having to rely on their unaided vision and the positioning of monoliths to make permanent records of the sun, moon, planets and 'fixed stars'. The study and practice of optics and of radar were to come.

The nature of the rocks and soil that comprised the earth was the next study. This was inhibited by the literal interpretation of Genesis, the creation confined to less than a calendar week. It was necessary also to know something of rocks far beneath the surface and in distant lands. This knowledge entailed much excavation and exploration.

The atmosphere was not any easier to observe or to measure, for, in contrast to the rocks and soil, it was volatile and never measurable until sensitive instruments of pressure and moisture were devised.

The ocean too, presented the same enigmas. It was an alien element. Only close to the surface could any observation of tides, currents, salinity, temperature and chemistry be made.

Until a firm basis of recorded observations was established, geography, a synthesis of all the above, was a vague subject.

Biology, or the study of life, is not any more easily separated into sections than the physical foundation. There are vital organisms which are neither animal nor plant but share some of the characters of both. There are organisms so tiny, like viruses that defy the filter and the microscope, that they are known only by their works, good or evil. Man has altered the natural world so fundamentally by artificial means and by exploitation that it has become totally unrecognisable from the natural scene at the end of the eighteenth century.

Nevertheless botany and its artificial by-products horticulture and forestry form a study separable to some extent from that of the naturalist who deals with animals, birds, reptiles, insects, fishes, etc.

The Scots inherited a homeland rich in natural life of all kinds and sad to say, like the Americans, and other colonists, they wantonly destroyed it. But there eventually arose a generation which knew not Cain and set an immense value on the study and preservation of nature, not only in Scotland but world-wide.

ASTRONOMY

James Gregory *(1638-1675)*

He has been noted in the chapter on inventors so it is only necessary to refer the reader to that article.

James Short *(1710-1768)*

He is also referred to in the note on Gregory, though he lived in the following century, but his work is of such importance as an aid to astronomers that we mention his career.

Short was born in Edinburgh, son of a carpenter. He was educated at Heriot's Hospital (now School). He early showed mathematical ability and this brought him to the notice of Professor Colin MacLaurin. He began to work for MacLaurin and turned to the study of optics, which entailed a considerable knowledge of mathematics. But theory was not sufficient. He learned how to cast and grind lenses of all requirements for reflecting telescopes of the Gregorian and other systems such as those of Newton and the Dutch artificers. These were of various alloys of metal. The high demands of astronomy for accurate work were met by Short's specula.

He now went to London where he was elected a Fellow of the Royal Society. He wrote many papers on subjects relating to astronomy. He was also a skilled surveyor and using his own field-instruments, plane-table, alidade, prismatic compass and clinometer he made a map of the Orkney Islands in 1739, a difficult task, as it entailed working in hazardous weather conditions.

James Ferguson *(1710-1776)*

He was born near Keith, Banffshire. His parents were poor and, as was normal, he made a few shillings tending sheep. This necessitated long spells of night-watching during the lambing seasons and led him to study the stars. Being of an ingenious mind he cut out a globe of wood and made a celestial map, as far as the northern hemisphere would permit.

He had a neighbour, also self-taught, from whom he acquired the elements of mathematics. He also took to painting portraits with Indian ink, and selling them to local celebrities. He thought of becoming a doctor but gave that up after a year or two.

At the age of thirty he invented the Astronomical Rotuli which related to the 26,000 year celestial cycle. He also published *Tables and Calculations* and a book explaining Sir Isaac Newton's principles. All this was acknowledged by his being made a Fellow of the Royal Society. He received a pension of £50 per annum from George III which he drew for thirteen years. He is said to have left £6000, owing to his frugal way of living. His motto could well have anticipated that of the RAF, *Per ardua ad astra,* through adversity to the stars.

Thomas Henderson *(1798-1842)*

He was born in Dundee, apprenticed to a legal firm in Edinburgh and as time went on moved up to be secretary to Francis Jeffrey, the well-known statesman and writer. But Henderson's hobby was astronomy and he delighted in calculations, copying the principles of Bessel, the eminent Prussian astronomer, who, among other triumphs, had calculated, from two-centuries-old notes, the orbit of Halley's Comet.

Henderson's legal work took him annually to London where he fell in with the enthusiasts then forming the Royal Astronomical Society. They quickly realised Henderson's value. For several years he gave his records of observations to the *Nautical Almanac*, without asking payment. Seeing astronomy as a career, he went in 1832 to the Cape of Good Hope to manage the new observatory there. He found the observatory to be in a savage and almost inaccessible region. It was badly equipped also and after a year struggling with all these handicaps he returned home. But he brought back an enormous volume of astronomical observations on which he worked for several years before publishing it.

On his return he was made Professor of Astronomy at Edinburgh and also Astronomer Royal for Scotland. He was put in charge of the Old Observatory on the Calton Hill, at an altitude of about 350 ft. above sea-level, but close to the centre of the city. This had been founded in 1818 by the Edinburgh Astronomical Association but was now taken over by the Government. Although the equipment remained very inadequate, in quantity and quality, Henderson did his best with it, and published many observations. The most notable of Henderson's contributions to astronomy was his first real measurement of the distance from the earth of *Alpha centauri.* It was the rapid movement and great brilliance of this star that drew his attention, as it had drawn others. So many false calculations had been made that Henderson's were suspected. But Henderson proved his accuracy from every angle although he delayed publishing his results for so long that Bessel published his, and the credit went to him, though the Scot, a great friend of Bessel's, did not complain.

Robert Grant *(1814-1892)*

He was born at Grantown-on-Spey and educated there and at Aberdeen University. He became interested in astronomy at an early age and thought he would write a history of astronomy. He worked as a clerk in a counting-house in London for some years while engaged in leisure time writing his book. When it was published, covering the whole span of astronomical history, it was readily credited as a standard work. He received the Gold Medal of the Royal Astronomical Society. In 1859 he became Professor of Astronomy at Glasgow where he laboured for twenty-one years on the observation of a large number of stars. The *Glasgow Catalogue of 6415 Stars* was published in 1883, followed nine years later by the *Second Glasgow Catalogue of 2136 Stars*, making a total of 8551 stars that belong to Glasgow.

Charles Piazzi Smyth *(1819-1900)*

He should be mentioned as the astronomer who was responsible for the initiation of the world-famous One o'Clock Gun fired from Edinburgh Castle. He was an authority on Time Measurement and published articles on this subject. The first time-signal had been a visual one, a large ball lowered on the top-mast of Nelson's Monument on Calton Hill. The gun was first fired, by an electric device from the Observatory to the Castle, on 7 June 1861.

He was one of the first astronomers to photograph the celestial bodies. He travelled widely in his astronomical observations and was a keen disciple of the great astronomer Herschel.

GEOLOGY

James Hutton *(1726-1797)*

He was born in Edinburgh and educated at Edinburgh University. At seventeen he was apprenticed to a lawyer but his employer set him free because he found his office being used as a chemical laboratory. He returned to the University, then went to Paris and Leyden. He completed his studies at Leyden and took his medical degree there.

He then left medicine and went to Norfolk to learn farming, but geology now took his fancy, especially after an exploration of Holland, Belgium and Picardy. For a few years he took a farm in Berwickshire but left it in charge of a manager and went on a geological tour of the Scottish Highlands. He eventually gave up farming and settled in Edinburgh.

He was named by a later geologist (Geikie) the 'Father of Geology'. When he began his investigations there was no such science; when he died, it had numerous schools and theorists.

Hutton set out to explain the creation of the earth in scientific terms. His theories are too complicated to present in a short notice, but his theory of creation known at the 'Huttonian' or 'Heat' doctrine, was presented first in 1785 in a paper read in the Royal Society of Edinburgh. The main title was *Theory of the Earth*. In it he propounds, on evidence observed by him in various areas, that the present rocks are formed out of the waste of previous rocks. He goes on to show that the Earth is a vast heat-engine and explains volcanoes as the safety valves.

He was opposed by other scientists, but his great triumph was to discover the igneous nature of granite. He also did researches into meteorology and

112

discovered the main principles governing rainfall in various regions of the globe. What is surprising is not that he was sometimes mistaken, but that he was so often correct, considering that he was working in a vast unknown field.

John Playfair *(1748-1819)*

We have noted him in the chapter on philosophers and mathematicians, but he was also an early friend of Hutton and his circle in the Royal Society of Edinburgh. When Hutton died in 1797 he took over many of his manuscripts out of friendship with a view to preserving them, but he found them nearly unreadable, not on account of the script but because of the unattractive and obscure style. After five years of unsparing labour he published the *Illustrations of the Huttonian Theory of the Earth*. The following year he published a book on Hutton's life and work. He was thus enabled to support Hutton's theory and to give it a wider and more permanent public. The opposing school of geology was the 'Neptunian'. Playfair's illustrations from geological specimens, especially those containing fossils, were strong witnesses against the Neptunians. But Playfair did more. He compared, from fossils, the gradual evolution of species from the strata of the distant past, and enumerated several species of animals now extinct.

When the war ended after Waterloo, Playfair set off on an expedition through the Alps to collect sketches for a second volume of *Illustrations* for the Huttonian Theory. He investigated the work of glaciers and the forms of lava. But he did not survive long enough to transform his notes into a complete book, and died, chiefly as a result of the 4000 mile excursion in support of his friend.

Sir James Hall *(1761-1832)*

He was of the famous ancient family of the Halls of Dunglass, east of Dunbar. He was educated at Cambridge and Edinburgh Universities. Being intended for an army career, he studied at the French military academy school for cadets at Brienne in 1782-3, where Napoleon Bonaparte was a fellow-student, though a few years younger than Hall.

He did not follow the military life but returned to Edinburgh and met Hutton and Playfair. He seems to have preferred Hutton's conversation to his written style, for he was won over to him and went on geological excursions to the continent to try out his theories. He and Playfair turned out to be the great buttresses of Hutton, supporting his theories by their diligent excursions and acute observations.

Hall was not a blind copier of Hutton. He preserved an independent view and had the advantage of accompanying an eminent French geologist Dolomien in the Alps and Apennines. In fact he found Hutton's views on glaciers incomplete and not logical. But he proved by experiment Hutton's theories of granite dykes.

He found Edinburgh a rich field for his geological work, particularly Arthur's Seat, the Castle and the several volcanic hills in the Lothian area.

He explained them to his own satisfaction by saying that these, and the great beds of boulder clay prevalent in the Lothians, were the result of a huge ocean wave sweeping from the Atlantic in remote ages. Actually, the rock forms of the district were subsequently confirmed to have been the work of ice, but Hall's was a very good guess. His son Basil, traveller and writer, is noted in 'Explorers'.

William Nicol *(1768-1851)*

Nicol was a popular lecturer in Edinburgh on science. He was the inventor of Nicol's Prism, an absolute essential in the study of rock elements. His work on fossil wood entailed making very thin slices of wood for the purpose of the microscope. He did not invent this technique but explained that he had learned it from the work of Sanderson, an Edinburgh lapidary, who prepared transparent sections of minerals and precious stones for his business. He had so improved on Sanderson that it opened up a new field of research in petrology and paleontology.

On his death all his instruments and specimens were left to a friend who continued the work but kept it to himself. It was not until 1870 that by chance an English petrologist saw Nicol's specimens and was able to tell his fellow scientists in England of a technical advance that had been lost for twenty years.

John MacCulloch *(1773-1835)*

He was born in Guernsey of Scottish parents, attended the medical school in Edinburgh and graduated as a doctor when twenty. Then he turned to chemistry and was appointed to the Board of Ordnance Survey when thirty. In 1814 he was appointed geologist to the trigonometrical survey. He became President of the Geological Society and was made a Fellow of the Royal Society of England.

His principal work was a geological survey of the Hebrides, which was of great importance in establishing that these are mainly composed of the most ancient rock strata on earth.

His geological map of Scotland, a work entailing a vast reassemblage of information, was published a few months after his death.

Robert Jameson *(1774-1854)*

He was born in Leith and naturally found himself in opposition to the school of thought based on its old rival Edinburgh.

As a youth he was not fond of study, and said in after days that Robinson Crusoe and Cook's Travels inspired him to play truant and wander far and wide on the hills, woods and shores of Lothian. He was a keen collector of all kinds of wildlife, crabs, insects, animals, birds, of which he made a domestic zoo.

To make a living he thought surgery a possible career so at eighteen he took a Natural History course at the University. After this he travelled for five years in the many islands and shores of Scotland, with an eye open for the spectacular geological forms seen there.

On his return he published an account of the minerals of the area and immediately set off to Germany to study geology under the leader of the school opposed to Hutton. This was the Saxon professor Werner, whose family for three centuries had been mining engineers in Saxony, in exploitation of minerals. He saw the whole world in terms of minerals and he delighted to tell his students all about this. His classification of minerals and rocks was similar to the classification of plants and animals already made by the Swedish scientist Linnaeus.

The bitterness of the conflict between the Huttonians or Plutonians and the Wernerians or Neptunians took on the aspect of a Holy War. Jameson's influence on Werner's behalf was profound and for fifty years he lectured and had many brilliant pupils, some of whom, while acknowledging Jameson's inspiration, formed theories contrary to his. To Jameson we owe the introduction of the term 'Old Red Sandstone', so well-known in connection with Hugh Miller, to be mentioned later.

Charles Darwin attended Jameson's lectures in his second year at Edinburgh and pays him this tribute. 'His lectures on geology and zoology were so incredibly dull that I determined never to read a book on Geology or to study the same.'

Charles MacLaren (1782-1866)

He was born at Ormiston, East Lothian, son of a small farmer, and moved with his family a few miles off to the hill parish of Fala, where he attended the small parish school and later was taught at Colinton, near Edinburgh. For a long period Scotland had been under the corrupt Tory rule of Henry Dundas, and no voice of radical dissent was allowed to be heard. MacLaren had, as a young man, joined a Society known as the 'Polymathic', where men of free-thinking mind met in debate.

This courageous group of young men started the publication of an anti-establishment paper entitled *The Scotsman*, in January 1817. MacLaren and Ritchie edited the first few numbers, then MacLaren worked as a clerk for a time, returning as editor in 1820, a post he held for twenty-seven years. In 1828 he began a series of twice-weekly geological articles to his paper and in 1839 he published his book *Geology of Fife and the Lothians*. To geologists the book was worthy of praise for its invention of the phrase 'Calciferous Sandstone', and for his description of the peculiar strata of the Pentland Hills.

His study of Arthur's Seat was most carefully done and distinguished the various volcanic products through the geological cataclysms. He even convinced Sir Archibald Geikie of some of his theories. Some of MacLaren's hypotheses were later disproved, but most are still acceptable to geologists.

An historic visit by Agassiz occurred in MacLaren's editorship. The Swiss professor came to view the parallel roads of Glen Roy, and his explanation of this phenomenon was printed in *The Scotsman*. The remark made in MacLaren's presence by Agassiz on seeing the glaciated rock-face in the Blackford Hill is still remembered by geologists as an epoch-making dictum. 'This is the work of the ice', which gave final credence to the theory of the glaciation of vast areas during successive ages.

Revd John Fleming (1785-1857)

He was a Fife minister with a great interest in geology. For many years he was one of Scotland's leading naturalists. He was a supporter of the Neptunian school and in the summer of 1827 he found wonderful evidence to support the theory that rocks were laid down as sediment. In the Old Red Sandstone stratum in Fife he discovered fossil fishes. He wrote on this to the *Fife Herald*, which however scarcely circulated in the scientific circles of Europe or America. He published his epoch-making find in the *Edinburgh Journal* but once again this was only of local reputation.

However, fame was to overtake Fleming in time. Agassiz complimented him in his lifetime by saying, 'It is beyond question that the first discovery of fossil fishes in the Devonian sandstone was made by the celebrated professor Dr Fleming of Aberdeen.' And, long after Fleming's death, Sir Andrew Ramsay, in his presidential address to the British Association in 1880, said 'In the year 1830 the Revd Dr Fleming of Edinburgh read a paper before the Wernerian Society in which he boldly stated that the Old Red Sandstone is a freshwater formation of older date than the Carboniferous Limestone.'

In Geology what greater reward could he have expected?

Sir Roderick Murchison (1792-1871)

He was born on his father's estate at Tarradale, Ross-shire, educated at Durham Grammar School and intended to be a soldier. As an ensign in his teens he fought with Sir John Moore in the Peninsular War and was in the battle of Corunna. In 1815, the war over, he married the only daughter of General Hugonin of the 4th Dragoons. She was to prove his faithful companion in his many travels.

The couple travelled in Italy studying art, then settled for a time at Barnard Castle, Durham, his wife's property, where he wasted some years fox-hunting. His wife prevailed on him to do something with his life so he turned to geology where he became eminent.

He was made a Fellow of the Royal Society in 1826. Then he explored Scotland, the Central Massif of France, Russia and the Alps. He worked in Wales for several year and concluded by establishing the Silurian System which forms much of the strata of Wales and the Southern Uplands of Scotland as well as many areas of the earth. The name Silurian is derived from the Silures, an old British tribe.

He now worked in South West England on the Devonian System. His work on *Russia and the Ural Mountains* gained him a knighthood and the Presidency of the British Association. Honours were heaped upon him from home and abroad. In his last year of life he founded a Chair of Geology and Mineralogy in Edinburgh.

Hugh Miller (1802-1856)

He was born in Cromarty where his father was drowned when Hugh was only five. He was educated at a dame-school and at Cromarty Grammar School and his favourite occupation was wandering on the sea-shore picking up curious pebbles and rocks. From seventeen he worked under his uncle in the stone-quarries of Cromarty. When twenty-one he went to Edinburgh as a mason but the dirty heavy work of rebuilding property after the great fire of 1824 affected his lungs and he came home. When recovered, he worked in Inverness as a monumental mason and published a book of poems. He left his mason work and became a bank-accountant. He was now recognised as a good writer and began to interest himself in church affairs, particularly on the very pressing question of patronage. He was asked to become editor of the *Witness*, a church paper. Here he began a series of popular articles on many topics, prominent being his series headed *The Old Red Sandstone*, which earned him the friendship of Murchison and Agassiz.

On reading Hibbert's paper on the fossil fishes in the Burdiehouse Limestone he recalled having found fossil fishes in the Cromarty rock, six years before Hibbert's discovery.

Hugh Miller was the man who did more to popularise geology in the whole English-speaking world than any other. This was undoubtedly due to his avoidance of the jargon which had crept into geology. Miller was faced with a dilemma. Geology had now shown the vast age of creation, extending back to many millions of years, to be an under-estimate. The Church, which Miller subscribed to, considered it blasphemy to contradict the fundamental view of creation and Miller was the subject of bigoted criticism.

This so affected his sensitive mind that, just as he finished correcting the proofs of his great work, *The Testimony of the Rocks*, a truly religious work in the most magnanimous sense, he was overcome by a mental storm and shot himself with a pistol in his home in Portobello, to the consternation of the British public. His funeral was attended by practically the entire population of Edinburgh, besides many famous scholars who came to pay tribute to the celebrated stone-mason.

Robert Chambers *(1802-1871)*

Though famed as a publisher and a general literary man, author of many popular and universally read books, especially his *History of the 1745 Rebellion, Traditions of Edinburgh* and his vast accumulation *The Book of Days* which killed him; he was also a noted geologist.

In the prejudiced atmosphere of the mid-nineteenth century, it was most unwise to publish anything in Scotland that could be construed as agnostic or atheistic. Therefore Chambers' *Vestiges of the Natural History of Creation* in which the main conclusion was that biological evolution must be admitted, was published anonymously. It was so popular that it went through eleven editions and placed its unknown author on the level of Hugh Miller.

Chambers, as a geologist, like MacLaren, is important for the part he played in emphasising the work of glaciers in forming the landscape. He travelled widely in search of glacial evidence in Switzerland, Norway, the Faroes and Iceland. In Scotland of course, the case for glaciation had already been proved.

James D. Forbes *(1808-1868)*

Although renowned as a physicist and recognised by being made a Fellow of the Royal Society, England, when only twenty-four, he also contributed to geology. By theodolite he measured the movements of Alpine glaciers and proved that they were fluid in movement, the middle moving faster than the sides, and the upper part faster than the lower. He also invented the first seismograph for measuring the severity and duration of earthquakes, and studied the variation of temperature below the earth's surface with thermometers up to forty-eight feet long.

Sir Andrew C. Ramsay *(1814-1891)*

Educated at Glasgow University and appointed to the Geological Survey of Britain when twenty-seven, he became Director of the Survey four years later and successively moved to these appointments: Professor of Geology, University College, London; Lecturer on Geology, Royal School of Mines; President of Geological Society; Director-General of Geological Survey of Britain. His published works cover many areas of Great Britain and his papers were translated into German and Italian. His work influenced Archibald Geikie's view of the effect of glaciation.

James Croll *(1821-1890)*

He was born in Perthshire and served his apprenticeship to a wheelwright. He then moved to Glasgow where he earned his living by his trade but published a number of articles on the cause of the glacial ages. In 1875 he combined his conclusions in a book entitled *Climate and Time*.

The problems which Croll tried to solve are still not answered. He considered that cosmic influences led to a succession of cold and warm periods over the whole earth and not, as had been thought, only over certain areas. Observers have recently begun to support Croll's theories, but until a cosmic catastrophe occurs which affects our atmosphere we shall never be sure of the phenomena of the ice ages.

He has been proved right in other directions. He considered that Orkney and Shetland and Caithness had suffered glaciation from the direction of Scandinavia. This was later corroborated by an examination of evidence from the sea-floor and sea-coasts.

James Bennie *(1821-1901)*

Bennie was another amateur like Croll who outshone many professionals. He was born in Glasgow to a working-class family and spent several years as a weaver and later as a warehouseman. In his leisure hours, which were few, he wandered about in the Clyde area picking up fossils from the carboniferous and glacial deposits. He was well known for his collection and in time he was asked to join the staff of the Geological Survey as a fossil-collector. James Croll was a friend of his.

With increased leisure and opportunity to travel he made many discoveries. One of his specialities was his minute inspection of washed sediment for microzoa, tiny fossils of prehistoric animals. These had hitherto defied the collectors. He found fossilised Arctic plants in the lake alluvia at Corstorphine, near Edinburgh, as well as remains of scorpions in other Scottish deposits, which showed the extremes of climate produced by the alternating ice and tropical epochs.

Archibald Geikie *(1835-1924)*

He was born in Edinburgh and educated at the High School and University. He was appointed at twenty to the Geological Survey where he was at once noticed by Roderick Murchison. Together they worked on some difficult formations of Highland rocks. Their first publication was a small geological map of Scotland.

In 1863 Geikie published his vindication of the work of the glaciers in Scotland. This was the first clear definition. His *Scenery of Scotland* in 1865 explained the landscape in terms of geological evolution.

He was elected Fellow of the Royal Society at a time when the Edinburgh school of geologists were emphasising the effect of denudation of land surfaces by running water. Geikie's book on Scottish scenery amply supported this view and he soon took a leading place in the Edinburgh school.

In 1867 a separate branch of the Geological Survey was set up in Edinburgh and he was made Director. He became Murchison Professor of Geology and Mineralogy in 1871 until he was made joint-director with Ramsay of the Geological Survey of Great Britain. He was also director of the Museum of Practical Geology in London until his retiral.

He travelled much through Europe and the USA especially among the canyons of Colorado and the volcanic regions of Wyoming, Montana and Utah. He was well known for his great contributions to volcanic geology.

He was President of the British Association and of the Royal Society. His textbooks were, for long, standard works.

James Geikie *(1839-1915)*

He was educated at the Royal High School and Edinburgh University, like his older brother Archibald, and he too joined the Geological Survey. James took a contrary direction, being interested in glaciers, while his brother was keen on igneous rocks. He published *The Great Ice Age* in 1874. This ran into three editions. He also wrote *Prehistoric Europe* and with these two great books he put his stamp on geology. He was Murchison Professor of Geology from 1882-1914 in Edinburgh.

Geikie pointed out the vast extent of the former ice fields in Europe, how great was the erosion and how many interglacial periods there were. He worked with European geologists in arriving at his conclusions and they in turn accorded him a position of eminence in their science. The German geologists dedicated their masterpiece *The Alps in the Ice Ages* to him.

From the above list of eminent pioneers it is evident that Scots played a large part in the development of geology. Other names could be mentioned in abundance, such as Peach, Horne, Macconachie and Tait but the pioneering work probably deserves most recognition so we end the section here.

METEOROLOGY

The Royal Society of Edinburgh had from its earliest days included the study of weather among its papers. James Hutton had delivered an address on *The Theory of Rain* and Professor Wilson of Glasgow had written on *Hoar Frost*. There were contributions from scientists of such eminence as Playfair, Rutherford, Brewster and Lord Kelvin.

In 1855, however, the Scottish Meteorological Society was founded by Sir John Forbes and David Home and others. It was inspired by the meteorological work of German, French and American researchers. Numerous Scots of distinction joined it and the Secretary was also Superintendent of Statistics for Scotland, Dr James Stark. In 1860, however, a man of outstanding merit was appointed Secretary who was to prove the most eminent meteorologist of the century, and whose name is still often quoted.

Alexander Buchan *(1829-1907)*

Before becoming Secretary of the Scottish Meteorological Society he had been a teacher in Dunblane and had already done much study in botany. He found out what had been done in meteorology and built on that foundation.

His first important paper was entitled *The Mean Pressure of the Atmosphere and the Prevailing Winds of the Globe*. It secured for Buchan a 'foremost place among the meteorologists of all ages.' Before his study was published it had been assumed by all European scientists that a purely theoretic system of pressure and winds obtained. But Buchan based his principles on observations taken simultaneously at various stations.

He was the first to show that European weather was dominated by pressure conditions around Iceland, and it is on Buchan's system that all weather data are now formed.

He spent his life to a great extent studying rainfall and problems connected with climate. He based his well-known 'Buchan's Cold Spells' and 'Warm Spells' on many years of observation. They are not meant to be more than guides to these peculiarities of weather, but they are based on scientific observations.

He worked with an eminent medical officer, Sir Arthur Mitchell, to prove some connection between the weather and mortality rates, but reached no conclusions.

Much of Buchan's work was incorporated in Bartholomew's *Atlas of Meteorology* published in 1899 in Edinburgh. During his later years he was busy with the work of the two Ben Nevis Observatories, one on the summit (4406ft. above sea-level) and the other at the base, nearly on sea-level. This great variation so close in distance on an Atlantic coast subject to streams of depressions, gave a very valuable aid to the meteorologists. It took great physical endurance to maintain the observatory on the summit and would not have succeeded but for the many amateur volunteers who braved the sub-arctic elements. It is interesting to note that Robert Louis Stevenson was so influenced by Buchan that he published a paper (1873) for the Royal Society of Edinburgh entitled *The Thermal Influence of Forests*.

Sir Charles Wyville Thomson *(1830-1882)*

He was born at Bonsyde, West Lothian, and educated at Merchiston School and Edinburgh Academy. He was Lecturer on Botany at Aberdeen, and Professor of Natural History at Cork and of Geology in Queen's College, Belfast and later of Natural History at Edinburgh.

He was director of the *Challenger* Expedition of 68,000 miles and though to some extent a meteorologist he is more famed as a biologist.

John Aitken *(1839-1919)*

He is noted for his paper to the Royal Society of Edinburgh on *Dust, Fogs and Clouds* (1881) and later for a paper on *Condensation* both of which were of great value to meteorologists in investigating the part played by solid particles in the production of rain. He also wrote a paper on *Dew* which was memorable because it demonstrated that the vapour which condenses on the surface on cold nights comes mainly from the ground, not from the atmosphere. He experimented on many subjects including the *Evaporation of Musk, Ocean Circulation* and *Thermometer Screens*.

Sir John Murray *(1841-1914)*

Between 1872 and 1876 HMS *Challenger*, a steamship, a wooden corvette of 2300 tons, was employed on a series of scientific voyages back and forth across the Atlantic and into the Antarctic and Pacific.

When the reports of this long voyage were at last published from 1880 to 1895 they extended to fifty volumes on all aspects of oceanography, with emphasis on meteorology and marine life. Sir John Murray, who accompanied the expedition, was main editor of the report, which was prepared in Edinburgh.

Murray was also the driving force behind the setting up of the Ben Nevis Observatories. The Government gave it little support. The Scottish public supplied the money and the personnel.

So many meteorological workers have spent their careers on this subject in Scotland that it is not possible to note them, other than the few leading figures mentioned here.

HYDROGRAPHY & OCEANOGRAPHY

Hydrography is the science of all the water on the earth's surface including rivers, lakes and other freshwater forms, as well as of all the oceans and seas. It does not deal with biology as oceanography does.

Alexander Dalrymple *(1737-1808)*

Born at New Hailes, near Edinburgh, he was brother of Sir David Dalrymple, Lord Hailes. Alexander was educated at Haddington and at fifteen sent to Madras as a clerk in the East India Co. He made several expeditions in the East Indies and studied the various sea-routes, taking soundings and observations and drawing maps and charts. He attempted to trade with Indo-China and Canton but was unsuccessful.

He came back to Britain in 1763 and tried to obtain a position as commander in Captain Cook's South Sea Expedition but again unsuccessfully, notwithstanding his experience of hydrography.

He went back to Madras and was in due course appointed hydrographer to the East India Co. and five years later to the Admiralty, a post he held until his death thirteen years later.

He wrote many treatises on his favourite study and published the following books which give some idea of the great extent of his work in what was then practically an unknown area of the ocean.

Discoveries in the South Pacific Ocean before 1764, South Sea Voyages, Collection of Charts, Expeditions to the West Coast of Sumatra.

'Edinburgh is the birthplace and home of Oceanography.' So wrote Professor Herdman of the University of Liverpool, in 1921. We have already mentioned Murray and Thomson in the chapter on Meteorology. We note them and several others in connection with their much more illustrious contributions to Oceanography, which rose strangely enough from the friendship of three medical students at Edinburgh University, not one of whom graduated in that faculty.

Edward Forbes *(1815-1854)*

He was born in the Isle of Man, of Scottish parentage. His mother owned an estate on the west coast in a good fishing area. This is where Edward during his boyhood made a large collection of shore marine life.

He went to London at the age of sixteen to study art but decided to change to medicine, so he enrolled at Edinburgh where he stayed for some years. There he met a number of brilliant young men including John Goodsir the anatomist, Balfour the botanist, and Sir Robert Christison the physician.

Forbes spent several summer vacations on his mother's estate using the sea-dredge which had recently been patented. He also explored the fauna and flora of the Isle of Man. He published the results of this a year or two later.

In 1839 he and Goodsir went dredging in the Shetlands and at a meeting of the British Association that year in Birmingham he roused enthusiasm by his paper on the strange sea-creatures he had found.

A Liverpool yachtsman took Forbes, Goodsir and their friends on dredging excursions around the British seas. His name was Robert MacAndrew, to be remembered for the early start he gave to oceanography.

In the Royal Society in Edinburgh in 1851 he and Goodsir presented a paper *On some Remarkable Marine Invertebrata new to the British Seas.*

He now extended his territory to Scandinavia, the Mediterranean and Aegean Seas. No longer was he confined to home water like the Firth of Forth, as he had been when a medical student. It was in 1841 that his great opportunity came when he was offered the post of naturalist on HM surveying ship *Beacon* in the Eastern Mediterranean. The results of his deep dredging brought him congratulations from the British Association.

He was appointed Professor of Botany in London, then various other posts in succession. His interest was in collating geology and biology and his most brilliant and original work was done in this mixed field.

In 1850 he prepared a most remarkable map of the distribution of marine life over the oceans, the first attempt to divide the oceans into provinces, on scientific grounds.

He was the most original, brilliant and inspiring naturalist of his day, a pioneer of Oceanography. His early death at thirty-nine was an immense loss to science.

Sir Charles Wyville Thomson *(1830-1882)*

Already mentioned as the leader of the renowned *Challenger* Expedition, he was the pioneer of deep-sea exploration. He made the discovery that many and varied living creatures have their habitat in the deepest parts of the ocean. Edward Forbes had stated erroneously that the zero of sea-life was about 300 fathoms but Thomson found life at 2500 fathoms.

As a medical student like Forbes he had collected sea-shore life by the Firth of Forth. He joined the Royal Physical Society (a society studying Natural History). As a result of ill-health he gave up his medical career and turned to science.

He heard of a remarkable starfish found in Norwegian seas and set off to examine it. He was shown other finds brought up from the depths of the Lofoten Fiords, and saw a resemblance between them and fossil animals long extinct. This interest sent him off to form an expedition to explore the Atlantic depths. The Admiralty were influenced by Thomson's friends to place a surveying steamer at their service. In his book *The Depths of the Sea* he describes what they found. It was in effect the first text-book of Oceanography.

He was elected Professor of Natural History in Edinburgh but the success of his first voyage encouraged him to approach the Government to furnish an expedition of the same nature but in a grand style. This resulted in the circumnavigation of the globe by HMS *Challenger*, which, it has been said, will rank in sea-history with the voyages of Vasco da Gama, Columbus, Magellan and Cook.

Soundings and dredgings were taken at 362 stations and enormous collections of marine organisms of all sizes, samples of deposits and water were brought home. The like had never been imagined, let alone seen. Sir Ray Lankester, President of the British Association said (something which may have suggested Churchill's war phrases), 'Never did an expedition cost so little and produce such momentous results for human knowledge.'

Thomson was appointed the Director of the Commision located in Edinburgh to investigate and publish the results. From all over the world marine biologists came to inspect the novelties of the *Challenger* collection.

In the practical work Thomson had the help of such eminent men as Professors Tait, Crum Brown, Chrystal and Sir Archibald Geikie.

Thomson was so occupied with administration that he had no time for research, but before his death, he arranged for an expedition to the Faroe Channel to investigate the remarkable difference in ocean temperatures only a short distance apart. When the expedition eventually found the cause of the variation, which was a great submarine ridge, Thomson had died. The ridge was named after him, so if anyone seeks his monument it stands forever 300 fathoms beneath the waves between Cape Wrath and the Faroes.

Sir John Murray *(1841-1914)*

He was born in Coburg, Canada, of Scottish descent and came to Scotland as a boy to complete his education. He met Forbes and Thomson in the medical classes but like them gave up that career. His first oceanographic voyage was in 1868 to Spitzbergen on a Peterhead whaler where as a medical student he was listed as ship's surgeon. This voyage gave him a fresh interest in ocean life, which he had first studied in Canada.

His inclusion in the *Challenger* Expedition was a chance in ten thousand. At the last minute one of the appointed naturalists dropped out and Professor Tait, who knew Murray's abilities, recommended him for the vacancy.

In addition to his part in the general duties of the expedition, Murray gave special attention to three subjects of general importance to oceanography. These were the plankton or floating life of the oceans, the ocean-bed deposits, and the formation of coral. His observations formed the basis of new theories. But, ever the practical Scot, Murray discovered something valuable of a marketable nature. He noticed that on Christmas Island in the Indian Ocean there was a great deposit of phosphate. The island was uninhabited so there was no disturbance of native life. After some years, due to the royalties and taxes on the sale of phosphate, the Government had recovered the entire costs of the *Challenger* Expedition. Sir Ray Lankester could afford to say 'Never did an expedition cost so little . . .' Thanks to Murray they got it gratis.

When the expedition returned, Murray was given the job of editing the reports assembled by Thomson. Over and above this he was always investigating general problems of oceanography and accumulating material for his final volumes summing up the expedition.

He also tried to set up a marine biological station near Edinburgh. One of his ideas was to rent or buy Inchcolm and convert the ruins of the old monastery into a laboratory with sea-water tanks. He leased an old sandstone quarry, instead, and near Granton, in the sea-water which had filled the quarry, he moored a canal-barge built into a house with laboratories. He called this the *Ark*.

Eventually the *Ark* was towed through the Forth and Clyde Canal and formed an annexe to the Millport Biological Station.

Murray explored the deep sea-lochs of the West Highlands and made the astonishing discovery of Arctic fauna in the deeper parts of Loch Fyne and Loch Etive.

His last voyage, in his seventieth year, was in the North Atlantic, the results being published in *The Depths of the Ocean*. After all these hazards he was accidentally killed near Kirkliston in 1914.

Natural History

Broadly speaking, these should include oceanographers whom we have noted in our previous chapter, but as these are very much concerned with the various physical aspects of the ocean, such as currents, salinity, depths and temperatures, we have located them among the hydrographers.

Naturalists have as many fields of study as there are species, but *fauna* and *flora* are the two main heads. *Fauna* comprise birds, animals, insects, fishes, reptiles and all the smaller creatures, such as the arachnids or spiders, and the multitudes of other invertebrates. *Flora* embody all the families of herbaceous plants, trees, grasses and ferns, mosses and parasites. Economically, the most important are those used in agriculture, horticulture and forestry, just as domesticated fauna are also of commercial interest.

Edinburgh's world-famous school of medicine was undoubtedly the origin and latterly the focus of all natural studies. Botany began with the need for drugs, obtainable to a certain extent from plants, and zoology was born in the anatomy laboratory. We shall first note the eminent botanists and gardeners, and later, foresters.

BOTANY

Sir Andrew Balfour *(1630-1694)*

His life story has been given in brief in the chapter on medical men. We deal here with his botanical work. The urgent need to systematize the *materia medica,* and to have a ready supply of drugs at a reasonable cost, induced Balfour and his colleague Sibbald, as head physicians, to make a botanical garden in easy reach of the city. Contrary to the geographical myths about Scotland's climate and Edinburgh's inclemency, the soil and climate were conducive to the healthy growth of a large variety of plants. In Balfour's time, any contemporary map or sketch of Edinburgh shows that large gardens extended down the southern and northern slopes from the houses in the Canongate. The valley between the ridge of what is now Princes Street and the High Street, for centuries in the Middle Ages used for gardens, had been dammed and made into the North Loch for defence against English invasion. Balfour purchased a piece of alluvial ground near the Watergate, not far to the west of Holyrood House. The soil is what is known as black loam, an alluvial soil which extends along both shores of the Forth. The site has long been used as the Waverley Station, but in the late seventeenth century, it was a secluded spot, inclined however to be marshy in places. It was a small plot, about a quarter acre.

Balfour had a small botanical garden attached to his own house. It was stocked with seeds of rare plants sent by foreign correspondents. In it he raised plants never before seen in Britain. He had a friend and pupil, Patrick Murray, of Livingstone, in whose estate was a garden with over a thousand species of plants. Murray died quite young and Balfour transferred all his plants to Edinburgh, which of course necessitated the breaking-in of the new garden at the Watergate.

At this point in 1676, with the help of Sir Robert Sibbald, an experienced botanist, James Sutherland was appointed head gardener.

James Sutherland *(1639-1719)*

Little is known of his early days. He was a self-made man, and by profession a gardener. He had, according to Sibbald, by his own efforts acquired a curious and exacting knowledge of plants. In 1683, after only seven years, he published a catalogue, in Latin, of the plants in the Physic Garden. The English names were also given. To make a living, he taught medical students the names and applications of the plants as they were seen growing. They paid a small fee. The city, renowned for its parsimony through the ages, paid Sutherland £20 per annum, which did not cover the rent, let alone the under-gardener's wages and the cost of new plants, which had to be brought tediously by bad roads and perilous seas from distant lands.

On top of all this, a catastrophe befell the garden. In the spring of 1689, when Claverhouse threatened the city, it was thought necessary to drain the North Loch. Workmen broke the dam and flooded the Physic Gardens for several days leaving it covered with mud and filth. Nearly all the delicate and costly plants collected by Balfour, Sibbald, Murray and Sutherland, were destroyed, and it took Sutherland and his underlings nearly a season to clear the ground.

He appealed to the Town Council and they awarded him £50 per annum pension. Being further helped by the Royal Treasury, he took heart and extended his garden towards Holyrood, and in the same year he raised a good crop of melons and fine and curious flowers not known before. He sheltered his garden with reed fences, built greenhouses, and grew oranges, myrtles and lemons under glass.

He had been elected Professor of Botany early in his career. His catalogue of exotic and indigenous plants is a great help to botanists who wish to know the origins of our present plant population.

Charles Alston *(1685-1760)*

Born in Lanarkshire, he studied medicine at Glasgow and Leyden. He took over the Physic Garden at Holyrood in 1720 and continued to give instruction on Sutherland's lines. He was appointed Professor of Botany in 1735 and by his teaching and influence Edinburgh gained a wide reputation for botanical science. His publication *Materia Medica*, was the best in Europe in its age.

His approach to botany was a novel one. He studied ventilation,

126

sanitation and other general principles of botany. At this time Linnaeus, the Swedish scientist, was preparing his system of arranging plants into genus and species, assigning two Latin names to each. His great work, giving the principles of his system, was published in 1751 when Alston was at the height of his powers. Several years earlier, Alston had read Linnnaeus' *Sexual System of Plants* which described the act of pollenisation. He disagreed with the Swede, as his own experiments had proved that in certain cases there is no necessity to have pollen as a fertilising agent. Alston was later proved to be correct, after many years. He was a man who lived before his time, and anticipated many advances in botany.

Sir John Hope *(1725-1786)*

He was born in Edinburgh, the grandson of Alexander Hope, Lord Rankeillor. He took over the old Physic Garden at Holyrood and encouraged his students by offering a beautiful medal for competition annually. He was a man of some wealth, which he used to advance his science. Using his political influence also, he sought out support to have the garden removed to a better site. The Treasury granted him £1330. 1. 2½, to make a new garden, and £69. 3. 0 for annual expenses. A very generous gift.

He had already chosen a good site about half-a-mile north of the city, on a gentle slope accessible by a good road. The soil was medium loam, inclined to be sandy, and, with manuring, quite fertile and well-drained. He supervised the laying-out in person and, the plants having been transferred, the Old Botanic Garden was left to the weeds and the vandals.

Hope died not long after, but through his influence, especially on his pupils, Edinburgh was remarkable for the large number of publications on physiological botany, written by men who made no pretence otherwise to be botanists. Hope was familiar with the work of all European botanists and, in contrast to Alston, he not only supported Linnaeus but introduced his system to Great Britain.

His sudden and early death left his work incomplete. He had been busy on a botanical treatise and left only the illustrations to suggest that it would have been invaluable. Like Alston he lived a century before his time. He was one of the great pioneers of vegetable study in this country, considering such problems as growth, effects of light (photo-synthesis), sap mechanism, and healing of plant wounds. One of his best ideas was the separation of the Chairs of Botany and Materia Medica, thus enabling the respective holders to concentrate on their subjects.

Daniel Rutherford *(1749-1819)*

Son of the 'Yarrow Doctor', John Rutherford of Selkirkshire, Daniel was educated at Edinburgh where he took his medical degree, his thesis being an argument for the existence of the gas now known as nitrogen. He studied for three years on the continent, then was given his doctor's certificate at Edinburgh. He was made a Fellow of the Royal College of Surgeons, then Professor of Botany, succeeding John Hope in that Chair. He was also physician to the Royal Infirmary. His interest in botany was on the chemical side. He established that plants exhale carbon dioxide. He was the brother of Sir Walter Scott's mother and as such was much admired by Scott.

Robert Graham *(1786-1845)*

He was another supporter of the Linnaean School and devoted his studies to the systematic examination of British flowers. He was a teacher of such ability that he shared his energy between lecturing and trying to be an efficient professor of clinical medicine at the same time.

John Hutton Balfour *(1808-1884)*

Balfour was fortunate enough to have the use of microscopes in his botanical work. Though known long before, they were too costly for class use until a new system of manufacture made them available. Balfour quickly adapted microscopic techniques to his botanical teaching and by his text books made a steady advance in the science.

We now leave the academic botanists for the practical gardeners, plant and tree collectors, and foresters. The 'Scotch Gardener' has long been a stock figure in fact and fiction. In one of the most loved children's books, *The Story of Peter Rabbit*, the gardener is Mr Macgregor, an irate foe of all garden pests. But the tradition of the skilled Scots gardener has a very wide basis of achievement.

James Justice *(c.1730-1763)*

The number of horticultural, botanical or arboricultural enthusiasts is impossible to estimate, in Scotland of the eighteenth and nineteenth centuries. Private gardens were given over to special hobbies and collections. For example, James Justice, an aptly named lawyer, owned the finest garden in Scotland at Crichton, ten miles south of Edinburgh. He had the only pine-stove in Europe where he grew pineapples to perfection in a Lothian garden hothouse six hundred feet above sea-level. He also had the largest European collection of auriculas. He published the *Scots Gardeners' Director* in 1753.

William Aiton *(1731-1793)*

He was born near Hamilton, Lanarkshire and was made a director of Kew Gardens under the ownership of Augusta, widowed mother of George III. Kew was owned by George himself in later years. It was an exotic garden and grew plants and trees from many parts of the world. Sir Joseph Banks had supplied American plants, Bruce sent plants from East Africa, via the Edinburgh garden. In 1789 Aiton published his catalogue of plants entitled *Hortus Kewensis*. He had effected many improvements at Kew, under munificent Royal patronage. George III does not receive many compliments, but his love of botany and his delight in his gardens should be remembered.

Aiton's son, William Tounsend Aiton (1766-1849), succeeded his father as director at Kew and published an enlarged version of *Hortus Kewensis*.

John Williamson (c.1780)

He was put in charge of the new Botanical Garden near Leith Walk. Sir John Hope had laid it out in plan, and, in honour of Linnaeus, he had erected a classical monument to him, inscribed *Linnaeus posuit Io. Hope* (erected to Linnaeus by John Hope). This monument may still be seen in the Royal Botanic Gardens at Inverleith, Edinburgh.

Williamson had five acres to maintain, with probably half-a-dozen assistants, chiefly labourers. By 1780 it was stocked with trees, affording shelter for delicate plants from the prevailing west (not east) winds, which cause most damage to vegetation in Scotland. The School of Botany was on the east side of the garden and contained 2000 species of plants, arranged methodically according to the Linnean style. Of rhubarb alone, grown for the roots chiefly, there were 3000 plants.

This botanic garden flourished for nearly half a century until the encroachment of the city and a nearby foundry rendered it unsuitable, after which the plants were transferred to the present large and beautiful site. In 1805, when Williamson was in full swing, we have a recorded appraisal of the garden by a German botanist named Frank. The 'order of the plants' appealed to the Germanic sensibilities, and he especially admired a beautiful *Ferula asafoetida* in full bloom. This is an umbelliferous exotic plant resembling fennel; it grows to six feet high, wide spread, and is not easy to rear in Britain. In medicine its product was a gum used to stimulate the stomach, lungs and nerves. It is also a source of vanilla for flavouring. Williamson was able to supply Kew Gardens, then being expanded from an old private garden under the direction of the English naturalist Sir Joseph Banks, and William Aiton, Scottish botanist.

Williamson built hothouses and dug a pond for aquatic plants. The conservatories were 140ft. long, but at first had slated roofs which drew the plants off the vertical. Glass was afterwards used to cover the conservatories. James Bruce, the explorer of the Abyssinian Nile, whose story was disbelieved in England, supplied John Hope with a number of Abyssinian plant seeds, which Williamson reared successfully. Amongst these was a plant which had cured Bruce of dysentery, a very useful addition to the *Materia Medica* of that period.

John Claudius Loudon (1783-1843)

He was the son of a farmer at Gogar, Midlothian, educated at Edinburgh. He worked for a time in the Old Botanical Garden at Leith Walk and wrote many books on his subject, besides editing several gardening magazines. He lived most of his time in London and in 1838 published his book on British trees. The Botanical Society of Edinburgh, formed in 1836, was one of those numerous British societies which appreciated the works of Loudon. He specialised in country estates, planted several cemeteries, and Derby arboretum. His wife published *The Ladies Flower Garden*, in six volumes, with superb colour plates.

Charles Lawson *(1794-1873)*

Charles was the son of Peter Lawson, an Edinburgh seed merchant. He travelled much, and introduced many useful trees and grasses into Britain. The larch tree had been introduced to Britain about 1770, as a popular plantation tree. It was a decided benefit as the wood of the larch does not readily rot in wet conditions and proves admirably suited to fencing in Scotland. But Lawson introduced the cypress which bears his name, *Cupressus lawsonii*, a beautiful ornamental tree with a perfumed timber somewhat resembling cedar in durability. He also introduced the Austrian pine. His book on British pine-trees still stands as a notable forestry textbook, and his book on British grasses was for long a standard reference.

George Walker-Arnott *(c.1799-1870)*

Born in Edinburgh, he was appointed Professor of Botany in Glasgow in 1845. He was notable as the co-author of two books; a *British Flora* and a text-book on Indian botany.

Hugh F.C. Cleghorn *(1820-1895)*

He was a medical graduate of Edinburgh and spent most of his life with the East India Co. We hear much today of the continuing denudation of tropical forests, which apparently no power on earth can stop. Cleghorn, nearly a century and a half ago, at the Edinburgh Assembly of the British Association, was responsible for setting up a Committee to make a report on the destruction of tropical forests. He drew up this report, the chief result of which was the inauguration of the Forest Department in Madras by the East India Co., which ultimately controlled all that sub-continent. Cleghorn was appointed Inspector-General of Forests in India in 1867 and is called 'The Father of Scientific Forestry in India'.

Francis Buchanan White *(c.1830-1880)*

White was a graduate of medicine in Edinburgh and one of the founders of the Cryptogamic Society of Scotland, which is interested in ferns, lichens and mosses. He also published books on the flora of Perthshire and on *British Willows*.

John Jeffrey *(c.1850)*

The Oregon Association, interested in Western American botany, was formed in Edinburgh for the purpose of sending botanists and foresters out to the Pacific coast to bring back seeds of the many magnificent forest species of the Rockies. John Jeffrey was sent out in 1851. He was an employee of the new Royal Botanic Gardens. He was responsible for awakening interest in America, and eventually, through his activities, many interesting conifers and other plants were brought to Europe for the first time. Many of these trees were planted at Benmore estate near Dunoon where the heavy rainfall (100 inches per annum) and temperate climate is almost the same as in British Columbia and Oregon mountain areas. The great sequoia and other American trees, a century and more in age, may be seen growing in Scotland as a result of the Oregon Society's initiative.

The influence of Scottish botanists extended over many parts of the world. We give an alphabetical list of only a few of these, with their position in the scientific world.

Thomas Anderson born Edinburgh, MD Edinburgh, (1853), Director of Botanic Garden in Calcutta, introduced medical plants to India, especially Cinchona and Ipecacuanha.

Robert Brown (1773-1858), medical student, Edinburgh, named by the eminent German geographer Humboldt 'the most eminent botanist of his time.' He accompanied Flinders on Australian exploration.

James W. Cathcart collected plants in the East Himalayas and had them beautifully drawn by native artists under his charge.

Nicol Dalzell, MD Edinburgh (1837), conservator of Forests in Bombay and worked with Alexander Gibson another MA of Edinburgh on a *Flora of Bombay* (1861).

Hugh Falconer, MD Edinburgh (1829), Superintendent of the Calcutta Botanical Garden. Introduced tea and cinchona to many parts of India.

Robert Fortune (1813-1886) worked many years in the Royal Botanic Gardens. Made an excursion to China and brought back many new trees and shrubs.

William Jameson was Professor of Chemistry and Botany at Quito. He wrote on the flora of South America and made many collections.

John Richardson, MD Edinburgh (1816) took part in Franklin's first Arctic expedition and in two subsequent expeditions to the Arctic, as naturalist and botanist.

John Scott foreman in the propagating department of the Royal Botanic Gardens, managed the Calcutta Botanic Garden with Thomas Anderson. He was a friend and correspondent of Charles Darwin.

Francis Buchanan was born near Callander. He took his MD at Edinburgh and was surgeon with the East India Company. He carried out botanical researches in the Andaman Islands and published a paper on the fishes of the Brahmaputra. He was assessor of the state of Mysore. He made a botanical collection in Nepal and was superintendent of the Botanical Gardens in Calcutta.

ZOOLOGY

As we have mentioned, Scottish zoology, entomology and ornithology began in the anatomy department of the Edinburgh School of Medicine, under Sir Andrew Balfour and Sir Robert Sibbald, towards the end of the seventeenth century. Already, earlier in that century, English zoologists had described the greater part of the fauna of Britain. There was a revival of interest in animal study in Europe about 1680 and Sir Robert Sibbald in his illustrated book, had attempted to tabulate the animals of all species. He also published the first book on British whales and other cetaceans.

We have already spoken of Alexander Dalrymple, hydrologist and geographer to the East India Co. He was also a skilled naturalist and gathered information about biology in the course of his duties. The same also applies to the African explorers James Bruce, Mungo Park, and William Baikie who was naturalist on the Niger Expedition of 1854.

The scientists in the *Challenger* Expedition, noted in the Oceanography section were of course naturalists. These were Edward Forbes, Charles Wyville Thomson and John Murray. The Revd John Fleming, noted as a leading geologist, was also one of Scotland's foremost naturalists.

We now come to a miscellany of men, not all of academic training, who made wild life their study, and in some cases, their life-long enthusiasm.

Alexander Wilson *(1766-1813)*

He was born in Paisley, son of a small distiller. He got the rudiments of learning at the local school but soon took to practical pursuits. For a time he was a weaver, for at that time Paisley was famed for its fancy textiles of all sorts. He then bought a pack and travelled round Scotland as a chapman or pedlar. He was naturally gifted at verse making, and his poems on comic Scottish life were at the time taken for the work of Robert Burns. Like Burns, Wilson was very adept at satire, and one of his targets, a Paisley magistrate, sent him to jail for his shrewd wit, in the year of the French Reign of Terror 1793. Wilson decided to quit his native land, like many others at that time, who objected to oppression. He emigrated to America where he worked at various jobs.

On the advice of an American naturalist, Wilson turned to bird-study, for which he had an inclination, as he had become familiar with the plentiful and varied birds of Scotland, as was Burns and most other Scots poets. He had taught himself etching so he wandered off to Niagara on foot, sleeping rough. He made a large collection of sketches of the birds of New York State and of neighbouring areas. He obtained a job in Philadelphia as assistant editor of *Ree's Encyclopaedia*. He now had the means to publish the first volume of his great work *American Ornithology*. To his disappointment, not many people were willing to subscribe, so he travelled all over the continent, sketching birds and asking subscriptions for his next two volumes. The winter of 1812-13 (which was also the time of a war between the USA and Britain) was spent by Wilson completing his next six volumes. He worked far into the night and paid the penalty, dying of dysentery due partly to his weakened constitution.

Others added volumes to his original ones and his genius was commemorated by the erection of a statue in Paisley in 1876.

Sir John Richardson *(1787-1865)*

Mentioned as an explorer in the Arctic during the search for Franklin, he was also a distinguished naturalist.

It is of interest in another direction that his father Gabriel was a neighbour and friend of Robert Burns in Dumfries, and that John entered Dumfries Academy on the same day as Robert, the eldest son of the poet.

132

Richardson studied medicine at Edinburgh, graduated in 1816, and joined Franklin as surgeon and naturalist on the Arctic Expeditions of 1819-22 and 1825-7. Here he made his explorations of the Mackenzie River and the Arctic Coast. He was thereafter appointed Fleet Physician, Inspector of Hospitals and knighted, within a space of eight years. He led an expedition in the vain search for Franklin and retired soon after.

He published in 1831-7 an account of the animals of Arctic America.

William MacGillivray *(1796-1852)*

He was born at Aberdeen where he studied medicine at King's College. At twenty-seven he was appointed Professor of Natural History at Edinburgh and eight years later became Curator of the Museum of the Royal College of Surgeons. He became Professor of Natural History and Botany at Aberdeen for the last seven years of his life.

His published works were well known and popular in his time. He was a recognised authority on many aspects of natural study. The celebrated Audubon, the American ornithologist, who brought out his Birds of America twenty years after Alexander Wilson's volumes on the same theme, came to Edinburgh to consult MacGillivray about the presentation of some of his work, and was given every help.

MacGillivray's own books were entitled as follows; *A History of British Quadrupeds, Molluscs of Aberdeen, Banff and Kincardine, Manual of British Ornithology,* and a very fine five volume edition of *British Birds.*

Queen Victoria requested that his *Natural History of Deeside,* which he had completed shortly before his early death, should be posthumously published.

John MacGillivray *(c.1820-1880)*

He was no relation of the above and studied medicine at Edinburgh from 1840-2. He sailed as naturalist and ship's doctor on an expedition to the East Indies. In 1846 he became naturalist on the *Herald,* but left it at Sydney to spend the rest of his days exploring and studying natural life in the many islands of the Australasian seas.

H.D.S. Goodsir *(d.1847)*

He was appointed naturalist in Franklin's last and fatal expedition. Only after a series of searches was the fate of the expedition revealed by the discovery of the skeletons, Goodsir's among them, along with equipment and records, in various encampments. An Eskimo woman witness of the last survivors said, 'They fell down and died as they walked.' Goodsir was one of the martyrs of natural history.

Sir John Kirk *(1832-1922)*

Born at Barry near Arbroath, a son of the manse, he took a medical course at Edinburgh and served during the Crimean War in the civil medical staff stationed in the Dardanelles, the Turks being our allies in that campaign.

When Livingstone's second expedition set out in 1858 for Central Africa,

Kirk was appointed physician and naturalist. For the next five years he was Livingstone's constant companion. With three other white men, including his leader, he beheld the mighty freshwater sea of Lake Nyasa. He was invalided home after five years, but with a fine reputation as doctor and naturalist.

He served in several political positions in Zanzibar before retiring. He was virtually ruler of Zanzibar. On his retiral he had much influence in suppressing the slave trade in Africa, and dealing with other controversial matters.

Many new species of flora and fauna in Central Africa were discovered by him, and he gave his name to no less than two animals and two plants; for example, a species of lemur, a lower primate, a long-tailed monkey, is known to us higher primates as *Otogale kirkii*.

John Muir *(1838-1914)*

Muir has already been noted as an explorer. His autobiography, published the year before his death, tells of his encounters with the natural world in East Lothian and later in the backwoods of Wisconsin. He walked for months all over North America, from the semi-deserts of Montana to the glaciers of Alaska, admiring particularly the huge and spectacular natural forests, mountains and prairies, where he was often the only human being for hundreds of square miles around. He was the American naturalist *par excellence*, no particular branch taking precedence over another.

Sir Patrick Geddes *(1854-1932)*

Born at Perth, he was trained in biology in the laboratory of T.H. Huxley, the eminent scientist, at University College, London. He then proceeded to various European universities and returned to London as demonstrator in Physiology. After appointments in Aberdeen and Edinburgh in zoology and botany, he was Professor of Botany at Dundee for many years, ending up as Professor of Sociology and Civics at Bombay, a completely novel departure.

His pioneer work was brought to light in his book *The Evolution of Sex* (1889), but from the first his interest was much broader than that of a pure biologist. He wanted to apply the science of life study to social problems.

He inaugurated the Outlook Tower on the Castle Hill of Edinburgh. This is an object of much interest to tourists and citizens alike becuase it contains a *camera obscura*, whereby, by means of an arrangement of mirrors, the visitor has the illusion of looking down directly upon the life of the city. This is a symbol of what Geddes intended. The Outlook Tower was the centre for many years of discussions and publications on social problems. In the midst of all his social studies at home and in India he still kept up his interest in botany and zoology.

Sir D'Arcy Wentworth Thompson *(1860-1948)*

He was the son of an eminent classical scholar and had a sound education, turning to science, not languages.

He probably did more than any other scientist to make the public aware of the marvels of nature. He was editor of many books and periodicals of naturalist interest. One of the problems which had occupied biologists since even before the age of Galileo in 1638 (who put forward a hypothesis) was to know the upper limit of organisms, whether plant or animal. Thompson treated these problems in a minute and comprehensive way in his treatise, *On Growth and Form*. It was most beautifully illustrated and clearly written, a remarkable piece of scientific synthesis.

J. Arthur Thomson *(1861-1933)*

He was born in East Lothian and educated at the Universities of Edinburgh, Jena and Berlin. He was for a time lecturer at Edinburgh in the medical faculty, in zoology and biology. In 1899 he was Regius Professor of Natural History at Aberdeen.

His chief work as a zoologist was in the study of certain corals. As a popular writer he did an enormous amount to popularise zoology. Some of his publications are; *Outlines of Zoology, Introduction to Science, The Wonder of Life, A New Natural History*.

He tried all his life to make science and religion more compatible.

William Spiers Bruce *(c.1867-1921)*

He studied natural history and medicine at Edinburgh and immediately after, in 1892, he was one of the first to begin a fresh wave of exploration in the Antarctic. In a whaler he conducted a naturalist cruise in the Antarctic. He was followed by a succession of Norwegian explorers and, as interest mounted in Antarctica, by Belgian, German and British expeditions.

In 1903 and 1904 he equipped a Scottish expedition to explore the Antarctic. The *Scotia* was the ship's name, commanded by Thomas Robertson. There was a large scientific staff, including naturalists, oceanographers and geologists. The Weddell Sea was extensively investigated in 1903 and, in the summer of 1904, land subsequently named Coats Land was sighted. Apart from the oceanographical discoveries in the Weddell Sea, the investigations of the *Scotia* generally in the Southern Ocean helped to solve many problems. There were many Antarctic expeditions in the beginning of this century. The South Pole, as all the world knows, was reached by Amundsen on 14 December 1911 and by Scott on 18 January 1912. Most of the explorers were content to sail as far south as the ice-barrier permitted, then to set up a base camp on the mainland of Antarctica for further exploration. Bruce's object was purely oceanography.

He also explored the Arctic Ocean, the difficulties not nearly as formidable as at the South Pole, where the great altitude of Antarctica makes for very low temperatures and unexpected blizzards. Accompanying the Prince of Monaco in his yacht *Princess Alice*, Dr Bruce made several valuable surveys and scientific observations on the ocean round Spitzbergen.

James Ritchie *(1882-1958)*

He was assistant Keeper of the Natural History Department of the Royal Scottish Museum when he published his monumental book *The Influence of*

Man on Animal Life in Scotland: a study in faunal evolution. (1920)

This book has a message for all ages and particularly for the present crisis in man's relationship to animal life. In his introduction he says, 'So sweeping are the changes wrought by Man and so swift are they in their action that they obscure and almost submerge the slow march of the other processes of nature.' His study is deliberately confined to Scotland, as it presents an epitome of man's conduct towards the animal world in every country. It is a strong indictment of man's callous indifference to his earth-born companions, be they animals, birds, reptiles, fishes or insects.

Ritchie records his indebtedness to one or two of the multitude of Scottish naturalists of all ages from mediaeval to modern times.

Seton Gordon *(1886-1976)*

A native of Aboyne, Aberdeenshire, he was interested in nature from his earliest days. His first published book, in 1904, was *Birds of the Loch and Mountain*. He studied at Oxford University where he took an honours degree in Botany, the award being mainly due to his brilliant description of alpine flora he had observed in the Cairngorms.

In 1912 he went to Russia with an Oxford friend who was a Russian Prince. He asked Gordon to be one of his foresters, but he refused, otherwise he might have been caught up in the Revolution, as Prince Youssoupoff was deeply involved.

In 1914 Seton Gordon was engaged in the Inner Hebrides, keeping a watch for German submarines from the Island of Mull.

After the war he and his wife spent many years at Aviemore, from which centre Gordon took most of his wonderful photographs of golden eagles and other wild creatures. He toured Britain continuously giving lectures and arranging for publication of his books, of which he wrote about thirty, the most comprehensive being *Highways and Byways in the West Highlands* and its companion book *The Central Highlands*.

In 1931 Seton Gordon and his wife decided to settle permanently at Upper Duntuilm in Skye, where they lived a quiet life on a large croft with sheep, cows, oats and potatoes. Here he wrote for several hours each day on his experiences with the natural life of his native land. He was active until after his ninetieth year, climbing the Cairngorms, in his kilt and Balmoral bonnet, to view his beloved mountains.

Sir Frank Fraser Darling *(1903-1979)*

After studying for two years (1928-30) in Edinburgh University's Institute of Animal Genetics, he was appointed Chief Inspector of the Imperial Bureau of Animal Genetics from 1930 to 1934. He was Director of the West Highland Survey from 1944 to 1950.

Apart from these official posts, he was always a keen observer of wild life, especially in his life on the Hebridean Island of Rona. He travelled widely abroad, in Alaska and South Africa, and issued numerous publications, illustrated by his own wonderful photographs and description, all advocating the conservation of the natural species that were in danger from the encroachments of modern civilisation. Ecology was a term largely attributable to Fraser Darling and his original contributions to Nature Study.

Invention

Most of the devices to which we are accustomed in our daily life, and accept without much thought, were at one time the invention of some genius whose name has been forgotten, perhaps for thousands of years. It would be unwise to assume that the people of Scotland, or of any Western European land, were in any way unable to live quite competently before the invention of wheeled traffic, of illuminated cities, of printed books or of preserved foods. The style of life of the urban or rural Scot during the late Middle Ages, in the time of Bruce and the early Stuart kings was in many respects ideal, had it not been for civil strife and English invasions. We know from contemporary literature that most households had adequate furnishing, humble though it was, in the shape of tables, stools, beds, butterchurns, pottery, metal kettles and pans, barrels and tubs, axes, saws and hammers, candles and lamps, pokers, tongs and shovels, spinning-wheels and looms. The farmer had his plough and harrow, harness for horse or oxen, hoes, rakes, seed-bags, pruning-hooks. The fisherman, forester, hunter, soldier, metal-worker, builder, slater all had varieties of gear and tools.

The splendour of the Middle Ages, the cathedrals, abbeys, churches and castles were all built by craftsmen accustomed to expertise in chiselwork, measurement, cementing, quarrying. Horticulture, beekeeping, conserving were fine arts. Such was the state of affairs, more or less until about the time of the Union of the Parliaments of Scotland and England in 1707. Then, it would seem, what had been normally a long state of belligerence between the two ends of the island developed, if not into a total acceptance of brotherliness as Britons, at least into a friendly rivalry. Many Scots opposed the Union but others saw in it a chance to expand and to take their ideas into a larger market and also to learn something from their former opponents.

A new spirit of enterprise in all human spheres of activity seemed to fill the minds of many Scots and, as we write in the chapter on poetry, they made an intellectual occupation of England in force, without, however, neglecting their own country's well-being. It is virtually impossible to separate the various inventors, so manifold were some of the ramifications of their fertile brains. For example, geniuses such as James Watt and Archibald Pitcairne, credited by fame respectively with the steam-engine and founding the great Edinburgh School of Medicine, have both very much more of invention and achievement to their credit, in quite other directions.

Mankind is too apt to think in general terms, and consequently to pay too little attention to what Thomas Carlyle said was the hallmark of genius, 'the transcendental capacity of taking trouble, first of all.' Not every person has the will power to return again and again, over weary years often, to the solution of a problem which has been given up over the ages. Yet that has usually been the method of inventors. Not always, however, for very infrequently, as in the cases of Watt and Fleming, a sudden flash has revealed a long-buried truth. Watt was walking on Glasgow Green one fine Sunday evening when he suddenly hit on the principle which made the steam-engine really efficient: Fleming was struck by the failure to escalate of some bacteria which had accidentally come in contact with moulds. A thousand persons would have passed by these phenomena without forming an association. Those who can complete the mental synapsis are the inventors.

Some inventors, like those primeval discoverers of the wheel and the lever, are so obscure that we could not find many details beyond their name. With others the credit has been claimed by someone else, in which case we acknowledge this if we know. This has often happened, as law-suits can show, such as in the celebrated case of the dispute early this century over the sleeve-valve in motor-engines, between the Daimler and Argyll companies, where the case went against the Scottish firm and helped to throw them out of the business. Many inventors have not troubled to patent their devices and fully as many, in all likelihood, have been deprived of their invention because it was brought to fruition in their employer's time. The Judgement Day will put this right?

John Napier *(1550-1617)*

He was the eighth holder of the estate of Merchiston near Edinburgh. He lived in an age of religious strife when civil war between the Catholics and Protestants was general throughout Europe, even touching upon Napier's own house and estate. He matriculated at St Andrews University when thirteen. After graduating there he went to Paris for further study, then variously through Italy and Germany.

He wrote on theology and was an influential member of church bodies. He was not in his day considered to be inconsistent when he mixed his Bible commentaries with the invention of secret instruments of war, preparing for an expected invasion of England by Philip II of Spain in 1596, eight years after the defeat of his Armada. Napier was living in London at this time and helping Elizabeth.

Towards the end of his life (he died a year later than Shakespeare) he was engaged in publishing the result of his new approach to mathematical calculation, the whole principle being to render easier the manipulation of large or small numbers. His book expounding logarithms was written of course in Latin for universal comprehension. Its title was *Canonis Descriptio* or a 'description of the principles'. The term logarithm was also his invention. In it he printed the logarithms of sines for every minute to seven figures, which gives some idea of the extreme particularity of his work.

He also invented numbering rods, later nicknamed 'Napier's Bones'. Two other aids to calculation were boxes of metal plates and a 'number game' to be played on a chessboard or *dambrod* as he called it.

There is no disputing his priority in this fundamental invention, nor of his being first user of the decimal point to separate integers from fractions, a simple but not obvious advance on Arabic numeration.

James Gregory *(1638-1675)*

Gregory was a relation of Rob Roy Macgregor. His family, because of the several Proscription Acts between 1603 and 1617 had been compelled on pain of death to change their names from Macgregor. They chose Gregory, as being distinguished in history and not far from the original.

Gregory was educated at Marischal College, Aberdeen, after attending the town grammar school. At the age of twenty-five he published his *Optima promota* describing his great invention, the Gregorian reflecting telescope. His book was of course in Latin so that it could be read by every European man of science. In 1665 he attended the University of Padua where he studied for a few years, publishing an erudite mathematical treatise on circles and hyperbolae. The following year, also at Padua, he published a book of rules for verifying and rectifying curves. He was elected an FRS and was Professor of Mathematics at St Andrews, then at Edinburgh, until his death at an early age.

Telescopes were invented by three Dutchmen about thirty years before Gregory was born. It was one of these early types of telescope that Galileo so improved that he was able to make observations which confirmed that the earth and the planets moved round the sun. The original telescopes were of great length, often up to 100 yards, but were not accurate. As Gregory worked out, the reflecting telescope was not only short but it cut out distortion. Gregory did not construct such a telescope, he only laid down the principles. Sir Isaac Newton, three years after Gregory's invention, also invented a reflecting telescope and other oculists succeeded in improving telescopes. It was not until the following century that James Short of Edinburgh, born in 1710, encouraged by Colin Maclaurin, Professor of Mathematics at Edinburgh, actually manufactured the Gregorian reflecting telescopes on the lines advised by Gregory. By his own modifications he was able to make them more accurate, so some of the credit is his.

William Ged *(fl.1690-1749)*

He was an Edinburgh goldsmith well used to delicate manipulation of materials. Although his invention of stereotyping does not seem to have much relationship to his craft he may often have wanted copies of designs to embody them in his own handicraft. Up to his time, sheets of copper had been engraved by a burin or carving tool, to be inked over and pressed upon a paper to produce a copy. This skilled and lengthy process was shortened by covering a metal sheet with wax and etching it; that is, by cutting away the wax with an etching pen and applying acid to the plate, thus producing a picture in the metal.

Ged's invention was this. He poured a soft paste of plaster of Paris on to the face of the forme, or original to be copied. When the plaster plate dried he poured molten metal such as pewter or lead upon it and so produced an exact replica from which any number of copies could be made.

He was commissioned by Cambridge University to make stereotypes of a Greek *New Testament*, an extremely difficult operation because Greek characters are difficult to distinguish. Ged, with infinite care, took plaster moulds and cast type metal plates from them. To his extreme disappointment the printers bungled the job and he returned in disgust to Edinburgh.

Ged's invention was revived half a century later, long after his death. In 1813 a David Bruce of Edinburgh went to America and established a stereotyping business. The first book to be printed by the new method was the *Westminster Catechism*, much in demand in New England. The printer was John Watts. Copies should be valuable today though at the time of stereotyping they were sold for a few cents.

James and Andrew Meikle *(c.1690-1760) and (1719-1811)*

They were father and son, born at Dunbar. Their trade was the setting up of water and windmills. They became the tenants of that great patriot, Andrew Fletcher of Saltoun, East Lothian. The Union of 1707 had spoiled his hopes of a political career, as he had bitterly opposed it, so he set his mind to matters near at hand. Seeing the expertise of James Meikle, he sent him at his own expense to Holland to study the devices used by the Dutch farmers. Meikle travelled far and wide, spying out the mechanisms of the Netherlands which he adapted and put to use by inventing his own version of a winnowing-machine, known popularly as a fanner. Fletcher set up a fanner factory at Saltoun with Meikle and his son in charge. They provided this very popular machine for Scottish grain-growers.

Fletcher did not stop at separating the wheat from the chaff. He encouraged Andrew Meikle to devise a means of decorticating barley, that is, removing the husks, firmly attached to the grain, by grinding. Meikle invented a mill for this purpose and Saltoun, or 'pearl', barley became famous.

Others copied Meikle's inventions all over Britain.

Sir Hugh Dalrymple, Lord Drummore *(c.1700-1755)*

With Sir Patrick Murray, Lord Elibank, he contests the honour of being the inventor of hollow draining, i.e. of sinking continuous tile pipes of varying diameters into water-logged ground to carry off surplus moisture and reclaim marshy and therefore sterile land. This agricultural invention brought immense areas of Britain into production both for forestry and farming.

James Small *(c.1730-1793)*

He was a Scottish carpenter who had worked in England. He set up a factory at Blackadder, near Duns, Berwickshire, for the manufacture of iron ploughs to supersede the cumbersome wooden ploughs in common use.

Small experimented for years until he had made an exact model of the machine. He took it to Carron Iron Works to have it cast. Some improvements followed, and by about 1784 he had a plough that was used without alteration for 150 years. It could be drawn by a pair of horses and guided by one man. He still had to encourage farmers to adopt it, which was an even harder task than inventing it. His great invention yielded him very little reward.

James Watt *(1736-1819)*

He was born at Greenock, son of a merchant who had been ruined by speculation. After a local schooling James worked in London for an instrument maker who overworked and underpaid him but gave him an opportunity to become expert at the trade. When he was twenty Watt returned to Glasgow and set up as a maker of precision instruments, but the closed shop policy of the city guilds prevented him from selling his wares. The University, however, elected him instrument maker.

Here he was befriended by Joseph Black, lecturer in chemistry, and discoverer of latent heat, who discussed with him the question of steam-engines, especially the Newcomen engine, an inefficient machine, used to pump water. Watt was given one of these to repair. This set him on a logical train of thought which resulted, a year later, in his great invention of the separate condenser, and other modifications. He did not take out his patent for four years during which he was trying out his new engine. With the co-operation of Mr John Roebuck, founder of the Carron Iron Works, Watt built his engine near Linlithgow.

Turning to civil engineering he planned harbours and canals in mid-Scotland, including the much-needed deepening of the Clyde. For the surveying he invented a simple micrometer.

In 1768 Watt met Boulton who owned the Soho engineering works at Birmingham. A partnership which was to become famous was formed, Watt doing the invention, Boulton the business. Now Watt's inventions continued, his first being to find a method of applying the reciprocating power of the engine to a rotary movement. His 'sun and planet' arrangement was patented, though Murdoch claimed it. But the centrifugal governor was Watt's, and many another invention made during his long life.

James Tytler *(1746-1804)*

The son of a Kincardineshire clergyman and related to a family famous in literary and legal circles, James Tytler demonstrated his inventive genius in very many ways, but all he got was ill-usage and ridicule in return.

He was one of the first to discover a cheap way of producing magnesia, which he put into practice; he was aware of the work of the Scottish chemist Joseph Black, Professor of Chemistry in Glasgow, who had separated magnesia from lime. Up to that time they had been considered to be identical. It speaks volumes for Tytler that in the 1780s (nearly forty years before a German chemist was producing almost pure magnesia), he was manufacturing it in Edinburgh.

Tytler, however, is famous as being the first man in Britain to ascend in a balloon. All his apparatus was made by himself, the balloon being barrel-shaped and lifted by hot air, made by an iron stove on the platform. In

August 1784, at Edinburgh, two months before a flight was made near Oxford, Tytler, at great risk (because he threw out the stove as the balloon ascended), made a flight of half a mile, rising, according to his line measurements, to 300ft. The heating source having been rashly discarded, the balloon descended rather rapidly but Tytler got off lightly as it fell into a swamp, in the area now occupied by the Meadowbank Sports Stadium.

While Tytler was jeered, the following year Lunardi, a conceited fop, was cheered to the echo by the Scottish crowds when he made a flight from Heriot's Hospital grounds to Fife. Burns knew Tytler very well and saw him often in 1786-7. He was sorry for the aeronaut and pitied his 'sky-lighted hat', but in his notes on Scottish songs he credits Tytler with another kind of invention. He was the author of that lively song, 'The Muckin' o' Geordie's Byre.'

Tytler wrote and edited many, perhaps most, of the articles in the second edition of the *Encyclopaedia Britannica*, of which the first edition was started in Edinburgh in 1768.

Despite his many-sided genius he was accused of sedition in the panic years following the Reign of Terror in France. He did not appear and was 'fugitated', that is to say, fled the country in 1793, and went to Salem in Massachusetts to escape the political witch-hunt. He died there by a drowning accident in 1804.

William Murdock or Murdoch *(1754-1839)*

He was born near Auchinleck. As a young man he decided to seek employment with Boulton and Watt in Birmingham. Murdoch was unable to afford a tile or 'lum' hat which at that time all respectable workmen wore, so he turned one out of wood and blackened it. He cut a poor figure at his interview in Birmingham and was dismissed. But as he turned to leave he accidentally dropped his hat. The noise startled his interviewer. When Murdoch explained his peculiar headgear he was taken on, as likely to prove an ingenious workman.

Two years later in 1779 he was sent to Cornwall to fit up Watt's engines. He began to experiment with the distillation of coal and by 1792 he was able to light with gas his cottage and office at Redruth in Cornwall.

To celebrate the Peace of Amiens between France and England in 1802, a part of the Soho factory in Birmingham was illuminated by coal gas, to the wonder and delight of all.

Although famed for his invention of gas-lighting, Murdoch's genius did not stop there. He invented an oscillating steam-engine and to the annoyance of Boulton and Watt he busied himself manufacturing a steam carriage for the highways. He also invented a steam slide valve, and earlier in his relationship with Boulton and Watt, the 'sun and planet' device in the steam-engine, which Watt patented, is thought to have been first demonstrated by Murdoch.

John Loudon MacAdam *(1756-1836)*

He was born at Ayr, emigrating at fourteen to New York, where he worked for his uncle as a clerk. He made a fortune and with it bought an estate in Ayrshire at Sauchrie near Maybole.

At that time the British highways were in bad condition. For example, it took a four-in-hand coach two days to travel from Glasgow to Edinburgh in winter or bad weather. Three-quarters of Britain was inaccessible by road, and stage-coach passengers often had to dismount to help extricate the vehicle from the soft road.

MacAdam was a man of wealth and resolution. He began to experiment with road-making on his own estate of Sauchrie where, as usual, he met with much active opposition from the conservationists. But as he was road trustee he carried on and discovered that his theories were workable. Put simply, his roads were made by laying a foundation of large stones and gradually decreasing the size until the surface was rolled over with gravel and grit. Allowance was also made for run-off of moisture and other drainage.

In 1798 he moved to Falmouth where he had a Government appointment to supervise roads. From there he went as Surveyor-General of the Bristol roads, published two books on road-making, and capped his campaign by being appointed General Surveyor of British Highways. He made a considerable fortune by his invention which showed a fair amount of shrewdness, for many inventors lost fortunes.

Thomas Telford (1757-1834)

Born at Westerkirk, near Langholm, Dumfriesshire, he was educated at the parish school and at fifteen was apprenticed to a stone-mason. He studied from whatever books he could obtain, often walking the six miles to Langholm for these. He published poems in the local Eskdale newspaper. In 1780 he went to Edinburgh where the magnificent New Town of North Edinburgh, planned by Craig, was being built. There Telford was employed for some years on the masonry of splendid freestone palatial houses. In 1793 he was appointed engineer of the Ellesmere Canal. Here was a task which enlisted all his genius for the canal had to be carried over the Vale of Llangollen by a gigantic aqueduct, to connect the Severn and the Mersey. This achievement established Telford as an eminent civil engineer. The canal has long been abandoned but the monumental aqueduct still stands.

He was now commissioned to report on the Highlands of Scotland and was appointed engineer of the Caledonian Canal and for the equally formidable task of making roads through 900 miles of mountainous and boggy country. The Caledonian Canal was designed to carry ships which had formerly had to face the dangerous Pentland Firth and the Minch. It has never come up to expectations but Telford made a valiant effort to overcome the great natural difficulties. Many years after his death, when a vast fortune, well over £1,000,000 had been spent, a series of weather extremes undid much of his labour.

Telford turned to the South and, besides improving the roads in South Scotland and Wales, he constructed the magnificent suspension bridge across the Menai Straits, and also the Conway Bridge.

Among his other successful conclusions of vast enterprises was the drainage of over 80 square miles of the North-east Fens, and the bridging of the great gorge of the Water of Leith at Edinburgh by the Dean Bridge, which rises over 100ft. above the river and still carries a busy main highway. He also built the Broomielaw Bridge over the Clyde at Glasgow.

Dawson *(c.1760)*

He was a tenant farmer of Frogden in Roxburghshire who took up the system of Jethro Tull, the English agricultural innovator who had been ridiculed and driven to the grave by his countrymen.

Dawson was not so much an inventor as a resurrector of a lost idea which is probably more meritorious. By his example of horse-hoeing, sowing artificial grasses, by cultivating turnips and by applying lime and marl he brought an infertile district to prosperity and was copied over the whole of Britain. Wight of East Lothian, shortly after Tull's publication in 1731, had practised horse-hoeing with success, except on wheat and legumes.

John Rennie *(1761-1801)*

He was the youngest son of a farmer at Phantassie, near Haddington. Like the Meikles, he was first engaged in the building of mills, in which he acquired a thorough knowledge of mechanics. But his genius expanded far beyond this specialised branch, to enable him to solve problems which had long defied the ingenuity of civil engineers. In the Fen country of Eastern England and on the Solway Firth he solved many problems of drainage and reclaiming lost lands.

He then turned his attention to bridge-building, for not only the carrying of roads but of canals. Had he been famed for nothing else, even one of his three London bridges would have served for not only a conspicuous, but a constantly useful monument. He drew the plans and supervised the erection of the Waterloo, Southwark and London Bridges, the last of which was so classical in its construction that it was taken piecemeal across the Atlantic and re-erected over, of all inappropriate places, a semi-desert in Arizona.

He was instrumental in constructing many harbours and docks from Wick to Torquay, as well as London Dock and East India Dock. The Government consulted him on the naval dockyards of Portsmouth, Sheerness, Chatham and Plymouth.

As a fitting consummation to this epic of a farmer's boy from Haddington, Rennie was buried in St Paul's, acclaimed by all his beneficiaries.

Charles Macintosh *(1766-1843)*

Born in Glasgow, Macintosh from the beginning proved himself possessed, not only of an inventive turn, but also of an astute eye for turning innovations into cash. At the age of twenty he went to Holland, which was the principal exporter to Glasgow of white lead, or sugar of lead, used for glazing and painting. Macintosh brought back the Dutch method of manufacture and set up such a successful industry that the tables were turned and sugar of lead was exported to Rotterdam. Chloride of lime, used in bleaching, was his next venture, then, by a happy application of naphtha to rubber sheeting

145

strengthened by cloth, he invented the fabric which commemorates him in all lands, the macintosh.

Macintosh's chemical research was the basis of some of the most extensive chemical works in the world, in the first half of the nineteenth century, the St Rollox works in North Glasgow, owned by Tennant and Knox.

Henry Bell *(1767-1830)*

He was born at Torphichen, West Lothian, He was apprenticed to his uncle, a wheelwright, then to a shipbuilder at Bo'ness. He tried his fortune in London where he worked for John Rennie the civil engineer. Returning to Glasgow for a time, he found occasional work as an engineer at Helensburgh. In 1812 he built a small steamboat of 25 tons and 3 h.p. capable of 7 knots and sailed it on the Clyde. It was named the *Comet* probably because of the long tail of sparks and smoke it carried.

Robert Fulton, the American, had sailed a steamboat earlier but he acknowledged the help he had received from Bell and others. Bell's initiative was rewarded by Glasgow, and a monument erected to him near Bowling. But, as he had neglected to patent his invention, it was promptly seized on by others.

It is uncertain to whom we owe the invention of the steamboat, for two enthusiasts had already sailed these successfully, on short voyages.

In 1788 **Patrick Miller** of Dalswinton not far from Dumfries had constructed a steamboat which he had sailed on Dalswinton Loch. In the same year he launched a steam-drawn paddle-steamer named the *Experiment* built by Allan and Stewart of Leith, which sailed for some miles on the Forth. At that time Burns was the tenant of Ellisland, to which he had been invited by Mr Miller. The poet was often in his landlord's house and it was only natural that he should be asked to embark on the first steamship ever to sail. Burns mentioned this exciting experience to some of his correspondents.

In 1789 another experimental steam vessel was tried out in the Forth and Clyde Canal and in 1802 **William Symington's** *Charlotte Dundas* towed barges there. The use of steam vessels for this purpose was later discouraged because of the effect of the wash upon the rather frail banks. A light railway for drawing barges was substituted for steam-ships but single horse-power on four legs was the normal sedate method.

Revd Alexander Forsyth *(1769-1848)*

He was a minister and like many Moderate clergymen he was fond of sport and seemed to see little harm in game-shooting, though Burns would have cursed him for it. At any rate Forsyth had so much trouble with the priming of his flint-lock fowling-piece, especially in wet or misty weather, that he turned his mind from religion to ignition. In the flint-lock a quantity of dry gunpowder was placed in a pan near the small entrance to the breech and ignited by sparks made by a small flint striking a steel plate. Far too often there occurred what was called 'a flash in the pan'. The powder charge in the breech failed to explode and the whole process had to be repeated. Forsyth succeeded in finding what he called a 'percussion powder', mostly composed of potassium chlorate, which explodes when struck by the 'dog-head' or hammer of the trigger mechanism. Some time later the percussion powder was put into a small metal cup, completely waterproof and easily handled. Forsyth's invention is considered to be almost as important as the invention of gunpowder itself. The paradox which springs to mind is; why should it have been a man of God who rendered killing so much more certain?

James Paterson *(c.1770-1840)*

He was a native of Musselburgh and came in contact with the many fishing-villages in the area, where fishing-nets were tediously made by hand. He enlisted in the army after serving as a cooper when a youth. He fought in the Peninsular War (1808-13) and was at Waterloo (1815) after which he was discharged.

Being mechanically inclined, he set about the invention of a machine for making fishnets from hemp twine. He had considered a system in 1812 on his temporary release from the army. He now set up a factory in 1820 but his machine was not quite perfect as the knots slipped too easily and allowed fish to escape. His machine too, was very complex, each mesh requiring a hook, a needle and a sinker, a most ingenious device.

Paterson was the first in Britain to succeed in making a practical machine. Some years before, the French inventor Jacquard had made one, to the amazement of Napoleon, who asked, 'Are you the man who pretends to do what God Almighty cannot – tie a knot in a stretched line?'

Walter Ritchie, also of Musselburgh, devised a method of making a handknot on machine nets, and in 1835, formed a flourishing net industry in the district. The modern nets of nylon are manufactured in enormous machines at incredible speed but Paterson deserves credit as the father of the process.

Robert Stevenson *(1772-1850)*

He was born in Glasgow, only son of a West Indies merchant. He attended Anderson's College and Glasgow University. His mother had been widowed, and remarried Thomas Smith, who was engaged in schemes to build lighthouses. So it is to a certain extent accidental that several generations of lighthouse engineers, with the astonishing by-product of a brilliant poet and writer, were created. At nineteen Robert was allowed to supervise the building of a lighthouse on the island of Little Cumbrae, a very necessary aid to shipping in view of the increasing trade of Clydeside. Smith was appointed engineer to the Commissioners of Northern Lighthouses. When he retired in 1797, Robert, at twenty-five, was appointed in his stead.

For nearly half a century Robert not only designed but supervised the difficult building of many lighthouses. One of the first and most perplexing was that on the Bell Rock off the mouth of the Tay. For centuries this hazard to shipping, both coastwise and from Dundee to the Baltic and North Sea coasts of Europe, had claimed hundreds of victims. A structure, supporting a bell, set a-going by the wind and waves, had been of little use so it was determined to build a solid stone lighthouse. Stevenson, on completing this seemingly impossible job, published a full account of it. As the rock was covered at spring tides (i.e. at intervals of a fortnight) to a depth of twelve feet, a solid base had to be constructed and dovetailed into the rock between tides. All the granite and sandstone was cut to exact shape ashore near Arbroath and shipped out the twelve miles to the site.

Stevenson's inventive genius devised a method of binding this great mass into one solid structure. He was also responsible for a new type of revolving light and a warning system by two large bells. As no less than seventy vessels had been wrecked on the rock in 1799 its completion was a great relief to sailors everywhere on the East coast.

The Skerryvore lighthouse had a completely different set of problems and these were solved by Stevenson's inventiveness and perseverance. The Atlantic storms, early in the construction, swept away many massive stones (2 tons each), which had been tied by iron bars and cemented. The work had to restart from scratch.

Stevenson was a prominent member of many learned societies. He was succeeded as a lighthouse engineer by his sons Alan and Thomas, the latter being the father of Robert Louis.

Sir David Brewster *(1781-1868)*

Born at Jedburgh, he is distinguished for his researches into the diffraction of light. One of his inventions in this connection was the kaleidoscope which, in a very simple form, was very popular for young and old in Victorian times. He was made an FRS at the age of thirty-four. The kaleidoscope was invented the following year. His most important work was the difficult one of persuading the British authorities to adopt, for lighthouses, a dioptric apparatus, invented by a European scientist. It took many years of argument to instal those lenses.

He edited and contributed to many scientific works.

James Smith *(1789-1850)*

Although Sir Hugh Dalrymple and Sir Patrick Murray contested the invention of hollow draining, the science of agricultural draining was not initiated until 1823 when James Smith of Deanston near Doune, Perthshire, put into practice the principles of draining that had been advocated by an English farmer, Blith, at the time of the Civil War, but had been forgotten.

Smith's scientific approach insisted on every field that was waterlogged being provided with parallel underground channels with a main receiving drain to carry off surplus water. He also invented various machinery to effect this, and put the system into practice at Deanston. He used stones to fill the drains but these were eventually replaced with earthenware tiles which were more efficient.

Smith's methods spread rapidly and thousands of hitherto useless acres were brought into production for the first time, adding greatly to the value of land, reducing the risk of famine and making cheap food available to the growing urban populations.

Draining, on Smith's principles brought up to date, has long been a legal obligation on landowners.

John Boyd Dunlop *(1789-1874)*

Dunlop was born on a farm at Dreghorn in Ayrshire. When a young man he was a veterinary surgeon in Belfast, with a large prosperous practice. In 1887 he made a pneumatic tyre for his son's tricycle and patented the invention the following year. Collaborating with Du Cros, the new tyres were produced commercially in 1890. After selling out to Du Cros, but retaining many shares, it was discovered that an inventor named Thompson had patented a pneumatic tyre in 1846. However Du Cros had certain supplementary patents which enabled him to retain the right to manufacture. Dunlop did not share in the vast fortunes made in the subsequent development of his company; and Thompson got much less.

Sir William Fairbairn *(1789-1874)*

Born at Kelso, son of a farm bailiff, he was educated in Ross-shire at a parish school. He was apprenticed as an engine-maker at a colliery at South Shields, then set up in business for himself in Manchester in 1817. His extensive use of iron increased his business. He developed the idea of using steel tube and erected many bridges of this.

He received many honours for his contributions of published papers and for his inventions relating to steam boilers and iron shipbuilding.

James Beaumont Neilson *(1792-1865)*

Born in Shettleston, Glasgow, he was educated at the parish school and went to work as a mechanic. He progressed steadily until he was appointed manager of the Glasgow Gasworks. Here he had an opportunity to experiment with coal as a fuel and in connection with the making of pig-iron. There were vast deposits of iron-ore near the Lanarkshire coalfield but, despite this great advantage, which reduced the transport of raw materials to a minimum, the production of pig-iron was very small. There was little demand for iron before the end of the eighteenth century and it was very expensive to produce. The smelting involved large quantities of charcoal in earlier centuries and, in Neilson's youth, about eight tons of coke for each ton of pure iron.

Neilson's invention was named the hot-blast. When the iron-ore, raw coal and limestone-flux had been assembled in the smelter, a bellows pumped very hot air through the mixture. Only about two tons of coal was needed to make one ton of pig-iron. The total production of iron in Scotland when Neilson was an apprentice in 1808 was just over 20,000 tons, concentrated between Glasgow and the Carron works, the latter, founded in 1760, supplying much the larger amount. Before Neilson died, the production topped a million tons, the impetus being given by the demands of railways and shipbuilding. Although other inventors such as Bessemer made improvements, Neilson's principle was the epoch-making breakthrough.

Thomas Drummond *(1797-1840)*

Born in Edinburgh and educated at the city High School he became a cadet at Woolwich Academy when sixteen and entered the Royal Engineers at eighteen. He was appointed to the trigonometrical survey of Great Britain. When surveying in Ireland in 1825 he invented a limelight apparatus (the Drummond Light), on somewhat the same idea as a heliograph, which enabled observations to be made of objects sixty-seven miles distant. He improved the heliostat and adapted it for use in lighthouses. As Secretary of State of Ireland he told the absentee Irish landlords very pointedly that 'property has its duties as well as its rights'. He took a large share in railway establishment in Ireland.

Revd Patrick Bell *(1800-1869)*

He was the minister of Carmylie, Forfar. He invented the reaping-machine, the principle of which was freely adapted by others in Britain and America. It eventually developed into the horse-drawn self-binder which cut, bundled and tied the standing corn and threw it out to be stacked in eights, tens or twelves by the reapers. After drying for a few days it was built into a large stack to be threshed by a steam-engine wheeled mill. The modern combine harvester dispenses with all these operations.

Thomas Graham *(1805-1869)*

Born in Glasgow and educated at Glasgow University, he refused his father's wishes that he make the ministry his career, and was cut off financially. At twenty-five he was Professor of Chemistry in the Andersonian Institution, and later in Edinburgh and London. He was made Master of the Mint and an FRS and first President of the London Chemical Society, then of the Cavendish Society.

He formulated Graham's Law on the diffusion of gases. His most important work was in colloid chemistry of which he has been called the 'father'. His book on *Chemical and Physical Researches*, published some years after his death, reveals the extent of his discoveries in what was then a little known field of science.

James Nasmyth *(1808-1890)*

He was born in Edinburgh, the youngest son of the eminent landscape artist, Alexander Nasmyth. Being well-to-do he started his own business in Manchester when twenty-six and after twenty years he was able to retire from a prosperous foundry business. During that time he was working on all sorts of ideas connected with the manipulation of iron and steel. He had a rather strange experience in 1842 when on a visit to the large Creuzot steel plant in France. He was seeking a steel-hammer large enough to forge the paddle-wheel shaft of the *Great Britain* steamship then being built. He found the very machine he needed in the French foundry but to his astonishment discovered that it was the steam-hammer he had himself designed and drawn on a scheme-book three years before. On further investigation it was discovered that James Watt had been working on the same lines many years before.

However, Nasmyths' fame does not rest on this rather insecure basis. He improved machine tools, and invented a machine, powered by steam, for shaping nuts, planing, pile-driving, and other uses. Even when retired he amused himself with astronomy and published a book on the moon, with the inspiring title, *The Moon considered as a Planet, a World and a Satellite*.

James Young *(1811-1883)*

He was the son of a Glasgow joiner and took up his father's trade for a time. He attended classes in chemistry etc. at Anderson's College and became assistant to the famous Thomas Graham. In 1837 Young was appointed to University College, London, and two years later became manager of a chemical works near Liverpool. At another works near Manchester he discovered more efficient means of producing stannate of soda and chlorate of potash. His greatest contribution to industry was his method of manufacturing paraffin wax on a large scale.

After experiments with shale and bituminous coal Young found that by slow distillation he could obtain paraffin oil and paraffin wax, both of which were in universal demand, not only for lighting and heating but for many industrial processes. He took out his patent in 1850. The same idea had been tried out in France earlier in the century but Young brought his initiative and perseverance to bear on the development of a great Scottish industry. It was of course located over the large shale deposits of Mid and West Lothian.

By 1862 the distillation plants began production and for over half a century 3,000,000 tons of shale and coal each year were mined and treated. The more easily produced crude oil from oil-wells made the shale industry unprofitable and, although efforts were made, especially during wartime, to continue production from shale, the mines and works were closed during the 1950s.

Enormous trapezia of burnt shale or 'blaes' resembling flat-topped mountains several hundred feet high are the monuments to this inventor. Much of the waste is used for various purposes in building and road-making and it is possible that when the marine hydro-carbons are exhausted Young's invention will come into its own again.

William J.M. Rankine *(1820-1872)*

Born at Edinburgh, he completed his education at Edinburgh University. As an engineer he worked on surveys of railways and harbours. At thirty-five he was appointed to the professorship of civil engineering at Glasgow. He was founder of the science of thermo-dynamics. He published the first book on the subject and presented many papers to the Royal Society on the discoveries and inventions he made in connection with heat-engines and machinery in general. He died at the early age of fifty-two, having collaborated with many British and European scientists to lay a sound basis for modern development.

William Thomson, Lord Kelvin *(1824-1907)*

Although born in Belfast, William Thomson's associations with Glasgow lasted throughout his long life, and though he was known in the peerage as Lord Kelvin of Largs he chose his title from the heart of Glasgow. His father was a teacher of mathematics and his son not only was properly educated in that subject but perhaps inherited a genius for it.

His father, when his son was eight, accepted the Chair of Mathematics in Glasgow University. At seventeen William started a brilliant course at Cambridge. He then studied the properties of steam at Paris, and at the remarkably early age of twenty-two he became Professor of Natural Philosophy in Glasgow, occupying this position for fifty-three years. During this time he was the inspirer of numerous scientific men.

When he was only twenty-seven his work on heat and energy conservation was universally praised, but his work on electricity outshone all else. In connection with the transatlantic cable, he invented several devices including a galvanometer. His articles in *Good Words*, a popular magazine of the times, set out to explain such mysteries as the mariner's compass, which he meantime completely reconstructed on scientific lines.

A man of humble and kindly nature, no one would have guessed the innumerable researches he conducted, or the huge advances in technology that are due to him. Even at the end of his career he was lecturing in England and the USA on such far-seeing topics as the wave-theory of light and the electronic theory of matter.

James Clerk Maxwell *(1831-1879)*

He was born at Edinburgh and educated at Edinburgh Academy. Like Kelvin and Gregory his brilliance showed up early in life. He was Professor of Natural Philosophy at the Marischal College Aberdeen when twenty-five and of Physics and Astronomy in King's College London at twenty-nine, when he resigned and retired to his estate in Kirkcudbrightshire. But an offer of an unusual kind tempted him back to Cambridge to be Professor of Experimental Physics, an innovation.

He died at the tragically early age of forty-eight.

It is on his extraordinary electrical discoveries that his fame as an inventor is based. His great book on *Electricity and Magnetism* was considered the finest single achievement by a scientific genius. In it he demonstrated how to control all electric and magnetic forces, thereby opening the way to a century of human achievement in this field.

Tod and Macgregor *(c.1838)*

After the first salt-water voyages of Henry Bell's ship the *Comet*, Glasgow turned more and more to steamships. These were at first made of timber because there was a strong prejudice against the use of iron in ships, although it was used on a large scale in bridges and railways. Ignorance was the chief obstacle and generally it was thought ridiculous that iron could float. Even eminent sea-faring men were strong in their condemnation of the idea. The shipbuilding firm of Tod and Macgregor on the Clyde decided to put the business to the test and laid down the hulls of two iron steamers, the *Royal Sovereign* and the *Royal George*. When the public, already sceptical, heard the latter name, they were not slow to quote Cowper's well-known poem, *The Loss of the Royal George*, which it will be remembered sank like a stone with all hands when being careened close to the shore in England.

The first iron-hulled ocean-going ships in the world were successfully launched and did good service on the Glasgow and Liverpool trade. They were found to be as light and buoyant as timber ships, as well as cheaper, more durable and rapid. Along with Napier's yard, Tod and Macgregor put Glasgow ahead of the entire world in ship-building for the next generation; from 1846 to 1852 iron ships, steam driven, almost equally divided between paddle and screw, outnumbered wooden ships by seven to one.

Sir James Dewar *(1842-1923)*

He was born at Kincardine-on-Forth. His early ingenuity is shown by an incident of childhood. He was fond of music but meeting with a mishap which stopped him from blowing the flute he practised making violins at which he became efficient. He was educated at Dollar and Edinburgh University where he was a pupil and later an assistant of Lyon Playfair, Professor of Chemistry. He studied at Ghent and was made Professor of Natural Philosophy at Cambridge.

As a member of the explosives committee jointly with Abel he invented cordite. His achievements were recognised in France, Italy and the USA. His activities were numerous in many directions, but he is best known for his work on the liquefaction of gases at very low temperatures and his researches on absolute zero. He invented a machine for producing liquid oxygen in quantity.

In his experiments he made the Dewar flask for the storage of liquid gases. This was commercially exploited as the Thermos flask. His best quality was in his manipulative skills, begun as a boy in making violins.

Alexander Graham Bell *(1847-1922)*

He was born in Edinburgh and educated at the Universities of Edinburgh and London. His health was poor, so with his father, an education lecturer, he went to Canada in 1870. He opened a deaf and dumb school and lectured on vocal physiology at Boston University. In 1876 he exhibited 'an apparatus for conveying sounds by electricity' which with subsequent modification became our modern telephone. He also invented the photo-phone, an instrument for transmitting sound by light. He was interested in mechanical flight. For a time he was President of the National Geographic Society and a member of many scientific societies.

Although Bell is credited with the invention of the telephone, there were several other experimenters working on the problem of speech transmission and there were long law suits as to the real holder of the patent, for some time after Bell filed his patent.

In 1874, two years before his patent was accepted, he had conceived and defined the principle on which successful telephones were to be based. He said, 'If I could make a current of electricity vary in intensity precisely as the air varies in density during the production of sound, I should be able to transmit speech telegraphically.' It is not in doubt that this principle was Bell's great contribution to the success of telephone communication.

Even if others like the Frenchman Bourseul and the German Reis had employed other systems (which had failed to work), Bell's principle, which proved successful, makes him the real inventor of the telephone.

Kirkpatrick MacMillan *(1813-1878)*

After many years of peculiar vehicles, such as the velocipede and the hobby-horse, or dandy-horse, all of which were a craze soon abandoned, the first practical bicycle was made by MacMillan in Dumfriesshire in 1839. He started with a dandy-horse and fitted cranks, driving-rods and pedals, and completed the machine by adding a saddle and handlebars. His prototype also had elaborate arm-rests which the modern bicycles have dispensed with. MacMillan rode the machine for many years without anyone attempting to copy it, with the exception of Gavin Dalzell, who studied MacMillan's invention and constructed another on the same principles with some improvements. As often happens when a man is before his time, MacMillan was prosecuted and fined for 'furious driving'. Nevertheless, these two Dumfriesshire men were the real inventors though that fact was so little publicised that many persons in the next two decades claimed the honour. Then, by the invention of the rotary crank by Pierre Lallement in Paris, bicycles became a commercial proposition.

Sir William Ramsay *(1852-1916)*

He was born in Glasgow and educated there to the age of eighteen. He spent a year at Tubingen University studying chemistry under a celebrated German professor. He returned to Glasgow to become an assistant at the Anderson College, teaching chemistry. At twenty-eight he was appointed professor at Bristol and followed this by becoming Professor of Chemistry at University College, London for twenty-six years. He was awarded a Nobel Prize in 1904.

His researches covered many and various fields; in inorganic and physical chemistry and molecular energy, he was chiefly responsible for the discovery of five rare gases, argon and helium, neon, crypton and xenon. He next studied radio-activity and analysed, with marvellous ingenuity, the substance radium.

He founded the Indian Institute of Science at Bangalore, which was the source of a spread of scientific interest to many other Commonwealth countries.

Sir Dugald Clerk *(1854-1932)*

He was born in Glasgow and educated at the West of Scotland Technical College. At the age of twenty-three he invented the Clerk cycle gas engine and became an authority on internal combustion engines. He was director of engineering research during the First World War and later was on the air inventions committee. He was elected FRS in 1908.

Ernest, Lord Rutherford *(1871-1937)*

Of Scottish extraction, he was born in Nelson, New Zealand, and studied at the University of New Zealand, presumably at Dunedin in South Island, the antipodean Edinburgh, home of many Scots. He came to Britain to do research in physics at Cambridge, then at the age of twenty-seven, became Macdonald Professor of Physics at McGill University, Montreal.

Eight years later he was appointed Professor of Physics at Manchester, after Cambridge the foremost English university in physics. He was simultaneously Professor of Physics at Cambridge and the Royal Institution, London.

As for his inventions and discoveries, they penetrated deeper into the secrets of the awful nature of the universe than any other physicist than perhaps Einstein. Rutherford investigated and confirmed the principles of radio-activity; the structure of matter and the nuclear structure of the atom, thus demolishing for ever the old theories of the physicists.

He was awarded the Nobel Prize for Chemistry in 1908 and was later President of the British Association and the Royal Society.

John Logie Baird *(1888-1946)*

He was born on 13 August 1888, in Helensburgh, the youngest of four children of a clergyman. He attended Larchfield Academy (then the Royal Technical College), and Glasgow University. Before he graduated as an electrical engineer, war broke out and he tried to enlist but was rejected because of bad health. He worked as a supervising engineer in the Clyde Valley Electrical Co. in Glasgow.

He was dismissed because of an experiment which went wrong. In an attempt to make diamonds out of coal dust, both being carbon, he caused a major fuse in the system, blacking out a large part of the city.

He never failed to find some new device, even building an automobile, but his chief interest was in television, even at that early period. He was of course encouraged by the success of the telephone and saw no reason to doubt the transmission of pictures. Meantime he experimented with various projects such as the making of jam and boot-polish, to earn a little money, moving to London to live with his sister.

His health was poor so he went to Hastings to recuperate. Here he worked with all sorts of photographic devices, using scrap materials to build up his inventions. In 1924 he transmitted a Maltese Cross on to a screen and was credited in the newspapers with the invention of television. Nobody believed it. He continued to experiment and was encouraged by a member of the Selfridge family.

On 30 December 1926 he demonstrated an infra-red television. A few days later he organised 2 TV, the first television station. On 24 May 1927 he made a transmission from London to Glasgow, but the big moment came on

27 August 1927 when he sent a picture from London to SS *Berengaria* in mid-Atlantic.

Many improvements have followed but there is no doubt that Baird's persistent work in spite of poverty and bad health added the third of the great inventions made by Scots – steam, telephones, television.

He is commemorated in his native town by the new name of the local primary school – the John Logie Baird School.

Sir Robert Watson Watt *(1892-1973)*

Born at Brechin, Angus, the son of a carpenter, he was nevertheless a direct descendant of James Watt, the inventive giant of the Industrial Revolution. Robert attended Brechin primary and high schools, then studied at Dundee University College, a branch of St Andrews University. Here he took his B.Sc. and at twenty was teaching physics.

In the early days of radio he became interested in the disturbing phenomenon known as interference and resolved to investigate. With the co-operation of hundreds of volunteer listeners he studied the reports of interference with a series of broadcast talks on 'Music and the Ordinary Listener'. These suggested the emergence of a logical pattern of 'Atmospherics'. To study these on a wider geographical basis Watt was allowed to travel on the HMS *Yarmouth* to the Bay of Bengal and to the Levant. The results were exciting so he approached the Government with his new theories.

At that time, the early thirties, the 'Death Ray' was engrossing the authorities and encouraging rumours which Watt firmly squashed. He offered a 'Direction Ray'.

He was appointed Superintendent of the new Radio Division of the National Physics Laboratory at Teddington. His next move was to set up a headquarters in Suffolk and by 1935 with the Nazis obviously preparing for action he had five local radio stations set up. Results proved his theories to be spectacularly accurate. By March 1936 his reporters were spotting approaching aircraft and other vehicles up to seventy-five miles off.

He and his wife went as tourists to Germany to spy on the war preparations in 1937 but could find no trace of radar development. Watt's plan was kept secret, being only revealed to the USA in September 1939 when war was declared by Britain on Germany.

The Battle of Britain in the late summer of 1940 proved the importance of Watt's invention. The 'first of the few' who constituted the British fighter squadrons were forewarned of German raiders who were puzzled at the ubiquity of the Spitfires and other fighters. Although the numbers of German victims were considerably exaggerated at the time, the attempt to master the air over Britain failed and the enemy tried night raids on the industrial centres and later, the centres of population. Once again Watt's system proved its worth.

In 1942 his merits were recognised in a knighthood, yet after the war when monetary rewards were being dispensed for services, the Government made itself contemptuous by an acrimonious resistance to Watt's request for recompense. He was finally given £52,000 for having saved his country from the Nazi threat.

Politics

In this broad category we include politicians, agitators for reform, and writers on politics. The Scots seem to have had a tendency to take on social responsibility despite the risks of failure, so the number of Scots statesmen, or men of affairs, is legion. At any period of history it is easy to name a dozen contenders for political power, usually vying with one another to the death. These were the domestic seekers after power. But there were many Scots who sought diplomatic distinction not only in England but in all the European countries and in the Old and New World. Their reputation had often gone before them and they became the bosom counsellors of prince and potentate.

In dealing with political men, naîveté never pays, honesty seldom, but courage and integrity and a high degree of intelligence are necessary to a modicum of success. These, to make the perfect diplomat, should be allied to presence of mind and the ability to produce the *bon mot*, or to refrain from saying it in certain cases.

Dr William King, one of the best known Tories or Jacobites of the early eighteenth century, having a wide personal friendship with the statesmen of that age, discussing the qualities that distinguish a man of affairs, says, 'Among all my acquaintances I cannot recollect more than three persons who were eminently possessed of this quality (presence of mind), Dr. Atterbury, Bishop of Rochester, the Earl of Stairs, who was our Ambassador in France at the beginning of the last reign, and Dr. James Munro, who was many years physician of Bethlem hospital.' The latter two were Scots.

To illustrate the point, here are two incidents involving the Earl of Stair. To test Stair's breeding, Louis XIV, the Grand Monarch, offered him precedence in entering the royal carriage. Stair made a bow and stepped in. 'A vulgar man,' said Louis, 'would have teased me with hesitations and excuses.'

Stair could be deadly when replying to insolence. He closely resembled the Duke of Orleans. The Duke wished to make an insulting reference to this similarity. He asked Stair, 'Was your mother ever in Paris?' Stair instantly replied 'No, but my father was.'

The English diplomatist Sir Henry Wotton made the punning definition of an ambassador, as true now as in his time (c. 1600). 'An ambassador is an honest man sent to *lie* abroad for the good of his country.' But there are degrees of honesty even in politicians. The Italians, of whom Machiavelli is a consummate example, were perhaps the most cynically unreliable politicians, the French not far behind them. But no nation could lay claim to

157

monopolise honest negotiation. The Scots were credited with a good mixture of shrewdness and audacity when it came to driving a bargain.

William Elphinstone *(1431-1514)*

Born in Glasgow and educated at the University, he was ordained priest and was Rector of St Michael's Church in the Trongate. He studied at Paris for four years and lectured at Orleans in Canon Law. In 1474 he returned to Scotland as Rector of Glasgow University. He became Bishop of Ross and an MP under James III. He was sent to France and England on Diplomatic missions. James IV also employed him to visit the Kings of England and France and the German Maximilian I. His most important Scottish work was the foundation of the University of Aberdeen. The Papal Bull for the founding was obtained in 1494. Through Elphinstone's influence this university became the most famous and popular of the Scottish universities.

As a statesman Elphinstone opposed the policy of hostility to England which culminated in the national disaster of Flodden. He died, partly of grief, like many others, the year following the battle. He was largely responsible for the introduction of printing to Scotland.

William Davison *(1541-1608)*

He was of Scottish descent. He was sent by Queen Elizabeth on a mission to Mary Queen of Scots in 1566. He remained in Scotland for ten years and went twice to Holland on diplomatic missions. He returned to England in 1586 to defend the action of his friend Robert Dudley, Earl of Leicester who had made himself Governor of the Low Countries without Elizabeth's sanction. He became MP for Knaresborough and assistant to Walsingham, the Queen's secretary.

When Mary Queen of Scots fled to England he was appointed a member of the commission set up to try her for treason. But he took no part in the trial and was not present at Westminster when sentence was passed.

The warrant for Mary's execution was entrusted to him and Elizabeth told him that she wished to be absolved of the blame for Mary's death. But Mary's gaolers would not take the hint that Elizabeth would have connived at Mary's escape and consequent assassination so the sentence was at last carried out by an order from the Privy Council headed by Lord Burleigh.

Elizabeth is alleged to have been furious on hearing of her cousin's execution and blamed Davison for having parted with the death warrant, which he had not done. He was put in prison but did not reveal, under trial, that Elizabeth would have preferred Mary to have been secretly done away with. He was acquitted of the serious charge but fined heavily and imprisoned for several years. It is clear that he was made the scapegoat for Elizabeth's disgracefully underhand conduct.

Mary, Queen of Scots *(1542-1587)*

Mary Stewart was the daughter of James Stewart, King James V of Scotland, and of Mary of Lorraine, a princess of the powerful family of Guise. From her birth to her death she was in the very vortex of a whirlpool of high drama in which she played her part with skill, dignity and courage. Her character was partly inherited from the Stewarts, originally a Breton family, who had played a heroic part in Scotland's wars for four centuries; and also from the Guises, an ambitious family from Lorraine who played an equally heroic role in the French wars against their continental rivals. The Stewarts had many virtues besides courage. They had charm, intelligence and good looks. They encouraged the arts and sciences and ruled with as much justice as their rude age permitted. The Guises were not so unscrupulous or as cynical as, for example, the Medicis, but they did not allow sentiment to stand in the way of their schemes.

With this genetic pattern an unwanted female child was born to Mary of Lorraine in Linlithgow Palace in 1542. James V was dying in a nearby room, his life closing on a chapter of military disasters for the Scots. When told of the birth of a daughter he is said to have encompassed the past and the future in a gnomic phrase, 'It cam wi' a lass and it will gang wi' a lass.' These were his last words.

He was referring to the fact that one of his direct ancestors, Walter the Steward, had married Marjory the daughter of Robert I, the Bruce, and by her right had acquired the throne of Scotland, which passed on to their son Robert II. As for the second part of his dying remark, it only expressed a fear which did not materialise. Because, far from losing the Scottish crown, Mary produced a son, James, who inherited the English throne and passed the United Kingdom to his direct successors for two generations, and to his indirect successors to the present day.

Princesses in past ages may have been undesirable options to princes, but they had their uses as bargaining pawns in high diplomacy. Even if of homely appearance they could be matched from infancy to form alliances with powerful states. But if to royal blood was added beauty, wit and charm, so much the better for a political alliance.

Scotland's too-near neighbour was England, ruled since 1509 by the blood-stained ogre Henry VIII. His infant son, later to reign as Edward VI, seemed a fitting bridegroom for Mary Stewart, so the Scots were approached to sanction this infant union. The Regent Arran agreed to the English proposal but the Scots Parliament had every reason to distrust Henry and refused his kind offer, seeing a trick to add Scotland to his domains.

Henry then embarked on what was subsequently named 'The Rough Wooing'. This was a typically English diplomacy, such as had been tried in France unsuccessfully, but successfully in Portugal. It consisted of indiscriminate massacre of the country people, burning of towns and destruction of abbeys and monasteries. A large English fleet disembarked near Edinburgh in 1544, burned the open town of the Canongate and pillaged and massacred far and wide.

The innocent cause of all this violence was safely removed from the coast and border, and grew up with her four Maries in various sanctuaries until she could be safely conveyed to France where she was betrothed to the Dauphin or heir apparent, Francis, thus strengthening the Auld Alliance between the two enemies of England. For ten years until her marriage Mary was under

159

the care of the Guises. In April 1558 she was married, and on Elizabeth's accession to the English throne in November of that year, Mary claimed that she was the rightful heiress, on the grounds that, in the eyes of the Catholic world, Elizabeth was a bastard. In France Mary changed the spelling of her name to Marie Stuart, as the letter 'w' was alien to French grammar.

Henry II, her father-in-law, ordered her and Francis to assume the arms of England in all their heraldry and plate, to proclaim to Europe their right to the English throne. But death was to play an unexpected part. Mary lost her mother Mary of Lorraine, her father-in-law Henry II, and her husband Francis II all within a year. She was now a widow of nineteen, no longer Queen of France, only a claimant to the throne of England, but entitled to be Queen of the Scots. Accordingly she set sail for her kingdom and arrived safely at Leith on a foggy August day in 1561 to be accosted, rather than greeted, by the austere Protestant leader, John Knox, who had called in the English armies of Protestant Elizabeth to drive out the French Catholic troops and establish a Protestant state.

Mary's diplomacy was much needed in face of such a situation. In short she had to pretend co-operation when she was bitterly opposed to the new regime which should by law have had her royal consent, but which she refused to acknowledge in retrospect. Though scarcely out of her teens she conducted her affairs with tact and courage and also with a cunning that would have earned the respect of her mother-in-law Catherine de Medici, to whom lies, deceit, and assassination were the breath of life.

A Catholic rebellion, which Mary might have been thought to support, broke out in the Highlands, led by the Earl of Huntly and the Gordons. Mary had to choose between her loyalty to her religion and her loyalty to the state. She chose the latter and the rebels were firmly punished by her bastard half-brother the Earl of Murray.

Mary was now being urged to marry again, and every suitor for her valuable hand had at least several supporters. Elizabeth had been privately advised by her surgeon that marriage, with the dangers of childbirth, would kill her, but she could not make this public and kept flirting all her life with hopeful lovers, with no hope of a succession. Nevertheless, like a dog in the manger, she could not endure the thought of Mary's offspring occupying the English throne and was very angry when Mary married her cousin Henry Darnley who had an inherited right himself to the English crown, being descended from a sister of Henry VIII.

Mary's marriage, by Catholic rites, started a religious war in Scotland, the Protestants being led by the Earl of Murray. But Mary was supported by the Earl of Bothwell and a force of Borderers, so Murray had to flee for safety to England where Elizabeth received him with hearty curses, for she was an accomplished swearer.

Mary was soon in trouble. Darnley tried to assume the crown because of his matrimonial descent and Mary strongly objected. She was backed by her favourite, the Italian David Rizzio, so Darnley schemed to get rid of his rival and induced a gang of desperadoes to murder Rizzio in Holyroodhouse, not far from the Queen's presence. Mary of course suspected her husband but

Sir Charles Napier (p.40)

(Portrait by John Simpson, National Galleries of Scotland, Edinburgh)

Andrew Duncan (p.88)

(Portrait by David Martin, National Galleries of Scotland, Edinburgh)

David Livingstone (p.100)

(Photo: Thomas Annan 1864)

Seton Gordon (p.136)
(Photo: Tom Weir)

Alexander Graham Bell (p.153)

(Photo: BBC Hulton Picture Library)

John Logie Baird (p.155)
(Photo: The Associated Press Ltd)

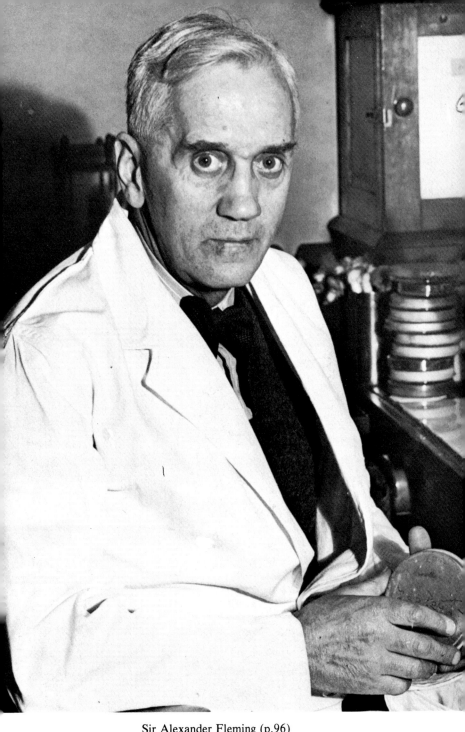

Sir Alexander Fleming (p.96)

(Photo: Popperfoto)

James Ramsay Macdonald (p.183)

(Portrait by Ambrose McEvoy, National Galleries of Scotland, Edinburgh)

Calum I. MacLean (p.216)

(Photo: by kind permission Mary MacLean)

Christopher Murray Grieve (Hugh MacDiarmid) (p.233)

(Photo: Gordon Wright)

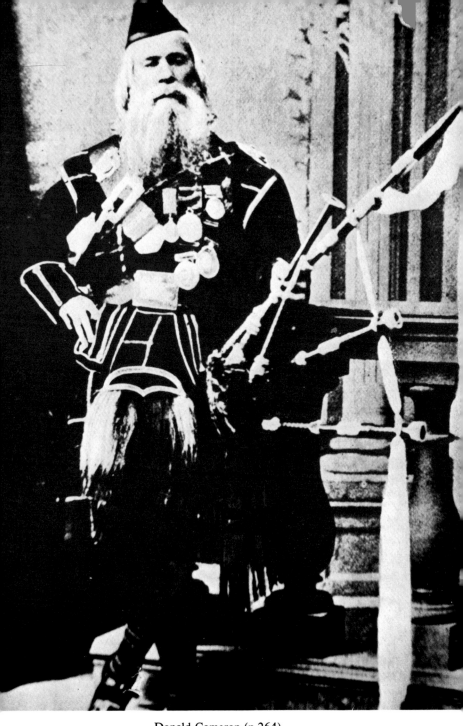

Donald Cameron (p.264)

(Photo: by kind permission Cpt. J.A. MacLellan)

Charles Rennie Macintosh (p.288)
(Photo: by kind permission The Royal Incorporation of Architects in Scotland)

Eric Henry Liddell (p.306)
(Photo: Glasgow Herald/Evening Times)

David Niven (p.296)
(Photo: Cornel Lucas)

Tom Morris (p.300)

(Portrait by Sir George Reid, by kind permission of the Royal and Ancient Golf Club of St Andrews)

Andrew Carnegie (p.320)
(Photo: Scotsman Publications Ltd)

though she kept silent she did not forget.

She had now turned for support to Bothwell, a bold warrior. On 19 June 1566, her son James was born and all seemed well for the marriage, but Darnley refused to attend the baptism and in other ways offended Mary by his behaviour.

He did not realise that Mary had the resolution of the Guises in her blood, and had looked unperturbed on the barbarous executions of hundreds of rebels when she was a young Queen of France. Darnley was lulled into a feeling of security and visited by the Queen in a house outside the city walls of Edinburgh, named Kirk o' Field. Later the same night a tremendous roar woke the city. Kirk o' Field had been blown to pieces by gunpowder but Darnley's and a page's bodies were found strangled in an adjacent garden; he and the boy had escaped the blast but been murdered by the assassins.

The scandal was widespread, but all were afraid to name Bothwell as the murderer. It was only when Mary married Bothwell three months later that the nation rose in protest at her conduct. A month after the Queen's marriage her army confronted the citizens at Carberry Hill, east of Edinburgh, and Mary was forced to give herself up, to be imprisoned in Loch Leven Castle, thought to be impossible to escape from. But after eleven months, with the help of a page, she escaped and raised an army of supporters. At Langside near Glasgow her army was defeated by a force under her half-brother Murray, and Mary fled south, crossing to England to seek protection from her cousin Elizabeth. Her interrupted reign had lasted seven years. She was now twenty-six, had been married three times, and had been forced to renounce the crown in favour of her infant son.

The next nineteen years of her tragic life is a long repetition of imprisonments and removals to fresh prisons, of conspiracies raised by gallant young men to rescue her, of secret messages passed to Catholic monarchs to invade England and place her on the throne of Elizabeth. Even accusations were laid against Mary of plotting Elizabeth's destruction. In the end the Babington Plot came so near success that Mary was removed to Fotheringay Castle, and the court of the Star Chamber met to try her in her absence.

On 1 February 1587 Elizabeth signed the death-warrant and a week later Mary was beheaded, betraying no sign of weakness nor of repentance. In her own mind she was a martyr for her religion and denied any plot against the life of Elizabeth. But she sent letters to Philip of Spain and to other Catholic monarchs to avenge her death. The Spanish Armada the following year showed all too clearly that Philip intended to conquer England and treat Elizabeth in as heartless a manner as she had treated Mary. But this threat came to nothing and even Mary's son James made no move to avenge his mother's death, as he anxiously awaited his invitation to take over the English throne. Elizabeth never gave that invitation. It came from the statesmen of England after her death in 1603.

It was Mary's misfortune to be born in an age of religious bigotry and to have been endowed with a passionate nature and a magnetic personality. Even as a young queen she outshone all the beauties of the court of France and earned the hatred of Queen Catherine de Medici by throwing her into comparative obscurity. The French poet, Ronsard, wrote of her at the peak of her career:

> Even as we see, snow blent with blushing red,
> Vesper-Aurora born as night is sped,
> So, far surpassing radiant beauties known,
> Blazes the Scottish princess from her throne.

James Elphinstone, Lord Balmerino *(1553-1612)*

He rose to power under James VI and accompanied him to London in 1603. He was made President of the Court of Session. In 1609 his earlier sins found him out. Through the evidence of an Italian cardinal he was proved to have sent a letter to the Pope in 1600 which had annoyed Elizabeth but which he had denied writing. James had him tried, attainted for treason and sentenced to death, but after a short term in the Tower he was released.

John Elphinstone, 2nd Lord Balmerino *(1590-1649)*

He published a petition offensive to Charles I and was also condemned to death. But popular protest rescued him. The poet Drummond of Hawthornden and others pleaded for him and he was pardoned. He was President of the Scots Parliament and a Lord of Session at the start of the Civil War. He died in the year of Charles I's execution.

George Mackenzie, Earl of Cromarty *(1630-1714)*

He rose on behalf of Charles II in the Glencairn Rebellion of 1654 and was forced into exile until Charles was restored in 1660. Then he was raised to the bench with the title of Lord Tarbet. He was opposed to the Duke of Lauderdale so was not appointed Lord Justice General until Lauderdale fell from favour in 1678. He was chief minister in Scotland for ten years and even when the Revolution came he held high office for over twenty years.

His grandson, George, rose with the Mackenzies in 1745 and forfeited his peerage. His son, Lord MacLeod, also supported Prince Charles and was pardoned only on giving up his title and estates. He went to Sweden and served in the army for thirty years. When he returned to Scotland he raised the Mackenzies to form what afterwards became the Highland Light Infantry (HLI). His estates were restored probably on that account.

Sir John Campbell, Earl of Breadalbane *(1635-1717)*

A supporter of the Stuarts, he raised a force in Glencairn's Rebellion against Cromwell in 1654. He urged Monk, after Cromwell's death, to restore Charles II. He sat in the Scots Parliament for several years. In 1678 he married the widow of the Earl of Caithness and with a mixed force of Campbells and Macgregors, the latter led by Rob Roy's older brother, he took over the Caithness estate after a battle in 1680. He became, after his relative Argyll, the most powerful man in Scotland, so when William III began his reign he tried to gain Breadalbane's support. Breadalbane now played a double game. After plotting to restore the Stuarts he sided with William and after the death of Claverhouse at Killiecrankie he was given the task of pacifying the Highland chiefs. All agreed to the terms except MacIan of Glencoe who was prevented from signing on a technicality. Argyll, Sir John Dalrymple (Lord Stair) and Breadalbane organised by treachery the massacre of the MacIans. By astuteness he managed to escape the consequences. He did not vote for the Union in 1707 yet was elected to the House of Lords in 1713.

Andrew Fletcher *(1655-1715)*

He was born at Saltoun, East Lothian, son and heir of Sir Robert Fletcher. A member of the Scottish Parliament which met in 1681, he was a fearless opponent of Lauderdale's repression of the Covenanters.

He went to Holland in 1682 and returned to England to assist in Monmouth's abortive rebellion but he left the army after killing one of Monmouth's advisers.

Not daring to return to Britain he travelled for years in Europe, engaging in wars against the Turks. When William of Orange took the throne of Britain, Fletcher had his estates restored to him but he became an ardent enemy of the English Government.

Angered by the failure of the Darien Scheme he did his best to secure civil and religious liberty for Scotland and was instrumental in passing the Act of Security which declared that Scotland and England could not have the same monarch until they were recognised as equal kingdoms.

After the Union of Parliaments he retired to his estates. His famous saying has often been misquoted. The true version is, 'I knew a very wise man... who believed that if a man were permitted to make all the ballads, he need not care who should make the laws of a nation.'

John Hamilton, Lord Belhaven *(1656-1708)*

He was the eldest son of Lord Pressmennan, born in East Lothian. In 1681 he was imprisoned for his opposition to the government of Charles II and for his contemptuous reference to the Duke of York (later James II). An anti-Jacobite, he asked William III in 1689 to take over the government in Scotland. He fought with Mackay at Killiecrankie, but escaped the slaughter. He was a member of the Privy Council of Scotland and a director of the Scottish Trading Company, which organised the Darien Scheme. The opposition which this scheme was met with in England, as well as from the Spanish and the Dutch, made Belhaven a bitter opponent of Union with England in the reign of Queen Anne.

In November 1706 he delivered a powerful anti-union speech which was later printed by Daniel Defoe in his *History of the Union*. In the corrupt Parliament in Edinburgh his speech was received to some extent with ridicule and opposition. On a pretext that he favoured a French invasion he was imprisoned and died in London shortly after.

William Paterson *(1658-1719)*

He was born at Tinwald, Dumfriesshire, at a period when religious persecution was about to envelop the South-West of Scotland. To avoid this he emigrated south, living first in Bristol. From there he went to the Bahamas where his activities are still a mystery. He was accused of piracy by some, praised as a missionary by others. He had already formed the idea of a Darien Scheme in Central America, but on return to England he could not persuade James II to engage in the scheme. He was no more successful in Amsterdam, Hamburg or Berlin, so he returned to Britain and amassed a fortune in business.

In 1694, when William III had superseded James II, Paterson, now a respected merchant, founded the Bank of England. It was based on the old Act, the Tonnage Act, but the new idea was Paterson's. The Bank was an immediate success for it supplied the Government with money and the investors with a good rate of interest. But Paterson fell out with his colleagues and resigned, to propose another bank, the Orphan's Bank, which failed owing to the jealousy of the subscribers to the Bank of England.

Paterson returned to Scotland to put his Darien Scheme into effect. This, put simply, was to establish a settlement on the Isthmus of Darien which would hold the key to a great international centre, a seaport and commercial centre for the world. Within three years the first expedition sailed to found the settlement. Paterson and his wife and child went with it. The tale of disaster is too well known. His wife and child died and Paterson nearly succumbed to disease. The opposition of the English, Dutch and Spaniards caused the settlement to be abandoned and the survivors returned to Scotland.

Paterson, undefeated, tried to persuade the King to start a new Darien Scheme but with no success. He busied himself to promote a Union of Parliaments and was actually elected as the Member for Dumfries. The Union of Parliaments indemnified those who had suffered in the Darien Scheme, and Paterson, after long delay, was awarded £18,000 for his losses.

He wrote many books on his studies of banking and on colonisation, all anonymous, but stamped with his enthusiasm and originality. His idea to include the English and Dutch in the Darien Scheme was opposed by his colleagues, otherwise it would have succeeded. He advocated Free Trade long before Adam Smith.

Simon Fraser, Lord Lovat *(1667-1746)*

Though he was more of an intriguer than a statesman, he ought to be noted, if only as a complete contrast to Duncan Forbes, a contemporary Scottish Highlander.

He was the third son of the 8th Lord Lovat and was educated at King's College Aberdeen. On leaving college he raised 300 Frasers to support William and Mary against the Jacobites.

The 10th Lord Lovat, a kinsman, having died early, Simon decided to secure that part of the Lovat estates by marrying his widow. She proving unwilling, he raped her and forcibly married her. This was only one of his notorious personal crimes. His unwilling consort's family went to law but Simon fled to France to the court of the Old Pretender against whom he had previously fought.

His plan to bring back the Stuarts was to enlist the aid of France by arranging a pincer movement, leading a French army simultaneously on the East and West coasts of the Highlands. But he was never trustworthy. When he went to find out the strength of the other Highland chiefs he revealed their confidential reports to the English government.

His intrigues were discovered in another plot and he was jailed in France for ten years, making his escape in 1714. He spent the next quarter-century in law-suits to recover his estates, and between appearances at court he intrigued both for and against the Jacobites.

In 1745 he assured Forbes of Culloden that he was strongly attached to the Hanoverians and when asked to explain why his son was leading a force of Frasers to support Prince Charles, he expressed his regret at the youth's rebellious behaviour. The truth was that he had forced the unwilling lad to go.

After Culloden he wandered about the Highlands and was at last arrested in a hide-out in Loch Morar. He was carried to London in a litter, being very crippled, and after a five-day trial, sentenced to death, though it could be argued that he did more harm to the Jacobites than to the Hanoverians. He was beheaded on Tower Hill along with more worthy men.

His son distinguished himself in the Seven Years' War and in the War of American Independence. He rose to be a British Major-General. As a reward he got back the forfeited Lovat estates.

John Law *(1671-1729)*

He was born in Edinburgh, son of a goldsmith. He studied mathematics, commerce and political economy in London. He killed an opponent in a duel, probably a fellow-Scot named Edward Wilson, and to escape the law, fled to Amsterdam. Here he studied banking-practice and in 1705 evolved a scheme for a national bank for Scotland. William Paterson caused it to be rejected, so Law applied to several European states but with similar results.

France had been reduced to bankruptcy by the ambitious wars of Louis XIV so the government of Louis XV clutched at Law's schemes. In 1716 he was given sanction to establish a National Bank of France. The capital was six million French pounds (livres) and the success was phenomenal. The issue of bonds rose to sixty million livres, the interest being a steady 4½%.

Law now extended his enterprise to Louisiana, the French province of Mississippi, Missouri and Ohio basins. Law's success here aroused jealousy in Paris and a rival company was formed. But he carried on and was appointed Director of the Royal Bank of France, backed by the King. He went further and set up an East Indian and Chinese company.

The British ambassador, Lord Stair, was worried and foresaw that his fellow-countryman's banking genius would ruin England's overseas trade. Law's ambition had now reached the point of his being put in charge of the Mint and of the managing of the finance of France.

Speculation became frantic and, as with the South Sea Bubble in England in the same period, the reaction set in when the public lost confidence. A panic ensued, Law was removed from office and his numerous enemies demolished his elaborate system.

Law was a very aristocratic man and defied all opposition. He had unbounded courage and even when his schemes to bring France to prosperity out of misery were frustrated, he turned on the mob who pursued him and called them 'Guttersnipes' to their faces, daunting them by his Scottish pride.

He wandered about Europe for several years after his disappointment and died at Venice, a financial genius, ruined by spite.

John Dalrymple, 2nd Lord Stair *(1673-1747)*

Second son of the Earl of Stair who was responsible for the Massacre of Glencoe, he was educated at Leyden and Edinburgh. As a youth he accidentally shot his elder brother some time previous to his father's heinous political act. When barely twenty he served as a volunteer under the Earl of Angus and was aide-de-camp to the Duke of Marlborough in the campaign of 1702. He commanded the Cameronian Regiment, formed of extreme Covenanters, and also the Scots Greys. A courageous soldier, he won distinction at the Battle of Malplaquet and Ramilies. His elder brother being dead, he became the Earl of Stair in 1707 on his father's rather early death.

He was now sent as British Ambassador to Paris to deal with Louis XIV, grown petulant in his old age. Here he forced Louis to keep the terms of the Treaty of Utrecht, against his will. He also supported the claims of the Duke of Orleans to be Regent of France. The Old Chevalier, who called himself James III of England, was in the French Court, so Stair had to find out what he was up to, and pass the information to the Hanoverian Government in London. Through his secret agents he got to know all the Jacobite plans and, had the British Government been active, he could have stopped the three rebellions of 1715, 1719 and 1745 without the loss of blood. Stair also compelled the Duke of Orleans to stop sheltering the Old Pretender and using his presence as a weapon against Britain.

The French did not like Stair's style of diplomacy, which was not subtle like theirs or the Italians. He told them bluntly what his terms were, never wavering in the face of strength, nor blustering before weakness.

In the introduction to this chapter we gave two anecdotes to show the character of this Scot. He was, of course, hated in certain areas of Scotland because of his father's crime, but he did a good service without treachery when a statesman.

Duncan Forbes *(1685-1747)*

Born at Culloden House near Inverness, he was educated for the law at Edinburgh and Leyden. At twenty-four he was advocate and sheriff of Midlothian. He was not Jacobite but supported the Hanoverians when George I came to power in 1715. Due to the Earl of Argyll's influence, Forbes rose rapidly. He was MP for Inverness when thirty-seven, Lord Advocate at forty and Lord President of the Court in 1737.

About this time he pleaded with the British Government to deal reasonably with the situation in the Highlands and to direct the warlike propensities of the clansmen into regular regiments, supplying them with equipment and arms and putting them under their own chiefs. But the English were afraid that the Celts would conquer England given these advantages. Nevertheless through Forbes' influence the original Black Watch (raised in kilts of dark green and blue tartan, hence the name), was expanded in the famous 42nd Highlanders who fought on the continent at Fontenoy and other battles.

When the Prince landed in 1745 Forbes hastened to Inverness and persuaded the chiefs of the MacDonalds and the Mackenzies to hold back their men from rising. As Lord Advocate, Forbes had the responsibility for keeping Scotland under law but he was given little encouragement from London. He spent much of his own money on supplies and arms and was never repaid.

After the inhuman cruelties following Culloden he exerted himself to the utmost to stop the ravaging of Scotland by the Hanoverians. Not only did his pleas go unheeded; they were the means of getting him into bad odour with London. His house at Culloden had been sacked by the Hanoverian troops, he had suffered financial loss and had fallen out of favour. These were his rewards for trying to save his country from the evils of a civil war. He was a man of great learning and high principles but he was opposed by the English establishment which was totally oblivious to either learning or Christian ethics. He died soon after Culloden. His statue by the famous French sculptor Roubilac stands in Parliament House, Edinburgh.

Arthur Elphinstone, 6th Lord Balmerino *(1688-1746)*

He was a captain in Shannon's Regiment of Foot and rebelled in 1715, joining the Old Pretender after the Battle of Sheriffmuir. He exiled himself in Europe but returned when his father secured a pardon for him. But he was among the first to join Prince Charles in 1745. He marched to Derby, fought at Falkirk and was captured at Culloden. But the days of clemency were over, as he found. Where his ancestors had been forgiven after sentence, Arthur was found guilty of treason and beheaded on Tower Hill on 11 August 1746. He behaved at his trial and execution with great presence of mind and courage. The line of Balmerino ended with him.

Adam Anderson *(1692-1765)*

His claim to fame is perhaps best founded on his account of the commercial interests of the British Empire. It was one of the earliest attempts to make a science of economics. Adam Smith consulted Anderson's book when writing the *Wealth of Nations*.

Robert Dinwiddie *(1693-1770)*

Born near Glasgow, for eleven years he was a customs clerk in Bermuda where he unveiled the corruption of the West Indian customs service. As a recognition of his integrity and with a view to preventing corruption in other ports he was promoted Surveyor-General of the 'southern ports of North America.' From 1751 to 1758 he was Lieutenant-General of Virginia where he carried out his duties so energetically and insisted so scrupulously on the payment of fees that he aroused the antipathy of the Virginians. At that time the French had a large hold on North America and were planning a rear-guard manoeuvre west of the Appalachians to unite their territory in Upper Canada with Louisiana by way of the Ohio valley. This would have cut off the western movement of the New Englanders and thrown open the prairies to French colonisation.

Dinwiddie perceived this danger and sent out messengers to ascertain the progress of the line of forts being built from the Lakes to the Gulf of Mexico. Washington was at this time a colonial soldier in the British service. Dinwiddie sent him to Fort Le Boeuf in 1753 as a commissioned officer with the rank of major, to negotiate with the French commander. There were only seven in the party, an interpreter, a scout, two servants and two traders. In a severe winter they reached Fort Le Boeuf, now Waterford, South of Lake Erie and were told bluntly by the French that nothing would stop their plan to take the Ohio.

After a perilous return, nearly killed by hostile Indians, Washington reached Williamsburg, Virginia, and delivered his message to Dinwiddie. Washington was appointed Lieutenant-Colonel of a provincial regiment under Colonel Fry and with 700 men set off to meet the French. Dinwiddie's war had started.

From a weak fort at Great Meadows Washington attacked a French force who brought a large party against him. He had to surrender but with his men was allowed to return home disarmed. Despite this reversal Dinwiddie made him a colonel and he was mentioned in the *London Gazette*.

Dinwiddie's warnings were heeded in Britain and two regiments of regular troops were sent to oust the French, with the aid of American colonial troops. All this cost money and Dinwiddie tried to raise funds from the colonists for military operations, but they obstinately refused so he urged the British government to pass an act to compel them to pay a tax. As this question finally precipitated the War of Independence over twenty years later, it may be said that Dinwiddie's integrity in money matters was a secondary cause of the American Revolution.

William Boyd, Earl of Kilmarnock *(1704-1746)*

He was son of William Boyd, a supporter of the Union of Parliaments 1707. When thirteen he succeeded to an estate heavily in debt and by riotous living got deeper into debt. He was at first neutral when the Rebellion of 1745 started, but after the Prince's victory at Prestonpans he joined the Royal Standard and was gladly received, made a general and a member of the Privy Council. He accompanied the Highland army to Derby and in their retreat and victory at Falkirk.

He was captured at Culloden and taken to London charged with treason and rebellion. He pleaded guilty along with Lords Cromarty and Balmerino but put forward a plea for mercy, on account of the many political services rendered by the Earls of Kilmarnock in the past. These petitions had no effect and with his fellow noblemen he was executed on Tower Hill at the age of forty-two.

John Stuart, Earl of Bute *(1713-1792)*

He was son of the second Earl of Bute and Lady Jane Campbell, daughter of the Duke of Argyll. Educated at Eton, he succeeded to the title at ten, on his father's death. He was elected a Scottish peer when twenty-four but kept out of politics, preferring to study agriculture and botany in the Isle of Bute. He had no political ambition; this was inspired by the merest accident.

He had lived in Edinburgh during the 1745 rising, and in 1747 he was present at the Egham races during a downpour of rain. He was invited to make a fourth at whist in the tent of Frederick the Prince of Wales. The Prince and Princess took a liking to him, and he was made a Lord of the Bedchamber. Frederick died in 1751 but Bute stayed on in the Royal Household, despite scandalous allegations regarding his association with Frederick's widow, never proved. Bute became the companion and guide of the young prince.

When George III acceded in 1760 Bute enjoyed his full confidence. The King proceeded to use Bute as his instrument in destroying the Whigs, in concluding a peace with France, and in making himself supreme over both Parliament and politicians.

A year later the King's schemes came to fruition and Bute was made Prime Minister. The post was highly unpopular because of Bute's nationality as well as because of his being a favourite of the court. The resignation of William Pitt roused the mobs to violence. Bute had to go about the streets with a bodyguard of prize fighters. His carriage was wrecked, he was cold-shouldered by society, but he remained faithful to the King. He secretly arranged a peace with France in 1763. He carried out a campaign of vengeance on the Whigs. He made a foolish mistake, however. He put a tax on cider. Shortly afterwards he resigned, his health undermined by the campaign of slander against him.

He spoke against the Government on the American question but he was not listened to, and the War of American Independence broke out with disastrous results for all concerned. He is probably the most unjustly maligned of all England's Prime Ministers, largely because he was a Scot, loyal to the King.

John Witherspoon *(1723-1794)*

He was born at Gifford, East Lothian and educated at Haddington Grammar School and at Edinburgh University where he studied theology. He was minister at Beith and later at Paisley. He was a popular preacher and was invited to minister in Dundee, Dublin and Rotterdam. The Scots Kirk had long been established in Holland. Witherspoon's sympathies were in America so he went to Princetown as president of the college, where he was more distinguished as a statesman than as a preacher. During the War of Independence he was a prominent member of Congress and the only clergyman to sign the Declaration of Independence. He died on his farm near Princetown, respected by the new nation.

Sir Robert Murray Keith *(1730-1795)*

He was the eldest son of the diplomatist of the same name who was a friend of the Empress Catherine of Russia. He was educated at Edinburgh High School and entered the army as a young cornet. At seventeen he was a captain in a Scots infantry regiment raised for service in Holland. He was commander of a Highland battalion which distinguished itself in the Seven Years War in Germany.

His statesmanship was manifested when he was made ambassador at Copenhagen in 1771. In that year the notorious Struensee had intrigued with the Queen Caroline Matilda, sister of George III and her weak husband, Christian. Struensee became so overbearing that the nobles and populace joined in overthrowing and executing him. The queen was about to share his fate, because of her association with him, when Robert Keith took it upon himself to tell the leaders of the rebellion that any injury to Caroline would bring on an immediate war with Britain. The queen was saved and later returned home. Keith's intervention was rewarded by a parcel which contained the Knight Commander Order of the Bath. No reason was given for its award but it represented George III's gratitude.

He was later made Ambassador at Vienna and a Privy Councillor.

Henry Dundas, Viscount Melville *(1742-1811)*

He was son of Robert Dundas, Lord President, born in Bishop's Close, High Street, Edinburgh. He studied law at Edinburgh and passed advocate when twenty-one. His political career was steady. He was Solicitor-General, then Lord Advocate, Treasurer of the Navy, Home Secretary, Secretary-at-War in succession. He was tried for misappropriation of Navy funds in the House of Lords in 1806, but not found guilty, carelessness rather than peculation being the general opinion. But he did not hold further appointments.

During the latter part of his political career he practically held all the Scottish votes in his pocket owing to his method of rewarding voters by placing their relatives in lucrative posts, particularly in India. In his favour it could be said that he remained a staunch Scots patriot and was often heard to express his dislike of English ways. He spoke with a broad accent and did not hide his political likes and dislikes.

In his domestic life he was unhappy, partly his own fault for spending too much time in social and parliamentary company, to the neglect of his young wife, who had brought him the title of Lord Melville and a large fortune. She left him and her family and ran off with Captain Faukener when she was twenty-eight. She was condemned by society, of course, such being the position of women at that time. But she lived to be ninety-eight, in Cornwall, and was completely forgotten and probably glad to be.

Sir John Sinclair *(1754-1835)*

Born at Thurso Castle, Caithness, he was educated at home by Logan, the minor poet, and at Edinburgh and Glasgow Universities. He became a lawyer at Lincoln's Inn and attended Oxford. He was MP for Caithness.

His idea for a statistical account for Scotland was perhaps his greatest claim to fame, but he was a voluminous writer on all subjects contributing to the benefit of Scotland in literature, agriculture, finance, military and naval science. He is credited with as many books as there are days in the year.

He gave Pitt, the Premier, advice in 1797 which enabled him to raise £18 million to carry on the war with France and his idea of Exchequer Bonds had previously prevented widespread ruin in Britain. He was responsible for the construction of roads and bridges in Northern Scotland where communications had been almost non-existent. His services to scientific agriculture were extremely valuable. He was, in fact, the ideal of a practical statesman. He even had a scheme for introducing nightingales to Caithness by hatching nightingales' eggs in the nests of local birds, but the young songsters migrated for good, preferring the warm South.

Lachlan Macquarie *(1761-1824)*

Born at Gruline, Isle of Mull, he entered the army at an early age and saw service in many campaigns, rising to be commanding officer of the 73rd Highlanders.

The penal settlement of Botany Bay, New South Wales, had been founded in 1788, when Australia was known at only a few places on the coast and was described in Britain as 'a sterile dumping-ground for convicts.'

After twenty-two years of settlement Botany Bay was a very unattractive area. Six thousand people lived in Sydney and the few settlements along the coast were occupied by groups of free pioneers who used the convicts as slave labour. Most of the coastal strip was a wilderness of gum trees. The whole colony was already in a state of decay and poverty.

Knowing this, the British Government chose Macquarie as a man of proved resolution, and backed him up with a regiment of his own Highland countrymen. He had no trouble with the convicts, his chief worry was with a group of freemen, known as the Exclusives, who sought to monopolise the resources of the settlement regardless of human misery.

Macquarie was a level-headed humanitarian and saw that the future of the new country lay in the hands of the thousands of convicted men and women who, after their term of transportation, had not the means to return to Britain and were compelled to make a new life down under. They should be treated as worthy citizens, and given a corresponding opportunity, stated Macquarie.

This doctrine annoyed the Exclusives who had much influence in London and registered their complaints there. But Macquarie carried on with his task and set about making laws to bring order out of chaos. Schools, banks, churches, roads and markets were superimposed on the area.

The British Colonial Office approved but as usual were niggardly and demanded that the new building should be paid for by New South Wales.

Outlawed convicts were robbing and murdering settlers so Macquarie gave them a chance to surrender to justice. As this offer was treated with contempt he sent the 73rd into the bush. They rounded up a number of ruffians and strung them up on the nearest gum-trees.

Perhaps this was the origin of the phrase, 'up a gum-tree'. At any rate peace was restored.

By 1813 the coastal strip had the nucleus of several towns of such Highland names as Argyll, Glencoe and Gordon. The Blue Mountain Range was now penetrated by explorers and the vast plains were open for ranchers.

The spite of the Exclusives finally drove Macquarie away from the land he loved for they procured a Committee of Investigation which gave a biased judgement on conditions. Though granted a pension when he returned to Britain he was refused recognition and a title. He died of disappointment but his gravestone in his native Mull claimed what all the world has since admitted, that he was the 'Father of Australia'.

Joseph Hume *(1777-1855)*

Son of the captain of a coastal trader at Montrose, he was educated locally and undertook a medical course at Edinburgh. He returned to Montrose as an apprentice surgeon. He was assistant surgeon in the East India Company and fought in the Mahratta war of 1803. He took up civil employment and retired with a fortune in 1808. He now could afford to travel in Europe, and translated Dante's *Inferno* in 1812. This shows his considerable ability in languages for a number of famous writers including Thomas Carlyle also published translations of the *Inferno*. Hume was MP for many seats for over fifty years.

He encouraged educational reform, savings banks, economy in national spending. He was a prominent Radical and fought the old Combination Laws aimed (on behalf of employers) at workmen's unions. He also protested in the Commons against flogging in the army, the press gangs for naval recruiting, and imprisonment for debt. He was very influential in promoting lighthouses and new harbours.

Henry Peter Brougham, Baron *(1778-1868)*

Born in Edinburgh and educated at the High School and University, he published two papers on light when still a student and became a Fellow of the Royal Society when twenty-five.

He took law as a profession but, after playing a few tricks on the sedate and pretentious Lord Eskgrove, he found the Scottish courts too dull and affording too little scope for ambition.

In 1808 he was called to the English bar. His brilliant literary work in the *Edinburgh Review* brought him to the notice of leading Whig politicians. His wit and gaiety made him popular in London.

He was an advocate of the abolition of the slave trade. He was always ready to act on behalf of clients accused by the Government and he successfully defended the essayist and poet Leigh Hunt and his brother on the charge of provoking a French invasion in 1811. This trial established Brougham's reputation.

He was notorious for his indiscretion in attacking his opponents and he did not hide his feelings when he felt he had been unjustly treated by his own party, the Whigs.

172

Queen Caroline, (at that time still Princess of Wales) had begun to seek his advice in her private affairs and in 1820 she appointed him Attorney-General. When a bill to depose her was brought before the House Brougham conducted her defence, helped by others. His winding-up speech had a terrific effect, and the Queen, although the bill was carried, came off triumphant, causing a nation-wide illumination in her honour. He refused the £4000 offered by the Queen, taking only the normal fee. But his income was great because of his extensive practice.

He was responsible for helping to set up the University of London, where entry, unlike Oxford and Cambridge, was free of all religious restrictions. He also helped to produce cheap popular books and magazines for the public.

He was offered the post of Lord Chancellor which he accepted along with the peerage.

The Reform Bill of 1832 owed much to Brougham. He now became a power on his own and took upon himself an unwarranted authority. Even King William IV became alarmed at Brougham's arrogance, and the Whigs fell from power. After this he became estranged from all his associates.

He lived to be ninety and his great distinctions and services were recognised and rewarded by Queen Victoria in 1860, especially in the abolition of slavery. He had been one of the most powerful orators of his age. His name was long perpetuated in the *brougham*, a one-horse closed carriage, with two or four wheels, to hold up to four passengers.

Mount Stuart Elphinstone *(1779-1859)*

He was fourth son of Baron Elphinstone. At seventeen he entered the East India Company's service at Calcutta. He was appointed to Poona, as assistant to the British resident and accompanied Sir Arthur Wellesley on a diplomatic mission to the powerful Mahratta Princes. War broke out in 1803 and Elphinstone acted as aide to Wellesley, being present at the battle of Assaye.

In 1808 he was sent as first British envoy to Kabul to make an alliance with the Afghans. This came to nothing for the Shah's brother took over and refused to ratify the terms. Elphinstone was given a more difficult task, to reside at Poona and deal with the treacherous leader of the Mahrattas. For seven years both sides wore the mask of friendship and Elphinstone's patience was rewarded by a declaration of war. At the battle of Kirkee, Elphinstone took over command of the British troops at a crisis and smashed the enemy, whose territories were annexed and governed by Elphinstone.

He was then made Governor-General of Bombay where he founded the system of state education in India. His services were recognised by both British and Indians; the first erected a marble statue, the second endowed the Elphinstone College.

On return to Britain he twice refused to be Governor-General of India. In his retirement he wrote a *History of India* and also an account of the British power up to the Mutiny. He lived long enough to see that terrible event, luckily from a distance. He had at least done his best to help the Indians.

William Lyon Mackenzie *(1795-1861)*

Born near Dundee he emigrated with his mother to Canada in 1820. He was a merchant in various towns in Upper Canada. The general discontent in the district drew him into politics and he expressed that feeling of annoyance by publishing the *Colonial Advocate* attacking the wealthy families who ruled the district of York. Mackenzie moved to Toronto and continued to attack the oligarchy. He met with no support but, on his press being wrecked by his opponents, and his action for damages being successful, he set up a larger press and published for several years.

In 1828 he was elected MP for York but expelled five times and as often returned, until the Government would not allow this turbulent Scot to stand for election. But he was popular and well received in Britain on a visit in Reform Year 1832.

Many reforms in Canada were due to his representation. He was elected Mayor of Toronto. For a time his party, the Reformers, were in a majority in Parliament, but the Tory party won in 1836 and he became embittered. He published a book advocating a republican government for Canada. Along with the French Canadian Papineau who planned a rebellion, he roused the populace in 1837 intending to set up a provisional government. Defeated, he fled for his life to the USA with a price on his head.

In Buffalo he raised a rabble, seized and fortified an island on the border and harassed the Canadians. His further career was turbulent. He was imprisoned but survived to join the Radicals in Parliament. He had many merits for all his turbulence. He could not be forced against his will either by bribes or threats. In 1832 when the British Colonial Secretary offered him a position of great power in Canada with £1500 per annum, he refused. He preferred to be free to fight the great evils in the early Dominion. He described the Queen as 'Victoria Guelph, the bloody queen of England' and her cabinet as 'Victoria, Melbourne's bloody divan.'

Sir James Douglas *(1803-1877)*

Born and educated in Lanarkshire, at seventeen he emigrated to Canada and four years later became the organiser of the Hudson Bay property west of the rockies. In 1830 he was transferred to Fort Vancouver where he built a line of forts to defend the company's property.

In 1843 he established a fur-trading post at Camosun, now named Victoria. This was the centre of the extensive fur-trading of the North of Canada.

In 1846 a treaty between Britain and the USA fixed the 49th parallel of latitude as the state boundary and the Hudson Bay posts in Oregon were abandoned in favour of British Columbia. Douglas was appointed senior officer of the Western Department and in 1851 was made Governor of Vancouver.

The San Juan or Haro Archipelago of about 200 square miles lies between Vancouver Island and the mainland. The USA and Canada could not agree as to who owned it and nearly went to war over it. But Douglas arranged an occupation by equal numbers of British and American troops.

In 1873 the Emperor of Germany was asked to arbitrate and he awarded the San Juan Islands to the USA. Douglas was made Governor of British Columbia and Vancouver for some years. He was one of the makers of Canada.

William Ewart Gladstone *(1809-1898)*

He was born in Liverpool, son of William Gladstone who had been a corn-merchant in Leith and was descended from a very ancient Scottish family who held lands in the Borders.

His father being now wealthy, William was sent to Eton, then, after showing brilliance there, he proceeded to Oxford where he again shone in debate. After taking a double first at Oxford, he was invited by the Duke of Newcastle to stand for Newark. He entered the House of Commons at the age of twenty-four.

He had aimed at a Church career and remained an earnest Christian all his days, scrupulously moral, often being satirised by his opponents. Disraeli said of him that he had not a single redeeming vice.

His rise was rapid. He became a Lord of the Treasury in 1834 and Vice-President of the Board of Trade in 1841. He carried through the great Railway Bill in 1844.

He had great strength and endurance, working for sixteen hours a day at full pitch. As the years passed, he gradually became the chief opponent, often in bitter debates, of Disraeli.

He became Chancellor of the Exchequer in 1859 and for the next fifteen years he enjoyed uninterrupted power and achievement. He passed many beneficial acts of reform before he suddenly dissolved Parliament in 1874 and lost the ensuing election. But, now an old man, he came back to fight a great campaign in 1879 and swept back to power, much to the displeasure of Queen Victoria, who hated him, but he never complained of her lack of support for his liberal policies at home and abroad.

Troubles in Ireland in 1885 helped to put him out of office but he came back at the age of seventy-six to astonish the world by his apparently inexhaustible energy. He tried and narrowly failed to pass a Home Rule Bill for Ireland. On his retiral from politics, he retired to his country estate at Hawarden, Wales, and began writing letters and reminiscences. At the great age of eighty-nine he died, and was buried in Westminster, remembered with love and respect by friends and opponents alike.

James Bruce, Earl of Elgin *(1811-1863)*

At the age of thirty he was made Governor of Jamaica where he improved the conditions of the workers. Slavery had been abolished years before but the negroes were still being badly treated by some planters. In 1846 Elgin was made Governor-General of Canada where he was well received as he was son-in-law of the former Governor, the Earl of Durham. But trouble arose very soon. He approved of a local bill to compensate those who had suffered in the rebellions of 1837. As some of these sufferers were French-Canadians whose countryman had led the revolt there was strong feeling amongst the English-speaking Canadians, and Elgin was openly attacked in the streets of Montreal. But he refused to give way to the mob as he had the full backing of the Parliament of Canada and of Britain, though Mr Gladstone condemned 'rewarding rebels for rebellion.'

Elgin had good relations with the USA and settled many questions in trade and fisheries before returning home after eight successful years. He shortly volunteered to accompany an expedition to China when the Opium War broke out, but he had reached Singapore when the news of the Indian Mutiny recalled his troops to Calcutta. He proceeded without them and sent an ultimatum to the Chinese Commissioner to surrender, which he did soon afterwards. The following year he concluded the Treaty of Tientsin, which gave the British many concessions. Elgin also visited Japan to conclude the Treaty of Yeddo, by which Britain began a friendship with Japan. Trouble broke out again in China and once again Elgin accompanied a united French and British force which took Pekin and sacked the Summer Palace. Another treaty was concluded after this gun-boat diplomacy. The Scots generals Sir Hope Grant and Sir Robert Napier led the British troops.

Elgin was made Viceroy and Governor-General of India. The Mutiny had been brutally suppressed and the East India Company superseded by direct British rule, so Elgin was subject to control from London and his authority weakened thereby. But he carried out wise and firm policies. His death occurred prematurely at a hill-station when he was on his way to put down a tribal rebellion on the North-West Frontier.

James Ramsay, Earl of Dalhousie *(1812-1860)*

Born at Dalhousie Castle, Midlothian, he was third son of the 9th Earl, who was one of Wellington's generals.

James spent his boyhood with his parents in Canada. Then he went to Eton and Oxford, spending some time abroad before marrying the daughter of the Marquess of Tweeddale. At twenty-seven he was MP for East Lothian.

His rise was predictable with these advantages. In spite of many offers of promotion at home he became Governor-General of India at the age of thirty-five.

His first report in 1848 was that, politically, everything was quiet. But before the report reached London the Sikhs were in open rebellion and two British envoys were murdered. Delaying for six months in order to raise a strong force, he sent Gough, who gained a decisive victory over the rebels. Dalhousie was thanked by Parliament and made a Marquess.

He now annexed the Punjab and took the young maharaja into 'protective custody'.

There was trouble in Burma next and when negotiations failed two military expeditions reduced the Burmese to order. Dalhousie set up a telegraph system to help pacify the annexed province.

He started the policy of annexing native states if there was a dispute as to heredity. He established railways, telegraphs, canals, roads and bridges. He also organised medical and equipment supplies for the army. He warned of the dangers to scattered English communities should rebellion threaten but

176

the home government seemed to see no danger.

He now set up a postal system and introduced cheap stamps. He reformed the jails, put down human sacrifice. He encouraged the culture of tea, the protection of forests and the preservation of ancient monuments. He set up technical colleges for Indians, and made the civil service more attractive.

He pacified the frontier states, Afridis, Waziris etc. by a mixture of subsidies and threats of military action. Shortly after his return through ill-health, the Indian Mutiny broke out and although he was blamed for it he refused to defend himself and ordered all his papers to be kept secret for fifty years. He died aged only forty-six.

Sir John Alexander Macdonald *(1815-1891)*

He was born in Glasgow of a Sutherlandshire family who emigrated to Canada in 1829, settling in Kingston, Ontario. At fifteen he entered the legal profession and was called to the bar in 1836, beginning a successful practice locally.

In 1844 he was elected as a Conservative for Kingston on the promise that he would maintain close ties with Britain. He was involved in controversy for many years over the Rebellion Losses Bill (mentioned in our article on the Earl of Elgin). Other issues were the move to secularise the clergy funds and the abolition of the ancient French seignorial tenure in Quebec, both of which, as a Conservative, he opposed. He was forced to form a Coalition Party with the Liberals. He became Prime Minister of Upper Canada in 1857.

When the Dominion was united in 1867 Macdonald became the first Prime Minister, a situation calling for much tact and perseverance. The North-West Territory was purchased from the Hudson's Bay Company and Manitoba established in 1870. The Treaty of Washington was concluded in 1871 and the apparently impossible building of a transcontinental railway was started. Charges of bribery in contract work led to Macdonald's resignation; for four years he was in opposition. He fought with Alexander Mackenzie the Liberal Leader, on the question of Free Trade, and won handsomely.

The Canadian Pacific Railway, built in five years, was regarded as Macdonald's greatest triumph. For fourteen years his influence was directed towards the organisation and development of the North-West. His career is, to a great extent, the history of the advance of Canada.

George Brown *(1818-1880)*

He was born and educated in Edinburgh. He emigrated with his father when he was twenty to New York and five years later he went to Toronto to publish *The Banner*, a paper inspired by the newly-formed Free Church of Scotland. This paper was supported by large bodies of Canadian Scots. In the following year, 1844, George issued the Toronto *Globe*, at first a weekly, then a daily. It influenced political opinion over the whole of Ontario. Brown entered Parliament, representing Kent County in 1851, and became well-known for his violent attacks on the Roman Catholic Church and its adherents, the French Canadians. He helped to make a long-sustained division in the region, which still persists. He argued against the religious influence on Canadian schools and tried to put them under non-religious guidance, but he failed to prevent the Catholics retaining their separate schools.

He succeeded in gaining the reputation of being an honest politician.

He favoured a federation of all British colonies in North America and was even willing to call a truce with a fellow Scot John Macdonald to accomplish this. Federation was achieved in 1867 but Brown was defeated in South Ontario and left the House.

He was behind the purchase of the North-West Territories and also the Reciprocity Treaty with the United States of America which the United States Senate rejected.

He refused the governorship of Ontario, and a knighthood, preferring to edit the *Globe*. He was assassinated by an employee whom he had discharged.

Sir James MacCulloch *(1819-1893)*

Born in Glasgow he emigrated to Melbourne to manage a business for a Glasgow firm. Member of the legislative council for Wimmera in 1854, he was soon Minister of Trade and Customs and became Prime Minister in 1862. He was involved in disputes regarding trade policies, resigning over a dispute regarding a grant. He was reinstated three times, finally defeated in 1877.

Francis Napier, Baron *(1819-1898)*

He was descended from the ancient family of Napier of Merchiston. He entered the diplomatic service when twenty-one and held posts in Vienna, Constantinople, Naples, Washington and The Hague. In 1860 he was Ambassador in St Petersburg and in 1864 in Berlin. In 1866 he was made Governor of Madras where a serious famine was taking place. He exerted himself to alleviate this by setting up public works, especially of irrigation. In 1872 Lord Mayo the Viceroy was assassinated and Napier took over his work. He then returned to Britain where he was created a Baron. He was a member of the London School Board and after the crofting troubles in the Highlands he was made Chairman of the Crofters' Commission, the result of which was the appointment of a permanent body to deal with problems entailing crofters and cottars.

Donald Alexander Smith, Lord Strathcona *(1820-1914)*

He was born at Forres, son of a merchant. His mother was the daughter of a famous Canadian fur-trader, John Stewart, after whom Stewart Lake and River are named. Through his uncle, Donald Smith became a junior clerk in the Hudson's Bay Company when eighteen, starting in Labrador. He had a rough time there, becoming an expert in trapping. More important, he proved by practice that potatoes and certain vegetables can be grown successfully on the bleak coast there. He wrote many letters and had ample reading time. By 1860 he was chief trader and factor on Hudson Bay.

Eight years later he was resident governor at Montreal and in the year of Riel's rebellion on the Red River he was sent to check the outbreak and discover the causes of discontent. His coolness avoided unnecessary bloodshed, and the rebellion ceased.

The Hudson's Bay interest in the North-West Territory was purchased by the Canadian Parliament in 1867 and, owing to Smith's handling of the compensation to traders, everyone was satisfied.

With partners he took over an insolvent railway line and formed the St Paul, Minneapolis and Manitoba company. Along with the Premier, Sir John Macdonald, Smith put all his wealth into the successful completion of the Canadian Pacific Railway and at Craigellachie, in the Rocky Mountains, he had the honour of driving in the last spike.

He was High Commissioner for Canada in 1896 and received many other honours, being raised to the peerage as Lord Strathcona.

During the South African War he raised and equipped a regiment of cavalry from the Canadian West, called Strathcona's Horse, which did good service. He gave large donations to Canadian and Scottish Universities and hospitals, improved the Canadian waterways and placed steamers upon them. He was a member of the Pacific Cable Board uniting Britain, Canada and Australia.

Alexander Mackenzie *(1822-1892)*

Born in Perthshire, he emigrated to Canada when twenty and worked as a stone-mason and builder in Ontario. In 1852 he became the editor of a Liberal paper. In 1861 he entered the Canadian Parliament as a Liberal under George Brown. In the first Dominion Parliament he led the Liberals, taking over the premiership from Macdonald in 1873. In 1875 he was offered a knighthood by Queen Victoria but declined. He was too canny to appeal to a new and vigorous community but he was widely respected for his integrity and industry and keen grip of practical affairs.

Sir Henry Campbell Bannerman *(1836-1908)*

Second son of the Lord Provost of Glasgow, Sir James Campbell of Forfarshire, he took the extra name of Bannerman on inheriting a property from his mother's brother Henry Bannerman. He was educated at Glasgow University and Cambridge and from the age of thirty-two represented Stirling as a Liberal in Westminster, continuously for forty years.

He was successively Secretary in the War Office, Secretary to the Admiralty, Secretary for Ireland, retiring from the difficult Irish office with credit, an unusual achievement.

In 1899 he was made Prime Minister, at the outbreak of the Boer War, to which he was strongly opposed. Despite this personal feeling he agreed to help supplies to South Africa, though he denounced the methods employed against the Boers, waging war against women and children and sweeping them into concentration camps. At a meeting in 1901, at the height of the war, he said, 'When is a war not a war? When it is carried on by methods of barbarism in South Africa.' This phrase caused a crisis in the Liberal Party.

After the war he supported Home Rule for Ireland. In 1906, on the sweeping Liberal victory he was appointed Premier. He was very popular, though not noted for brilliance or originality. He was supported because of his sincerity and courage, even if his statements went against popular ideas.

Had his principles been put into effect in South Africa, granting independence to the Boer States after the war of 1899-1902, the present situation in South Africa would never have arisen.

Sir John Mackenzie *(1838-1901)*

Born at Ard-ross in East Ross-shire, son of a crofter, he emigrated to Otago, South Island, New Zealand, when twenty-two. He was for some years a working shepherd at Puketapu, Palmerston South. In 1865 he was clerk to the local committee and in 1871 was elected member of the Council of Otago.

Ten years later he was elected to the New Zealand House of Representatives where he sat for twenty years. He had a large responsibility for the early development of New Zealand, being in charge of land management and agriculture.

Charles Thomson Ritchie, 1st Baron *(1838-1906)*

Born in Dundee but educated at the City of London School, he went into business, then was elected a Conservative MP for a working-class district in London. In 1885 he was made Secretary to the Admiralty and in 1887 was in the Cabinet.

He was responsible for the institution of Parish Councils, though the majority of the conservatives have always owed him a grudge for creating the London County Council which has been a Trojan Horse in the City for nearly a century.

He was President of the Board of Trade and Home Secretary under Lord Salisbury, and became Chancellor of the Exchequer. He was a Free Trader. He was made a peer a few weeks before his death.

Sir Robert Stout *(1844-1930)*

Born at Lerwick, Shetland, he became a student teacher, emigrating to New Zealand when nineteen. There he continued teaching but left it to study law, becoming a barrister and solicitor. He was solicitor and MP in Otago and formed the Liberal Party of New Zealand. Then he became Attorney-General and Minister for Immigration and Lands. In two parliaments he was Prime Minister, with other offices. From 1899-1926 he was Chief Justice for New Zealand. He passed many measures establishing hospitals, Land Tax and Civil Service as well as Court Procedure.

Sir George Houston Reid *(1845-1918)*

Born at Johnstone, Renfrewshire, he emigrated when seven and a half with his family to Australia. He practised as a barrister in Sydney and was elected to the Parliament of New South Wales in 1880. He was in turn

Minister of Education and of the Free Trade Party.

He was Prime Minister of New South Wales from 1894 to 1899 and a member of the first Commonwealth Parliament in 1901. For a short time in 1904 he was Leader of Parliament. He was High Commissioner for Australia in 1909 and a London MP when he received the KCMG.

Archibald Philip Primrose, Lord Rosebery *(1847-1929)*

Son of Lord Dalmeny, he was born in London and educated at Brighton and Eton. He early showed his interest in horse-racing by being sent down from Oxford when he was twenty-one rather than give up his stud of racehorses. But this did not worry him as he succeeded his grandfather the same year to the earldom and estates. (His father had died when Archibald was four.)

After some years in travel he bought a house called the Durdans near Epsom which he adorned with 'turf' portraits. He won the Derby three times. He married the only child of Lord Baron Rothschild.

He supported Gladstone and was foreign secretary, though their views differed. He gave wise advice on many foreign matters. He was made Prime Minister by Queen Victoria for one year. He was a fine writer and a witty public speaker. His biographies of Pitt, Cromwell and Peel are classics.

Arthur James Balfour, Earl *(1848-1930)*

Eldest son of Balfour of Whittinghame, East Lothian, and Lady Cecil. Educated at Eton and Cambridge. Represented Hertford in Parliament from the age of twenty-six to thirty-seven, as a Conservative. He wrote on philosophy. He gave the impression of being indolent if clever. But at heart he was far from lazy. Lord Salisbury, his uncle, made him Secretary of State for Scotland, then later, for Ireland, where the Nationalists received him with ridicule, but soon discovered that he was fearless in his application of the Crimes' Act, aimed at assassins and other penal offenders. Crime was reduced to vanishing point.

In 1891 he returned to London to become Lord of the Treasury and Leader of Parliament. He was in charge of the Foreign Office for a time before the Boer War. He succeeded his uncle as Prime Minister in 1902, with other offices. The Conservatives now split over trade policies, Protection or Free Trade. Winston Churchill went over to the Free Traders.

An incident in the North Sea when Russian warships fired on British fishing-vessels by mistake, nearly led to war with Russia, but Balfour diplomatically avoided this step.

In 1906 the Conservatives were heavily defeated by Campbell-Bannerman's Liberals. At the outbreak of war in 1914 Balfour became First Lord of the Admiralty. He will perhaps be best remembered in world history for his support of the establishment in Palestine of a national home for Jews.

Sir Leander S. Jameson *(1853-1917)*

He was born in Edinburgh, son of a Writer to the Signet and educated for medicine at University College Hospital, London. After overworking in his profession his health impelled him to settle in Kimberley, South Africa in

1878. There he met Cecil Rhodes and through his influence the British South Africa Company was formed and Jameson gave up practice to support the Company.

The pioneers occupied Mashonaland and a greater part of Manicaland to which Portugal laid claim. Jameson was made administrator of 'Rhodesia', the new colony.

Jameson was popularly acclaimed when he visited Britain but the world was astounded to hear, on 31 December 1895, that he had led a force of 600 in a raid into the Boer territory of the Transvaal, hoping to start an anti-Boer rebellion.

The force had to surrender and were handed over to the British Government by President Paul Kruger, the Afrikaaner, for punishment. They were tried in London and Jameson got fifteen months in jail. He returned, a hero, to Rhodesia, where he and Rhodes worked together.

After the Boer War he was elected Prime Minister of Cape Colony. In later years, to promote a union of Boers and British, he said he was willing to serve under Louis Botha. But the Dutch would not accept this union, so Jameson attempted a union of English-speaking people in South Africa. After two years as the leader of the 'Unionist' party he returned to be honoured in Britain with a knighthood and KCMG.

James Keir Hardie *(1856-1915)*

He was born at Legbrannock, Lanarkshire, to a boyhood of great hardship, being a mine-worker from ten years old. Though a Liberal in politics at the start, he became an ardent Socialist and published with his associates the *Miner* which was afterwards entitled the *Labour Leader*.

As a delegate of the Ayrshire miners to the Trades Union Congress in 1887 he led the attack on the Liberal Government. His allies were Tom Mann and John Burns. In 1888 he entered politics against the wishes of the Trade Unionists, calling his party the Independent Labour Party. He struggled for votes and for a long spell was MP for South West Ham. He represented the Welsh mining community of Merthyr in 1900. He now had prevailed on the TUC to enter candidates for election and in 1906 twenty-nine Labour men were returned to the Liberal-ruled House. This rose to forty by the addition of some Labour miners' representatives. He had a problem to draw the party together but his campaign to spread Socialist principles to every industrial area was successful. His was a strength which declined to compromise over Socialist principles. He was warm-hearted and honest but unfortunately could not stop the world-madness of 1914 by combining with French and German Socialist parties.

Andrew Bonar Law *(1858-1923)*

Born in New Brunswick, he came to Scotland as a young boy and went to Glasgow High School. He went into business and when forty-two he was elected Conservative MP for Blackfriars, Glasgow. He supported Chamberlain in opposition to Free Trade and was defeated along with the party in 1906 and again in 1910. He was re-elected and strongly opposed Lloyd

George's reforms. He defended Balfour the party leader. He was elected opposition leader in 1911.

He opposed Home Rule for Ireland and this problem was left unsolved when the war of 1914-18 broke. He advocated the Derby scheme in 1916 for calling up fresh recruits. He partnered Lloyd George more or less in conducting the war 'to bring Germany to her knees'.

After the war he was faced with many problems at home and abroad. He was Prime Minister of a predominantly Conservative Party for under a year, and died as a result of his war years of strain.

James Ramsay Macdonald *(1866-1937)*

Son of a labourer, he was born at Lossiemouth on the Moray Firth. Educated at Drainie School in the vicinity, he became a student teacher. He came to London as a clerk, earning 12/6 per week. He aimed at a scientific career but turned to journalism.

He joined the Independent Labour Party, founded by Keir Hardie, and stood unsuccessfully as a Socialist candidate for Southampton. He was elected to the London County Council and married a niece of Lord Kelvin.

He travelled much abroad, all over the English-speaking world. He attended the Second Socialist International.

His political career began with his persuasion of the Trades Unions to form a political Labour party in 1900. In 1906 twenty-nine MPs were returned to Westminster. In 1918, when universal franchise was adopted, the party had over three million members.

He was leader of the party in 1911 and when Earl Grey declared war on Germany in 1914 he was deserted by his party when he opposed the war. For several years all through the war, he was denounced as a traitor, though his aim was humanitarian as all the world has come to realise.

He came back to favour and in 1924 was made Premier and set about the settlement of post-war Europe, inviting co-operation from the Germans and the French. He tried to make a treaty with Russia and aroused hostility from the Press who accused him and his party of being Bolsheviks. His party was defeated in the 'Red Letter' election, by a political trick, and he resigned.

In 1929 he was again Prime Minister with a talented Cabinet. He carried out several domestic and foreign improvements but the world slump of that year worked against these. He was Prime Minister of a Coalition Party in 1931, though most of his colleagues resigned rather than be seen to desert their socialist principles.

Sir Eric Geddes *(1875-1937)*

Sir Eric was born in India, educated at Merchiston Castle School, Edinburgh, and at Oxford.

He worked for some years in America in lumbering and railways, then on Indian railways. He was General Manager of the North-Eastern Railway in England when the Great War started. As a business man he was put in charge of munitions and communications to the front line in France. Then he was made First Lord of the Admiralty after a preliminary experience as

Controller of Shipping.

After the war, he helped with the demobilisation, then transport, including railways. His last administrative job was to effect economies in Government spending, where he felt he had not done as much as he was credited with. He was chairman of Imperial Airways and Dunlop Rubber.

Sir Aukland Geddes *(1879-1954)*

Sir Auckland, Sir Eric's younger brother, was born in Edinburgh and educated at Watson's College and Edinburgh University, where he studied medicine. He was engaged in the South African War.

In 1916 he became Director of Recruiting and Minister of Natural Science. After the war he was President of the Board of Trade and helped to restore trade and industry. The great coal strike of 1921 followed his term of office. He was British Ambassador to the USA at a critical post-war period.

William Downie Stewart *(1878-1942)*

Born in New Zealand of Scots descent, son of a politician, he trained to follow in his father's footsteps. He was elected MP for Dunedin West in 1914 but joined the Otago regiment and saw service with the Anzacs in the World War. He returned in 1919 and resumed his seat until 1935. He was Minister of Customs, of Internal Affairs, of Industry and Commerce, of Finance, and concluded by acting as Prime Minister in 1926.

John MacLean *(1879-1923)*

He was born in Pollockshaws, Renfrewshire, the sixth child of working-class parents, both of whom were of Highland origin and had been victims of the notorious Clearances, coming to the Glasgow area to seek work and subsistence.

His father died when John was eight, of a disease caused by his work, but his widow, realising John's ability, scraped and saved to send him to secondary school and teachers' training college. At twenty-one he was appointed assistant master at Strathbungo School and joined the newly-formed Progressive Union whose aims were the improvement of the members mentally and morally, and to encourage discussion of present-day problems. John gave lectures in public on such themes as *Poverty, Drink and Crime* and *Plato and the Republic*. He fell out with his headmaster over what he considered the hypocrisy of Bible teaching, for he was a convinced atheist, though he eventually realised that such a negative attitude was non-productive and began preaching Socialism. By private study, out of school hours, he took his MA at Glasgow University.

He joined the Social Democratic Federation, a Marxist body of Scottish origin, one of whose members was James Connolly, the Irish patriot and martyr, but a native of Edinburgh.

In 1914 when war came, most of the anti-war Socialists of Europe changed to war-mongers but MacLean led the Clydesiders in protest against the world-madness. By 1916, the opposition to war led to the arrest and imprisonment of MacLean and his associates. Following wide protests

MacLean was set free after a year and a half.

MacLean was not intimidated. He travelled over the country preaching support for the Bolshevik revolution and was again arrested and tried for sedition. He was sentenced to penal servitude for five years.

Riots broke out in Glasgow causing hundreds of injuries. MacLean in Peterhead prison went on hunger-strike and was forcibly fed. The Armistice was signed, but MacLean was not released until huge demonstrations in London and elsewhere forced the Government to give in.

After the war, with Revolution in the air, MacLean led the movement for reform by calling a General Strike, but after the occupation of Glasgow by English troops, the unrest petered out.

The latter years of MacLean's life, until his early death in 1923, were filled with controversy, which still persists. MacLean was again imprisoned for twelve months for inciting the unemployed to protest. His last days were passed in poverty and ill-health.

A cairn to his memory was erected in 1973 in Pollockshaws.

Thomas Johnstone *(1881-1965)*

He was born at Kirkintilloch and educated at Lenzie Academy. He started the publication of the Socialist newspaper *Forward* in 1906 with a capital of £60. It was a great success for many years, but owing to its condemnation of warfare in 1916 it was temporarily suppressed and only allowed to be republished after Johnston had interviewed David Lloyd George, the Premier.

The History of the Working Classes in Scotland, published by Johnston in 1920 was a very searching study of the real history of Scotland never before presented.

While at Glasgow University in 1908 Johnston backed James Keir Hardie for the Rectorship, unsuccessfully.

Johnston himself was made MP for West Stirlingshire from 1922 to 1924, then sat for Dundee in Westminster from 1925 to 1945. In that period he was Under-Secretary of State for Scotland, then Lord Privy Seal. He was Secretary of State for Scotland from 1941 to 1945 and despite these being war years he pushed through the North of Scotland Hydro-electricity Bill and also initiated the Scottish Tourist Board. A humble man, he refused a peerage in 1945.

James Maxton *(1885-1946)*

A native of Pollokshaws, Glasgow he inherited a teaching tradition from his parents and after his education at Hutcheson's Academy he graduated MA in 1909 at Glasgow, where he was also a good athlete. He joined the Independent Labour Party in 1904 and became a fiery Socialist orator, much beloved by all, friend or foe, for his wit and gentlemanly behaviour. He called a strike in Glasgow in 1916, and was imprisoned with others for sedition. The military repressed the strike with much violence on Clydeside.

In 1918 he won a large support from the Bridgeton ward, and was eventually made MP for that division in 1922. He was the liveliest member of Parliament for many years, speaking his mind freely and eloquently.

Law

The earliest recorded laws of Scotland were those of Malcolm II (1004-1034) who was succeeded by Duncan, slain by Macbeth. This was before the Norman Conquest of England so the laws have no connection with the feudal system. Malcolm, and his successors, Duncan, Macbeth and Malcolm III (Canmore) etc. held a 'King's Court' comprised of 'all the barons and dignitaries of the realm.' The chief justice was named the 'Justiciar', later called the Lord Justice General. An official of scarcely less importance was the Justiciar's Clerk, later named the Lord Justice Clerk. A team of judges with the territorial title of Lord, latterly amounting to five, supplemented the Court. Sheriffs were also appointed to dispense justice in the shires, distant from the centre of government.

The King's Court dealt with all cases, civil and criminal, and in early days there was a Justiciar for the Highlands and a separate one for the Lowlands. This was because the former was a Gaelic-speaking region and the latter mainly English-speaking. For a period a third Justiciar was appointed for Galloway where Pictish and Gaelic were spoken.

In the reign of Mary Queen of Scots all Scotland was under one justiciary and it had been the custom for some years that the monarch should sit in the Court to add authority and dignity. The young queen travelled through the Highlands extensively, dispensing justice, and she was certain to have acquired a knowledge of Gaelic in the Court.

In those early days law was not always impartial. The barons and the chiefs could evade punishment despite the royal will to enforce it. A bad feature, too, was the conflicting authority of other courts, of which the most powerful was the Privy Council, often an instrument of the King's personal feeling. As obstructive were the Courts of Regality, Church Courts and on occasion the Court of Session. The Lords of Regality had unlimited hereditary powers, called the powers of 'pit and gallows'. They could imprison or execute without reference to anyone; even the King himself could not interfere unless the crime was treason or witchcraft. The Highland chiefs held such powers as well as the Lowland barons.

In 1672 this confusion was put to rights by a Royal Commission of Charles II, though the old institution of hereditary jurisdiction was so strongly defended that it required the great political crisis of the 1745 Rebellion to put an end to it. Those holders of this power who had rebelled were forfeited and the loyalists were compensated out of the forfeited estates.

The Scottish legal system is still evolving to suit a changing nation but its progress from primitive justice to a settled and fair system, irrespective of personal influence, is a matter for national esteem. Despite continuous English attempts to weaken the authority of the Scottish system and to make it conform to a code based on a chaotic and anomalous assemblage known as Common Law, it holds its ground and asserts its tried and trusted principles.

Scots law was founded on Roman law with certain modifications. Scots studied law in Holland, France and Italy. The Dutchman Van Groot, or Grotius (1583-1645), despite religious persecution, had written his great book on international law entitled *The Laws of Peace and War*. It was written in Latin for universal understanding. But even before Grotius a Scottish lawyer had published a book of wide application.

Sir James Balfour *(c.1520-1584)*

Sir James Balfour had written *A System of the more ancient laws of Scotland*, in which he also refers to the very old *Visby Sea-laws* which had originated in the Baltic in the hey-day of the powerful Hanseatic League. Balfour may be called the father of Scots law. Unfortunately, his political career brings his character into disrepute, however brilliantly logical were his legal arguments.

He was born in Pittendreich, son of Sir James Balfour, probably about 1520, and educated for the legal branch of the Church of Scotland, then Catholic. He was involved with John Knox in the murder of Beaton, captured and kept in jail for two years. In 1549 occurred the first of his many betrayals. He renounced the reformers and went over to Mary of Guise, the Catholic Queen Mother. Then he joined the Protestant Lords of the Congregation before betraying their plans to the Catholics.

When Mary Queen of Scots arrived he became her greatest favourite, second only to Rizzio who was later murdered. The conspirators also intended to murder Balfour but he escaped and assisted in the murder of Darnley, Mary's husband.

He was always rewarded for his treacheries. He was made Governor of Edinburgh Castle for his share in Darnley's murder but when Bothwell, who had married Mary, got into hot water, Balfour surrendered the Castle to the Reformers.

After a long series of betrayals he was trusted by nobody. He was even thought to have betrayed Mary's secrets to Elizabeth and is proved to have been responsible for the death of Regent Morton.

His career was one of the blackest in the chronicles of politics and crime yet he was the greatest lawyer of his day. The law is supposed to be based on justice and truth but the above tale of treachery and murder no doubt helped to give rise to the old Scots proverb, 'Hame's hamely,' quo' the Deil, when he found himself in the Court of Session.

Admiral Alexander King *(c.1550-1610)*

Admiral Alexander King, shortly after the death of Balfour, and before the Union of the Crowns in 1603, published a tract on the Laws and Customs of the Sea. As Balfour's System of Laws was not published until about 1754, King's book was the first published on this subject.

William Wellwood *(c.1540-1620)*

William Wellwood, Professor of Civil Law at St Andrews, published *The Sea Law of Scotland* about 1590 in which he started an argument about the rights of shipping, which roused Grotius to reply so many years after that Wellwood was past caring. The row is still going on four centuries later.

Sir William Barclay *(1546-1608)*

Sir William Barclay was another Scot who wrote on law. He was born and educated in Aberdeenshire but took his degree at Bourges. Not long after, he was appointed Professor of Civil Law at Port-a-Moussin where he taught for nearly thirty years. Shortly before his death he was elected to a chair at Angers. He wrote several works on International Law and a commentary on the summary of Roman Law collected by the Emperor Justinian in the sixth century. This work had a strong influence on future Scots jurists.

Lockharts of The Lee

An ancient Scottish family renowned in legal and state circles. Their seat is Lee-castle near Lanark.

Sir Simon Lockhart (c.1329) accompanied Sir James Douglas in his attempt to carry Bruce's heart to the Holy Land.

Sir James Lockhart *(1600-1674)*

In legal matters the Lockharts first came into prominence with Sir James, during the Civil War, when he tried to rescue Charles I from the Cromwellians. For taking part in the Battle of Prestonpans, he was deprived by Cromwell of his offices and banished. Still rebellious, he was captured in an engagement and sent by Cromwell to the Tower. At the Restoration he was made a Privy Councillor and Commissioner of the Exchequer, then appointed Lord Chief Justice.

Sir William Lockhart *(1621-1675)*

Eldest son of Sir James he was also a great Royalist but after being defeated at Preston with his father, he fought for Charles at Worcester. Once again on the losing side he switched over and joined the Commonwealth party, and married Cromwell's niece. Naturally 'Old Noll' appointed him to a good position. He was made Commissioner for the Administration of Justice in Scotland, and for the first time for many years justice was seen to be done. He was made Governor of Dunkirk and refused to open its gates to Charles II so at the Restoration he lost his position. However he changed sides again and was made Ambassador to the German state of Brandenberg where he died.

The famous talisman 'The Lee Penny' has been in the possession of the Lockharts since the days of Robert the Bruce. It was used to cure disease in the days of superstition. It is a small triangular stone set in a silver shilling of

Edward I and is *The Talisman* round which Sir Walter Scott wrote his novel of that name.

Sir George Lockhart *(1630-1689)*

Sir George Lockhart was the second son of Sir James. He studied for the bar and was in favour with Cromwell, being appointed an advocate at the age of twenty-eight. But like his brother (or the Vicar of Bray in the satire) he thought it only right to go over to the king at the Restoration. He was a most elegant lawyer and acquired an extensive practice. He took part in many debates which brought him into conflict with Charles II, but he later made his peace with the king. He became Lord President of the Council, a Privy Councillor and Commissioner of Exchequer. He was instrumental in helping King James II to relieve Roman Catholics, which made him unpopular, as James was suspected of being a Catholic himself.

Lockhart's death was one of the greatest sensations of the times. A man of very violent temper, Chiesly of Dalry, a good estate near Edinburgh, had fallen out with his wife and had separated from her. She sued for alimony. The case was heard before Sir George Lockhart. To Chiesly's great annoyance Lockhart awarded the lady the small aliment of £93 per annum out of the estate. Six months later, in London, Chiesly swore to an advocate friend that he would go to Scotland before Candlemas and kill Lockhart, who was soon warned of this open threat to his life, but paid no attention.

On Easter Sunday, 31 March 1689, the assassin followed Lockhart home from St Giles and shot him in the back at his own front door. He died instantly. Chiesly was taken red-handed and put to the torture, to confess if he had any accomplices. He had none, so he was executed with all the barbarity of the age and hanged in chains with the pistol round his neck, for murdering a just judge who forced him to do the decent thing and maintain his wife and family.

George Lockhart *(1673-1732)*

Son of the above and like him an active supporter of the Stuarts, he was made a Member of Parliament in the Scots Parliament in 1703. He was strongly opposed to the Union of Parliaments but when through bribery the Union was effected he took part in negotiations to represent Scottish feelings in London. He was Member for Edinburgh in the new Imperial Parliament, where he opposed the highly unpopular Malt Tax for Scotland. In 1715 he supported the Jacobite Rebellion and was imprisoned in the Castle. He had already incurred the displeasure of the Government by trying in 1713 to repeal the Act of Union. He was set free for a time until it was discovered by a secret agent that he was corresponding with James III, the Old Pretender. He went into hiding until he could escape abroad. Through the Duke of Argyll's influence he was allowed to return but his restless nature caused him to fall foul of an opponent, who shot him dead in a duel.

He wrote privately *The Memoirs of Scotland from 1702 – 1707* exposing the underhand proceedings that led to the Union of Parliaments. It was published without his consent and made him further disliked in London.

Alexander Lockhart, Lord Covington (c.1700-1782)

Alexander Lockhart was the son of the above. He was one of the ablest lawyers of the age, as one would expect from his heritage and upbringing, yet he was never allowed to become a judge. This was due to the spite of the Government, because of his gallant defence of the Jacobite prisoners at Carlisle in 1746.

The Highland army, on its retreat through Carlisle, had been orderly and peaceful and had caused no disturbances to the populace. Yet when Jacobite prisoners were brought to Carlisle for trial, having become detached from the main army, they were disposed of by completely unjust measures and about seventy of them were put to a barbarous death in the human shambles in front of the Castlegate. These prisoners-of-war had been guilty of no crime but that of wearing tartan. Any man in this garb was sure to be sentenced to death by the hatred of the jury.

Lockhart and his rival advocate Fergusson, indignant at the treatment of the Highlanders, decided to employ a stratagem to show up the rancour and barbarism of the Carlisle butchers. They at first set off for Carlisle to offer their services to the unhappy Jacobites. Lockhart was to examine the evidence and Fergusson to address the jury. Their pleading had not the slightest effect. The evidence was discarded and the prisoners sent to the slaughterhouse.

Then the device was put into effect. One of the advocates dressed his servant in tartan and sent him off to skulk about in the environs of Carlisle until he was arrested and accused of being a rebel, as usual. He was immediately condemned by the English jury and would have been executed had his master not claimed him as his servant and proved beyond all doubt that he had been in his close service during the whole of the Jacobite campaign.

The Carlisle jury were staggered and Lockhart applied his caustic tongue to them in such a manner that they were careful in future. But the mischief had been done to the Highlands (and Lockhart) for the Hanoverian butchers, from Cumberland down, never forgave him for publicly exposing their injustice and savage cruelty to political opponents.

Lockhart, perhaps soured by his long neglect and positive discrimination by the authorities, had a pretty rough temper in his latter life. A young advocate, who later rose to Lord Chancellor of England, owed his eminence to Lockhart, through unusual circumstances.

In a case in Edinburgh, the young advocate, Alexander Wedderburn, who had been drudging for a year or two, trying to earn a few guineas, was opposed by Lockhart. Wedderburn argued so skilfully that Lockhart called him 'a presumptuous boy' (he was twenty-four). The court was then treated to such a torrent of abuse from the 'boy' that it was shocked to the core. Lockhart got up and threatened him with vengeance, but he got more than he bargained for. Wedderburn replied with scorn, 'I care little for what may be said or done by a man who has been disgraced in his person and dishonoured in his bed.' Lockhart had been horse-whipped by an opponent and his wife was known for her gallantry.

Wedderburn, highly excited, would not withdraw his remarks, took off his gown, laid it coolly on the bar, bowed to the judges and left the court never to return.

James Dalrymple, Viscount Stair *(1619-1695)*

James Dalrymple was born at Drummurchie, Ayrshire, educated at Mauchline and Glasgow University, and after seven years at Glasgow he was admitted as advocate in Edinburgh. In 1649, the year of Charles I's execution, Dalrymple was sent to Holland by the Scots to ask Charles II to return as king. Charles refused then, but was met by Dalrymple in Aberdeenshire when he changed his mind. After the defeat at Preston Charles fled. Dalrymple refused to acknowledge the rule of the Common-wealth in Scotland but, befriended by General Monk, he was appointed a Commissioner of Justice along with Sir William Lockhart.

After the return of Charles II he was knighted and made a judge, but as he refused to say that the National Covenant was unlawful, he resigned. Charles allowed him, however, to make a qualified declaration and he resumed his office.

A family tragedy of a highly dramatic kind occurred in 1669. His daughter Janet, about twenty, had fallen in love with Lord Rutherford, and they had become engaged. But apparently her father disapproved and insisted on her marrying Dunbar of Baldoon, whom she detested. On the wedding night she stabbed her husband and when the attendants rushed in she was found insane, hiding in the chimney-place. She never recovered. The incident was used by Sir Walter Scott in the *Bride of Lammermoor*.

The following year Stair went to London to discuss a proposed Union of Parliaments. The next year he was made President of the Court of Session. Despite the high position, he knew that, as a Covenanting supporter, he was liable to suffer the same fate as the Earl of Argyll, i.e. to be executed for his opposition to the Crown. He went to London to see Charles, but the Duke of York, the future James II, prevented this and displaced him from his judge's office. However, he retired to his estate and busied himself with his famous book *The Institutions of the Law of Scotland*, which is a clear and logical presentation of its subject, comparing and contrasting Scots law with that of the neighbouring countries, much to the detriment of English law, which is shown by contrast to be chaotic and illogical.

Dalrymple was resident with his wife and some of his younger children in Holland from 1684 to 1688. During this exile he wrote two legal books of importance. But an attempt was made by Sir George Mackenzie, the notorious prosecutor, to attaint Dalrymple with treason. This however was circumvented by the appointment of Dalrymple's son, a friend of James II, in place of Mackenzie.

Dalrymple came back to Britain with William of Orange and seemed about to reap his reward as a supporter of the anti-Jacobites. He was created Viscount Stair in 1690 and his son assumed the title of Master of Stair. But an outrage of the greatest kind occurred which cast both father and son into universal loathing, though the father had no direct hand in the event. This was the Massacre of Glencoe which occurred in February 1692, when a small Highland clan, the MacIans or MacDonalds were treacherously slaughtered, man, woman and child, by a detachment of soldiers under the command of Robert Campbell of Glenlyon. But the Master of Stair was fully responsible; Campbell, though not unwilling, was only an underling.

The entire British nation was shocked by the barbarism, though it was no worse than many similar incidents in the Highlands, before and after. An enquiry was set up and eventually in 1695 the Master of Stair was directly accused. His father died, doubtless of shame, and his son succeeded to the title, ever after an infamous one. But he refused to attend Parliament, though he was made a Commissioner in 1705 for the projected Union. He died in the year of that Union, 1707.

Sir George Mackenzie *(1636-1691)*

Sir George Mackenzie was born at Dundee, grandson of Lord Mackenzie of Kintail. He was educated at Dundee Grammar School, at Aberdeen, St Andrews and at Bourges, famed for centuries in France as the seat of the study of law. He became an advocate when twenty-three and in 1677 he became King's Advocate, at a time when the Covenanting troubles were at their highest. He was involved in some of the worst cruelties against the Covenanters and fully earned the title of 'Bloody Mackenzie'. The courts at that period employed various tortures, such as the thumbscrews and the boot, to extract confessions, and Mackenzie quite callously supervised these scenes.

He was a confirmed Royalist and by his own lights no doubt he did no wrong in suppressing both Presbyterians and Catholics who were against Charles II. He enforced the penal laws against Catholics just as severely as against the Covenanters, for which even Charles had him removed from his office for a time. When William of Orange took the throne he was urged to dismiss Mackenzie but refused, perhaps believing him to be a very erudite lawyer, which of course he had proved by his many publications.

After the death of Claverhouse at Killiecrankie, and thereby the destruction of the Jacobite cause, Mackenzie retired to Oxford to do literary work.

As a young man he wrote well on romantic and moral topics, but his most important legal works are on Criminal Law and Customs in Scotland, and his *Institutions of the Law of Scotland*. The latter is not considered to be as lucid as Dalrymple's work on the same subject. He actually published a *Vindication of the Government of Scotland during the reign of Charles II*, although that period has been universally condemned as a period of misrule, equal to the worst persecutions of religion in any country in Europe at that time. It is considered that 18,000 innocent persons perished by persecution in the South-West of Scotland during Mackenzie's term as King's advocate though only a small percentage came up for trial.

His tomb in Greyfriars Churchyard in Edinburgh was for long thought to be haunted by his ghost and it was a test of courage to approach it after dark and shout through the doorway, 'Bloody Mackenzie, come oot if ye dare.'

John Erskine of Carnock *(1695-1768)*

The families of Erskine produced many illustrious men in Scottish affairs for three centuries, in legal, military and church careers. In law, John Erskine was an authority. He was passed as an advocate when twenty-four, held the Chair of Scots Law in Edinburgh for nearly thirty years and retired to prepare his monumental volume on his life-study *The Institutes of the Law of Scotland*. He did not live to see it published. He had earlier written a more concise book on the *Principles of the Law of Scotland*. Both books are considered to be authoritative works.

Henry Home, Lord Kames *(1696-1782)*

He was born at Kames in Berwickshire. Educated privately, he studied at Edinburgh and passed as advocate when twenty-eight. He had a good deal of unwanted, because unpaid, leisure as a young advocate but spent it profitably by writing the *Remarkable decisions of the Court of Session from 1716 – 1728*. As this was a very disturbed political time, covering the arrival of the Hanoverian George I and the consequent Jacobite rising of 1715 with the ensuing confiscations and executions, Home had many strange findings to report, not all bringing credit to Scots justice.

In 1752 he was made Lord Kames and later Lord of Justiciary Court.

He was a man of wide interests, one of these being agriculture. He published *The Gentleman Farmer* as a guide for landowners to improved methods. He was, on the strength of his interests, appointed a trustee on a Committee dealing with Fisheries, Arts and Manufactures. He was also a philosopher in an age when Scotland led the world in that study, when Hume and Adam Smith and a host of others were his associates, either friends or foes. He would have been wiser to stick to law, where he was on known ground, for his assertion that man had freedom of will so alarmed the Calvinists in the Established Church and outside it, that Home found it sensible to withdraw the proposition, thereby showing the world that even an eminent man of law had no freewill in a bigoted age. Home was an eccentric and his favourite term of endearment was used when he turned to his fellow-judges on retiral, 'Fare ye weel, ye auld bitches.'

William Murray, Lord Mansfield *(1705-1793)*

His life occupied nearly all of the eighteenth century and his career was entangled with most of the troubles of that age of political strife.

Born at Perth, fourth son of Lord Stormont, he went to London with his parents when three. He returned for his first schooling to Perth Grammar School, then he entered Westminster School when fourteen and Oxford four years later. He took his second degree, MA, when twenty-five and then, like most aristocratic youths, made the Tour of Europe for a year or two. There were no passport difficulties, and wars did not exclude British travellers. He was called to the bar at Lincoln's Inn and, being a good scholar, he mingled with the literary lights of the age, having a close friendship with Alexander Pope. He was a Tory and a Jacobite; therefore, although he was a friend of such brilliant men as the Tory Dr King of Oxford, he had not his enemies to seek among the Whigs.

He was known as 'Silver-tongued Murray', which proves that he had acquired an English accent, otherwise he might have suffered the fate of James Erskine, Lord Grange, the notorious judge who had his wife abducted and imprisoned on St Kilda. Lord Grange had the ambition to sit in Parliament, to supplement his judge's salary. He was a very able speaker and his maiden speech was much applauded, but as was said at the time, 'the House would not long endure his Scotch accent', and refused to attend when he was due to speak.

Murray, by reason of his pleading, rose to eminence in his profession.

In 1736 he had a chance to prove his ability and patriotism. During the Porteous Riots in Edinburgh, a mob drawn from all ranks of society had executed Captain Porteous after a 'Kangaroo' trial. The obvious organisation of the riot gave the government and the Crown great offence, and a Bill of Pains and Penalties was aimed to deprive Edinburgh of civic rights and to impose a heavy fine. Murray defended the city and the Bill was mitigated. He was thereafter very popular in Scotland.

Murray became Solicitor-General and was MP for a Yorkshire constituency. He supported the highly gifted Duke of Newcastle against Pitt the Elder, which made him an object of hatred for the opposition, who accused him of being a Jacobite, though he had helped to condemn Lord Lovat after the Battle of Culloden. Lovat, however, was a treacherous and unscrupulous schemer, difficult to defend on any score.

Murray, in 1756, was made Lord Chief Justice of England and raised to the peerage as Baron Mansfield. He was also a member of the Cabinet and Speaker of the House of Lords.

He aimed at moderating the acrimony between the parties but still incurred the hostility of the mysterious 'Janius', whose letters remain as brilliant as they were anonymous. One of Mansfield's cases was the famous 'Douglas Cause' where he defended the claims of Lady Jane Douglas to the disputed title and inheritance.

His greatest achievement was in bringing his clear and logical Scots intelligence to bear on Commercial Law, reducing it from a chaotic tangle to an exact science. However, in attempting to apply his expert acquaintance with Roman and Continental Law to English Common Law, with its mass of inconsistencies, he had to admit defeat. After he had been buried in Westminster Abbey, with a fine monument, for nearly a century, English lawyers tended to admit his principles and adjust English law accordingly.

Robert MacQueen, Lord Braxfield (1721-1799)

Born at Braxfield, Lanarkshire, he became an advocate in 1744. Almost immediately he was involved in the cases arising out of the forfeiture of Jacobite estates following Culloden. He was an expert on Feudal Law, of which Sir Thomas Craig of Riccarton was a student in the seventeenth century. He became Lord Braxfield in 1773, Lord of Justiciary in 1780, and Lord Chief Justice in 1788.

In the following year the Bastille fell and the French Revolution began. Scotland and England were affected by the new spirit of equality, and societies such as 'Friends of the People' were formed. The country was in a political ferment. The poet Burns was involved with Thomas Campbell and others. The Government decided on repressive measures. The Habeas Corpus Act was suspended and anyone suspected of libertarian feelings was arrested and tried. Braxfield was notorious for his savage manner on the bench. He was credited with the remark, on viewing a suspect, that he would be 'nane the waur o' a hanging'.

On being reminded, at the famous trial of the reformers, Muir, Skirving and Margarot, that Christ, too, had been a reformer, he retorted, 'Muckle guid he made o' that. He was hangit for it.' Braxfield was named the 'Hanging Judge'.

Robert Louis Stevenson took Braxfield for the model of *Weir of Hermiston* in his unfinished novel of that name and no doubt some of Braxfield's domestic character of cynical coarseness was founded at least on reliable hearsay.

But as a judge he had integrity and as a man he had plenty of courage, for in the heights of the riots of 1793 and 1794, when Edinburgh was a very rough Gothic town, Braxfield used to walk at midnight, without a guard, from the Law Courts to his house in George Square, through the toughest area of the city.

David Dalrymple, Lord Hailes *(1726-1792)*

Eldest son of Sir James Dalrymple of Hailes near Musselburgh, he was born in Edinburgh and educated at Eton, Edinburgh and Utrecht. He became an advocate at twenty-two. His hobby was Scottish antiquities, particularly the ancient poetry of Scotland, which had been sorely neglected and indeed misrepresented. He ascended the Bench as Lord Hailes when forty, and ten years later became Lord of Justiciary. His published works are *Memorials and Letters* of the reigns of James I and Charles I; *Godlie and Spiritual Songs, Ancient Scottish poems,* and *Annals of Scotland.*

During his old age his daughter faithfully attended him and acted as charming hostess to his many celebrated guests in his town house in New Street, off the Canongate. His estates and house were at Musselburgh but it was customary for landed men to have a town residence also. On his death no will could be found, a very remiss business for a lawyer. The male-heir, a relative rather remote, was due to inherit all the estate, to the exclusion of the daughter. She was almost ready to quit the house when by chance she found his will behind a shutter, where he had put it expecting her to find it when she covered the windows at nightfall. She enjoyed her unexpected heritage for forty years.

Alexander Wedderburn, Earl Rosslyn *(1733-1805)*

Under the article on Alexander Lockhart we have referred to the incident in Edinburgh which turned Wedderburn's talent to England. He was the eldest son of Lord Chesterhall, a member of the Bench, and was born in East Lothian. He was educated at Edinburgh and entered at Temple Bar.

He was called to the Inner Temple and, like the 'Silver-tongued Murray', he was forced to abandon the 'auld Scots tongue' at the beginning of his career of forensic art. He engaged Thomas Sheridan, the famous Dublin-born elocutionist and actor, to teach him oratory. He was friendly with Lord Bute and Baron Mansfield, fellow Scots. He suggested to Bute that Dr Samuel Johnson should have a pension, which probably extracted little gratitude from that disliker of Scots.

Wedderburn's political career was very complicated but he did not hesitate to use all the influence he had, to advance himself. He also married an heiress. In an age of political intrigue he proved as slippery as anyone and changed sides more than once. He also was the target for the pseudonymous 'Junius', who said of him, 'There is something about him which even treachery cannot trust.' In the end he supported Pitt in his opposition to the French Convention; and the declaration of war with France was supported by him. When Pitt resigned in 1801, Wedderburn received the Midlothian title of Earl of Rosslyn and retired. He was buried in St Paul's, having held high offices including the Lord Chancellorship of Great Britain.

As a pleader he was the most eloquent speaker of his time, his chief excellencies being his clear diction and his marshalling of facts. His judgements also were lucid and fair. He was quick and unruffled in debate, but in private company he was extremely dull, perhaps on purpose, to act as a foil to the brilliant wits he mingled with.

Henry Erskine *(1746-1817)*

Henry Erskine was the younger son of the 10th Earl. Born in Edinburgh and educated at St Andrews, Edinburgh and Glasgow, he became an advocate at twenty-two. He soon, by his brilliance and wit, gained a large practice both in civil and ecclesiastic cases. In the Church he supported the 'High Fliers' or Evangelical party against the Moderates. He succeeded Henry Dundas as Lord Advocate in 1783.

The story is told of his encounter with Dundas on that occasion. Dundas was noted for his corrupt political practices, using bribery and more subtle devices to secure votes.

On the morning of Erskine's appointment he gaily addressed Dundas, 'I must be off now and order my silk gown,' that being the official costume of his new office.

Dundas drily and discourteously replied, 'It is hardly worth your while for all the time you'll want it. You had better borrow mine.'

Erskine replied smartly, 'From the readiness with which you make me the offer, Dundas, I have no doubt the gown is made to fit any party; but it shall never be said of Harry Erskine that he put on the abandoned habits of his predecessor.'

Dundas's remark proved true, however, for a sudden change of government soon deprived Erskine of his appointment.

Thomas Erskine *(1750-1823)*

Thomas Erskine was the younger brother of Henry Erskine, born in Edinburgh, educated at the High School and at St Andrews Grammar

School. He went into the navy as a midshipman, then, still in his teens, became an ensign in the army, being two years stationed in Minorca. He found promotion too slow so he left the army and married the daughter of an MP. By chance, he met Lord Mansfield, who suggested he try the law. He was called to the bar when twenty-eight. He was lucky immediately, being called to defend a man accused of libel against Greenwich Naval Hospital. Erskine, having been a sailor, could speak with knowledge. He also spoke with eloquence, skill and courage and won his case. His fortune was now assured and doubly so when he successfully defended Lord George Gordon against treasonable charges.

He stood as MP for Portsmouth but was never successful in Parliament. He was inspired when addressing juries and conducted many famous defences, notably in defence of a bookseller, Stockdale, who published a pamphlet supporting the famous Warren Hastings. But Erskine made one unfortunate mistake. He defended Thomas Paine, author of *The Rights of Man*, on the principle that, had he refused to defend Paine, he would thereby have judged him. He lost his position as Attorney-General to the Prince of Wales, later George IV, but George made him his chancellor to recompense him.

He became very popular by his defence of several 'Friends of the People' in 1794, and they were discharged. This was in contrast to the injustices Braxfield was inflicting on the reformers in Edinburgh. As Lord Chancellor he was a failure and he now fell on evil days. But his powers were revived in his defence of Queen Caroline in the trial of the Queen for adultery in 1820. Erskine's popularity was assured for the rest of his life when Caroline was acquitted and the whole of Britain celebrated the event with street illuminations. His eloquence and courage, keen reasoning and power to command attention from juries made him the greatest advocate England has ever known.

Sir James MacIntosh *(1765-1832)*

Sir James MacIntosh was born at Aldourie, near Inverness, son of a veteran Highland soldier. He was educated at Fortrose and at King's College Aberdeen. He took his medical degree at Edinburgh and, on being forced to sell his inherited estate, he tried unsuccessfully to set up a practice in the South of England.

He turned to law and politics and defended the French Revolution in reply to Burke's condemnation. He joined the 'Friends of the People' and wrote their *Declaration* which antagonised the Government and led to prosecutions.

He was appointed Recorder of Bombay and knighted. He became Whig MP for Nairn and Professor of Law at Haileybury College. He wrote many articles to the new *Edinburgh Review* and represented Knaresborough for several years in Parliament.

His great legal work was his effort to improve the Criminal Code which contained many mediaeval laws, relating to theft, forgery and poaching. He held enlightened views on Slavery, Catholic Emancipation, Parliamentary Reform and Jewish Emancipation. The Parliamentary Reform took effect in the year of his death, the others soon after.

He became a member of Privy Council and Commissioner for India. He wrote on ethics and history.

Joseph Bell *(1770-1843)*

Joseph Bell was born at Fountainbridge, Edinburgh, an elder brother of Sir Charles Bell, the famous anatomist. He attended legal classes at Edinburgh University and became an advocate at twenty-one. He specialised in the laws of bankruptcy, a condition attended by many inconsistencies and injustices at that time. In 1804 he published his *Treatise on the Law of Bankruptcy in Scotland*, a work which many years later he expanded into a book of the highest excellence, praised by all lawyers in Britain and Europe. He was made Professor of Scots Law in Edinburgh and put in charge of a commission to inquire into bankruptcy law, as a result of which valuable changes were made. His name is still cited in Scottish courts as one of the four authorities on points of law.

John Campbell, Baron *(1779-1861)*

He was born at Cupar, Fife, son of Dr Campbell, minister. Educated at St Andrews and as a student of law at Lincoln's Inn, he was a journalist with the *Morning Chronicle* for a time before being called to the bar. Here his journalism aided him in his reports of jury trials which cover ten years and gained him wide credit.

After one unsuccessful attempt, he became MP for Stafford. In Parliament he spoke without eloquence or spirit, but with sound common sense which enabled him to promote great improvements in clarifying the law.

Success was now rapid. In the Reform year 1832 he was knighted and made Solicitor-General. Two years later he represented Edinburgh and was Attorney-General.

In Parliament he spoke powerfully for more equity in affairs of the Church and of marriage laws, and advocated legal defence in felony cases. He defended the right of the House of Commons to publish Hansard's reports, irrespective of any action of slander.

He published his own speeches and also the *Lives of the Chief Justices of England from 1066*. He sat in the House of Lords from 1841 to 1849 and was made Lord Chancellor in 1859.

Henry, Lord Cockburn *(1779-1854)*

Born in Edinburgh, son of a baron of the Exchequer, he was early marked out to follow a legal career. He was educated at the High School and University of Edinburgh. He became a member of the Speculative Society where he met Walter Scott and the Whigs Brougham and Jeffrey. He became an advocate at twenty-one and, rather against his own interests, followed Whig principles. He had been made Advocate-Depute in 1806 but his friendship with the radicals caused his dismissal in 1810. However he continued to have extensive clientele and for many years was considered the most formidable speaker in the courts.

He was made Solicitor-General in 1830 and four years later was made

Lord Cockburn. His mansion, which is still to be seen, was at Bonaly, at the foot of the Pentland Hills, a mile or two from the city of Edinburgh. There he held his friends enthralled by his conversation which was noted for its clearness, pathos and simplicity, like his court utterances.

His famous autobiography, though not claimed as such, is entitled *Memorials of his Time* and gives a vivid picture of the metropolis in the stirring 'Golden Age' when Edinburgh attracted geniuses from all quarters of the globe to mingle with her own galaxy of literary, legal and philosophic men and women.

Sir Alexander Cockburn *(1802-1880)*

Sir Alexander J.E. Cockburn of the ancient Scots family of that name, was son of the British minister to Colombia and a French aristocratic mother. Educated at Cambridge for the law and called to the bar in 1829, he practised in Devonshire. He was elected MP for Southampton as a Liberal in 1847 and his first speech was so appreciated by the Premier that he was made Solicitor-General, then Attorney-General.

He took part in many famous trials, being agent for the Crown in the case of William Palmer, the Staffordshire poisoner. He was Lord Chief Justice of England for twenty-four years, dying in harness.

He had a great reputation as a judge, being brilliantly clever and rapid, so much so, that many people of slower modes of thought accused him of making up his mind before he heard the evidence. But he was on the whole thought to be fair. He tried all cases, big or small, with thoroughness, courtesy and dignity. One of his summing-ups, in the famous Tichbourne trial, lasted for eighteen days. The case was one of the most sensational of the century.

Roger Charles Tichbourne 9th baronet, a great adventurer, who mountaineered in the Andes, sailed from Rio de Janeiro in April 1854. The ship was lost, all hands drowned. The insurance was paid and the will approved. His younger brother took the estate but died in 1866. The dowager had always refused to believe Roger was dead and unwisely advertised for news of his survival. In 1865 she got word from Australia that a man answering Roger's description had turned up in the shape of a small butcher at Wagga Wagga, Queensland. Lady Tichbourne 'recognised' him as her son.

The other Tichbournes protested that the lost son was merely Arthur Orton, son of a Wapping butcher. The case came for trial in 1871, and after 100 days and as many witnesses Orton was proved to have committed perjury. He came up before Chief Justice Cockburn who, through the indiscretion of Orton's counsel and testimonies of Orton's sweetheart, was enabled finally to present the above mentioned long summing-up to the jury. Orton got fourteen years.

Cockburn's greatest occasion was abroad when, at Geneva in 1872, he represented the British Government in the *Alabama* case, when the United States sued Britain for damages done to American Federal shipping by three men-of-war fitted up by Britain for the Confederate States who were at war with the Federals. The *Alabama, Shenandoah* and *Florida* did immense damage to Federal ships and Britain was blamed for all of it, though indirectly involved.

Cockburn fought the arbitrators, who were neutral representatives, step by step, to the very last decision, but his arguments, though skilful, were ineffective, and Britain had to pay the United States fifteen and a half million dollars.

His famous dictum on the duties of a lawyer was, 'He ought not to use his powers of argument as an assassin but as a warrior, reconciling his clients' claims with truth and justice.'

Colin Blackburn, Baron *(1813-1896)*

Born in Selkirkshire and educated at Eton and Cambridge, he was not generally known to the public though he had a long experience of commercial law and edited eight volumes on his subject. He was considered the highest authority in England or, of course, elsewhere, in Common Law.

In 1876 he was made a peer and nominated a member of a commission on improvement of Common Law. His standard work is entitled *Sales*, a guide to the intricacies of Commercial Law for many years.

Allan Pinkerton *(1819-1884)*

Born at Glasgow, at twenty-three he emigrated to Chicago and the following year to the town of Dundee, Kane County, Illinois. In Dundee a gang of counterfeiters was at work so Pinkerton set about running them to earth. When he had got them convicted he was appointed deputy-sheriff of Kane County and soon after of Cook County with his headquarters in Chicago.

There he recruited a force of detectives of athletic build and stout character to catch thieves who were stealing from the extensive railyards. This organisation expanded and became much in demand. It was entitled in 1852 the Pinkerton National Detective Agency. It did not restrict itself to petty crime discovery but took part in industrial disputes. One of Pinkerton's major successes was the capture of the key men involved in the robbery of 700,000 dollars from the Adams Express Company in 1866.

A more remarkable exploit was Pinkerton's discovery of a plot to assassinate Abraham Lincoln when he was President-elect and was on his way to Washington via Baltimore. Pinkerton was of course a dedicated Federal man and during the Civil War he sent spies into the South to bring back military secrets to Washington. From this nucleus he developed the Federal Secret Service.

The 'Molly Maguires' was a widespread American Irish secret society recruited from the poorer classes of Irish immigrants. As far as it went it was relatively law-abiding, aiming only to preserve a national identity and to harass landlords and rent-collectors. But a lawless gang got control in the Pennsylvanian coalfields. They intimidated Welsh, English and German miners and tried in many ways to get rid of overseers and police. They did not stop at murder but were cunning enough to see that the murderers were brought in from a distance.

By 1875 the Molly Maguires dominated the coalfields. They forced a general strike. Despite all the efforts to bring the criminals to justice they continued to defy the law.

Pinkerton was brought in. He sent one of his detectives, an Irish Catholic named McParlan, into the coalfields. He joined the Molly Maguires and even rose to be secretary of the most notoriously criminal lodge. His evidence broke up the society by leading to the arrest, conviction and in some cases the execution of proved assassins or murderers.

Sir Thomas Barclay *(1853-1941)*

Born at Dunfermline, he studied at London, Paris and Jena. He was sent by *The Times* as a correspondent to Paris in 1876. After six years he resigned to study French law and its practice. He was the principal agent in cementing the *Entente Cordiale* between Britain and France which was also so much favoured by Edward VII. In 1903-4 he visited the USA and advocated a mutual treaty to improve Anglo-Saxon relations. He continued his efforts to secure a peaceful future for the western world by visiting Berlin in 1905, at the invitation of the Germans.

He was elected MP for Blackburn in 1910. He wrote many books on international law and on the possible solutions to international disputes and it must have been a source of great disappointment when the war of 1914-18 was succeeded in his long life by the outbreak of the Second World War in 1939.

Scholarship

Scotland can lay claim to eminence among the European nations in certain fields of scholarship and research. Edinburgh was the birthplace and nursery of several encyclopaedias, notably the *Encyclopaedia Britannica*. Not only were these conceived and brought into being in Edinburgh, they were also printed and published there.

In what has variously been termed the Golden Age, or the Scottish Enlightenment, there were several historians who set the tone of Europe in their interpretation of the past. In theology the Scots excelled, reducing the study of the Bible and of the works of churchmen to an exact science, as far as this may be done. Translators of famous European works were busy too, not neglecting their own poets and writers.

Students of language, often of languages so little known as never to have had a printed grammar or vocabulary, were numerous among the Scots as among other European nations, at a time when Latin was the common medium of communication. In more modern times, with the extension of travel, many Scots came into contact with Asiatic and African languages and turned to comparative philology, on which the German professors were enthusiastic. Scotland had three or four languages all through the Middle Ages and most students used three of these, their own vernacular, either Gaelic or Scots, or both; Latin, Greek or French. Southern English was generally known among students, many of whom travelled to study at Oxford or Cambridge. These tongues were a good foundation for a study of other Indo-European languages.

The following notes on the lives of the scholars, historians, lexicographers and classical students, are necessarily brief. Where some interesting events or circumstances are connected with them the notice includes this.

John Fordun *(1330-1390)*

He was probably named, after the style of that age, because of his birthplace, Fordun, Kincardineshire. He was a canon of Aberdeen and wrote the *Chronicles of Scotland* from the earliest times up to 1158, the reign of Malcolm IV. He was not able to complete more than five books, but he left notes to bring the history up to 1384, which were completed, enlarged and unfortunately corrupted, by Walter Bower fifty years after Fordun's death. The history of early Scotland is largely based on Fordun's work, which is a great deal more accurate than the later history of Boece.

Andrew Wyntoun *(1360-1430)*

He was a canon of St Andrews and Prior of the monastery of St Serf, an island of Loch Leven. He was one of the first historians of Scotland and his *Orygynale Chronykil of Scotland* is written in verse. It is in nine books and goes back to the very beginning of things, tracing the Scottish nation back to Adam and Eve.

In the *Chronykil* the early books are mythical but the later ones are fairly reliable. Wyntoun's account of Macbeth introduces the three weird sisters and other inventions which will not bear investigation, although they were used by Shakespeare. Wyntoun gives the English a reputation for treachery, especially in their capture of the future James I. He says that no treaty can be made of however sacred obligation, but the English will find a way to break it. In his own lifetime, he had innumerable proofs of this, and Scots often wonder if nearly six centuries of history have changed Wyntoun's verdict.

Hector Boece *(1465-1536)*

He was born at Dundee, educated there, and later studied at Paris to such effect that he was appointed Professor at the College of Montaigu, where he formed a friendship with Erasmus of Rotterdam, the great humanist philosopher and writer, who thought highly of Boece.

On returning home he aided Elphinstone, Bishop of Aberdeen, in founding the university and he was made first Principal. Here he worked successfully with the learned men of the Church. This was, of course, before the religious wars of the Reformation.

Boece wrote a history of the bishops of Moray and Aberdeen, but his most famous work, which he claimed was based on ancient chronicles from the monastery of Icolmkill, is his history of the Scots from their origins. This was written in good style, based on the Latin of Livy. It has been criticised as fabulous and it certainly contains as much romance as fact. For us the most interesting point is that it was a source-book for the English historian Holinshed, but, more important, Shakespeare got the plot of Macbeth from Boece's version. This explains how Macbeth is so falsely portrayed in the play, for Boece obtained his history from a prejudiced source. Still, the nineteen books, published in Paris, gained universal attention for the Scottish nation and gave the Scots a somewhat exaggerated origin going back to Biblical times.

John Major *(1469-1550)*

Born near North Berwick, he was educated at Cambridge, Oxford and Paris, where he was much appreciated as a lecturer in the Montaigu College in Logic and Philosophy. He was perhaps the last and the greatest of the mediaeval Schoolmen who disputed the fine points of theology and whose skill in Latin was never equalled in modern times.

Major wrote many commentaries on the works of Peter Lombard whom later churchmen considered a heretic. But, as a historian, Major's best work was the chronicle of events in England and Scotland up to his own time, that is, the beginning of modern history about 1500.

Among his pupils at St Andrews between 1523 and 1525 were John Knox, George Buchanan and Patrick Hamilton, whose influence on Scotland was to be so marked.

Major was of the old school whose attitude to life and learning is absolutely defunct, and does not have any meaning in the modern world, but his intellectual ability was remarkable and his *Historia Majoris Britanniae* is an enlightened truth-seeking history fully as sceptical as David Hume's history written over two centuries later.

John Bellenden *(1490-1550)*

He spelt his name also Ballantyne or Bannatyne. He was educated at St Andrews and Paris and worked in the finance department of James V. He undertook the translation into Scots of the Latin History of Hector Boece, *Historia Scotorum*, the history of the Scots which had been published in Paris not long before. He also translated several books of Livy, the Latin historian. Bellenden's *History and Chronicles of Scotland* is remarkable for its vigorous and easy style, showing the old Scots tongue as a language well established to deal with all subjects.

John Leslie *(1526-1596)*

Son of the rector of Kingussie, he studied at Aberdeen, Paris and Poitiers. He was a zealous supporter of Queen Mary and joined her in her imprisonment at Tutbury in 1569, when he suffered because of his loyalty. He went to France and did not return.

As a historian he is noted for his Latin *History of Scotland*, published in Rome in 1578 and translated into Scots some years later by a Scottish Benedictine, Father James Dalrymple.

Robert Lindsay *(c.1532-1578)*

He was born on his estate at Pitscottie, near Cupar, Fife. His style is quaint but his facts pretty reliable. He wrote the *Chronicles of Scotland* (1436-1565) dealing with the stirring events of the reigns of the Stuarts from James I to Mary Queen of Scots.

Not much is known for certain about Lindsay, not even the period of his life. His *Chronicles* are written in Scots and are a fine example of the pithy Scots style of the Pre-Union Kingdom. He is never dull, often humorous, shrewd and witty.

George Bannatyne *(1545-1608)*

A native of Newtyle, Forfar, he became a merchant in Edinburgh and was made a burgess in 1587. The story of how he came to collect his world-famous book of ancient Scottish poetry is rather strange.

In 1568 there was an outbreak of plague in Edinburgh and other cities, due to the filth of these rookeries. George retired, as many did in such cases, to the countryside of his birth, and amused his vacant hours by collecting and making copies of poems of the old makars such as Dunbar and Lindsay.

He made up 800 folio pages, divided into five sections. Luckily his work was preserved by his family and passed on to the Advocates Library (now the National Library).

The whole text was published by the Hunterian Club (1873-1902) and Bannatyne's name perpetuated in the famous Bannatyne Club founded in 1823, of which Walter Scott was a member.

William Bellenden *(1555-1630)*

He lived in the reign of Mary and her son James VI and I, and held an important post in the court. Most of his life was spent in Paris where he was a professor in the University and a lawyer in Parliament. His knowledge of Latin, French and English (as well as Scots) enabled him to publish a treatise on regal government based on the principles of Cicero. It was probably as well for his safety that he did not publish it in Britain where James believed in the Divine Right of Kings, a principle not supported by Cicero.

A similar erudite work on Roman politics followed, but Bellenden's *Outline of World History* (in Latin, of course) was an early attempt to collate the scattered chronicles of the nations. His greatest scholarly feat was, unhappily, to be uncompleted at his death. It dealt with the works of the most illustrious Roman writers. Even the uncompleted work was further abridged by much of it being lost on the way to Britain. Bellenden was a scholar of world-wide repute, unknown in Britain for nearly two centuries, until his works were discovered by Dr Parr the English scholar and conversationalist.

John Spottiswoode *(1565-1639)*

He was educated for the church in Glasgow. He had a strong church career, being in turn Archbishop of Glasgow and St Andrews and finally deposed and excommunicated a year before his death.

His chief work is *The History of the Church and State in Scotland*.

John Cameron *(1579-1625)*

He was born in Glasgow and educated there, where he taught Greek in the University for a year, after which he went to France. He lectured at Bordeaux and Sedan and was appointed Professor of Divinity at Saumar, the centre of Protestant education.

Civil War in France drove him to Britain, where King James VI appointed him Principal of Glasgow University. He was a man of moderation, prepared to avoid religious strife and for this he was hated at home and abroad. He was a scholar and wrote in French and Latin on religious subjects. He was opposed to Calvin on several points, especially on free will. He was stabbed to death on the streets of Montauban by a religious opponent.

Arthur Johnston *(1587-1641)*

Born at Caskieben, Aberdeenshire, he studied medicine in Scotland and in

Europe, graduating MD at Padua at twenty-three. He visited many seats of learning and practised as a physician in France. He was also a famous classical scholar and the fame of his original poems in Latin spread over Europe.

In 1625 he was appointed physician to Charles I in London.

He translated the *Psalms of David* into Latin verse and published them in Aberdeen. He also helped to publish and made contributions to the Latin collection of *Most Illustrious Scots Poets of the Age*. A man of many parts, long obscured.

Gilbert Burnet *(1643-1715)*

He is noticed at length in our chapter on Churchmen. His historical works are; an explicit account of the Church of Scotland, a History of the Reformation, a posthumous *History of my own Times*. He also wrote biographical sketches of the Earl of Rochester and Sir Matthew Hale.

Living much of his life in England as Bishop of Salisbury, his style and vocabulary were said to be indistinguishable from those of an Englishman, a great achievement in the Augustan Age of English Literature.

Thomas Ruddiman *(1674-1757)*

Born near Banff he graduated MA at Aberdeen when twenty, was schoolmaster at Laurencekirk for five years and then appointed assistant in the Advocates' Library, Edinburgh. He edited several Latin works and in 1714 he published his famous *Rudiments of the Latin Tongue* which became the most used classical textbook for many generations of scholars, perhaps causing more infantile anxiety than any other schoolbook, methodical though it was.

He edited the works of George Buchanan, Livy, Virgil, and Drummond of Hawthornden. He was succeeded as Head Librarian of the Advocates' Library by David Hume.

Alexander Gordon *(1690-1750)*

Born in Aberdeenshire, he travelled in his early days in Italy, as a tutor. He returned home to devote himself to antiquarian work. He was secretary to the Society for the Promotion of Learning, and of the Society of Antiquaries.

His best known work was his *Itinerarium Septentrionale* or *Northern Journey* wherein he described the antiquities of Northern Scotland. Walter Scott used this interesting character as the main thread of his novel *The Antiquary*, displaying the quaint humour and hobby of this erudite Aberdonian.

Thomas Blackwell *(1701-1757)*

Born at Aberdeen and principal of Marischal College for ten years before his early death. His scholarly works are on the Life and Writings of Homer, a treatise on Mythology and a memoir of the Court of Augustus, the first Roman Emperor. These all show great erudition.

Alexander Cruden (1707-1770)

Born at Aberdeen, son of a prosperous merchant and magistrate, he was educated there and took his MA at Marischal College with a view to entering the ministry. An unhappy love affair upset him so much that he became demented and had to be confined by his friends.

On his restoration to a right frame of mind, he left Aberdeen for London. He tutored privately for some years at Ware, then worked as a bookseller and printer's corrector. He was highly esteemed for his conscientious work, and obtained the post, ill-paid, of Bookseller to the Queen.

In 1737 he finished his enormous task of composing a *Bible Concordance* and presented the first copy, with a dedication, to Queen Caroline, who smiled on him and promised recognition. But she died two weeks later, leaving Cruden to meet the cost of his *Concordance* by selling off his shop and stock of books.

Understandably his dementia returned and he was, against his will, confined in an asylum by order of Dr Munro, one of the famous Scots doctors practising in London. Cruden escaped and brought a legal action against his captors, but failed to obtain damages. He returned to proof-reading and several editions of Greek and Latin books owe their accuracy to his skill.

His eccentricity developed to such an extent that he extended his correction of books to correction of the morals of the nation. He had a hard task, for the English were notable in the eighteenth century for swearing and Sabbath-breaking, the two sins Cruden attacked.

For all his foibles he was a kind Christian, spending much of the gain from his sale of *Concordances* in charity. He published, in Aberdeen, a *Scripture Dictionary* just before his death.

John Campbell (1708-1775)

He was born in Edinburgh. His chief historical work is *Lives of the British Admirals*, a very comprehensive list of these up to the period of his life. He also wrote on the military history of Prince Eugene and John Churchill, Duke of Marlborough, and a *Political Survey of Britain*.

David Hume (1711-1776)

Although noted in the chapter on Philosophers, Hume is also well known as a historian. His *History of England* gave him a high place among historians, though it has been criticised on the grounds of being prejudiced. Dr Johnson saw a number of Scotticisms in it, which to his eyes, of course, was a fault, no matter how well it was otherwise written.

William Robertson (1721-1793)

He has been noticed as a Churchman. His historical books are *History of Scotland 1560–1603* and *History of Charles V* and *History of America*. The first had a remarkable sale, running to fourteen editions in the author's lifetime.

Sir William Hamilton *(1730-1803)*

Younger son of Lord Archibald Hamilton of Riccarton, Linlithgow, he was an officer in the Guards in his youth and Equerry to George III. He married an heiress, became an MP and was Ambassador to the Kingdom of Naples. Here his antiquarian studies began. He made a long and intense study of Naples and Vesuvius, and prompted the excavations of the submerged cities of Pompeii and Herculaneum. He sent accounts of the finds to Britain and made a valuable collection of Greek and Etruscan vases, publishing a description with illustrations.

1791 was his annus mirabilis. At sixty-one he was made a Privy Councillor and achieved everlasting notoriety by adding to his collection of articles of vertu the enchantress Emma, afterwards the mistress of Nelson.

His publications, sumptuously produced, include *The Antiquities of Etruria, Greece and Rome, Mount Vesuvius, Campi Phlegraei* (the description of the buried cities of Pompeii and Herculaneum, the strange title being a classical reference to a district in Macedonia where the gods, led by Vulcan, are supposed to have destroyed the giants by lightning).

Colin MacFarquhar *(1745-1793)*

Though little is known of MacFarquhar's birth or education, he was a young man of wide and deep knowledge. At the age of twenty-three he arranged with Andrew Bell, an engraver, to publish the *Encyclopaedia Britannica* in Edinburgh. The editor was William Smellie (1740-1795) a printer. MacFarquhar, according to Archibald Constable, was the actual projector of the *Encyclopaedia*.

The first numbers were published in December 1768. The second edition was edited by James Tytler MA, mentioned in our chapter on Inventors. He is said to have written many of the scientific and historical articles and almost all the minor articles. The third edition was edited by MacFarquhar himself as far as the article *Mysteries*, when he died, 'worn out by fatigue and anxiety of mind'.

Hugo Arnot *(1749-1786)*

He was born at Leith, son of a shipmaster named Pollock. He changed his surname to Arnot, that being the name of a small family estate in Fife. A whole volume could be made of the eccentricities of this gifted but afflicted man.

He was educated for the law and passed advocate when twenty-three. His chronic asthma had not yet reduced him to the meagre shape he afterwards had to endure. He made advances to a young society lady, sister of a future Marquis of Tweeddale, but was not finally accepted. In his lodgings in St Andrew Street he used to ring a bell to call his valet with the shaving water. His neighbour objected to the noise and asked him to call his servant in a different manner. He obliged by firing a pistol each morning.

His great work was *History of Edinburgh*, fully illustrated with drawings of historical buildings long since demolished. It was a source-book for all future historians. He also published *Criminal Trials* not without interest for students of Arnot's time.

In his short life he suffered much from the ridicule of his fellow-citizens but he persisted in his labours as a historian.

James Currie *(1756-1805)*

As a doctor he is known as the first to use the thermometer in clinical medicine; as a collector he was the first editor of Burns' works, which he published in 1800, less than four years after the poet's death, the proceeds to be devoted to Burns' widow and children. He had been an acquaintance of Burns from 1792, being a native of Kirkpatrick-Fleming in Dumfriesshire. His edition of Burns has naturally been the subject of criticism by later Burns exponents, but at least it had the merit of being produced when Burns' reputation was still under a cloud.

John Pinkerton *(1758-1826)*

He was born in Edinburgh of an old East Lothian family. Educated at Lanark Grammar School, he worked in a lawyer's office for a number of years, then settled in London.

He was an industrious and accomplished but irritable writer. He was an antiquary and historian who wrote on miscellaneous subjects, poetry, literature, geography, history, geology, medals, ethnology.

Many amusing encounters took place between him and George Chalmers on Scottish history. He also exchanged scurrilities with an equally quarrelsome historian Joseph Ritson over the original races and languages of Scotland.

John Jamieson *(1759-1838)*

Son of a minister, he was born in Glasgow and educated at Glasgow and Edinburgh Universities. He was licensed to preach in 1789 and became pastor of an Anti-burgher or Session Church in Forfar. He brought about the Union of the two Session Churches in 1820.

Important though his church activities were, he is remembered with gratitude by students of the Scottish language for his scholarly work *An Etymological Dictionary of the Scottish Language* (1808).

Thomas McCrie *(1772-1835)*

A native of Duns, Berwickshire, he studied for the ministry at Edinburgh and was ordained a minister of the Anti-burgher Associate Synod (Auld Lichts) there. His researches covered much ground and were very particular. He published a life of John Knox, another of Andrew Melville, both reformers, and was naturally an apologist for some of their more rebellious acts and Calvinist vigour. He attacked Sir Walter Scott's picture of the Covenanting zealots (in *Old Mortality*) but Scott had drawn his information and characteristics from the works of Peden and other enthusiasts and defended himself against the charge of excessive portrayal. McCrie also wrote a *History of the Reformation in Spain.*

James Mill *(1773-1836)*

Born at Montrose, son of a shoemaker, he studied for the ministry after much privation on the part of his poor parents. However he gave up the church in favour of literature, settling in London. He edited and wrote for many periodicals but his great work, published in 1806, was his *History of India*.

In 1829 he obtained the post of district examiner with charge of the Revenue Department with the East India Company. He wrote many articles on the administration of India.

He was a man of profound and original thought, deeply read on all subjects. He influenced many young men of his time, including his eldest son, the great political economist John Stuart Mill.

Alexander Murray *(1773-1813)*

Son of a Galloway shepherd, he was self-taught as he lived in a remote area far from a school. He had an excellent memory and was well versed in Scripture. He began to teach neighbours' families when he was twelve and attended a school at Minnigaff, some miles away. He learned the elements of Greek, Latin, Hebrew and French, as well as Arabic. He was a prodigy and as such was given a free run of University classes in Edinburgh. Having mastered the Abyssinian language he undertook to prepare for Constable, the publishers, a new edition of the travels of James Bruce, the Abyssinian explorer.

He took to divinity and was appointed assistant to the talented Dr Muirhead, minister of Urr parish, the only man who, by a severe reply to Burns' satire on him, actually got under the bard's skin. Murray did not long remain in the upland parish. He was elected Professor of Oriental Languages in Edinburgh and made a Doctor of Divinity. He burned himself out and died at forty-three. His publications are, *Outlines of Oriental Philology* and *A History of European Languages*.

Robert Jamieson *(1780-1844)*

He made an important contribution to the preservation of Scottish tradition. In 1806 he published his *Popular Ballads and Songs from Traditional Manuscript and Scarce Sources*. Sir Walter Scott held Jamieson in high esteem for his wide knowledge of his subject and his zeal in preserving much oral music and song that would otherwise have perished.

Allan Cunningham *(1784-1842)*

Born in Dumfriesshire, he worked as a stone-mason's apprentice. His father was a neighbour of Robert Burns, when the poet farmed at Ellisland, so Allan knew him. He also knew James Hogg, the Ettrick Shepherd. These connections turned him to writing verse and songs himself.

He went to London and worked for Chantrey the sculptor for thirty years. Cunningham's publications include, *Lives of British Painters, Sculptors and Architects, Tales of the Peasantry, Works of Robert Burns, Songs of Scotland, History of Literature 1770-1830*, etc.

John Ramsay McCulloch *(1789-1864)*

Born at Whithorn, Wigtownshire, he edited *The Scotsman* newspaper during its early stages for a year and began writing on the 'dreary science', political economy. He published a work on the principles of the study and was accordingly made professor at London. He became also Comptroller of the Stationery Office where he introduced reforms. His monumental works are, *Dictionary of Commerce and Commercial Navigation,* and *Statistical Account of the British Empire (1837)* the year the Victorian Age began.

Patrick Tytler *(1791-1849)*

Younger son of law-lord Lord Woodhouselee, he was born in Edinburgh and studied there for the law but turned to literature.

He wrote for *Blackwood's Magazine*. His first book was on the life of the Admirable Crichton. Then came his life of John Wycliff. He was recommended by Sir Walter Scott to write a history of Scotland. This, when completed, covered the story from 1249 to 1603, and was recognised as the best Scottish history up to Tytler's time. He also wrote *Lives of the Scottish Worthies, Life of Henry VIII, England under Edward VI and Mary, Discovery on the Northern Coasts of America* and *Life of Walter Raleigh*.

Alexander Dyce *(1798-1869)*

Born in Edinburgh, educated at the High School, he graduated from Oxford when twenty-one, intended for the clergy. But he settled in London as a literary man in 1825 and devoted his life to producing editions of English classical poetry. He was well known for his wisdom and learning.

He was the first to collect and publish the works of the Elizabethan dramatist Peele. He also published the dramas of Greene, a contemporary of Peele.

Other publications, concentrated on the same glorious period, were of Webster, Shirley, Middleton, Beaumont and Fletcher, Marlowe and Shakespeare.

Hew Scott *(1800-1872)*

Born in Haddington and educated for the ministry in Edinburgh, he was an enthusiast for the research of early parish records and personally visited hundreds of parishes in Scotland to collect these details. He was minister of the East Fife parish of Anstruther Wester. His record of the Church of Scotland occupied most of his life and he died shortly after completing it. The Latin title of this immense work which has of course been continually revised over the last century is *Fasti Ecclesiae Scoticanae*.

Robert Chambers *(1802-1871)*

A Peebles native, younger brother of William Chambers. They founded the famous publishing house. Robert, while still a young man, with the personal encouragement of Sir Walter Scott, compiled the very entertaining *Traditions of Edinburgh* as well as *Illustrations of the Author of Waverley*. These were rapidly followed by his *History of the Rebellion of 1745*. His *Picture of*

Scotland is a graphic description of a walking tour he made all round Scotland, bringing in local history and description. He was then only twenty-five.

He published the *Popular Rhymes of Scotland, Life of James I,* a *Dictionary of Eminent Scotsmen,* and *Life of Robert Burns.* The last was a discretionary tale, as it was for the benefit of the bard's family.

The *Book of Days* is an enormous assembly of all kinds of curious knowledge and narrative, written to entertain the Victorian reader. It is still a mine of curious fact and fancy. It was said that the vast amount of research for this two-volume compendium shortened his life.

His most notable achievement was an anonymous scientific study, anticipating Darwin's theory of Evolution, entitled *Vestiges of the Natural History of the Creation*, published in 1844.

Henry Glassford Bell *(1805-1874)*

Born in Glasgow and trained for the law, he was ultimately chief Sheriff of Lanarkshire. He was a brilliant contributor to *Blackwood's Magazine* and noted for his wit and humour. His one notable contribution to history was his vindication of the unhappy queen, Mary of Scots. In this history he defended her with strong emotion and sympathy and it is due to Bell that the Queen is preserved in history as a long-suffering victim of religious and political spite.

John Stuart Blackie *(1809-1895)*

He was born in Glasgow, educated in Edinburgh, Aberdeen, Germany and Italy, and intended to enter the Church. His studies abroad gave him a change of heart; he studied law and passed advocate in Edinburgh.

He had acquired a taste for classics and literature and at twenty-five he published a popular translation of Goethe's *Faust*. At thirty he was made Professor of Latin at Aberdeen. His ability in Greek led to his appointment to that chair at Edinburgh where his general enthusiasm made him very popular with the students. He wrote many student songs in Greek, Latin, Scots and English, some of which are still sung.

He adopted a pronunciation of Greek based on his own visits to Greece. At home he was mainly responsible for the establishment of a Professorship of Celtic in Edinburgh. He did more to present scholarship in an attractive light than any other learned man.

William Forbes Skene *(1809-1892)*

He was born at Inverie, Loch Nevis, the second son of a friend of Sir Walter Scott, Skene of Rubislaw. He was educated at Edinburgh High School, in Germany and at St Andrews and Edinburgh Universities. He studied for the law and became a Writer to the Signet, but his interest was in obscure areas of Scottish history. He had learned Gaelic while residing at the Manse of Laggan, Inverness-shire, so he was able to write with insight and knowledge on Celtic Scotland. He succeeded Hill Burton as Historiographer Royal.

His published works are chiefly, *The Highlanders of Scotland, their Origin, History and Antiquities, Celtic Scotland, The Dean of Lismore's*

Book, Chronicles of the Picts and Scots, and *The Four Ancient Books of Wales*.

Skene was considered by European scholars to be the greatest Scottish archaeologist of last century.

John Hill Burton *(1809-1881)*

Born in Aberdeen, he was educated there and in Edinburgh where he took up literary work.

His first historical work was *The Life and Correspondence of David Hume*, followed by the *Lives of Simon Fraser and Duncan Forbes*, two men of diametrically opposed character, noticed in our chapter on Statesmen. He wrote a history of Scotland in two separate books, the first dealing with the first half of the eighteeenth century, the second dealing with all the previous eighteen centuries. Needless to say, the first book was more accurate than the second, being better documented.

He also wrote the *History of the Reign of Queen Anne,* and *The Scot Abroad*, telling of the exploits of Scots in Europe. His style is accurate and its pedanticism relieved by flashes of Aberdeen pawky humour.

Joseph Robertson *(1810-1866)*

Born at Aberdeen and educated there and at Marischal College, he worked for Oliver & Boyd for some years in Edinburgh. He was author of a book on Aberdeen, *Book of the Bon Accord* and founded the Spalding Club dealing with the history of the North-east of Scotland.

He was Curator of the Historical Department of the Register House for the last ten years of his life.

Among his publications were *A Cartulary of the Black Friars of Glasgow* and *Catalogue of the Jewels of Mary Queen of Scots*. He also wrote on the little-known aspects of Church History.

John Muir *(1810-1882)*

Born at Glasgow and educated there and at Haileybury. He was with the Civil Service in India for twenty-five years. His great work was *Original Sanskrit Texts*. He also wrote *Metrical Translations from Sanskrit Writers*.

William Muir *(1819-1905)*

Younger brother of the above, he also spent much of his illustrious career with the Indian Civil Service, being Lieutenant-General of the North-West Frontier, then Finance Minister for India. He published a *Life of Mahomet, The Early Caliphate,* and a *History of the Marmelukes or Slave Dynasty*.

David Masson *(1822-1907)*

He was born at Aberdeen and educated at the Marischal College and at Edinburgh University. When twenty-five he lived in London writing for reviews and encyclopaedias and editing *MacMillan's Magazine*.

He became Professor of English Literature in University College London and thirteen years later in Edinburgh, where he taught for thirty years.

His *Life of John Milton* in six volumes is the most complete biography of any Englishman. Masson also wrote a work on British novelists, and on *Recent British Philosophy*. His biographies of Drummond of Hawthornden and of De Quincey, followed by an edition of the latter, were very popular.

He edited the Registers of the Privy Council of Scotland, a work requiring much skill as an archivist and scholar. He was made Historiographer Royal for Scotland in 1893.

John Francis Campbell *(1822-1885)*

Born in Islay, educated at Eton and Edinburgh University, he worked as a minor government official. He spent years of holidays and other leisure journeying round the Gaelic-speaking areas of Scotland, chiefly the Western Isles and Coasts. He collected, translated and edited the folk-lore of the Scottish Gael. He published *Popular Tales of the West Highlands* in four volumes from 1860-62, a collection invaluable to students of Gaeldom. He also invented the sunshine recorder used in British meteorological stations.

James Gairdner *(1828-1912)*

Born at Edinburgh, he entered the Public Record Office London to become assistant keeper. With erudition, accuracy and good judgement he edited many historical documents and also published *The Houses of Lancaster and York, Life of Richard III, Studies in English History*, and *Henry VII*.

Sir James A.H. Murray *(1837-1915)*

Born at Denholm, near Hawick, and educated locally, he went to Edinburgh University where he graduated at the mature age of thirty-six. Before this he had been teaching, chiefly at Hawick. After many years studying and teaching, his reputation as a philologist had increased to such an extent that he was asked to undertake the editing of the long-projected *New English Dictionary*, the materials for which were enormous in bulk alone, weighing several tons.

Murray got together a team of readers but only his encouragement and enthusiasm held them together. In 1885 he gave up teaching at Mill Hill School and set up his famous 'Scriptorium' in Oxford where the colossal work went on, year after year. He was personally responsible for about half of the alphabet but he inspired others to complete it. He was honoured by the British Academy and by the Crown for his mental brilliance and stamina.

Sir William W. Hunter *(1840-1900)*

Educated at Glasgow, Paris and Bonn, he entered the Indian Civil Service at twenty-two. He was appointed superintendent of public instruction in Orissa, when he wrote the *Annals of Rural Bombay*, and a *Comparative Dictionary of the non-Aryan Languages of India*.

He became the Director-General of the Statistical Department, his first task being the census of 1872.

He retired in 1877. His publications include *The Imperial Gazetteer of India*, in fourteen volumes; *Orissa, Assam, A History of British India*.

Andrew Lang *(1844-1912)*

Born at Selkirk, he was educated at Edinburgh Academy, St Andrews and Oxford. Although described as the greatest journalist of his age, he wrote history from a romantic point of view. He wrote on Mary Queen of Scots, John Knox, a history of Scotland (AD84-1746). He also was interested in French history, especially Joan of Arc and the mystery of the *Man in the Iron Mask*. His studies of Homeric poems were well received.

William Robertson Smith *(1846-1894)*

Born at Keig, Aberdeenshire, he graduated at Aberdeen and studied theology at Edinburgh, Bonn and Gottingen. At twenty-four he became Professor of Hebrew and Old Testament studies at Aberdeen Free Church College.

In 1870 he wrote the article *Bible* for the *Encyclopaedia Britannica* and was accused of heresy, but acquitted. Immediately on his acquittal, another article in the *Encyclopaedia Britannica* on the Hebrew language caused him to be removed from his professorship.

He gave lectures on Old Testament subjects and became Editor-in-Chief of the *Encyclopaedia Britannica* in 1887. He was made Professor of Arabic at Cambridge and was an authority on the religion of the Semitic peoples. He died aged only forty-eight.

Peter Hume Brown *(1850-1918)*

A native of Haddington, he studied for his degree in Edinburgh. He published the biographies of George Buchanan and of John Knox and wrote a *History of Scotland* which was shortened for use in schools. His style has been called severe, and unrelieved by the human incidents which endear history to the reader. He was perhaps affected by his subject, Ancient Scottish History and Paleography, of which he was the first professor in Edinburgh. He was, however, an authority in his day, though much of his history has been challenged.

William Laughton Lorimer *(1885-1967)*

Son of the Free Church minister of Mains and Strathmartine in Angus, he succeeded to a scholarly tradition for his forebears had high reputations in the world of learning and religion.

He was educated at Dundee High School and at Fettes College, and won a scholarship in classics to Oxford in 1904. Following a nervous illness he stayed a winter in Italy where he acquired perfect fluency in Italian. He returned to Oxford in 1906 and became Greek assistant in 1910 at St Andrews.

In 1914-15 he was in the Army, suffered pneumonia, and worked in the Intelligence Department of the War Office until 1919. He taught Latin in Dundee before taking the Chair of Greek in St Andrews in 1953.

His professional and domestic life alike were full of disappointments but he never wavered in the demands he made upon himself in his scholarship and his relations with his fellow-men.

His great contribution to Scottish letters and religion is his translation of the New Testament into Scots. The enormous amount of work involved consulting all translations of the New Testament in twenty languages, including many minority languages such as Flemish and Frisian. The result has proven a gratifying success, surpassing all previous work in Scots prose. Moreover, it raises hopes for the future development of a resurrected Scots tongue.

Douglas C.C. Young *(1913-1973)*

He was born at Tayport, near Dundee, but spent part of his childhood in Bengal, learning to speak Urdu. He was educated at Merchiston Castle, St Andrews and Oxford. He taught Greek at King's College, Aberdeen, from 1938 to 1941.

He began writing poetry in Greek, Latin, Scots and English, proving himself as widely learned in foreign tongues as the mediaeval Scots scholars. His great height and beard gave him a distinguished appearance and he was a close acquaintance of many academicians and gentry.

He courageously resisted the authorities who sought to enlist him for the Second World War, and was jailed for a year, spent not unpleasantly reading Greek classics.

From 1947 to 1968 he taught classics at Dundee and St Andrews, going to the USA as a Classics Professor.

He died suddenly in 1973, in North Carolina, in the full vigour of mind and body, with a book of Homer open before him.

His publications consist of poems in Scots and prose writings in English. His translation of *The Frogs*, by Aristophanes, into Scots was a successful drama in a comic vein.

Calum I. MacLean *(1915-1960)*

He was the third son of Malcolm MacLean, tailor of Raasay, and Christina Nicolson of Braes, Skye. From them he inherited a love of oral and written lore and of song-making.

He attended Portree Secondary School and graduated MA with First Class Honours in Celtic at Edinburgh under Professor I.C. Watson. On two scholarships he studied Old Irish and Mediaeval and Modern Welsh in Dublin.

He was appointed Collector of Folklore in the Gaelic-speaking area of Connaught and in 1946 he continued this labour of love in the Hebrides, making, in only four years, the largest collection of folk-tales since the work of J.F. Campbell of Islay, a century before.

His appointment in 1951 to the newly-established School of Scottish Studies in Edinburgh began a decade of great activity in the collection and storage of folk-lore from many areas of Scotland both Gaelic and Lowland. This enormous work involved MacLean in much hardship, especially after the loss of his left arm in 1957.

Future scholars of many nations will have reason to bless the conscientious skills of a man who, with intense love of his country's traditions, did not spare himself to record Highland history and contemporary life from the unique point of view of the Scottish Gael. He published many articles and a unique book, *The Highlands*.

Poetry

Scotland has a poetic tradition going back to pre-history. Each of the constituent tribes of the future Scotland had its distinct style of poetry. The earliest poets of the Britons, or Strathclyde Welsh, are known by name, and several poems have survived. They wrote heroic verse for tribal enjoyment. Arthur was known personally to them and is mentioned in their ballad of disaster, the *Gododin*, the epic of heroes who died fighting the Angles. But these invaders from Europe also had their bards or skalds who sang of tribal heroes who lived in the fourth century in Europe. The Anglo-Saxon poems of adventure, such as *Widsith* (The Wanderer) and *Beowulf* are full of striking phrase and vigorous rhythm. The Gaelic Scots brought a great wealth of poetry from Ireland, including the Ossianic poems, composed in the third and fourth centuries. Many refer to places in Scotland so they must have been composed after the immigration. Sir James Macgregor, Dean of Lismore, wrote these early Gaelic poems in phonetic Gaelic in 1512. The original is in the National Library of Scotland. As for the poems of the Picts and Caledonians, they were obliterated by the Scots, except for one epic translated from the Pictish original into Old Irish Gaelic in the seventh century, shortly after the battle of Dunnichen in AD 685, which it commemorates. It celebrates the destruction of the Anglian King and his invading army.

Scottish poetry, as usually understood, i.e. written in a form of Northern English quite distinct from Southern English in syntax and grammar, begins in the thirteenth century with Thomas Learmonth of Earlston, often called Thomas the Rhymer. His tale of adventure, *Sir Tristrem* was published by Sir Walter Scott, who credited Thomas with the authorship, though some critics think the original language had been altered a century later. The Rhymer's prophecies are wide-spread over Scotland, and there is no doubt he was well-known for his strange abduction into Fairyland, a tale generally believed in mediaeval days.

Although there was a state of war between England and Scotland at the end of the Middle Ages, during most of the fourteenth, fifteenth and sixteenth centuries, there was much communication between scholars, poets and courtiers. The Scots poets were quite familiar with the works of the Southern English poets of the age of Chaucer, who died in 1400, and no doubt this was mutual. As an instance, when James I was held captive in England, he acquired such skill in poetry that he was held in high esteem in both countries. After Chaucer, poetry declined in the south, but flourished in Scotland, and a whole school of court poets brought a renaissance to the reigns of the first five Jameses for a glorious century.

But sadder days followed with the wars of religion, and the stern faith of the Presbyterians. In the words of an earlier fragment of lament of the thirteenth century, 'Our gold was changed into lead'. Even though innumerable ballads in Scots were sung by the people, poetry by individuals could not avoid dwindling into dialect, often not understandable outside the region where it was sung. Poets who aimed at ambitious themes turned more and more to writing in the 'King's English'.

Then with the genius of Allan Ramsay, Robert Fergusson and Robert Burns, came a great revival of Scots, though a much-watered-down language compared with the masterful tongue of the fifteenth century. With a few exceptions the poets following Burns produced only trivial imitations. Yet, despite the general opposition to it from most quarters, Scots continued to be spoken and written, and a new effort, bravely named a renaissance, was made in the twenties of this century by Hugh MacDiarmid and others to restore the old tongue. It is not yet clear whether this could be called a re-birth or a long series of galvanic twitches.

Scots have also written good poetry in English, as indeed they have also done in Latin and other acquired tongues. Perhaps the best work in English was done in the eighteenth and early nineteenth centuries by Thomson, Blair, Beattie, Campbell, Scott and Byron. Their work differs little from the writings of Englishmen, and some anthologists have excluded them from collections of Scottish poetry, even though to a trained ear, a native Scot's English can be detected, either by its artificiality or by its echoes of Scotticisms.

There was also a revival of Gaelic poetry in the seventeenth and eighteenth centuries which seems to have been inspired rather than suffocated by the severe persecutions of the Jacobites after Culloden.

It is no exaggeration to count Scottish poets in hundreds. It was said of most Scottish towns, such as Paisley and Hawick, that the poets out-numbered the police. It is impracticable here to give notices of all Scots poets, even if all were known, for many good poets have remained private and have consequently never reached the anthologies. In any case poetry is so difficult to assess that poets, lauded to the skies in one generation, have been completely forgotten in the next. Consequently it is a distorted view that one gets looking at poets from the present time backwards, as many who loom large today will have dwindled to insignificance a century hence, and vice versa. Certain poets, however, have stood the test of time and we list them here with a brief note of their life and achievements.

Thomas Learmonth (Thomas the Rhymer) *(c. 1220-1294)*

There is no historical record of his birth but his name appears in a charter of about 1260 and again in 1294. He wrote the romance of *Sir Tristrem* and also numerous rhyming prophecies which survived orally among the people for centuries. He is supposed to have been spirited away to Fairyland and to have been given the gift of poetic speech by the Queen of the Fairies. He gained a great reputation by actually prophesying the death of Alexander III the day before it happened.

John Barbour (1316-1396)

He was born near Aberdeen and studied for a Church career, becoming Archdeacon of Aberdeen. He travelled through England on several occasions, being granted a passport to go to Oxford or to the continent. He was in favour with the court of David II and Robert II and this perhaps prompted him to write his great epic poem the *Bruce*. This is of 14,000 lines in rhyme; but only in places, as in his praise of freedom, does it rise to the height of poetry. But it provided a basis for the hero-worship of Robert Bruce and is an enjoyable romance, full of incident, covering the career of the second liberator of Scotland. William Wallace is not mentioned but that omission was rectified by a later poet.

James I (1394-1437)

At the age of twelve he was sent by sea to be educated at the court of France, but was treacherously captured in time of peace by an English ship off Flamborough Head, and spent the next eighteen years in captivity, much of the time in the Tower of London. He was not ill-treated but had a chance to study general subjects, including literature and the laws of England. He brought back as his bride Joan Beaufort, great grand-daughter of Edward III, but the Scots had to pay a ransom of £40,000. James did not prove a good bargain, and his stern measures to build up the royal fortunes made him so very unpopular that it was no surprise when he was assassinated. His wife took a fearful revenge on his enemies.

He was credited with several poems but *The King's Quair*, or *Book*, is his finest work, full of love and chivalry. Of his six daughters three were married to European monarchs and in an age when educated women were scarce, they all proved to be excellent poets.

Robert Henryson (1425-1506)

He was educated partly in a Scottish university and partly abroad, perhaps in Paris. He became a member of Glasgow University in 1462 and was schoolmaster in Dunfermline. He was of the Benedictine Order. Although a thorough student of Chaucer, who died in 1400, Henryson wrote in an original way. His pastoral poem *Robene and Makyne* (Robin and May) is the first poem of its kind in the English language. Its humorous appeal is as fresh today as when written. Henryson's fables of animals are equally bright and witty. In them he made satirical comments on the society of his age.

Blind Harry (or Henry the Minstrel) (c.1430-1493)

His birthplace is not exactly known but he wandered around Scotland reciting his long epic on the life and deeds of William Wallace.

Although he professed to be unlettered and is said to have been blind, his verse shows that he was well enough educated and keen-sighted enough, in one sense, to have read Chaucer. Even less historical than Barbour's *Bruce*, nevertheless the *Wallace* was popular reading right up to the time of Robert Burns, who says that the first two books he ever read were Blind Harry's *Wallace* and the story of Hannibal. But the version Burns read had been translated in 1722 from the Old Scots of Henry the Minstrel into a more modern Lowland Scots, otherwise the Scots of Burns' day would have found it hard to follow.

The *Wallace* is a rhymed poem of over 11,000 lines, like the *Bruce* full of incident, but decidedly more savage and full of hatred of the 'Auld Enemy'. But with all its faults we owe to it the 'flood of Scottish prejudice' which Burns said 'poured into his veins'.

William Dunbar *(c.1460-1513)*

He was born in East Lothian and graduated at St Andrews University when nineteen. He became a Franciscan, an order dedicated to poverty and preaching. Yet he says he made good cheer preaching in every town in England from Berwick south. After a visit to the continent he threw off the friar's habit and became an ambassador for James IV to foreign courts. On a visit to London to arrange the King's marriage to Margaret Tudor he wrote a poem in London and dined with the Lord Mayor.

Dunbar did not write for the people but for the court. Consequently his poems were forgotten for two centuries after his death, and it was Sir Walter Scott who called him the 'darling of the Scottish muses'. His variety of theme and treatment show him to be as broadminded as Burns and as liable to shock the prudish reader. His most remarkable poems are *The Dance of the Sevin Deidly Synnis* and the *Tua Mariit Wemen and the Wedo*; the latter shows woman's views on sexuality with no hold barred. His *Lament for the Makaris* (poets) is perhaps the most memorable poem of pathos in any language.

Walter Kennedy *(c.1460-1508)*

He probably held a church office in Ayrshire and had been well educated for that post. Apart from one or two shorter poems of note, such as 'In Praise of Age' he is chiefly remembered for his part in the highly amusing duel of abuse with William Dunbar. It is entitled 'The Flyting', a Scottish term for a scolding match. The two contestants used the most scurrilous expressions but actually they were good friends. Dunbar, in the *Lament for the Makaris*, speaks of 'Good Master Walter Kennedy lying at point of death, which is a great sorrow to all'.

Gavin Douglas *(1475-1522)*

He was born at Tantallon Castle in East Lothian, third son of Archibald Earl of Douglas, 'Bell the Cat'. He was educated for the Church at St Andrews and Paris. After holding several prominent church posts he fled to England because of the feud between the Douglasses and the Duke of Albany. He was proscribed as a traitor, but died of the plague in London.

His best-known work is a translation into Scots of Virgil's *Aeneid*, the first classical Latin poem to be translated into 'English', though of the Northern variety. He admits to using Latin, French and Southern English words where they make better sense than his native Scots.

Sir David Lyndsay *(1490-1555)*

It is not certain if he was born in Fife or East Lothian but he was educated at St Andrews and employed at the court of James IV. He was with the King at church in Linlithgow when an apparition appeared and warned James not to set off on his fatal invasion of England that led to Flodden. The young James V knighted him and sent him as ambassador to Europe.

His poems are racy, coarse and humorous, giving a vivid picture of his age. His works were the most popular in Scotland for two centuries until Burns succeeded him as the poet of the Scottish people. He satirised the failings of the Church and encouraged John Knox to be a preacher. His most notable work, dramatised for the Edinburgh Festival some thirty years ago, was *Ane Pleasant Satyre of the Thrie Estaites*. It was first played in the open air before the court, the bishops and populace at Linlithgow, Cupar and Edinburgh about 1540, where its frequent indecencies were fully appreciated.

Alexander Scott *(c.1525-1584)*

Very little is known for certain of this gifted poet, but, we may infer from his humorous satire, *The justing and debait up at the Drum*, that he was a Lothian native, probably of Dalkeith, which lies in a valley a mile or two below the Drum estate.

Another of his longer and traditional poems in the old alliterative style has a peculiar historical interest. It was addressed to Mary, Queen of Scots, greeting her on her arrival from France, and is entitled *Ane New Yere Gift*. She could not have been altogether pleased with Scott's gift, for most of the poem of 224 lines is a complaint against the Roman Catholic abuses and the injustices suffered by the poorer Scots before the banning of Catholicism in 1560. Mary remained all her short life a staunch Catholic. But there was one pleasing part in the poem wherein Scott put into a verse an old prophecy that from Mary would spring a bairn who would rule all Britain. This ultimately came to pass, though it seemed very unlikely in 1562. But four years later Mary's son James was born, to fulfil the prophecy in 1603 by succeeding Elizabeth.

Ane New Yere Gift, though of historical and social interest, and revealing the excellence of Scott's technique, was not his best achievement. He is remembered for his three dozen love-lyrics in all humours, light, passionate and earthy, so excellent that they were not approached in poetic quality until the following century when the English Carolingian poets Herrick, Waller and Lovelace wrote their immortal songs.

Alexander Montgomery *(c.1556-1610)*

He is reputed to have spent his youth in Renfrewshire and to have resided for a time in Galloway. He was a favourite of James VI and had an appointment at Court. Although he gratified the low tastes of James and his courtiers by indulging in a flyting with Hume of Polwarth with the normal abuse, he also wrote religious poetry. His poetical masterpieces, full of a fresh description of nature, are his *The Cherrie and the Slae* and *The Banks of Helicon*.

222

He was the last of the grand generation of makars, writing their poems in the style and against the background of old Scotland.

Anonymous Ballad-makers *(13th to 18th centuries)*

Although the author or authors of the many famous Scottish ballads are not known, there is no doubt that they are far superior to most of the acknowledged poets. The best-known of these popular tales, which were composed to be sung or chanted, not read, are *Sir Patrick Spens, The Young Tamlane, The Wife of Usher's Well, Otterburn, Kinmont Willie, Mary Hamilton.* As Andrew Lang said, 'Praise is superfluous. They charm all ranks in all ages'.

William Drummond of Hawthornden *(1585-1649)*

He was born at Hawthornden, a few miles from Edinburgh, son of the first laird of that estate. He attended the High School and University of Edinburgh and then studied law in France. On his father's death in 1610 he succeeded to the estate and was able to devote himself to poetry.

Drummond was an accomplished classical scholar with a knowledge of Italian, Spanish, Hebrew and French. He was also an associate of several English poets such as Drayton and Jonson. In 1613 on the lamented death of Henry, the elder son of James I, Drummond wrote an elegy, *Tears on the Death of Meliades*, which showed his Royalist sympathies. His beloved wife, Mary Cunningham, died suddenly soon after their marriage and Drummond published a collection of poems in many forms to lament his loss. These are all in Southern English, some being models of Italian sonnets and other verse forms. He could write in Scots but rarely did, though one of his disputed productions is a comical poem in a mixture of Scots and Latin entitled *Polemo-Middinia* or a treatise on middens, an unlikely topic for him.

At Christmas 1618 he entertained Ben Jonson at Hawthornden and made a record of their conversations which may still be read. In 1623 appeared his *Flowers of Sion. Cypresse Grove*, a prose work of unique style, revealed an amazing command of powerful and musical English. He also wrote several other prose books of history and political argument in favour of the Royalists, especially the Marquis of Montrose, a personal friend. The death by execution of Charles I is said to have so shattered Drummond that he died later that year.

Allan Ramsay *(1684-1758)*

He was born in the highest village in Scotland, Leadhills. He was the son of a leadmine manager. On the death of his parents, Allan, having had a good village education, was apprenticed to an Edinburgh wig-maker. After a full apprenticeship he set up on his own. He was appointed poet-laureate of the 'Easy Club', one of Edinburgh's many social clubs. His poems became very popular. He gave up wig-making for publishing, and produced a collection of Scottish songs entitled 'The Tea-Table Miscellany'. Encouraged by its reception he embarked on an edition of ancient Scots poems, of such writers as Dunbar and Douglas, for which he was quite unqualified, as his knowledge was restricted to his own, now debased, dialect. He redeemed his reputation by returning to known ground and publishing *The Gentle Shepherd*, a realistic picture of Scottish rural life as he knew it.

His attempts to open a theatre were thwarted by the bigoted Presbyterians. Otherwise he had a prosperous and respected life. It was his initiative and love of the old Scots life of good humour and liveliness that began a revival of Scots poetry when so many of his contemporaries were turning their backs on it in favour of Southern English.

Robert Blair *(1699-1746)*

He was born in Edinburgh, son of the minister of the Old Church, and was educated for the ministry. Having a private income he was able to complete his education in Holland. The Church of Scotland early in the eighteenth century was extremely Calvinistic and constrained. It exercised a strong tyranny over the people, arresting for Sabbath-breaking and publicly rebuking all human weaknesses. Blair was tinged by what has been called 'the good old Saxon gloom'. He chose *The Grave* as the subject of his masterpiece, begun when he was in his late twenties.

Fortunately for his readers, the long poem of 800 lines did not turn out as horrifying as expected. It contains many striking and dramatic and of course poignant passages, It is noteworthy that Robert Burns counted *The Grave* amongst his favourites. He often quoted passages from it in letters to his friends and lovers, particularly the following:

> Tell us, ye dead, will none of you in pity
> To those you left behind disclose the secret?
> O, that some courteous ghost would blab it out
> What 'tis you are and we shall shortly be.

Blair's interest in nature in all its moods, and in small creatures such as birds roosting in hedges at night, shows his powers of observation as well as his wide sympathy. Little doubt this influenced Burns in his poem 'To a Mouse'. It is thought that the famous English poet Edward Young may have had Blair's poem in manuscript before commencing his long poem *Night Thoughts* on similar lines. Both poems were published about the same time. Robert Burns could recite from memory most of *Night Thoughts* and doubtless got the material for 'Address to the Deil' from one of Young's satires. *The Grave* and *Night Thoughts* were to be found in most houses in Scotland and many in England.

James Thomson *(1700-1748)*

He was the first Scotsman to be ranked by Englishmen among the great English poets. Another distinction is that he was the forerunner of a host of Scots who in many fields were sufficiently conspicuous as to constitute a Scottish intellectual occupation of England in force.

Thomson, like Blair, was a son of the manse, born near Kelso. His father moved to Southdean, a very sequestered parish in the Cheviot Hills, a perfect environment for a young poet, who was writing good lines when only a schoolboy. He was meant for the church but on his father's death went to London to make his fortune. Here he was helped by his college friend David Mallett, who introduced him to influential people. His *Seasons*, descriptive of nature through the year, quickly were recognised as a completely new approach to poetry. He travelled on the continent and was generously treated with pensions and sinecure appointments.

Unluckily, at the peak of his fame, when his long poem *The Castle of Indolence* had been completed, he caught a chill and died. His death was universally mourned for he had been very popular, being by nature kindly, easy, cheerful, indolent and, above all, modest. He gave the English a very acceptable picture of a 'Kindly Scot'.

Robert Fergusson *(1750-1774)*

Son of a poor clerk, he was born in the Cap and Feather Close in the Old Town of Edinburgh. His delicate constitution was evident from his schooldays at the High School, but his ability won him a bursary to Dundee Grammar School and St Andrews University. After three years, during which he became a great favourite of William Wilkie, Professor of Natural Philosophy and a poet, Fergusson was forced to discontinue his studies owing to his father's death. He visited a wealthy uncle in the North but was refused any help, so he became a drudge in a legal office in Edinburgh. After writing several English poems for the theatre he realised that his strength lay in writing, as Ramsay had done, in Scots. His poems became very popular and Edinburgh society read them eagerly as they were published. At the height of his fame he took a severe illness, aggravated by a fall. He was confined to Darien House, the Edinburgh Lunatic Asylum, where he perished miserably.

But his example inspired Burns to some extent, and Burns generously acknowledged his debt by ordering a headstone for Fergusson's unmarked grave in the Canongate Kirkyard, when he visited Edinburgh in 1786.

Robert Burns *(1759-1796)*

A vast literature surrounds the life and associations as well as the poetry of Burns. Everything has been investigated. Few poets have had the searchlights of critics so constantly turned on them. But still there are mysteries unsolved. His ancestry has not been traced back for certain, beyond five generations, when he was discovered to be the descendant of a Highland poet who fled from Argyllshire to the Episcopalian area of Kincardineshire. Burns was born in a humble cottage near Ayr, his father having been a gardener and latterly a small farmer. Robert was the eldest of seven children. The Burns family knew the hardships of poverty and the anguish of seeing their father failing to establish himself profitably even when he worked himself literally into an early grave. Burns meantime realised a growing power within him and was soon locally famous for his lyrical and satirical pen. His early education he got from his father and from John Murdoch, a young man employed by neighbouring families as a tutor. By the age of twenty-six he had such a marvellous miscellany of excellent verse that he thought of publishing, with a view to realising some capital, as his lady friend Jean Armour was pregnant, and Burns wished to marry to avoid scandal. To his anger her father tore up the written acknowledgement of Burns' paternity.

Desperate, the poet arranged to emigrate to Jamaica as a book-keeper on an estate. To meet the expenses he had a volume of poems printed. *Poems chiefly in the Scottish Dialect*, known as the Kilmarnock edition, was published in July 1786. The whole course of Burns' life was altered.

He arrived in Edinburgh and was feted by the gentry and intelligentsia and bore himself so well that he was treated as an equal even by titled persons such as the Duchess of Gordon. But the question of his future career had to be settled. In 1788 he married Jean Armour after a romantic association with Mrs Maclehose, who was not amused by his subsequent marriage, though she herself was not free to marry. Burns now tried farming at Ellisland in Dumfriesshire where he wrote the immortal 'Tam o' Shanter'. But he was so pestered by visitors that he could not manage the farm. He obtained a post in the Excise, stationed in Dumfries. His republican sympathies with the French are thought to have stood in the way of promotion.

At any rate, for the last two short years of his life, though he persisted in writing and collecting Scottish songs, gratis, he was in a permanent mood of depression, aggravated by a rheumatic condition that affected his heart. His death took place in tragic circumstances. His wife was far advanced in pregnancy; he received a letter dunning him for a small debt; he knew he was dying and leaving no provision for his family.

It was many years before a real assessment of his work was made. He has been long acclaimed as the foremost Scottish poet, and can stand comparison with any poet in any nation, in any age.

Carolina Oliphant, Baroness Nairne *(1766-1845)*

Daughter of a Perthshire laird and like her father a staunch Jacobite. She was born in the 'Auld Hoose' of Gask, her maiden name being Carolina Oliphant. She married her second cousin who, some years later, became the sixth Lord Nairne.

She wrote pseudonymously on Scottish themes, especially Jacobite laments for the lost cause. She comes next to Burns, a very close second, in the number and perfection of the lyrics, which vary in mood from the tragic 'Land o' the Leal', an old favourite at military funerals, to the humorous 'Laird of Cockpen', the ludicrous and unsuccessful wooing of a Scottish country gentleman. 'Will Ye No' Come Back Again?' is perhaps the best known of her Jacobite songs. Like Burns she wrote her songs in English with a Scottish flavour. She could not do otherwise, for she was a lady born, and her 'Scots' was the diluted tongue of one accustomed to speaking English normally; whereas, Burns, if he had wished to restrict his audience to the west of Scotland, instead of speaking to the wide world, could very well have written all his songs exclusively in his native dialect.

James Hogg *(1770-1835)*

He was born in the lonely valley of Ettrick and spent his youth herding sheep. He had no schooling. When he was twenty he subscribed to the Peebles Lending Library and taught himself to read and write. It was the delight he felt at reading Allan Ramsay's *Gentle Shepherd* and the modernised version of the *Wallace* that decided him to become a poet. He says that, in 1797, when he was out on the hills he met a half-daft man called John Scott who recited to him the whole of *Tam o' Shanter*. Scott told him all about Burns, the ploughman who had been born on 25 January 1759 and had died the previous summer. Hogg immediately took a notion that as he himself had been born on 25 January and was a shepherd, a profession far above a mere ploughman, he would 'succeed Burns as the poet of Scotland'.

There is little doubt that Hogg was a natural genius, a born poet, his imagination always active, his powers of description often unbelievable. He was a friend of Walter Scott and of the many eminent men in Scott's circle, and he made himself free of their acquaintance, not always to his advantage, for they sometimes resented his presumption.

Yet both his poetry and prose were outstanding. His study of a murderous fanatic, *The Confessions of a Justified Sinner* is a novel of obsession which compares in power with Dostoievsky. The writing is so masterly that it was attributed to Lockhart for no other reason than it seemed quite beyond the powers of a naive shepherd from Ettrick. But critics of his age generally agreed that James Hogg 'was the greatest poet next to Burns who ever sprang from common people'. The 'Queen's Wake' is his most admired poetic work, but his two Jacobite songs, 'Cam' ye by Athol' and 'Flora Macdonald's Lament' are eternal favourites.

For the less romantic reader we can recommend his practical book on sheep-rearing, still consulted by pastoral men. Its unpoetic title is *Hogg on Sheep*.

Sir Walter Scott *(1771-1832)*

Born in Edinburgh, the son of a lawyer, his paternal ancestors were the Scotts of Harden, a famous old family of Border raiders. When a young boy he was smitten by a fever which left him lame so he was sent down to the Borders, to Sandyknowe, overlooking the lower valley of the Tweed. There he heard old Border ballads and tales of superstition and daring deeds, in somewhat the same style as Robert Burns had heard from an old woman in his youth.

Scott returned to the High School in Edinburgh and took part in all the escapades that Edinburgh boys indulged in, climbing Arthur's Seat, the Castle Rock, or risking life and limb in street battles with sticks and stones. At fifteen he was apprenticed to his father and the following year, in 1787, he met Burns at a social gathering where he had the great distinction, for a stripling, of being thanked by Burns for being able to name the author of a pathetic verse on a war-painting in the room.

He was able in pursuit of his legal business to travel into remote parts of the Borders and the Highlands of Perthshire where, in the latter, he made the acquaintance of people who remembered Rob Roy.

In 1797 he married Miss Charpentier, a French emigrée, and entered a period of great happiness and poetic and business activity. This was the poetically fruitful part of his literary work, and although his famous novels belong to his maturer years, his gift of poetry never left him as he grew older and he carried it into all his novels to his last days.

But it is as a poet that we must regard him in this chapter. His poetry could be divided into three styles, the song or lyric, the narrative ballad based on the traditional Border ballad, and the long historical poems based on episodes in history. Of Scott's poems most are in English except the ballads.

His lyrics, of which perhaps the most magical is the short 'Proud Maisie' are comparable to Shakespeare's. His imitations of the old ballads are so artistically done that it is impossible to distinguish the original from Scott's stanzas in the *Border Minstrelsy* which he researched and edited. His long poems, like *The Lay of the Last Minstrel, Marmion*, and *The Lady of the Lake*, are full of action and splendid scenic description. In all his verse of whatever kind, he was a popular poet. That is to say his language is direct and intelligible to all at the first reading. His rhythm and rhyme carry the reader along from start to finish.

But his poetic popularity came to an end rather suddenly, not for want of material or inspiration, but because Lord Byron came on the scene with his romances which took not only Britain but Europe by storm. To this day the Europeans hold Byron above Shakespeare or any other English poet.

In another chapter Scott's prose works will be noted.

Robert Tannahill *(1774-1810)*

He was born in Paisley and spent his early life at the loom. He was one of a family of seven. With a younger brother he travelled to Lancashire in 1800 where he stayed for two years, returning because of the news of his father's illness. His father blessed him and died.

Tannahill was an enthusiastic reader of Ramsay, Fergusson, and Burns, and from his youth had composed poems both in English and in Scots. Like other poets in Scotland he was not in his element in English and was advised by a musical friend to write songs in Scots. Of the first edition of poems and songs nearly all were sold in a short time.

Tragedy seemed to hang over the Tannahill household. Of the original nine, including the parents, only three remained and Robert himself was far gone in consumption, due no doubt to long hours in the weaving mill. The final blow came in 1810 when Constable the publisher returned a new collection of his poems. Robert, ill and despairing, burnt a hundred new songs, went out unnoticed and drowned himself in a canal.

Some of his songs rival all but the best of Burns in popularity. Of such are 'The Braes o' Balquhidder', 'The Braes o' Gleniffer', 'The Flower o' Dunblane' and 'Gloomy Winter's noo awa'.'

Thomas Campbell *(1777-1844)*

He was born in Glasgow, youngest of eleven children, at a critical period in his family's history, for his father, a Virginia trader in tobacco and other American exports, was ruined by the outbreak of the American War of Independence in 1776. But fellow-merchants came to the rescue and with a thrifty mother the family managed to send Thomas to the grammar school, then to the University of Glasgow. He was a brilliant scholar, excelling in Greek and poetry. He was an admirer of the French Revolutionaries which got him into trouble later, as it did Burns. He was a private tutor and worked for booksellers to support himself. At the age of twenty-one he published his poem *The Pleasures of Hope* which brought him fame and wealth. He had composed it while walking round Arthur's Seat and the Calton Hill and other heights near Edinburgh accompanied by his poetical companion the 'Amiable James Grahame', a fellow Glaswegian, author of *The Sabbath*, another popular book. Some passages in *The Pleasures of Hope*, in which Campbell shows his anger and horror at the Russian destruction and enslavement of Poland, belong to our own age.

Campbell now visited the continent which was in the midst of war. He actually witnessed the Austrian cavalry charging the French at Ratisbon and missed seeing, by a few weeks, the battle of Hohenlinden, which, however, he described splendidly, two years later. His patriotic poems, *Ye Mariners of England* and *The Battle of the Baltic*, written in Germany, took the country by storm, but on the other hand his poem supporting the Irish rebels, *Exile of Erin*, put him under suspicion of being an Irish spy and he was arrested and questioned in Edinburgh on his return home.

In London he lived with Thomas Telford, the eminent engineer from Dumfriesshire, and made his living by literature. His works are many and varied and include well-known short lyrics like 'Lord Ullin's Daughter', which was at one time included in every school-book along with his war pieces. Obviously, like Scott and Burns, he aimed at being a popular poet and succeeded beyond hope.

He helped to found the University of London.

George Gordon, Lord Byron *(1788-1824)*

He is perhaps the most controversial figure in English literature, for, although half a Scot, his contributions to Scottish literature are small. But they include that splendid song, 'Dark Lochnagar'. A Victorian critic said of him, 'the moment people begin to write about Byron they either lose their heads in uncritical admiration of him, or else an itch for disparagement attacks their fingers.' We shall try to give a fair description of his poetic achievements without emphasising his personal reputation, which was too briefly summed up by Lady Caroline Lamb, one of his lovers, as 'mad, bad, and dangerous to know.'

Byron was born in London of an ancient family who came over in the Norman Conquest. His immediate ancestors on the paternal side included his great-uncle 'the wicked Lord Byron' who was killed in a duel when young Byron was ten, and old enough to remember. The man who killed the wicked Lord was the grandfather of Mary Chawarth, one of Byron's first loves, to whom he dedicated rather indelicate boyish verses which had to be suppressed. Byron's father was even more notorious. He seduced the

Marchioness of Carmarthen, borrowed her money, eloped with her, and completed her bad luck by marrying her. The only child of this marriage was Augusta, Byron's half-sister, whom he loved. Byron's father married again, once more to secure a fortune, for his wife was the rich heiress, Catherine Gordon of Gight, in Aberdeenshire. The only offspring was George Gordon Byron. His parents separated, Captain Byron leaving his wife and son to subsist on a pension of less than £3 per week in the town of Aberdeen.

Byron was born lame yet tried hard to be athletic; he was an excellent boxer and swimmer, said to have swum the Hellespont, between Asia Minor and Europe. But his boyhood in Aberdeen was a psychological disaster. He learned all sorts of wickedness from a female servant before he fell heir to the Byron title. Then with his mother he moved to England and attended Harrow, then Cambridge. Wicked dandies, or bucks, were all the rage during the Regency and Byron tried to become one of them.

As a result of his two years of travel in Europe, visiting many areas of the Mediterranean, he wrote *Childe Harold's Pilgrimage*, which was autobiographical. It took the public fancy and as he said, 'I awoke one morning to find myself famous'.

A grave scandal connected with his marriage forced Byron to leave England. He travelled about, drifting into Venice, Ravenna, Pisa, to associate with all sorts of debauched characters, but nevertheless producing a constant stream of poetry, including *Don Juan*, and the satire *A Vision of Judgment*, aimed at George III. *Don Juan* is a splendid triumph which captured the imagination of Europe, despite many English attempts to denigrate his achievements by such phrases as 'among the great writers of the world no place can be found for Byron.'

He caught a fever, when on an expedition to assist in the liberation of Greece from the Turks, and died at Missolonghi. His body was brought for burial to the family vault in England.

Robert Louis Stevenson (1850-1894)

Probably the best-loved of literary men, especially in the USA, was born in Edinburgh of a well-established family of famous lighthouse engineers. His father expected Robert Louis (baptised Robert Lewis but changed because of his father's aversion to an Edinburgh councillor named Lewis) to follow in his footsteps, but for various reasons this came to nothing.

Stevenson was delicate from birth and much cossetted by his mother and nurse. He could not face the rough and tumble of ordinary school but nevertheless attained Edinburgh University. His family had a country house in the Pentland Hills, quite close to the city, and there Stevenson spent much of his youth, learning to love the 'hills of home' and to listen to the traditional tales and verses of the uplands. His first book was an account of the Pentland Rising of 1666. It was privately printed in a small edition but does not show much promise, being a very good boyish effort but mostly consisting of quotations.

Stevenson is most valued as one of the finest stylists in the English language, an excellence which he attained by 'playing the sedulous ape' i.e. imitating various English authors. We shall note his prose works in another chapter, but his poems are so memorable and so universally quoted that he ranks, if not as a great poet, at least as a popular one.

His *A Child's Garden of Verses* is justly celebrated for its charm, which opened up a new approach to the study of children and led to many modern developments in education, disposing for ever of the old idea that a child was merely a small adult.

His poem dedicated to the novelist S.R. Crockett, beginning 'Blows the wind today and the sun and the rain are flying' was written in nostalgic mood when he was a voluntary exile, for his health, in Samoa where he died not long after. *The Vagabond* is equally redolent of the gipsy life that he loved, and his *Requiem*, which adorns his hill-top tomb in Samoa, is the last utterance of an optimistic and gallant spirit.

> Under the wide and starry sky,
> Dig the grave and let me lie.
> Glad did I live and gladly die,
> And I lay me down with a will.
> This be the verse you grave for me:
> 'Here he lies where he longed to be;
> Home is the sailor, home from sea,
> And the hunter home from the hill.'

Although the late Victorian age and the early twentieth century saw many poets of purely internal Scottish interest, and one or two exiles in England like James Thomson, author of *The City of Dreadful Night*, John Davidson and Andrew Young, writing in English, few were outstanding. None caught the popular imagination as the masterpieces of Burns, Scott and Campbell had done. The old tug-of-war went on between English and Scots as the medium for verse. One unfortunate result of this private quarrel was an acrimonious exchange between Edwin Muir (1887-1959) and Hugh MacDiarmid (the pseudonym of Dr Christopher Grieve)(1892-1978).

Muir believed that Scots was obsolete and, as he himself thought to demonstrate in his pessimistic verses, English was the language for future Scots poets. He speaks in *Scotland 1941* of Burns and Scott, 'sham bards of a sham nation', a bitter line, for he was a dedicated patriot.

Popular poets whose most notable work was either in dialect or in a revival of Middle Scots (as in the cases of Pittendrigh MacGillivray and Lewis Spence) really belong to the nineteenth century in both body and spirit, but they lived on vigorously, well into the twentieth.

J. Pittendrigh MacGillivray *(1856-1939)*

MacGillivray's poems *Abasshyd* and *Mercy o' Gode* distinctly anticipate MacDiarmid's resurrection of the mediaeval world of superstition and magic.

John Davidson *(1857-1909)*

Born at Barrhead, Renfrewshire, son of an Evangelical clergyman, he received a good education and was an omnivorous reader, especially of poetry. The writings of Thomas Carlyle were particularly influential in the formation of Davidson's life philosophy. After a spell as a laboratory assistant he took up school-teaching, following a desultory session at Edinburgh University. He found teaching 'hellish drudgery' and left it in 1888 to seek his subsistence in journalism, but with no better relish. In Glasgow he came under the strong influence of John Nichol, Professor of English Literature and biographer of Carlyle. Before leaving teaching Davidson had written much poetry and several plays in both prose and blank verse. His poetry is forceful, graceful and exuberant.

In London, to which he moved in 1890, he had mixed success with his poetic and dramatic publications but he became acquainted with the prominent literary men, Richard le Gallienne, Max Beerbohm and George Gissing. Critics and the public gave his poems a good reception.

The initial success did not last and a series of misfortunes, financial, domestic and personal, brought on a state of depression which his removal to Sussex did not alleviate. But he had good friends who helped him, especially the publisher Grant Richards who brought out Davidson's books despite losses. Edmund Gosse, the distinguished critic, and Sir William McCormick, secured a Civil List pension of £100 per annum for the poet. Despite this help he became more and more pessimistic and cut himself off from society. He still tried to be the prophet of a new evangel for mankind and continued to write his books and poems on the grand irony of existence. He exiled himself to Cornwall and after leaving a note of intention he disappeared. His body was recovered from the sea after six months and buried there, off Penzance, at his own written request.

Davidson was of Highland pedigree and his poems are largely Celtic in spirit, especially 'A Loafer' and 'In Romney Marsh'. He was infected by the decadence of the nineties, but only slightly. The prevailing character of his writing is his Carlylean total acceptance of the universe, a vast inter-mingledom of good and evil, beauty and filth, the intricacy of science and the simplicity of nature. He had a strong influence on younger writers, later to become famous; T.S. Eliot, Ezra Pound, D.H. Lawrence and Hugh MacDiarmid.

Violet Jacob (1863-1946)

She was the poetess of Angus, her native county. Her sincere and colourful poems of the soil and the sea 'Tam i' the Kirk' and 'Baltic Street' brought a fresh rush of life to Scots Verse.

Charles Murray (1864-1968)

The bard of the North-east, though condemned hastily by MacDiarmid as 'one who never did and never could write a single line of poetry', nevertheless wrote energetic and tuneful poems, evocative of the Buchan countryside.

Marion Angus (1866-1946)

A good poetess in her mother tongue, she departed into English on a moving sentimental excursion which depicted the softer side of the life of Mary,

Queen of Scots, entitled 'Alas! Poor Queen'.

Lewis Spence *(1874-1953)*

Like MacGillivray he wrote some verse in old Scots, including a notable sonnet also in the well-trodden field of Mary Stuart. The modern reader of Scots would need a very large glossary to help his reading. Spence dabbled in magic, writing on Druidism and other occult matters.

Sir Alexander Gray *(1882-1968)*

Equally at home in Scots, English and Germanic tongues his best poems are the Spartan 'Scotland', and the translation of Heine's *Du hast Diamenten und Perlen.*

Andrew Young *(1885-1971)*

He was born at Elgin and educated at the Royal High School and University in Edinburgh. He took a degree in divinity and was minister at Berwick and later at Temple, Midlothian. He became a Church of England minister, residing in Sussex.

Young was a keen naturalist, being author of two botanical books. His poems reflect his superb powers of observation and remind one of his poetic models which include James Grahame, John Clare and Thomas Hardy. His poems, mostly in English, are simple yet imaginative.

Helen B. Cruickshank *(1886-1975)*

She was a complete mistress of the Scots of her native Angus and is notable for the realism, allied to sympathy, with which her poems bring to life the world she was brought up in. 'Shy Geordie' is perhaps the best known.

Edwin Muir *(1887-1959)*

A farmer's son from Orkney, he moved with his family to Glasgow where circumstances forced him to the depressing and dirty labour of bottling beer and grinding bones. His elder brother died of consumption and another brother of a brain-tumour. He escaped a similar fate, moving to London as a journalist.

With his wife, Willa, he settled in St Andrews and translated several German classics. He was on the staff, later, of the British Consul in Edinburgh, Prague and Rome. He was warden at Newbattle College, Midlothian for a period.

His poems show a mastery of technique and use of words, but they lack passion and realism. They are gentle, subtle and unearthly, probably a reaction to his traumatic experiences in Glasgow.

Christopher Murray Grieve (Hugh MacDiarmid) *(1892-1978)*

He was born at Langholm and educated first at Langholm Academy where he fell under the influence of F.G. Scott, the composer, who afterwards set

Grieve's poems to music. From Langholm he proceeded to Broughton Junior Students' Centre, Edinburgh, where George Ogilvie, his English master, exerted a very strong influence on the young poet and was worshipped in return. On the death of Grieve's father he gave up teacher training and worked as a journalist in Montrose. He edited the three volumes of *Northern Numbers* between 1920 and 1922. Up to this time he was opposed to writing in Scots. In 1922 he was converted to it, however, and a remarkable series of lyrics, using evocative old Scots vocabulary and strange outlandish imagery, showed his mastery of the new medium.

In 1926, with the aid of F.G. Scott, he pieced together a number of fragmentary verses and published them under the title *A Drunk Man Looks at the Thistle*. This is accounted his masterpiece. It is a didactic and in many ways a self-contradictory picture of Scotland set in time and space. It embodies Grieve's philosophy.

Most of his subsequent verse was in English, with a few exceptions which remind one of the early inspired lyrics in Scots. But the best of his work puts him in line with William Dunbar and Robert Burns.

William Soutar *(1898-1943)*

He was a Perthshire native who contracted an obscure disease while on war service which condemned him to a lingering death, bed-ridden. He saw himself as a major lyric poet and from as early as his student days at Edinburgh he published many splendid lyrics, all however tinged with melancholy. During his confinement to bed he wrote many humorous and whimsical poems in Scots of epigrammatic quality. Paradoxically, his diary of this period is a brave, optimistic book.

Joseph MacLeod (Adam Drinan) *(1902-1983)*

He was educated at Oxford and called to the Bar in the Inner Temple in 1928. Ezra Pound, the American poet, recommended T.S. Eliot, his fellow poet, to publish a long poem by MacLeod. During the war years (1939-45) he was well-known as a BBC announcer, his poetry being published under the pseudonym Adam Drinan, a name taken from a village in Skye, home of his ancestors. His poems show great economy of words and express humour as well as deep feeling. They are influenced by the superb technique of Ezra Pound.

Robert Garioch Sutherland *(1909-1981)*

He was born in Edinburgh and educated at the Royal High School and Edinburgh University. He worked as a teacher until he was called up in 1939. He was captured at Tobruk, his experiences as a prisoner-of-war being recalled in *Two Men and a Blanket*. After teaching in Kent he returned to Edinburgh where he produced many poems in all genres, in Scots and English, many being in translation from Italian. His humour is gently satiric and he was an anarchist at heart, who enjoyed deflating the pretentious. He was a skilled musician and his technical construction of all kinds of metrical forms, classical and native, reveal a poet of the highest order.

Sydney Goodsir Smith *(1915-1975)*

A New Zealander by birth, he adopted Edinburgh and the Scots language with enthusiasm. His poems such as *Under the Eildon Tree* are conspicuous for his frank self-revelations as well as for his wide-ranging knowledge of exotic places and literature. His use of Scots is remarkably descriptive and incisive, revealing strong passion and vision.

George Campbell Hay *(1915-1984)*

He was born in Argyll the son of John MacDougall Hay, novelist and author of the powerful novel *Gillespie*. He was educated at Oxford and served in the Middle East in the war of 1939-45 where his experiences made a deep impression on his life and poems. He was a sensitive poet and wrote in Gaelic, Scots, English, Italian and Norwegian. In 1983 he won the Writer's Award of An Comunn Gaidhealach.

Among his best poems are 'Flooer o' the Gean' (Scots) and 'Song' (English).

Gaelic Poets

Gaelic is a language common to Ireland and Scotland. During the Middle Ages most of the poetry and prose was written in Irish Gaelic, rather different in many ways from Scottish Gaelic. The exception to this rule was the *Book of the Dean of Lismore*, written in Roman letters, phonetically. James Macgregor was the author, and beside including well-known Irish poets, he also gives the poems of Scottish bards. Some of these early poets are Allan MacRorie, Calum MacAulay, John of Knoydart, Finlay MacNab, Duncan Macgregor and Campbell of Glenorchy. The *Book* also gives very ancient Ossianic poems written in Ireland and Scotland as far back as the pre-Christian era.

Before the remarkable renaissance of poetry which followed the brutal repressions after Culloden, there were two well-known poets.

Mary MacLeod *(1588-1693)*

She was bard to Sir Norman MacLeod of Bernera. The remarkable thing about her best poems was that they were written after she was seventy. She lived to be 105.

Her finest pieces are dirges and songs of praise relating to the MacLeods.

John Macdonald (*Ian Lom*, Bald John) *(c.1620-1710)*

Macdonald wrote poems which had an extraordinary effect in his lifetime. Like Mary MacLeod, he was a clan bard and decidedly partial in his poems. This partisan spirit is best shown in his two famous poems, one on the murder of a Macdonald heir, and the other on the Battle of Inverlochy where he was present and rejoiced in the slaughter of the Campbells, his hereditary enemies.

Alexander Macdonald (c.1700-1780)

He was the son of an Episcopalian clergyman. He attended Glasgow University but an imprudent marriage ended his divinity studies and he became a Presbyterian teacher. His was the first Gaelic book to be printed. It was a vocabulary.

He fought in the 1745 Rising but his songs were more useful than his sword. In 1751 he printed his poems in Edinburgh, love-songs, nature poems and Jacobite songs. His masterpiece, by far the longest, is *The Birlinn* (Galley) *of Clanranald*, excelling in description of the stormy Hebridean seas.

John MacCodrum (1693-1779)

He was born in North Uist and was bard to Sir James Macdonald of Sleat. For this he received free rent of a croft for life, plus provisioning. He was one of the last of the professional bards. He had a considerable gift for satire which can be seen in his poem 'In Dispraise of Donald Ban's Pipes'. He also gave a fairly full description of Highland dress in his poem 'Song to the Highland Dress'.

Robert Mackay (Rob Donn) (1714-1783)

He was born in Sutherland. His strength lay in satire, though his love poems were well admired, and he also wrote elegies. He had a very sharp tongue like his contemporary John MacCodrum.

Dugald Buchanan (1716-1768)

Buchanan was born in Strathyre, Perthshire, son of a miller. His education was patchy and he tried several trades. Stewart of Killin asked him to help with the first version of the *New Testament in Gaelic* (published 1767). In the same year Buchanan published his own poems. Both these publications have proved, for different reasons, to be the most requested books in Gaelic. His poems are undoubtedly inspired by his religious anguish, the two most popular for many generations being the *Day of Judgement* and *The Skull*, both revelling in the torments of Hell as much as in the ecstasy of Heaven.

Duncan Ban MacIntyre (1724-1812)

Unlike Alexander Macdonald he was a poor man with no education in English letters. He fought on the Hanoverian side at Falkirk (1746) and afterwards was a gamekeeper in Breadalbane and later in Rannoch.

His address to his wife *Mairi Bhan*, Fair-haired Mary, is thought to be the best Gaelic love-song, but he had a very wide variety of songs and poems, the finest descriptive poem being *In Praise of Ben Dorain*, a great mountain known intimately to him for many years. His poems were first published in 1768 and were always very popular. In his old age he was a member of the Edinburgh Town Guard, his pay being sixpence a day. He is buried in the North Yard of Greyfriars in Edinburgh.

William Ross *(1762-1790)*

He was born in Strath, Isle of Skye, where his ancestors had lived for centuries. His father was John Ross, a humble farmer and his mother had come from Gairloch on the Ross mainland. Probably William inherited his poetic ability from her for she was the daughter of John Mackay, the blind poet, piper to the Gairloch family.

William was sent, along with his only sister, to school in Forres, where he distinguished himself by his all-round ability. Schooling completed, he went with his parents to live at Gairloch. William was tall and handsome, of a frank, intelligent and humorous character but of a weak constitution which, as so often at that time, rendered him a victim of tuberculosis, of which he died at twenty-eight.

In his short life he worked as a schoolmaster and devoted his spare time to the study of Gaelic. He travelled about Scotland and composed many poems on his impressions. An unhappy love affair is said to have hastened his end.

His main literary influence was the lyrics of Burns, his contemporary, and he adopted Burns' methods of composition, basing his lyrics on melody and metre, in most instances either singing the air or playing it on the violin, as Burns did, before fitting in the words.

Ross was the first Gaelic poet to devote most of his enthusiasm to love songs, which laid him open to satirical parodies from aspiring rhymesters who failed to appreciate Ross's genuine genius and deep feeling.

William Livingstone *(1808-1870)*

At the beginning of the nineteenth century every district in the Highlands had a bard, an outstanding example was William Livingstone, a native of Islay.

He sustained a burning hatred of the English up till his dying day, looking upon them as enemies of Gaelic civilisation, as indeed the centuries of vandalism of Celtic art prove them to be. Livingstone's poems have been published in many editions both before and after his death and are remarkable for their spate of vehement rage and deepest sorrow for the deliberate suppression of the Gaelic world by the Saxons or Sassunach, a term which also includes the Lowland Scots.

One of his finest poems is *Eirinn a' Gul*, 'Ireland Weeping', in which is this verse linking the two Gaelic lands.

> Today I see your skyline unaltered
> Over the sea from the wave-beaten shores of Islay;
> But dreary it is to describe your present condition.

A bitter poem on the Highland Clearances is *Fiosthun a' Bhaird*, 'Message to the Bard'. Here is his description of the present desolation and its causes.

> Injustice, Rent Extortion and the Sassunach
> Have triumphed. The mottled adder has coiled
> On the floor where noble folk of ancient times
> Who were my Kinsmen, were prepared for life.

Prose

Although a great school of poets were writing in Scots (which they called Inglis to distinguish it from Gaelic or Ersche) from the middle of the fourteenth century or earlier, there was very little Scots prose, apart from some legal documents and correspondence. Most of the literate people were connected with the Church and were educated from a very early age to write and speak in Latin, although Scots was their mother tongue. Latin was the language common to all Europe and to ensure a wide audience for treatises and theses of whatever nature, religious or scientific or political, the author had to be well-versed in the classical Latin writers. It was from Cicero and Livy and a host of others, resurrected from monasteries in the Renaissance of the fifteenth century, that the language of scholars got its vocabulary, phrases and ideas. The first declaration of Scottish Self-government, that from Arbroath in 1320, was in Latin, largely composed of phrases from Sallust, a master of splendid invention and memorable description with a taste for Greek idioms.

To show the ability of the Scots in this unhomely medium, the most extraordinary illustration is in the meteoric career of James Crichton, called 'Admirable Crichton', but better described as the 'Wonderful'. In his brief life of twenty-two years, when he travelled through Europe, he acquired such eloquence in Latin that he took on any challengers in debate in France or Italy, on any hard questions, and beat them easily. He learned his Latin at St Andrews University where he graduated MA at fourteen. He was stabbed fatally in a duel in 1582.

That year also marked the death at seventy-six of George Buchanan, of a Highland family, unlike Crichton, who was a Lowlander. Buchanan's mother tongue included Gaelic, if it was not all Gaelic, but it made little difference to his ability to master Latin. He wrote very little in Scots. The first accomplished writer in Scots had been John Knox but his Scots was largely interspersed with Southern English. His religious enemies, who were many, accused him of 'Knapping Suddron' or speaking affected English. But all his writings, although very salty and wryly humorous, were propaganda for the Calvinist cause and lose interest for the uncommitted reader. Far more entertaining, though at second hand, because translated from French, is Sir Thomas Urquhart's rendering of the first two books of Rabelais, *The History of Gargantua and Pantagruel*. Urquhart writes in English with an occasional Scots word, so his books were read as eagerly in England as in Scotland.

Such famous characters as the 'Bloody Mackenzie', Sir George Mackenzie, persecutor of the Covenanters, and Andrew Fletcher of Saltoun, the patriot statesman, wrote in English and from the Union of the Parliaments (1707) onwards, English, with reported speech in Scots, was the medium of Scottish writers. The language was still coloured by Scottish modes of speech, which many of the authors tried, without notable success, to eliminate.

In all fields of prose literature, fiction, history, philosophy, scientific exposition, native Scots, while still speaking their mother tongue, were increasingly taking over many fields of literature, culminating in Scott's Waverley Novels in fiction, in Carlyle's histories and philosophical essays, in Stevenson's *belles-lettres*. But they were still able to write a racy authentic Scots when they chose, even at the grave risk of being unintelligible to English and foreign readers.

George Buchanan *(1505-1582)*

Born at Killearn, Stirlingshire, of a branch of the ancient family of Lennox, he attended Killearn School and studied for two years at Paris where he learned Latin and Greek. Scotland was in a state of civil war, with bodies of French troops supporting the Duke of Albany, with whom Buchanan sided. At Aberdeen he fell in with the learned John Mair who took him again to Paris.

He wrote a description of student life in Paris, with which he was disappointed, owing to poverty, long hours and poor prospects. He, nevertheless, stayed in Paris for eleven years and wrote against the Franciscans. This induced James V to ask him to satirise the friars on his return to Scotland; Buchanan regretted doing this, as he was imprisoned for it. He escaped to Bordeaux where he met Montaigne and doubtless influenced that immortal essayist. He was imprisoned in Portugal and in jail wrote a Latin version of the Psalms.

Mary, Queen of Scots, had returned to Scotland to find that by Act of Parliament Catholicism was illegal. Buchanan, now safe to return, was appointed tutor to the eighteen-year-old queen. He took a prominent part in the Reformed Church and gained a great reputation for learning.

On the political side he was not so commendable and there are strong reasons for suspecting him of sustaining the charges which, after his death, led to the execution of Mary. He was tutor to her son, James VI, despite her objections. His severity as a royal tutor caused James life-long nightmares.

His great political work, arguing that the people had a right to punish unjust kings, was early condemned by James VI and was burnt at Oxford as late as 1664. His famous history of Scotland was written 'to purge sum Inglis lyes and Scottis vanite'.

Sir Thomas Urquhart *(1611-1660)*

He was the son of Sir Thomas Urquhart of Cromarty, his mother being a daughter of Lord Elphinstone. His first education was at Aberdeen University then, like many young men of his age he travelled in France, Spain and Italy. In politics he was a strong Royalist and rose for the King in

1639 when he had the satisfaction of drawing first blood in the Civil War in Scotland by defeating a force of Covenanters at the 'Trot of Turriff' in Aberdeenshire. He was knighted shortly after by King Charles I. He began to write tracts and books on many dissimilar topics, such as *Epigrams*, *Logarithms*, and a proposed universal language. He was on the Cavalier side at the Battle of Worcester in 1651 and was taken prisoner after the Royalist defeat. He was wounded and lost nearly all his precious manuscripts, but in the following years he was as busy as ever rewriting and publishing.

There is little doubt of his genius, eccentric even to the borders of madness. For example, he traces his family back, with all the particulars, to Adam and Eve. He also wrote, from the Episcopal point of view, a vindication of the honour of Scotland from the infamous character given it by the Presbyterians. He is very lengthy on the exploits of Scots abroad, learned men and men of war alike, generous characters even to the length of giving their heart's blood for the land of their adoption. He blamed the narrow-minded Kirk of Scotland for the reputation Scotland got for a love of money, particularly those Scots who went to London to feather their nests by hook or by crook. He calls some of his fellow-countrymen wolves, foxes and cannibals.

He was obviously the best man to translate Rabelais, for he also had the same out-spoken humour, satiric, quaint, coarse and quite unrepentant. He is said to have fled to Europe during the Cromwellian tyranny and to have died in a fit of uncontrollable laughter when he heard of the Restoration of Charles II to the throne in 1660.

John Arbuthnot *(1675-1735)*

He was born at Arbuthnot in Kincardineshire, son of an Episcopalian minister who had been put out of his living after the Presbyterian return to power. John went to London and made a living by teaching mathematics.

He attended Oxford University then graduated as a doctor at St Andrews. His paper on *The Usefulness of Mathematical Learning* (1701) made him a Fellow of the Royal Society and a friend of many literary and scientific men.

He became a fashionable doctor and, later, physician to Queen Anne, but it was for his genius as a literary man that he became famous. One of his best works was the *History of John Bull* a satire on the times, aimed especially at the Duke of Marlborough.

He was acknowledged to have given numberless hints to Pope, Swift and other great wits and satirists of that age, and some of his writings were indistinguishable from Swift's best work. His life of the fictitious Martin Scriblerus ridiculed false taste in writing and was a great force in correcting literary fads.

Arbuthnot did not seek literary fame though he was perhaps the wittiest writer in a brilliant circle, never surpassed in any age.

The death of Queen Anne ruined his court connection as a physician but he still had a large practice amongst the aristocrats. He remained a Jacobite all his life, never forgiving the religious bigotry that had ruined his father.

240

Tobias Smollett *(1721-1771)*

He was the son of Sir Jas. Smollett of Bonhill, Dunbartonshire. His father died early and Tobias was brought up by his grandfather, a promoter of the Union of 1707. He studied at Dumbarton Grammar School and at Glasgow University, then was apprenticed to a doctor. He had written a drama entitled *The Regicide* based on the assassination of James I in 1437. Armed with this he set off for London to set the Thames on fire. But nobody would even read it, no doubt because the English were as totally ignorant of Scottish history then, as ever since.

Smollett was starving so he applied for the last resort of any self-respecting medico, a post of surgeon's mate, a very bloody business in 1741. So it proved, for the 80-gun man-of-war HMS *Cumberland* was involved in the abortive and expensive siege of Carthagena.

At Jamaica he had fallen in love with Nancy Lascelles, a planter's daughter, so he left the navy to return to England. He set up a doctor's practice but got few patients so he returned to literature.

In 1748 his novel *Roderick Random*, based on his naval experiences, was an immediate hit. He portrayed the British sailor as he had never been before, with such veracity that he was instantly recognised as a supreme craftsman. But as he had not put his name to the book it was attributed to Fielding, the author of *Tom Jones*. However, this was soon put right and Smollett, trying again to be a doctor by taking an MD, brought out his *Peregrine Pickle*, describing among other adventures of low and rough life, his experiences at Carthagena.

His literary work was staggering, both in amount and variety. He seemed to have an inexhaustible energy, despite poor health. He translated *Don Quixote*, wrote a *History of England* and many articles to magazines. One of these, denouncing an admiral at Carthagena, put him in jail for three months, with a fine of £100.

The death of his only daughter at fifteen drove him heart-broken to seek comfort in travel in France and Italy. His book of travels gives a vivid picture of Europe in 1760 and he foreshadows the French Revolution in his description of the misery of French people under the Bourbons.

After hearing of the success of his last novel *Humphrey Clinker*, he died aged only fifty at Leghorn.

Smollett's poetry was only incidental to his novels but in his *Tears of Scotland*, written in indignation after the butcheries following Culloden, he shows the *praesertim ingenium Scotorum*, despite his exile in search of literary fame.

Smollett never worried about being indiscreet and is as blatantly vulgar and grossly humorous as Burns or Dunbar. Nothing that showed humanity in all its moods was beneath his notice. His influence on Thackeray and Dickens is very noticeable.

James Boswell *(1740-1795)*

Born in Edinburgh, son of the lawyer Lord Auchinleck, whose estates were in Ayrshire, he was educated at the Edinburgh High School and at the

Colleges of Edinburgh and Glasgow.

Having a good allowance from his father he was able to indulge himself in all sorts of amusement in London at the age of twenty. He seemed to be irresistably sociable with all classes and was acceptable to the ladies, though not reliable as a lover. He had, from boyhood, an incurable itch for writing, taking copious notes of every circumstance. His visit to Holland, intended for study at Utrecht, was divided between books and dissipation. He then went on *Le Grand Tour* through Germany, Switzerland and Italy and of course met the élite, amongst them Voltaire and Rousseau.

After his return to Edinburgh he passed as advocate and conducted some cases with success. Domestically he made a happy, if unexpectedly sober choice, by marrying his cousin Margaret Montgomery, a canny Scots lass who bore him seven children and turned a blind eye to his flights of fancy.

But, as the world knows, his fame rests upon his long friendship with Dr Samuel Johnson whose biographer he became. Johnson had a prejudice against the Scottish nation which he was not at pains to conceal, but he had several Scots friends whom he loved and admired. He was also a strong Tory and had a soft side for the Jacobite cause.

Boswell encouraged him to make a journey to Scotland and to see for himself the scenes of Prince Charles' adventures after Culloden. The Journal of this tour is one of the great factual books of the eighteenth century, full of day to day incidents, revealing the character of the travellers and the Highlanders.

Many have accused Boswell of faults of character; of being a sycophant, a lecher, a drunkard, a fop. Some of the mud is sure to stick but at least he was the frankest writer in English, equal to Montaigne in revealing all his inmost thoughts. They reveal his admiration and love for the literary monarch of England, Johnson, whose immortality is doubly assured by his biographer.

Henry Mackenzie *(1745-1831)*

Born in Edinburgh, son of a doctor, he was educated at the High School and University and aimed at a career in law. His fame was assured when, as a man of only twenty-six, he published his first novel *The Man of Feeling*. He was mistakenly known by that title all his long life, and after. Actually he was a shrewd Scottish lawyer, respected by a wide circle of literary men in Edinburgh. He had a keen sense of merit in others, and Scotland owes him much because he was foremost in recognising the outstanding genius first, of Burns, then of Scott. Many a spark that might have developed into brilliance has been allowed to die away for want of a little fanning.

He wrote other novels, *The Man of the World* coming out two years after his first success, to contrast the simple gullible anti-hero, Harley, with a harder character. As with Smollett, another author was credited with *The Man of Feeling*.

The false claimant was Eccles of Bath who brought forward several manuscripts to support his claim. But subsequent work by Mackenzie corroborated his authorship.

Although he wrote a good deal afterwards, and edited two Tory magazines in Edinburgh, the *Mirror* and the *Lounger*, an imitation of the famous *Tatler* and *Spectator* two generations before, his fame, apart from his early novels, rests on his influence and associations with the Golden Age of Edinburgh. He rendered a great political service to Pitt the Younger for which he was awarded a lucrative Government post. He had his portrait painted by Raeburn. What more could a man ask?

Sir Walter Scott *(1771-1832)*

In the chapter on Poets, Scott's biography has been sketched. Here we propose to mention the outlines of his prose romances.

After giving up poetry, more or less, on the appearance of Byron, he came upon some discarded notes of nine years before, and on examining them seemed to see the chance of a lifetime. The novel which resulted was named *Waverley*, the forerunner of a long series called the *Waverley* novels. *Waverley* or *'Tis sixty Years since*, was written in three weeks and it set the pattern for most of the others. Scott's greatest achievement for Scotland was his healing of the centuries-long breach between the Celts and the Saxons which was begun at the Battle of Harlaw and aggravated by the Wars of Montrose and the savage onslaughts of the Gaelic forces under Sir Alexander MacDonald. Scott's theme in *Waverley* was the Jacobite Rising of 1745-46. He goes behind the scenes to show the nobility of the Highland Jacobites and to sympathise with them in the harsh repressions they suffered. The *Legend of Montrose* and *Rob Roy* were set respectively in two other periods where the cultures clashed. Scott, a member of a Border clan famed for its restlessness, gives a fair unbiased picture of both half-nations.

In *Old Mortality* he was subjected to severe criticism by the protagonists of the Covenanters, especially for his pictures of ludicrous fanatics like Habbakuk Mucklewraith and Mause Headrigg his female counterpart. But his knowledge of historical trials and contemporary correspondence was used to draw these portraits from the originals.

Ivanhoe and *The Talisman* were set in the Middle Ages and although full of incident and coloured background are recognised as pure romances, not at all historical.

Scott's strength is in his native land, in the humour of his characters and their racy conversations. Particularly is this so in his dramatic novel *The Heart of Midlothian* where he depicts a domestic drama of a young Edinburgh girl falsely accused of infanticide and rescued from the gallows by her sister's fortitude. More than any other of the *Waverley* novels set in Scotland, this story, based on an actual incident takes the reader right into the flesh and blood pathos of real life in 'mine own romantic town' during the Porteous Riot days. His novels are always healthy and fresh, like the ocean and the mountains. Carlyle thought that his countryman was superficial, and did not attempt to get at the heart of existence. There is some truth in this, but on the other hand Scott's vigour would have been lost had he indulged in psychoanalysis and philosophical musings and he would not have been swept irresistibly into the affections of readers all over the world.

John Galt *(1779-1839)*

Born at Irvine, Ayrshire, son of a West-Indian sea-captain, he moved with his family to Greenock in boyhood. Until twenty-five he worked as a clerk in the customs, sending verses to the local press and learning the craft of writing. He met with initial failure in business when he went to London, and became a law student. Always ready to chase some fresh project he took up writing *The Life of Wolsey* but, falling ill, he went voyaging to see if he could implement a scheme to smuggle British goods into Europe to beat Napoleon's blockade.

He met Byron in Gibraltar and again in Greece. He travelled over Asia Minor and after a time in Gibraltar he returned to England after Waterloo. His literary works were many but not profitable. His first break-through was when he began to write about his own life in the West of Scotland. *Blackwood's Magazine* published a humorous correspondence, fictitious, of a Scottish family that had settled in London. This was *The Ayrshire Legatees*. It was popular, but his next publication, *The Annals of the Parish*, with which his name is always associated, assured his success. It had been written twelve years before, and rejected by the very publishers who afterwards had such a success with *Waverley* and *Guy Mannering*. The reason given for Galt's rejection? 'A novel entirely Scottish would not be acceptable to the public.' The same prejudiced excuse was being put forward a century later.

Galt's production of novels of the same genre was remarkable. *Sir Andrew Wylie* and *The Entail* were most popular at that time, the pawky humour of the characters giving rise to the accusation, in later generations 'that knew not Joseph', that Galt had been the father of the 'Kailyard School' of writers.

At his best he is as good as Scott in his scenes of Scottish humble life and his characterisation is more credible.

Amazingly this energetic man now emigrated to Canada to establish the Canada Company and here he belongs more to a different category of famous Scots. He founded the town of Guelph and had a town named after himself. But he felt disappointed at a lack of confidence in him and returned to Britain where he based his novel *Lawrie Todd* on his experiences as a pioneer. He wrote several other novels, acted as editor and wrote a short but successful *Life of Byron* which, as usual, attracted criticism because of various reasons unconnected with the writing.

He worked right up to his death, which took place at Greenock.

Susan Ferrier *(1782-1854)*

She was born in Edinburgh, youngest of ten children of an Edinburgh lawyer, who was a factor to the Argyll estates. Although Susan spent most of her life in Edinburgh she frequently resided at Inverary Castle. Between these two places she was able to observe the society of her age, in all classes. A niece of the Duke helped and encouraged Miss Ferrier in many ways. Their correspondence shows that some of the characters in the subsequent novels were recognisable as persons in Argyll and Edinburgh.

Susan's first novel *Marriage* was published anonymously when she was thirty-six. From her style and approach she seems to be the Scottish parallel to Jane Austen, lively, practical and penetrating; humorous, caustic but not cynical. In 1818 Scott was in the middle of his most prolific novel-writing period and some critics assumed that *Marriage* was from Waverley's pen as he wrote pseudonymously under that name.

Her second novel *The Inheritance* followed in 1824 and her best and last, *Destiny* in 1831, the secret not yet revealed. They were very popular in Scotland. But reported conversations which in novels dealing with society, filled much of the books, were written in broad Scots. This would never be understood in England, far less would the subtle humour be appreciated. Who, for example, but a Scot would know what was meant by this remark by Mrs Violet MacShake in *Marriage*? '... a wheen puir feckless windlestraes' or 'It's ae mercy I see ye hae neither the red head or the muckle cuits o' the Douglases'.

Susan Ferrier was a great friend of Scott and left a record of her acquaintance unpublished at her death, *Recollections of Visits to Ashiestiel and Abbotsford*. His opinion of her was very high. He called her his 'sister shadow' and thought she was as capable as he of 'gathering in the large harvest of Scottish character and fiction.'

Thomas Carlyle *(1795-1881)*

He became the most influential man of English letters in two centuries, vastly more so than the Englishmen Coleridge, Pope or Dr Johnson. He was born in the little Dumfriesshire village of Ecclefechan. He was the second son of a stone-mason who had built his own two-storey house, still standing, and the Mecca of literary pilgrims from all over the world. His parents saw to it that he had a good grounding in the alphabet and in arithmetic. At the age of seven the village school-inspector declared Thomas 'complete in English'. His further schooling at Annan Academy made him acquainted with Latin and French, though he was bullied by unmannerly oafs.

When fourteen he walked to Edinburgh to matriculate at the University of Edinburgh which he described as 'out of England and Spain it is the worst of all hitherto discovered universities'. After an arts course of four years he left without taking a degree.

He took up school-teaching of mathematics in Annan and then in Kirkcaldy. He then decided that it was better to perish than to continue teaching. However, he did several years of well-paid private tuition, translated a geometry book from French, and took up the study of law. This was the most miserable time of his life for he was a life-long sufferer, like Burns from a nervous illness. In Carlyle's case, dyspepsia.

Now occurred a remarkable change in his fortunes. He was suddenly filled with a defiant spirit and resolved to face up to any danger or difficulty whatsoever. This may have been a crucial point in his personal life, for he met Jane Baillie Welsh, one of the most vivacious young ladies in and around Edinburgh, who had scores of admirers.

With the family he was tutoring he visited London for the first time and met Coleridge, Thomas Campbell, Hazlitt and Allan Cunningham. He lodged with Edward Irving, later to become the most popular preacher in London. In 1826, after much hesitation from both parties, he married Jane Welsh, who was descended from both John Knox and William Wallace, a formidable combination. They lived in Edinburgh, but found it expensive. They lived for six years on Mrs Welsh's property at Craigenputtoch, an isolated house on the Solway moorlands, where Carlyle wrote many famous essays, including a splendid one on Burns. Here, too, he created his remarkable *Sartor Resartus*, putting out his philosophy of existence. The outspoken Jeffrey told him 'Bring your blooming Eve out of your blasted Paradise'.

In 1834 the Carlyles took the bold step of moving into 5 Cheyne Row in Chelsea, which was to be their life-long home. Here Carlyle wrote his great histories of the *French Revolution* and *Life of Frederick the Great*, as well as all kinds of biographies and essays. Against his nature, but to make a little money, he delivered lectures to the intelligentsia of London, which were later published. The Chelsea house was the focus of London's literary and scientific life. Jane was a charming and witty hostess and drew many admirers. She was a prolific letter-writer, as was her husband, and her colloquial style marks her as one of the most accomplished women of the age. Two such brilliant characters were often self-abrasive but they were both wholly in love for all that. When she died Carlyle lived in a dark world, still writing and becoming more opinionative. He received many awards, including the Prussian Order of Merit, which he accepted, and the offer of a baronetcy and Grand Order of the Bath, which he refused. His last request was to be buried beside his family near Ecclefechan, not in Westminster as offered. Jane's grave is in Haddington.

John Brown *(1810-1882)*

He was born at Biggar, son of the minister there and grandson of the famous John Brown of Haddington, author of the *Bible Dictionary*. He was taught by his father up to the age of twelve. Then his family went to Edinburgh. John was educated at the High School and University. He began medical studies at eighteen, being pupil and assistant to the great surgeon, James Syme. In 1832 occurred the terrible Asiatic cholera epidemic which brought a minor Black Death to Britain. Brown was surgeon's assistant at Chatham and saw danger at first hand. Dr Brown then set up a practice in Edinburgh but not with great enthusiasm. His zest was for literature. He contributed to many papers and magazines.

He wrote very little and often under great persuasion, but his style was of such superb charm, on the simplest and commonest subjects, that it is reminiscent of Charles Lamb. Humour and pathos are found together, skilfully blended in the highest degree in his veracious story of *Rab and his Friends*, the tale of a faithful dog and his master, a rough country carrier. Brown's *Marjory Fleming* is a unique book, telling of the precocious and quaint Edinburgh girl, friend of Sir Walter Scott, who died at the age of eight. He wrote with feeling of his native hills and moors as well as of his boyhood life in Edinburgh with his pet dogs. His essays on art, contributed at an editor's request, to criticise Ruskin's *Modern Painters* are forced and he loses his touch when he writes biographies, or on education. But his works, noted above, on nature, children and dogs, are not likely to be forgotten.

George Macdonald *(1824-1905)*

He was the son of a farmer, born and educated at Huntly, Aberdeenshire. His ancestors were from Glencoe, having fled from the massacre of 1692. He took his Divinity degree at Aberdeen and studied for the Congregational Ministry at Highbury, London. He was a minister in Arundel and Manchester, but settled in London and turned to writing.

His first publications were verse of a varied kind, romantic and pleasing, but he won success with a long series of novels based on his knowledge of the North-east of Scotland. The best of these are perhaps *David Elginbrod, Alec Forbes* and *Robert Falconer*.

To a modern reader all of Macdonald's novels are heavy-going, being wordy, didactic and religious. But this was the taste of the mid-Victorian age. His style is faultless, looked at from a literary point of view. The rhythm and choice of expression show a highly intelligent and sensitive writer. His characters come to life and express themselves in flawless native idiom, not over-clotted with dialect, and therefore no obstacle to most British readers. His tales for children are free from sermonising and his weird novel *Lilith* is said by W.H. Auden to be even more blood-chilling than Edgar Allan Poe.

William Alexander *(1826-1894)*

Macdonald had a contemporary who was his equal in portraying the Aberdeenshire folk with a vivid exactness. He was William Alexander, editor of the *Aberdeen Free Press*. His great book *Johnny Gibb of Gushetneuk* was an outstanding success, which epitomised and outshone all his other works.

Both these genuinely literary men presented a dignified picture of the Scottish life and character of their time, with no great pretence at the drama or historical highlights that had electrified Scott's novels of his native land. They must, on this account, be completely dissociated from the writers of the Nineties who traded on J.M. Barrie's sentimental successes in what is called the 'Kailyard'. Macdonald and Alexander survived to see this decline in the portrayal of Scottish rural life, though there is no record of how they reacted to it. The former attained his eightieth year and saw the publication of George Douglas Brown's *House with the Green Shutters*, of which bitter aloes he perhaps disapproved as strongly as of the sugary dill of Crockett and MacLaren.

Mrs Margaret Oliphant *(1828-1897)*

Born at Wallyford near Musselburgh, Midlothian, she travelled with her father, a business man, to Liverpool and Glasgow. She had a disturbed education which did not help her literary ambitions.

At twenty-one, however, she published *Passages in the Life of Mrs Maitland*, not a very exciting title. But in mid-Victorian times it was immediately popular in a number of domestic circles. Similar novels of

Scottish life and character followed, one every year. They were published as serials in *Blackwood's Magazine*. They appealed to the feminine readers, having a wealth of domestic detail and quiet fun as well as emotional restraint.

She married her cousin, an artist. He was consumptive and died a few years later, leaving her deep in debt, with two sons and a daughter.

She was proud and independent, as well as optimistic. She knew that she could only earn by her pen, and set herself, year in, year out, to the formidable task. She liked to live in luxury and to give lavish hospitality, but she had a hard struggle to maintain this front of respectability. Life in the Oliphant household had its glimpses of Hell. She sent her two sons to Eton and Oxford. Her daughter died in late childhood and her sons both died as young men before they could repay her for bringing them so elegantly to manhood.

Her early style now clarified and she achieved a real success as a literary woman with her novels about English dissenters. The *Chronicles of Carlingford* and *Salem Chapel* were as good as anything by Anthony Trollope. She also, as a relief from fiction, wrote the life of Edward Irving, the friend of Carlyle, and of her late husband. Her other works of history and biography cover St Francis of Assisi, Dante, Cervantes, Joan of Arc and the Brontës. She wrote a *Child's History of Scotland*.

It is hardly surprising that she earns censure as a stylist. But she entertained her age and no doubt the millions of British and English speaking readers overseas relieved their burdens by relaxing over some of her two hundred and fifty volumes.

Robert Buchanan *(1841-1901)*

Though born in Staffordshire he was the son of a Scottish schoolmaster and socialist who moved to Glasgow when Robert was young. He was educated at Glasgow High School and University where his bosom-friend was the ill-fated David Gray, a poet.

In 1860 they set out for London full of ambition. They endured poverty in a garret in Blackfriars, accentuated by Gray's having contracted tuberculosis following a chill, while sleeping rough. He died within the year, but Buchanan published two volumes of poems which were well received. His *London Poems* in 1866 were a great success. For several years he wrote on all sorts of themes, European and American. He now turned to prose and engaged in a bitter controversy with Rossetti and Swinburne. A whole series of popular novels followed as well as dramas which were presented successfully in London theatres in the eighties and nineties.

He is a good example of a Scot who found success and also notoriety in London when he would have been less appreciated in Scotland. In this respect he resembled J.M. Barrie and John Davidson who at that time also achieved success in London.

Robert Louis Stevenson *(1850-1894)*

In 'Poets' we have appraised his verses but it is for his *belles-lettres* that he is universally acknowledged.

He was an omnivorous reader in French and English and had a great admiration for the ancient and quaint styles of Sir Thomas Browne, Hobbes, Urquhart, Cervantes (in translation) and Montaigne. He early copied every literary trick. At that time, the Seventies of the last century, Flaubert had started a craze for *le mot juste* or 'the fitting word'. Stevenson caught the infection and throughout all his writing there is a certain preciousness, a self-conscious striving, which is not to be found in the very best authors. But he redeems this by his refined and penetrating insight into men's minds, and his energetic writing. The English essayist Hazlitt was a factor in the formation of his style. Only in his later illnesses does he show an understandable laxity and dullness.

His first venture into published prose was the result of a canoe trip which he made with his friend Walter Simpson through the canals of North France and Belgium. Its title is *An Inland Voyage*. This gave him a limited reputation. A year later, as a result of a hike with a pack-donkey through the Cevennes in the South of France he wrote and published the enchanting *Travels with a Donkey*, famous still for its pictures of the young Stevenson sleeping out in the woods puffing his cigarette and munching his chocolate.

In France, he met a Californian lady, Mrs Osborne, whom he afterwards married. To rejoin her he made a trip in 1879 to California. Despite his delicate health, to save money, he crossed the Atlantic in an emigrant ship with all its horrors, then over the prairies with all its accompanying hardships. He spent the following winter in the utmost misery of body and mind. He tells all this in *Across the Plains*.

In California he married Mrs Osborne and with her and his stepson Lloyd he returned in a happier humour to Europe. His health forced him to live in Davos, a Swiss health spa. There his genius began to bear fruit in a book of essays *Virginibus Puerisque*, the title rather bookish, being a quotation from Horace's poem beginning 'I hate the vulgar throng, I sing to youths and maidens'. Stevenson certainly appealed to them in his epoch-making *Treasure Island* which appeared in 1882. *The New Arabian Nights* followed, with other popular works.

He now puzzled and shocked his generation with *The Strange Case of Dr. Jekyll and Mr. Hyde*. There is no doubt that this book is based on Stevenson's own double life in Edinburgh when he, out of curiosity mainly, was attracted to the taverns and brothels of the Old Town of Edinburgh. With Henley he composed plays, one on Deacon Brodie, an ambivalent Edinburgh villain, rather like Jekyll and Hyde.

Stevenson now turned to Scottish history as Scott had done, but his first task was to find areas which Scott had not visited. He did this successfully, beyond expectation, in *Kidnapped*, set in 1752 and based on an actual political murder, never solved, though a Highland chief was unjustly hanged for it. *Catriona* was the sequel, somewhat flat after the sustained action of *Kidnapped*. *The Master of Ballantrae* was well received but Stevenson died before he could finish the powerful *Weir of Hermiston*. He wrote, amongst these, several other historical romances of which *St. Ives* a tale of French prisoners-of-war in Edinburgh in the Napoleonic times, written in

249

his last months, shows his failing powers.

He died in Samoa, aged forty-four, a boy at heart. He had bought ground and built a home and interested himself in the Samoans. He was much admired by them, being given a native name 'Tusitala' the teller of stories. Whom the gods love die young.

The Revd John Watson (Ian Maclaren) *(1850-1907)*

He preached in Liverpool and was unashamedly of the pious lugubrious brotherhood. His deathbed scenes, especially of gifted youths, are unbearable. But he was popular. *The Starling, The Days of Auld Lang Syne, the Bonny Brier Bush*, and others were in every humble Scots home along with the poems of Burns, the Bible, the Shorter Catechism and James Grahame's *Sabbath*.

But these writers, strange to say, were also acceptable in England and America and laid the success of Harry Lauder, *Brigadoon*, and a host of comic postcard artists.

Mary Mackay (Marie Corelli) *(1854-1924)*

She was the daughter of Charles Mackay, a Perth native, who was one of the most industrious and popular journalists of his day; for some years he was editor of the *London Illustrated News* in which many of his finest songs were printed.

It is little wonder that his daughter, child of his second wife, achieved an enormous success in her melodramatic romantic novels. She was educated in a French convent school and had originally been intended for a musical career but she followed her father's bent for literature.

At thirty she suddenly burst into the limelight with her novel *Romance of Two Worlds*. She created for herself an immense crowd of avid readers and did not disappoint their appetite for a constant supply of novels. The titles indicate the sensational nature of the writing; *Vendetta, The Soul of Lilith, Barabbas, The Sorrows of Satan, The Mighty Atom, The Master Christian*. She had many critics who sneered at her 'bad style' and others who accused her of blasphemy and cheap emotionalism. But that was what was wanted at the close of the Victorian Age. The ordinary reader was tired of the semi-religious dullness of the ordinary novel and found relief in Marie Corelli's sincerity and strong, if rabid, convictions. She lived long enough to see her novels rapidly becoming obsolete and ridiculed by a cynical postwar generation. Like Mrs Oliphant she served her day.

Sir Arthur Conan Doyle *(1859-1930)*

Born in Edinburgh, son of Charles Doyle, an artist, who was a clerk in the Exchequer Office. He came of a very talented family, his uncle being the famous Richard Doyle who designed the original cover for *Punch*. Arthur was educated at Stonyhurst and Edinburgh University where he was taught medicine. One of his professors was an expert at deduction and, after the examination of a patient he would ask his students to tell all they could from the evidence. He would then astound them by his acute reasoning. This professor, Joseph Bell, is acknowledged by Conan Doyle to have been the original of his Sherlock Holmes.

Doyle had a varied medical experience, including a voyage to the Arctic, but he early practised writing and as a student had articles published in *Chamber's Journal*.

His first successful books were of crime and adventure. *A Study in Scarlet*, *Micah Clarke* and the *White Company*. His *Rodney Stone* was a story set in Regency times and *The Adventures of Brigadier Gerard* was a popular series of the Wars of Napoleon. Then he took up a more active life.

During part of the Great Boer War he was a doctor with the troops and returning before the end of the war took up politics, standing in the Unionist interest, unsuccessfully, for an Edinburgh constituency.

Conan Doyle's name is however most closely associated with Sherlock Holmes. This imperturbable logician first appeared in *A Study in Scarlet,* in 1887 when the author was in his late twenties. *The Adventures of Sherlock Holmes* appeared in serial form in the *Strand Magazine* in 1891, followed by *The Memoirs of Sherlock Holmes* in 1893. Though they were not the first detective stories (for Edgar Allan Poe had written on these lines) they started a vast movement, still filling the libraries.

The public refused to agree to the death of Holmes in one book and he had to be resurrected in *The Return of Sherlock Holmes*.

Conan Doyle was a prolific writer in other modes and wrote several successful plays, and histories of the Boer War and First World War. In his later days he was a convinced spiritualist and wrote and lectured on this controversial subject.

Kenneth Grahame *(1859-1932)*

He was born in Edinburgh but spent most of his life in England where he wrote his studies of childhood in an English countryside setting. He was a descendant of the Revd James Grahame, a well-known religious and native poet of the early nineteenth century, a Glaswegian and friend of Thomas Campbell. Little doubt that Kenneth inherited his ancestor's lyricism.

His first book, *The Golden Age* (1895) was very popular as also was the sequel *Dream Days* (1898) but neither of these has immortalised Grahame with children and adults like *The Wind in the Willows* (1908) with its well-known animal characters.

Sir James Matthew Barrie *(1860-1937)*

He was born in Kirriemuir, Angus, and early showed his literary bent, being able to write before going to the village school. As a 'Lad o' pairts', or of promise, he was sent to Edinburgh University, though this meant strict economy for his parents, who were not well off. He found employment for his talents in Nottingham as leader-writer for the *Journal*. While there, he had an article accepted by *St James's Gazette*, London, which started a completely new trend in writing about Scotland. Its subject was *An Auld Licht Community* which described life in Kirriemuir where most of the people belonged to the non-juring Associate Synod of the Kirk, a sect ridiculed for hypocrisy and bigotry by Burns a century before, but still surviving despite that satire.

Barrie moved to London, encouraged by the editor of the Gazette, and published a brilliant satire on London Journalistic life in 1887, entitled *Better Dead*. *Auld Licht Idylls*, presenting a picture of whimsy, wit, pathos and tragedy, came next, and has been blamed for starting a spate of imitators of little humour and abundance of bathos known collectively as the 'Kailyard School'. We shall refer to them later. *A Window in Thrums*, being on the same subject as the *Idylls* about life in Thrums, a nickname for the weaving town of Kirriemuir, came out in 1888. Barrie was now established as a perfect portrayer of Scottish provincial life. English readers must have had trouble with the dialogues, modified though they were, but they still enjoyed the books. *My Lady Nicotine*, a humorous book on smoking, and *The Little Minister*, a romance of early days in Kirriemuir, completed the first phase of Barrie's writing.

He now turned to what was to be an enormously successful field, writing for the theatre. In the miracle years, 1903 to 1908 he had as many as three plays running at the same time in London. The most famous of these were *Peter Pan*, *The Admirable Crichton* and *What Every Woman Knows*.

As the years went on his fantasies increased until in *A Kiss for Cinderella*, *Dear Brutus* and *Mary Rose* the line between Fairyland and everyday becomes impossible to be drawn. He has been likened to the Hans Andersen of the theatre, to whom the tragedy of life was as attractive as the comedy.

Barrie has been blackened by Scottish critics much more than by English. J.H. Miller in his *Literary History of Scotland* published in 1903 when Barrie was about to enchant the world with his plays, says bitterly of him, 'His cynical disregard of true art—the studied "playing to the gallery"—has been a prominent feature in all Mr. Barrie's subsequent work.' But, despite this disparagement from a Scots carp, he went on to delight children as they had never been before, and to earn an immortal place in British theatre.

The Kailyard School *(c.1893-1900)*

The success of Barrie's Kirriemuir books attracted other writers to follow him, which they did with no waste of time. In 1893 Crockett, a minister of Penicuik in Midlothian, turned to writing and published *The Sticket Minister*, a collection of short stories of Scots rural life. A sticket minister is one who, failing to complete his divinity studies, turns to school teaching or some other employment. In 1894 John Watson a minister of the Presbyterian Church in England, at Sefton, Liverpool, published a sentimental novel *Beside the Bonnie Brier Bush*, the title being a quote from a well-known Scots song of the Jacobites. The relevant line is 'There grows a bonnie brier bush in our kailyard.' The last word in the line gave the critics of these domestic writers a handy stick to use on them, though it hardly applied to all their work.

Samuel Rutherford Crockett *(1860-1914)*

He was the historian novelist of Galloway and as it was his early stamping ground he wrote his novels with an intimate knowledge of country and people. His books achieved an instant success and he turned out more than twenty before he exhausted the vein. Some of these were set abroad and some in Scotland. The most realistic, grimly humorous and full of authentic scenes in the Old Town of Edinburgh, is *Cleg Kelly*, the tale of a Scoto-Irish guttersnipe. There was little sentimentality here.

Neil Munro *(1864-1930)*

He was born near Inveraray in Highland surroundings, and was early influenced by the writings of R.L. Stevenson. His first novels, dealing with minor events in Highland history, were *The Lost Pibroch, John Splendid, Gillian the Dreamer* and *Doom Castle*. These have vigour and movement. He used a new medium, more popular, with his *Para Handy* stories, which still appeal by their wit and humour. The first of these was *The Vital Spark*. *The Daft Days* and *Ayrshire Idylls* are also amusing, though published seventy years ago.

George Douglas Brown *(1869-1902)*

Born in Ochiltree, Ayrshire, he early showed his potential by winning in competition a Snell foundation at Oxford. After gaining his BA, he turned to journalism where he was competent but not exceptional. However, when twenty-seven he contributed a very fine essay on Burns to *Blackwood's Magazine* in commemoration of the centenary of the poet's death. His critical articles were all noteworthy but he would never have been remembered above a month except for his work of a lifetime, *The House with the Green Shutters*. He died at thirty-three not long after he had written it.

Perhaps it was deliberately written as a bitter tonic to counteract the cloying effects of the novels of Maclaren and others, but it was also a masterpiece of realism and energetic prose, inclined to be bitter, as if to gratify some personal hatred. It tells the story of the battle between a hard self-made Scottish businessman and the community which he had dominated. Brown wrote the book from his personal knowledge of life in a small Ayrshire town of the late nineteenth century and it is not a pretty picture. He also depicts the life of a student in Edinburgh with its mixture of hardship, boredom and debauchery.

Readers could make up their minds whether to believe Brown or Maclaren. The truth probably lay halfway.

Brown too had his imitators, many of them, right up to the middle of the century, with such works as *Hatter's Castle* by A.J. Cronin, *Gillespie* by the Revd Hay, *No Mean City* by Alexander McArthur and H. Kingsley Long, and *Man's Chief End* by Edward Albert. The glittering granite stone that the earlier followers of Barrie had set up was lifted at intervals to show the crawling and slithering creatures that hid beneath it.

John Buchan *(1875-1940)*

Born at Peebles, he early took to literature and wrote his first novel at the age of eighteen. His most prolific novel-writing period was from 1915 to 1923 when he was engaged on the staff of the British Army in France and later as Director of Information under Lloyd George.

His best novels are *The Thirty-nine Steps*, *Greenmantle*, *Mr. Standfast*, adventures of spying. They have been filmed successfully but they now have an outmoded flavour.

Buchan's more serious literary work was in the biographies of such varied heroes as *Montrose*, *Sir Walter Scott*, *Julius Caesar* and *Oliver Cromwell*. He was Governor-General of Canada from 1935 until his death.

David Lindsay *(1878-1945)*

Son of a Scottish father, he was educated at Blackheath and worked in Lloyds until he served in the Grenadier Guards during the First World War. He is chiefly noted for his mythical and metaphysical novel *A Voyage to Arcturus* (1920), which was inspired by George Macdonald's allegoric novel *Lilith*, published in 1895.

J. MacDougal Hay *(1881-1919)*

He was born at Tarbert, Loch Fyne, and took an arts degree at Glasgow, proceeding to Ullapool as schoolmaster.

After a crippling bout of rheumatic fever he left teaching and became a minister at Elderslie, Renfrew, where his arduous parish duties did not help his health.

In 1914 he published his strongly written novel *Gillespie*, on the same theme of conflict in a small town, as Brown's *The House with the Green Shutters*. It contains some powerful descriptive scenes and it is a remarkable achievement for a minister, unsparing in its realism.

Florence Marian McNeill *(1885-1973)*

A daughter of the manse, she was born in Orkney, where she spent her childhood and acquired deep impressions which served for the matter of her writing. She was educated at Holm Parish School, and at High Schools in Kirkwall, Glasgow and abroad. She graduated MA at Glasgow, then did social work in London and lexicography in Aberdeen.

Her first publication in 1920 was a history of Iona. Her second, in 1929, is likely to be her memorial for generations. Its title is *The Scots Kitchen*, a collection of traditional recipes.

Always an ardent Scot, she published a four-volume work on Scots folk-lore and festivals, *The Silver Bough*, completed in 1968. She identified herself with Scotland's long struggle to achieve political independence.

O.H. Mavor (James Bridie) *(1888-1951)*

He was a native of Glasgow and qualified there as a doctor, serving in both World Wars in the RAMC.

His first success as a playwright was with *Tobias and the Angel* in 1930.

It had a long run in London. Many other successes followed, the most notable being *The Anatomist, The Sleeping Clergyman* and *Mr Bolfrey*. These have a strong moralistic note, also apparent in *John Knox* and *The Queen's Comedy* written not long before his death.

Neil Gunn *(1891-1974)*

Born in Caithness, son of a skipper, he was educated at the village school of Dunbeath. He entered the Civil Service in 1906, working in London, Edinburgh and Inverness.

In 1937 he left the Civil Service because of his success in novel-writing. His first novels, *The Grey Coast* and *The Lost Glen*, deal with Highland life. But *Morning Tide, Sun Circle* and *Butcher's Broom* were greater novels, full of myth, poetry and also passionate sympathy with tragic events. *Morning Tide* and *The Silver Darlings* are also novels of universal human interest.

George Blake *(1893-1961)*

He was a Greenock native who began to read for law in Glasgow, was wounded at the Dardanelles, and took up successful journalism in Glasgow and London. He edited *John o' London's Weekly* and then the *Strand* magazine, and was a director in Faber & Faber, publishers.

He wrote powerfully, especially on the scene he knew best, the industrial world of the Clyde where he was sure of his material.

Eric Linklater *(1899-1974)*

Although born in South Wales, he was of Orcadian stock. He was educated at Aberdeen Grammar School and University and served with the Black Watch as a private from 1917 to 1919. In the Second World War he was an Engineer Fortress Commander in the Orkneys. He was a man of the North, as his novels show, but he could also depict such foreign backgrounds as appear in *Juan in America, Juan in China* and *Poet's Pub*, all comical and vigorous. *The Men of Ness* and the Norse story *The Saga of Thorlief Coalbiter's Son* show another aspect of his talent. But comedy was his strong suit and he had a series of successes in *The Impregnable Women, Laxdale Hall* and *Private Angelo*. In serious vein he wrote a survey of the Orkneys and Shetlands.

J. Leslie Mitchell (Lewis Grassic Gibbon) *(1901-1935)*

He was born on a farm near Auchterless, Aberdeenshire, but when young went with his parents to Kincardineshire where at school, under the guidance of a kind teacher he was advanced to Stonehaven where he left the Mackie Academy after a stormy scene. As a young Glasgow journalist his irregular behaviour earned him dismissal. A spell in Central Asia, Persia and Egypt with the RASC after the 1914-18 war gave him a distaste for the army, but he worked as a clerk in the RAF leaving in 1929. From then till his early death he wrote prolifically. His books were didactic, argumentative and fictional. His finest story, however, is the historical account of

Spartacus, the leader of the slave revolt against Rome.

His best work was based on his early life in the Mearns, or Kincardine. It formed a trilogy of novels surrounding the life-story of Chris Guthrie, daughter of a crofter. The title is *A Scots Quair*; and the separate parts are named *Sunset Song*, *Cloud Howe* and *Grey Granite*. The books are passionate and energetic but rather overwritten. Mitchell's writing is seen at its finest in a book of selected essays and stories, *A Scots Hairst*, published in 1969.

Tom Douglas Macdonald (Fionn Mac Colla) *(1906-1975)*

Macdonald was a fiery protagonist of the ancient Gaelic world. In his novels *The Albannach* (1932) and *And the Cock Crew* (1945) he unsparingly condemns the genocide of the West Highland people in the various 'Clearances'. His realism is often hard to bear, but it rings true to anyone familiar with the harsh realities of history of the past two centuries. *Scottish Noel* graphically depicts the all-too-often repeated incursions of the English barbarians into the Scottish Lowlands. He also wrote the strong polemic books *At the Sign of the Clenched Fist* and *Too Long in this Condition*, leaving readers in no doubt as to his crusade against injustice and political apathy.

Robert Kemp *(1908-1967)*

He is chiefly notable for his adaptation of Robert Lindsay's *The Thrie Estaites*, a mediaeval morality satire first staged in 1540 and presented in 1948 in Edinburgh with enormous success. Kemp also wrote a popular play based on the flirtation of Burns and Mrs Maclehose, entitled *The Other Dear Charmer*.

James Kennaway *(1928-1968)*

He was born in Perthshire and educated at Oxford, serving during the Second World War as an officer in the Cameron Highlanders.

From 1951 to 1957 he gained valuable literary experience as editor with Longmans Green, publishers, which stood him in good stead when he left to become a full-time writer. He was looked upon as one of the key novelists of the fifties and sixties. His early death in a car accident was considered by the literary world to be an irreparable loss. His favourite novel was *The Cost of Living Like This*, which portrayed his poetic talent and insight, and is set in contemporary Scotland.

Music & Song

Music was the breath of life to all the ancient tribesfolk of Scotland. The Gaelic Scots from centuries BC, before they crossed from Ireland, were entertained by harpists on various forms of the clarsach. So famed was the Irish harp through all Europe from the seventh century that it was adopted as the symbol of the Irish nation. But the Gaels of the Western Isles of Scotland also enjoyed the harp. In the sixteenth century George Buchanan, the scholar wrote, 'They delight very much in music, especially in harps of their own sort.' The harpist most famed in early Scotland was the Lewis man Roderick Morison, named Rory Dall or Blind Roderick (1656-1714). He was reputed to be the only minstrel in Gaelic Scotland. He was domiciled at Dunvegan Castle, home of the Macleod chiefs, where he played along with Patrick Og MacCrimmon the piper and James Glass the fiddler. These three instruments were the main source of accompaniments in Scotland for centuries. The harpists were contemptuous of the fiddlers and the Lowlanders in general were averse to the pipes, but this was prejudice, for each instrument had wonderful performers.

In court circles there was a great variety of musical instruments, many of French or other European origin. In the reigns of James IV and V and Mary, additional to the native harps, fiddles and pipes, there were trumpets, lutes, virginals, viols, all kinds of drums, recorders, cornets, flutes and organs.

The Reformation put an end to much of this and along with all forms of art, music was not tolerated either within or without religious services. The effect of this repression continued with severity for two centuries and is still felt.

The disestablishment of the religious foundations, many of which had already been destroyed by the English, especially so in the Borders in the reign of Henry VIII by the invasion of the Earl of Hertford, meant that Scotland lost all opportunity to develop the grand oratorios, fugues and organ and choral music which were the glory of the European cathedrals. Yet it had been a Scot born in the late tenth century who was prominent in Europe in the theory and teaching of music. We mention this outstanding genius of the early Middle Ages, after which there is a gap of seven centuries before any individuals are noteworthy.

Aaron Scotus (c.980-1060)

He was born probably in Ayrshire, Argyll or perhaps the Ulster area about AD 980. He was Benedictine Abbot of St Martin, Cologne, Rhineland. Pope Leo IX (1049-54) had composed a new service of music named the

'Office of St Gregory (the Great)' and it was recommended to be used throughout Christendom. Aaron, as Abbot, decreed that the new service be used in St Martin, to replace the previous 'Common of Confessors'.

He also wrote a chronicle of music and a treatise on singing and psalmody, entitled *De Utilitatis cantis vocalis' (On the usages of vocal music)*. Several other works on music were composed by him.

John Garve Maclean *(c.1590-1650)*

He was the Laird of Coll, considered to be a good composer and harper. A devout Royalist, he composed a lament for the death of Charles I entitled *Caoincadh Rioghail*, the Royal Lament. After his death, the Macleans of Coll maintained harpers, clothing and feeding them, until about the time of the 1745 Rising, after which there was an English proscription on all things Highland.

Roderick Morrison (*Rory Dall*, Blind Rory) *(c.1660-1712)*

He was born in Lewis, son of a tacksman or small farmer. He was intended for the church but while a student at Inverness he took smallpox and lost his sight, so gave up a church career. He turned to music for a living, having a gift for it.

Though he played other instruments, the harp was his choice. He was trained by one of the known harpers and his skill introduced him to many well-known patrons. He went to Ireland, the old home of the harp, for further instruction and returned to Scotland in 1681 where he met the Chief of MacLeod, known as Iain Breac, who asked him to be clan harper.

He stayed at Dunvegan, the MacLeod residence, until 1693 when Iain Breac died. The successor did not want his services so Rory eventually returned to Lewis where he died.

Rory was a bard as well as a harper and wrote poems in favour of Iain Breac and also two against the heir who had turned him out.

The Scots taste in music was for melody rather than harmony and no instrument was as congenial to popular Scottish airs as the fiddle. Consequently there are many famous fiddle composers and players, though most of them remain unknown outside their native land.

William McGibbon *(1690-1756)*

He was born in Edinburgh, son of Malcolm, a professional oboeist in the city. William went to London as a young man to study violin and composition with the musician William Corbett. On his return to Edinburgh he became professional violinist in the Edinburgh Musical Society for twenty years.

He was the leading Scottish composer of that time, named the late Baroque Period. He had a very large output of tunes in the popular folk-style. His violin playing was so famous that, sixteen years after his death, he was commemorated in Robert Fergusson's poem, *Elegy on the Death of Scots Music* (1772).

Neil Gow *(1727-1807)*

He was born in Dunkeld, Perthshire, and lived there most of his life, giving rise to a dynasty of famous fiddlers. He was largely self-taught and came to the art in the severest time of proscription of all things Highland, after Culloden. He took a few lessons from a local fiddler, John Cameron, and then went on to compose reels and strathspeys by the dozen. His brother Donald accompanied him on the 'cello.

One of his best known airs is a slow march, 'Neil Gow's Farewell to Whisky', a touching lament.

Neil Gow had four sons, William, Andrew, John and Nathaniel, who were all accomplished fiddlers.

Nathaniel Gow *(1766-1831)*

Nathaniel was the youngest and proved to be the best of a very fine quartet. Like his brothers he studied under his father, but his teachers also included a Robert MacIntosh and MacGlashen. His repertoire is an extensive one of reels, strathspeys and jigs, perhaps his best known tune, however, is none of these, but the sublime 'Caller Herrin' for which Carolina (Baroness Nairne) wrote the fine words. The tune was inspired by the church bells of St Andrew's Kirk and the cries of the Newhaven fishwives.

Neil Gow, son of Nathaniel, showed great but unfulfilled promise to be a worthy holder of his grandfather's name. In his short life he composed the airs 'Bonnie Prince Charlie' and 'Flora Macdonald's Lament', words to both being supplied by James Hogg, the Ettrick Shepherd.

Daniel Dow *(1732-1783)*

Born in Perthshire, he became a teacher of music, including the guitar. He published a book of *Twenty Minuets and Sixteen Reels* (1775), and another on *Ancient Scottish Music for the Violin* (1768). His best known works are the strathspeys 'Monymusk' and 'The Duchess of Gordon', and the reels of 'The Brig of Perth' and 'Athole House'.

His son John Dow was also a popular violinist.

William Marshall *(1749-1833)*

He was born at Fochabers, Strathspey, of very poor parents. He had little education, but by attention to what books he could obtain he taught himself well enough to become butler to the Duke of Gordon and eventually factor on the extensive estates. He became a JP and was also a clockmaker and surveyor.

He made an outstanding contribution to folk music, writing 257 original dance tunes, but, the slow strathspey being his favourite form of composition, these were found unsuitable for dancing. He best-known piece is 'Miss Admiral Gordon's Strathspey', which Burns fitted to the words of 'O' a' the airts the wind can blaw'.

Isaac Cooper *(1755-1820)*

A native of Banff, he went to Edinburgh as a teacher and composer, where he became the most versatile musician in the country, teaching every instrument then known, in a very sophisticated society. He published a set of reels in 1783, and composed several well-established popular airs including 'Miss Forbes' Farewell to Banff', and the strathspey 'Mrs Rose's' or 'Ben Lomond'. He also wrote a slow air, 'The Death of Nelson'. He died obscurely in extreme poverty, and details of his life were almost impossible to find.

Robert Petrie *(1767-1839)*

Born in Kirkmichael, Perthshire, he was a talented violinist, teacher and composer. He won the Silver Bow prize for violin playing in Edinburgh against much competition. He composed the violin tune 'Comin' through the Rye', the words being originally from an old song but rewritten by Burns.

Petrie was accidentally drowned one stormy night returning from a musical evening.

Robert Archibald Smith *(1780-1829)*

He was the son of a Paisley weaver who, because of lack of employment at home, moved to Reading, where Robert was born. As a youth Robert was an apprentice weaver when the family returned to Paisley. Here at an early age his musical talent was recognised by his being made precentor in Paisley Abbey church. From this he was appointed choir-master in St George's Parish Church, Edinburgh.

He was an extremely modest man of great talent, his compositions including both church and lay items. As a Paisley man he felt it his privilege to set to music the poems of the Paisley poets Tannahill and Motherwell. He published *The Scottish Minstrel* (six volumes, 1821-1824), *The Irish Minstrel* (1825), as well as *Flowers of Scottish Song* and *Devotional Music*.

He also composed fifteen anthems and ten doxologies and the sacred music 'How beautiful upon the Mountains'. 'Jessie the Flower o' Dunblane' and 'On wi' the Tartan' were popular Scots airs for a century.

It was said of him by a music critic, 'His music is entirely free from the scientific pedantry which forms the prevailing vice in the modern (mid-Victorian) English school.'

George Hogarth *(1777-1870)*

Born at Carfraemill, Lauderdale, he moved to London when a young man and contributed as music critic to various papers. He had married the daughter of George Thomson, the friend of Robert Burns, for whom Burns contributed freely a large number of songs. That was fame enough, but Hogarth's own daughter, Catherine, went one better. She married the young Charles Dickens in 1836, a marriage that was not to prove the happiest.

George became a famous critical writer and was appointed Musical Critic to the *Daily News* in 1846, a post he held for twenty years. He also edited the *Musical Herald* and was secretary of the Philharmonic Society. He published a comprehensive volume on *Musical Criticism, History and*

Biography. He was kindly, impartial and scholarly. He died in the same year as his famous son-in-law.

James Scott Skinner *(1843-1927)*

Born at Banchory, Aberdeenshire, he became a pupil of Dr Mark of Manchester and was probably the most famous violinist of the century, performing to huge audiences in Great Britain, the USA and Canada. He was also a poet, composer, teacher and editor.

His best strathspeys are 'The Miller o' Hirn', and 'Glenlivet'; his reel, 'Jenny's Bawbee' is very popular; and his march 'The Bonnie Lass o' Bon Accord' sets feet tapping everywhere.

George Learmonth Drysdale *(1846-1909)*

Born in Edinburgh, he was organist in Greenside Church before moving to London where he became sub-organist at Kensington. He was a student at the Royal Academy of Music from 1887 to 1892 where he won the Lucas Medal.

He returned to Scotland in 1904 as a teacher in the Athenaeum School of Music (now the Royal Scottish Academy of Music).

He has been named the 'Scottish Grieg' because of the essentially national feeling of his music (though Grieg was himself of Scottish origin).

Drysdale's compositions include 'Spirit of the Glen' (1889), 'Thomas the Rhymer' (1890), 'Through the Sound of Raasay' (1890). His best known work is 'Tam o' Shanter'. His 'Border Romance' was written at the request of Sir Henry Wood.

Sir Alexander Campbell Mackenzie *(1847-1935)*

He was born in Edinburgh. His great-grandfather and grandfather were both noted Scottish musicians, his father being leading violinist in the Theatre Royal.

When only ten he studied music in Germany, and as a youth played second violin in the Sonderhausen Orchestra, where the performances included the works of Liszt, Berlioz and Wagner. In 1842 he won a scholarship in London for the Royal Academy of Music. Returning to Edinburgh he obtained the much prized appointment as precentor of St George's Parish Church and became the conductor of the Scottish Vocal Music Academy. In 1879 he went to Florence to study, and while there composed 'The Bride', a cantata, and also 'Columba'.

His composition 'The Rose of Sharon' was voted the best work in England for 1884. He now became conductor of the Novello Oratorio Choir.

In 1880 he was Principal of the Royal Academy of Music. He introduced Tchaikovsky and Borodin to London musical circles but many of his own compositions were based on Scottish subjects, including themes from Burns and other poets.

He toured Canada and was given the D. Litt. of McGill University. He was made a Knight Commander of the Victorian Order in 1922.

Hamish McCunn *(1868-1916)*

Born in Greenock, the son of a ship-owner, he was a precocious pianist and composer and won an open scholarship to the Royal Academy of Music when only fifteen.

He never returned to Scotland from London, but it was obvious from his compositions that his heart was in Scotland.

He was Professor of Harmony at the Royal Academy of Music from 1888 to 1894 and taught composition to many students, among whom was the celebrated Liza Lehmann.

McCunn made his main income by conducting, chiefly in the Opera House, the most famous operas being *Siegfried* and *Tristan*.

In 1910 and 1915 he conducted the Beecham Company. He was noted for his tact and assurance and efficient professionalism. His overtures and cantatas of the most eminence were 'Land of the Mountain and the Flood' (1887) and 'Jeanie Deans' played by the Carl Rosa Company. He wrote music for lyrics by Burns, Scott, Moore, George Macdonald and Robert Bridges.

Francis George Scott *(1880-1958)*

Born in Hawick and educated at Edinburgh University and Moray House Training College, he took the Mus.B. at Durham in 1909.

He was appointed first to Langholm Academy where he taught Christopher M. Grieve (Hugh MacDiarmid) and formed a life-long friendship with him. He afterwards taught in Dunoon and Glasgow. He was appointed lecturer of Music in Jordanhill Training College, Glasgow, from 1925 to 1946.

He was largely influenced by Bartok and Schoenberg. He made fine settings of poems by Burns and Dunbar but his best music is of the lyrics of MacDiarmid; 'Watergaw', 'Eemis Stane', 'Milkwort and Bog Cotton'. His conspicuous skill lies in his synthesis of words and music. He has a strong idiomatic style.

Erik Chisholm *(1904-1965)*

Born in Glasgow, he studied at the Scottish Academy of Music from 1918 to 1920. He then toured Canada as a pianist, and on return studied composition with Professor Tovey at Edinburgh University. He promoted the music of Bartok and Hindemuth, and was conductor of the Glasgow Grand Opera Company from 1930 to 1939. He founded many musical societies and was Musical Director of Celtic Ballet during 1938 and 1939, Conductor of the Carl Rosa Opera in 1940, and of the Anglo-Polish Ballet from 1940 to 1943. In 1946 he went to South Africa to direct the South African College of Music in Cape Town, whereby his talents greatly enriched South African cultural life.

He used Celtic musical idiom from early in his career but also was influenced by Hindu music. His best composition was 'The Pardoner's Tale' inspired by Chaucer.

Cedric Thorpe Davie *(1913-1983)*

Though born in London he was of Scottish provenance and devoted his career to Scottish music as a composer, organist and pianist.

He studied at the Royal Academy of Music and the Royal College of Music as a contemporary of Vaughan Williams. He then went to Europe to be taught by Rilpinen and Petri. He joined the staff of the Royal Scottish Academy of Music and was for many years (1945-73) Master of Music in St Andrews University. He was also Professor of Music.

His compositions include the operatic score for *Gammer Gurton's Needle* and a 'Fantasia on Scottish Airs'. The incidental music for *Ane Satyre of the Thrie Estaites* (1948) was his work.

Bagpipes in various forms have been played all over the world for thousands of years, and for the last thousand years the Highland bagpipe has been very popular in the Gaelic areas of Scotland and Ireland. Every clan chief had his piper, who held an honoured place in society and enjoyed many privileges.

A skilled piper could make his instrument convey every human emotion from tenderest love to fiercest anger. There were few occasions which did not give rise to a composition on the pipes. The sound of the pipes was most influential in battle, and in the last uprising of the clans under Prince Charlie, every battle was accompanied by a fierce pibroch. After Culloden, when a proscription was imposed on all things Highland, the playing of the pipes was severely condemned. Nevertheless, they were played in defiance of the law and when the ban was lifted in 1782 the bagpipes flourished. Not only Scots, but many nations now have pipe-bands, male and female, from North America to Nepal and Arabia.

In literature the bagpipes have been praised both in verse and prose. For example, the American poet J.G. Whittier, at the time of the Indian Mutiny, wrote his wonderful tribute, *The Pipes at Lucknow*. Robert Louis Stevenson, in *Kidnapped*, describes a piping contest between his hero Alan Breck Stewart and Robin Oig Macgregor in which the latter boasts he is 'as good as a MacCrimmon', the supreme claim to piping excellence.

The MacCrimmons are a legend which has aroused much controversy, especially as to their origin, which some believe to have been Italian. Recently, however, the document of an agreement between Lord Lovat and his piper David Fraser, made in 1743, has been found in the Scottish Records Office, in which Lord Lovat agrees to send Fraser to Skye 'to be perfected by the famous Malcolm MacGrimon'.

In the records of the Scottish Judiciary there are only two persons of such a name. They are Donald and Finlay MacGrumen or MacGrimen who lived in Perthshire. So the MacCrimmons, or MacGrimons, really did exist, and are of Scottish origin.

The most famous of Highland pipers from the later sixteenth century are as follows:

Donald Mor MacCrimmon *(1570-1640)*

He was piper to Sir Roderick MacLeod, famed as Rory Mor. MacLeod sent him to Ireland to join a company of twenty-five students in a course of piping instruction. MacCrimmon was so keen to learn that he hid himself so that he could listen unobserved to each of the other pipers having private tuition and was able to return with all their skills to MacLeod.

This was the era of the Elizabethan conquest of Ireland. MacCrimmon returned there to join Hugh O'Donell in the uprising and composed a lament for the death of the Earl of Antrim. He was a man of vehement temper, which caused him to avenge his brother's murder in violent reprisals as well as in the pipe-tune 'A Flame of Wrath for Patrick Caogach'. He had a great reputation among the pipers of his age.

John MacGregor *(1708-1789)*

He was born in the MacGregor clan lands of Central Perthshire and probably was trained in piping in the MacGregor School at Drumcharaig, near Fortingall. He joined Charles Edward Stuart at Glenfinnan in August 1745 and became his personal piper and attendant. At Culloden he was wounded in the left thigh but made his way back with most of his clan to Fortingall, where he later became piper to Campbell of Glenlyon.

He had four sons, all of whom were good pipers, and his descendants, down to John MacGregor VI, a century later, were prominent in Championship Meetings. John's own successes were chiefly in his old age. At seventy-three he won Third Prize in the first competition held (before the ban was lifted) at Falkirk in 1781. At seventy-five he attended the meetings in Falkirk and Edinburgh in the honourable position of 'an Intermediary between the Judges and competitors', which showed he was considered the highest authority on the *piobaireachd*, pibroch.

Charles MacArthur *(fl. 1750)*

He was the only piper who could boast that he was better than the MacCrimmons. This arose from the fact that he was a pupil of Patrick Og MacCrimmon, at the School at Borreraig in Skye for eleven years. This made him so good a performer that Patrick Og's son Malcolm sent his son Donald Ruadh, or Red Donald, to MacArthur for the finishing touches.

MacArthur was second at the Falkirk Tryst in 1781, being piper to the Earl of Eglinton at the time. Patrick MacGregor was given first prize.

MacArthur's best compositions were 'Abercairney's Salute' and 'Lament for Sir James MacDonald of the Isles'. His grave is on the headland of Duntuilm in Skye.

Donald Cameron *(1811-1868)*

A native of Maryburgh, Dingwall, he was tutored by Angus Mackay of Raasay and John Ban Mackenzie. An apt pupil, he beat Angus Mackay in Glasgow to win a set of pipes, in 1841. Cameron went on to great successes, winning the Highland Society's Prize Pipe in 1844 and the Scottish Society of London Gold Medal in 1849 with his favourite tune 'The Blue Ribbon'. Perhaps his best years were from 1859 to 1867, when he won the Pipers Champion Gold Medal (where the set piece was 'MacIntosh's Lament') followed the year before his early death by the Gold Medal for Gold Medallists.

Angus Mackay *(1813-1859)*

The tutor of Donald Cameron, he studied hard for some years until, aged only twenty-three, he was awarded the Prize Pipe out of thirty competitors, when he played 'Lament for the Union'.

At twenty-six, when piper to Campbell of Islay, he published his famous book of pibrochs.

He now blossomed in another direction, winning both prizes, for dancing and being the best-dressed Highlander, in Glasgow in 1841. His reward came two years later when he was made Piper to the young Queen Victoria. His end was very affecting, for, following these triumphs, he developed mental illness and, after seven years of confinement, he died in the Crichton Hospital, Dumfries.

Malcolm MacPherson *(1828-1898)*

He was late in achieving recognition. At thirty-eight he won the Prize Pipe at the Northern Meeting and in 1871 won a Former Winner's Gold Medal for his rendering of the Jacobite air 'My King has Landed in Moidart'. He had four sons whom he trained in his own skills. When his chief, Cluny Macpherson, died in 1885, Malcolm composed 'The Lament for Cluny MacPherson'. His teaching skills were considerable and pipers came from far and wide to study under him.

John MacDonald *(1866-1953)*

He was taught by his father and later by Malcolm (Calum) MacPherson, Cluny's piper. He was probably the foremost pibroch player of his day and also the most famous teacher of pibroch this century, giving tuition to at least fourteen Gold Medalists.

At twenty-four he won the Gold Medal for Pibroch at the Northern Meeting and for over forty years his playing swept the boards. He won the Open Competition at Oban no less than nine times.

He taught candidates for appointments as Pipe Majors, in the Regular Army. He conducted these classes in Edinburgh, London, Glasgow, S. Uist and Inverness. He was Honorary Piper to King George V, King Edward VIII and King George VI and was awarded the MBE for his extensive services to piping.

Archibald Campbell *(1877-1963)*

He was born at Kilberry and had many tutors, perhaps the most influential being John MacDougall Gillies. He devoted his whole life to the complete study of the history and music of the pipes. His great ambition was to resuscitate the *Ceol Mor*, that is, the Great Music, or Classical music of the pipes. As a proof that he was successful in this may be adduced the large number of different tunes to be heard today in competition.

He was a founder member of the Piobaireachd Society and its musical

265

editor until his death. He was well known as one of the greatest authorities of the Highland Bagpipe.

Angus MacPherson *(1877-1976)*

The youngest son of Malcolm and one of a long line of pipers, he was born near Castle Cluny. At twenty-one he was invited by the multi-millionaire Andrew Carnegie to be his piper at Skibo Castle. There he lived and entertained many of Carnegie's guests, including Edward VIII. He was still judging competitions at the great age of ninety-six. He was awarded the MBE for his services to piping.

William Ross *(1879-1966)*

A native of Glen Strathfarrar, Ross-shire, he was taught by both his parents. He enlisted at the age of seventeen in the Scots Guards and served with distinction in the South African War, being awarded the Queen Victoria Medal and King Edward VII Medal, both with clasps. He was Pipe Major of the 2nd Scots Guards from 1905 to 1918, serving in the war of 1914-18 until he was invalided out. He then became Instructor of the Army School of Piping at Edinburgh Castle for nearly forty years. He was not only a supreme performer, he was also an excellent teacher and composer. He was Champion All-round Piper of Scotland for several successive years and was indeed the best-known piper in the world. He published five books of Pipe Music, accepted universally as authoritative. He was awarded the MBE and had a pibroch composed in his honour by Angus MacPherson.

George Stewart MacLennan *(1884-1929)*

A native of Edinburgh, he took to the pipes at an early age. He was taught by his father and his maternal uncle, John Stewart, and at the age of ten played before Queen Victoria at Balmoral Castle and was amateur Champion of Great Britain. He joined the Gordon Highlanders when he was fifteen and at the age of twenty-one became Pipe Major of the Gordon Highlanders. He was a brilliant composer of innumerable pibrochs; 'Lochaber Gathering', 'Pipe Major John Stewart', 'Mrs MacPherson of Inveran' and 'Alick C. MacGregor' are some of these. Many consider him to have been the finest player of Marches, Strathspeys and Reels of all time. He retired from the army in 1922 and started business as a bagpipe maker in Aberdeen. He died at the age of forty-five shortly after publishing a book of Pipe Music.

Robert Reid *(1894-1965)*

Another of John MacDougall Gillies' pupils, he became Pipe Major of the 7th Battalion, Highland Light Infantry, and served in Palestine and France from 1915 to 1918. He was a masterly player of the pipes and won every available prize from 1921 to 1949, including Gold Medals in Inverness and Oban Meetings and First in the Open Piobaireachd in Oban in six competitions from 1923 to 1947. He had a bagpipe-making business in Glasgow and was well known as a prominent teacher.

Robert Urquhart Brown *(1907-1972)*

Born in Aberdeenshire, as a young man he was invited to Balmoral Castle by King George V to be a piper-ghillie and he remained there until his retiral. He was a pupil of John MacDonald of Inverness and he had a world-wide reputation as an excellent tutor. He travelled extensively, giving recitals and tuition. He was awarded an MBE for his services to piping.

Donald MacLeod *(1917-1982)*

A man short in inches but in all other respects a giant. He was born in Stornoway, Lewis and joined the Seaforth Highlanders when he was twenty. He was captured at St Valery in 1939 but escaped during the march into Germany. He was appointed Pipe Major of the 7th Seaforths in 1941, in which capacity he returned to France with the battalion in 1944. He is famous for disobeying his commanding officer, who had prohibited the playing of the troops into battle with the bagpipes. But Donald played them into the assault crossing of the Rhine in March 1945.

He won many competitions after the war, then he left the army to become a partner in a pipe-makers in Glasgow. He was a brilliant composer and published six books of Ceol Beag as well as a collection of his own pibrochs. He received an MBE for his services to piping.

The most celebrated Scottish singers last century are commemorated on a monumental plaque on the Calton Hill, Edinburgh.

John Wilson *(1800-1849)*

He was born in Edinburgh where he was a precentor. He was a pupil of Lanza and Crivelli and became a distinguished tenor. He took the leading part in the opera *Guy Mannering* in London in 1830. His Scottish songs were always a great success. He published a book of these. He also composed several songs, the best being 'Hail to the Chief'.

John Templeton *(1802-1886)*

A native of Kilmarnock, he was a most renowned tenor who took lessons in London from Welsh, De Pinna and Cooke. For the higher parts he had an excellent falsetto. From 1833 to 1836 the famous Madame Malibran would have no one else to partake in duets. He made tours of the USA with great success. His four brothers, who sang alto, tenor and bass were almost as gifted as John.

David Kennedy *(1825-1886)*

He was born at Perth and acted as precentor in an Edinburgh church. A famous tenor, he gave concerts, especially of humorous Scots songs and travelled with his gifted family of three sons and five daughters, all over the world; America, New Zealand and Europe. His sons were tenors and baritones, his daughters contraltos. A terrible tragedy in 1881, brought grief to his old age. A son and two daughters died in a fire which destroyed the Opera House at Nice, where they were performing.

Mary Garden *(1874-1967)*

She was born in Aberdeen but emigrated as a child to Brooklyn where she sang at church fêtes. After a short spell back in Aberdeen, the Gardens returned to Chicago where American friends financed her tuition in Paris. When the dollars stopped, the teachers were so impressed that they gave lessons gratis. Some jealous performers at this time put about anonymously a slander on Mary Garden's private life but she ignored it. In this dark hour she was generously supported by an American singer Sybil Anderson, also working in Paris.

Her fortunes now began to mend. She was, to her surprise, offered the leading part in the opera *Louise* by the director Albert Carré. The world-famous composer Debussy hated the opera but was hypnotised by Mary's singing. After this triumph Debussy offered Mary the leading part in *Pelleas and Melisande*, written by Maeterlinck, but the music composed by Debussy. Maeterlinck was very annoyed. He had some other leading lady in mind, but he had to admit to Mary's genius.

For eight years Mary Garden was the toast of Parisian opera addicts. Her greatest success was in *Extase* by Debussy.

Joseph Hislop *(1884-1977)*

He was a native of Edinburgh and as a boy sang in the St Mary's Cathedral choir. He trained as a photographic printer but abandoned this to study music and singing in Stockholm, where he made his debut as Faust in the Royal Opera in 1914.

He then studied in Italy. He gained further acclaim in 1920 in Covent Garden for his part as Rodolpho in *La Bohème*. He was recognised world-wide as a superb tenor.

He had a distinguished opera career and made world tours from 1936 to 1949 along with such famous singers as De Luca and Pasini. He was enthusiastically welcomed in South America, in Buenos Aires particularly, as in South Africa, Australia and all over Britain and Europe.

He made many recordings on HMV from 1921 to 1933, though these failed to convey the full richness of his voice.

He was a teacher of singing for much of his long later life.

Isobel Baillie *(1895-1983)*

A native of Hawick, Roxburghshire, of a long line of Border ancestors. Her father, a master-baker, took the family to Newcastle in 1900. They then moved to Manchester where he owned five shops. Isabella, as she was then named, attended Princess Road Board School. Her father died suddenly and the family of five had a hard struggle. Isabella won a scholarship to Manchester High School where the principal told her she would never make a living as a singer. She sang at church festivals for a 7/6 fee. She was now tutored by Manchester's top singing mistress, Madam Sadler-Fogg, and paid for lessons when she could.

Recognised as early as fifteen, she sang in the *Messiah* and earned fees of from £2 to £5.

She married Harry Wrigley in 1917. He was twice invalided home from Flanders but survived. Their daughter Nancy was born in December 1918.

Success followed her until she retired forty years later. She broadcast before the BBC was formed and she sang under the conductorship of Sir Henry Wood, Hamilton Harty and Toscanini. She performed at the Hollywood Bowl, Handel Festival, Alexandra Palace and with the London Symphony Orchestra.

Isabel toured New Zealand, Malaya and South Africa, the backbone of her repertoire being the oratorios of Bach, Handel and Haydn.

She is said to have sung the *Messiah* one thousand times, but she never enjoyed broadcasting. She taught in her latter years and was made a Dame of the British Empire in 1978.

Jeannie Robertson *(1908-1975)*

She was born in the Gallowgate, Aberdeen, where her mother kept a small shop. But her people for centuries had been nomads, probably made up of outlaws and disinherited Highlanders from Clan Stewart, Clan Donnachy and Clan Gregor, in whose blood ran what Sorley MacLean considers the finest song-making in Europe. Every year Jeannie left the city in spring to join her folk by the campfires and to commit to memory the hundreds of songs and tales of ancient feuds and loves. She readily composed her own original ballads based on these.

It was not until Jeannie was in middle age that her great art of ballad-singing was more widely known and soon attracted thousands of enthusiasts from all over the world. Dr Hamish Henderson was one of the first to recognise Jeannie's unique character and genius and to record and promote her ballads and tales through the medium of the School of Scottish Studies.

She was invited to sing in folk-song clubs all over Britain, and was awarded the MBE in recognition of her unequalled contributions to Scottish music and oral literature.

Art

In common with the rest of Europe, particularly the Spaniards, Flemish and Dutch, Scots enjoyed a revival of painting in the early seventeenth century. Even if confined to one or two artists the quality of their work was comparable to the Dutch masters.

George Jamesone *(1588-1644)*

He was born in Aberdeen, son of a master-mason, architect and burgess of the city. In May, 1612, he was apprenticed to his uncle, Anderson, a painter in Edinburgh.

Little is known of his early life, except that he painted a portrait of the Lord Provost of Aberdeen in 1620. This showed a masterly technique, as yet immature. It is possible that Jamesone went to Antwerp in 1618-19 to study under Van Dyck and Rubens, for his early style seems to show some influence of Dutch study. His name is not on the Antwerp Guild of Painters but as Rubens did not register all his pupils, this is no proof.

Van Dyck came to England in 1621 and 1630, but even before 1621 Jamesone had attained his characteristic style, independent of the Dutch influence.

He painted portraits of many of the famous Scots of his time, including Charles I, James Grahame (Duke of Montrose), the Duke of Argyll, Warriston and General David Leslie. His portrait of Lady Mary Erskine, Countess Marischal, is in the National Portrait Gallery of Scotland. Perhaps his *chef-d'oeuvre* is his portrait of Maister Robert Erskine.

He visited Italy in 1633 but his style appears not to have been much affected by his Italian visit.

Despite his popularity, painting sometimes miniatures, often full-length, he charged very small fees. Twenty marks, or £1.20 was a normal charge, though he sent Lord Haddington a bill for £32 for a magnificent full-length portrait.

He left a fortune, perhaps on account of the large number of his commissions. For example he made sixteen portraits of Colin Campbell of Glenorchy, which that wealthy laird could well afford at Jamesone's minimal fees.

Scotland can boast in all truth that in this Aberdeen artist she produced a native painter of original merit long before England.

William Aikman *(1682-1731)*

He was the nephew of Sir John Clerk of Penicuik and Forbes of Newhall, both great patrons of art and industry. Aikman, to their gratification, turned out to be the most notable British painter of the early eighteenth century. His father, a Forfarshire laird, can get no credit, however, for he forced him to pursue a legal course, aiming at becoming an advocate. Only on his father's early death, when William was nearly of age, did he turn to studying art under Sir John Mediṇa.

He sold the family estate in 1702, and went to Rome for eight years, studying art treasures and techniques. He also voyaged to Constantinople and the Near East before settling as an artist in Edinburgh under the patronage of the Duke of Argyll.

His fees for portraits were £10 a head, not out of the way, but this safe livelihood palled and at Argyll's request he went to London in 1723, taking a studio at Leicester Fields, an area later to be made famous by the presence of the great Hogarth.

Aikman was a favourite in the literary circles of that Augustan Age. He was an intimate of Sir Robert Walpole and many leading Englishmen.

Sorrow struck suddenly in the midst of this splendour. His only son died suddenly and he did not long survive the shock. Both are buried in the Greyfriars Burial Ground, Edinburgh.

He was lamented in verse by the Scottish poets who knew him, David Mallet, Allan Ramsay and James Thomson.

Aikman's most famous portraits are to be seen in all their splendour in Scottish and English galleries. Notable are those of Allan Ramsay, the poet, Sir John Clerk, 6th Earl of Lauderdale (in armour), Principal Carstares, Sir Hew Dalrymple and the Duke of Argyll (in Holyrood Palace).

Allan Ramsay *(1713-1784)*

He was the son of Allan Ramsay, poet, who encouraged his artistic leanings from the age of twelve, until he went to London at twenty to study under William Hogarth. The English genius took a liking to Allan and thought so much of him that he dedicated his twelve engravings, illustrative of Butler's *Hudibras*, to the young Scot.

In 1736 Ramsay travelled through Europe to Rome, being shipwrecked on the way, near Pisa. At Rome he studied at the French Academy under two celebrated painters, Solimena and Imperiale. He enjoyed Roman society and entertained them by writing verse, sonnets, odes, epigrams in various languages.

In 1738 he returned to Edinburgh for two years and began a series of very fine portraits, especially of the 2nd Duke of Argyll. He found Edinburgh society fully as famous as London's and made friends with David Hume, Adam Smith, William Robertson and others of that brilliant coterie.

In 1756 he returned to London and was on terms of intimacy with top society, painting portraits of many of them. He painted several portraits of the young King George III and Queen Charlotte for presentation to foreign monarchs and statesmen. So much was demanded of him that he employed the young Scots painters, David Martin and Alexander Nasmyth, to assist him.

In 1775 he had an accident in Italy which prevented him from painting and affected his health, so he retired to Rome, leaving an assistant to finish off the portraits of no less than fifty pairs of assorted kings and queens, with which Europe at that age was surfeited.

In 1784 he felt so unwell that he left Rome for England. On reaching Dover he died.

The strangest exclusion from fame was his. He was never asked to join the Royal Academy. The reason was perhaps he was not primarily a painter. He was an intellectual man, a friend of Voltaire and Rousseau, as James Boswell was; interested in Greek and Roman archaeology. He perhaps excited envy by his social success.

His best portraits are of his wife, of the Countess of Kildare, and of Mrs MacLeod of MacLeod dressed in Rob Roy tartan.

David Allan *(1744-1796)*

Born at Alloa, at eleven he was expelled from school for making a caricature of the master. At twelve he studied art at the Foulis Brothers Academy in Glasgow.

His friends sent him to study in Italy for the long space of eleven years, where he was attracted to subjects from history and mythology by the famous galleries of Rome, Florence, etc. He won the Gold Medal at the Academy of St Luke, Rome, for his large painting in the allegorical style of *The Origin of Painting* (in the National Gallery of Scotland).

From 1777 to 1780 he practised in London, making many political portraits of wealthy people and prospering thereby. But he returned to Edinburgh and among others he painted Craig, the architect of the New Town.

He now returned to Scottish domestic scenes and started a new demand for these.

His *Penny Wedding* (National Gallery of Scotland) gives a humorous account of this peculiarly Scottish gathering, and is most attractive for its portrayal of contemporary rural life. *The Repentance Stool* is equally attractive, showing the reverse side of the coin in the sanctimonious Presbyterian picture of a ceremony which Burns satirised in verse.

Sir Henry Raeburn *(1756-1823)*

Son of Robert Raeburn, an Edinburgh yarn-boiler, he was educated at Heriot's Hospital (now School) and at fifteen was apprenticed to a goldsmith. His fine work attracted David Martin, a leading portrait painter, who offered to help him but, for some reason not clear, Martin left Raeburn to his own devices.

For some years Raeburn painted portraits for commission and had a wide clientèle amongst whom was a wealthy young woman with whom he fell in love. In 1778 they were married and Raeburn's financial footing was assured. The Raeburns travelled to Italy in 1785, calling on Sir Joshua Reynolds, the eminent artist, on their way south. Reynolds was doubly generous, giving the young Scot letters of introduction and sums of money.

After two years of study in Italy Raeburn and his wife returned to

Edinburgh where he set up his studio in George Street from which he sent forth portraits that assured him of the foremost place in Scottish art. His life henceforth was an unbroken success apart from a small financial embarrassment in 1809. He painted everyone of importance. In fact his portraits tell the story of Scotland in Napoleonic times.

Although he was frequently advised and often begged to go to London he remained in Edinburgh. Nevertheless he was elected an Associate of the Royal Academy in 1812 and a full Academician in 1815, honours he did not solicit. The Academy of Florence and two American Academies also elected him a full member.

In 1822, on the visit of George IV, he was knighted at Hopetoun House and appointed King's Limner for Scotland. His cup was running over, but he died before he could enjoy it, in October, 1822.

He was a man of many interests, mechanical science, architecture, legal business, angling, archery, gardening and golf, but of course painting was his passion. Sometimes he had four sittings in a day. He readily helped young artists with advice and money.

His best-known portraits are of Dr Hutton, the geologist; Professor Black; Mrs Ferguson and her children; Neil Gow; Sir John and Lady Clerk of Penicuik; Sir John Sinclair; Admiral Duncan; Macdonald of Clanranald and Mrs James Campbell.

Alexander Nasmyth *(1758-1840)*

Born in Edinburgh, he was apprenticed to a coach painter and employed in painting and drawing armorial bearings on the coaches of local gentry. Allan Ramsay found this talented lad employed on an unworthy task and induced his master to break his apprentice indentures. Ramsay took him to London and trained him along with David Martin, in technique.

Nasmyth returned to Edinbugh in 1778 and found a patron in Patrick Miller of Dalswinton, the landowner, who was interested in steam navigation. He employed Nasmyth to draw the projected mechanism for his steam-boats. Miller did more; he lent Nasmyth money to go to Italy to study art.

The young artist was two years in Italy and on return was able to repay the sum borrowed. His time had been well employed and he came back in 1784 to paint excellent portraits of Scots clients.

When Burns visited Edinburgh as a celebrity in 1786 he naturally got in touch with Nasmyth whom he had previously met at Dalswinton in company with Miller. It was shortly afterwards that Nasmyth painted his well-known portrait of Burns. This is however not his finest portrait, splendid though it is. His *Miss Burnet*, ill-fated beautiful daughter of Lord Monboddo, is thought to be Nasmyth's best work in this genre and, if a comparison may be tolerated, it seems an echo of the best of Gainsborough's portraits.

Nasmyth lived in an age of political turmoil when bitter animosity over the French Revolution split the nation. He was very outspoken in favour of democratic principles and by this frankness he antagonised many of his aristocratic clients. He gave up painting portraits on this account and turned to landscapes where he found more peace of mind in the portrayal of the Scottish scene.

Revd John Thomson *(1778-1840)*

Born at Dailly, Aberdeenshire, son of the parish minister, he was trained for his father's calling and did indeed succeed his father for a time in Dailly, but in 1805 he was ordained at Duddingston, a picturesque village immediately beneath Arthur's Seat and only a mile from Edinburgh, but completely rural.

Here Thomson soon became a prominent figure in the society of the capital and his manse a centre of literary and artistic gatherings. In fact this popularity was detrimental to his painting for he had continual interruptions from garrulous lionisers, as Burns had at Ellisland a generation earlier. Thomson had an octagonal tower of two storeys built in stone by the lochside close to the manse but out of sight. He christened it 'Edinburgh' and used the top storey as a studio. He left word at the manse that if an idle caller asked for him there, he was to be told that the minister was in Edinburgh and would not return before nightfall.

His pictures were in great demand because of their magnificent treatment of romantic Scottish landscape. His income from these was £1800 per annum. His style was at first in the Dutch manner, then inclining to the French, but he put his own genius into it and he was the greatest Scottish landscape painter of his age. Especially admired for its wild beauty is *Fast Castle*. Others equal in mastery are *Newark Castle, Graves of the Martyrs* (inspired by his Ayrshire origin), *Aberlady Bay,* and *Castle Baan*.

Sir David Wilkie *(1785-1841)*

Born at Cults, near Cupar, Fife, son of the parish minister there, he studied art at Edinburgh when only fourteen at the Trustees' Academy. After a very poor start he eventually gained a prize for a class competition drawing. This set him on the road to fame. At nineteen he made sketches of the many rural characters who attended his father's kirk. From these sketches he made a wonderful composition *Pitlessie Fair* which stands forever as a true record of an old Fife community. The young artist did not get much credit for this in his own parish, as the sketches were if anything somewhat satirical and did not amuse the congregation.

He studied at the London Art School in 1805 and when only twenty-one became immediately famous for his painting *The Village Politicians* which started a new epoch in British art. He followed this success with many similar paintings of the humour and pathos of rural Britain. He received indirectly his highest compliment when the great Turner copied his style in *The Blacksmith's Shop* (1807), but it was Hogarth who had really initiated this picaresque portrayal of British domestic life many years before.

Wilkie was made an ARA in 1809 and an RA in 1812. He was appointed Painter-in-Ordinary to George IV and knighted by William IV in 1836. On a projected visit to the Holy Land in 1841 he died suddenly on board ship off Gibraltar.

His most loved paintings are *The Reading of the Will, Blind Fiddler, Village Festival* and *Penny Wedding*. He also specialised in historical scenes and Spanish compositions.

Sir John Watson Gordon *(1788-1864)*

Son of a naval captain he was destined for the Royal Engineers but he met David Wilkie and determined to turn to art. He never studied abroad and, on the death of Raeburn in Edinburgh in 1823, he stepped into that master's shoes and took over many of his clients. There are traces of Raeburn's influence in Gordon's work, as in his portraits of *Lady Nairne, Dr Andrew Duncan, John Taylor golfing, James Hogg, and Lord President Hope*.

In an age which thought rather poorly of Velasquez, Gordon alone proclaimed him one of the greatest of all portrait painters.

Robert Scott Lauder *(1805-1867)*

He was the inspirer of a large group of Scottish artists who have collectively been termed 'The Master Class'. Their work was not always fully appreciated south of the Tweed at the time, but much of it has since been universally acknowledged as being well in advance of its age.

Horatio McCulloch *(1805-1867)*

He was born in Glasgow and apprenticed to a house-painter. From this humble profession he graduated to one that was so much in vogue in Regency times; that of a painter of snuff-boxes, in Cumnock, many of the motifs being taken from Burns' poems. His next step in art was to the Edinburgh establishment of W.H. Lizare, RSA, the famous engraver. Here McCulloch coloured anatomical and other plates, a non-creative job. Tiring of this he returned to Glasgow to paint landscapes within travelling distance of the city. His work was recognised in 1824 when he was elected an Associate of the Royal Scottish Academy and four years later an RSA.

His pictures were very popular, being of Scottish scenes in the Lowlands and Highlands very minutely observed and rendered. But once again he did not appeal to England.

Sir Noel Paton *(1821-1901)*

Born in Dunfermline, Fife, he is noted for his powers of invention. He wrote good poetry and was a man of wide interests, especially in literature and history. On the practical side he was a first class modeller and archaeologist.

In the Victorian age he appealed to the current British taste for pictures that told a sentimental or romantic story. His best paintings, showing fantasy and delicacy of execution, were inspired by Shakespeare's *Midsummer Night's Dream*. These formed a pair, *The Quarrel* (between Queen Mab and Oberon), and *The Reconciliation*.

His historical scenes were partly contemporary as in *Home from the Crimea*, and partly from European history as in *Luther at Erfurt*. He illustrated scenes from Tennyson and from the Border Ballads. One of his famous large paintings is a version of *The Last Supper*.

275

He was made an RSA in 1850 and Her Majesty's Limner in Scotland in 1866.

William McTaggart *(1835-1910)*

He was born in a small farm at Macrihanish in the South of Kintyre, Argyll. For a time he worked for a local doctor at Campbeltown, then at sixteen he went to Edinburgh and studied drawing and painting under R.S. Lauder. During his summer vacations he went to Ireland and travelled around with his easel, selling his landscapes to earn his keep. A year after leaving Lauder's care he was recognised by being made an RSA, though the full award was not given until 1870. He was made Vice-President of the Water-Colour Society also.

Although he was then little known outside Scotland there has never been any doubt that McTaggart was a unique artist, a really great artist whose sense of light, space and movement was undreamt of by any of his predecessors.

Whence this wonderful ability came is impossible to say, though he was early influenced by the Pre-Raphaelites. He seems to have anticipated the Impressionists. One has only to see his *The Bathers, Wind and Rain* or *Whitehouse* to be amazed at his genius. He was perhaps the first, certainly the foremost, to put the Celtic magic upon canvas.

Sir William Quiller Orchardson *(1835-1910)*

Born in Edinburgh, he worked at the age of ten in the Trustees' Academy in Glasgow where he was the earliest and later the oldest of Scott Lauder's pupils. His early paintings belong to the Scottish School. *Broken Tryst*, a rural idyll, is in Aberdeen Art Gallery. His *Flowers of the Forest*, not about Flodden but a woodland scene, is in Southampton Art Gallery.

In 1862, along with John Pettie and Graham he went to London to paint historical canvasses. He was amongst the most meticulous of artists, his motto being 'Art is not fine unless refined'. Consequently his pictures have details of background, including carpets and costumes, rendering them a true record of Victorian high family life. His best subject pictures are the *Mariage de Convenance* series.

He often visited the Salon in Paris, collected French furniture, and the continental influence is pronounced in his works. He thought his best picture was *Master Baby* showing the doting mother and her child. He was a worthy successor to Raeburn and Watson in portraiture.

His last picture was *The Last Dance*, appropriately unfinished.

John Pettie *(1839-1893)*

He trained at the Trustees' Academy from sixteen, being sponsored by John Drummond, the history painter, who met him at his birthplace, East Linton, where his father was a shopkeeper. He was inspired by Massonier, the French artist. In Edinburgh he was employed by the editor of *Good Words*, Norman MacLeod, to illustrate this. On *Good Words* moving to London in 1862 the illustrators also moved south, where Pettie lived in Pimlico.

His first success, at twenty-six, was *A Drumhead Courtmartial* exhibited at the Royal Academy in 1865. *Arrested for Witchcraft* followed in 1866. All his historical pictures were very popular especially *Treason, Tussle with a Highland Smuggler* and *Rob Roy*. His best Highland painting was *The Chieftain's Candlesticks* inspired by Sir Walter Scott. *Hamlet and Ophelia* is world-famous.

William York Macgregor *(1855-1923)*

He was the leader of the 'Glasgow Boys', a group of young men, twenty-three in all, who flourished from 1880 to 1895. They were not all Glaswegians but came from various parts of Scotland and England. They were influenced by continental artists but produced brilliant original work. Macgregor's dictum was 'Hack out the subject as you would were you using an axe and try to realise it; get its bigness. Don't follow any school. There are no schools in art.'

His most characteristic painting is *The Vegetable Stall* in the National Gallery of Scotland. John Paterson was his chief disciple. D.Y. Cameron and Sir John Lavery were also of the Glasgow School.

The Scottish artists of the late nineteenth and mid-twentieth century are too numerous to detail. Among the most distinguished were:

Sir David Y. Cameron *(1865-1945)*

Born in Glasgow where he studied art for a time in association with William Y. Macgregor. He also studied art in Edinburgh but lived in Glasgow until 1898 when he moved to Kippen, Stirlingshire, for a time.

He soon became renowned, especially for his etchings of landscape. He travelled much over England and Europe in his painting and etching. He was knighted in 1924 and appointed King's Painter and Limner in 1933. He was internationally acknowledged for his original etchings.

Samuel J. Peploe *(1871-1935)*

Born in Edinburgh, he studied from an early age at the Trustees' School and at the Royal Scottish Academy. He then stayed in Paris with Robert Brough where he was influenced by the new school of painting. His works are conspicuous by his use of brilliant tones, reminiscent of Cezanne and Gaugin. He exhibited at the Royal Academy from 1902 onwards. Much of his best work was done during the many years he resided in Paris and Provence.

He was made an RSA in 1927.

Jessie M. King *(1875-1949)*

Her father was the minister of New Kilpatrick, Glasgow. Despite his disapproval she studied at the Glasgow School of Art whose principal, a man of European outlook, encouraged her to follow her romantic bent towards gossamer treatment of flowers and nature. This was the period of Beardsley and Macintosh, of Oscar Wilde and Morris, and Jessie's work was much appreciated. She exhibited and published and won a Gold Medal for book-cover design. After her marriage she painted in France until the 1914 outbreak of war, then she returned to her beloved Galloway and Arran. She did not claim greatness but posthumously achieved it.

Sir David Muirhead Bone *(1876-1953)*

Born in Glasgow, he studied at the Glasgow School of Art before going to London in 1901. He was early acknowledged as a very talented draughts-man and illustrator. His work was exhibited in the Royal Academy when he was twenty-four. He contributed to the RA from 1900 to 1904. But his magnificent book of illustrations *Old Spain*, the fruit of his travels there, assured his fame.

He worked all over Europe, in Holland, Italy, Spain and Sweden. He was appointed official war artist in both the World Wars, depicting the horrific effects of these in detail for the Imperial War museum. He was knighted in 1937.

Stanley Cursiter *(1887-1976)*

Born in Kirkwall, Orkney, he studied at the Edinburgh School of Art. He exhibited widely, at the Royal Academy, the Royal Scottish Academy, the Royal Society of Painters in Watercolours. He was appointed RSA in 1937.

He had been Keeper of the National Gallery of Scotland from 1924 to 1930 and was Director from 1930 to 1948. In the latter year he was granted a CBE and made King's Painter and Limner in Scotland.

Anne Redpath *(1895-1965)*

Born at Galashiels, she studied at the Edinburgh College of Art where she won a scholarship to Paris, Brussels and Florence. She lived in France from 1919 until 1934 and though she painted little in that time, she was making notes for future work. She held her own show in 1947 when her genius was widely appreciated. After that she exhibited freely. She was given an OBE in 1955.

Sir William G. Gillies *(1898-1973)*

Born at Haddington, he studied art at Edinburgh Art College from 1919 to 1922. A scholarship took him to France and Italy. He exhibited widely in Scotland, his studies of landscape in the Borders and Lothians being highly impressive.

He was made an RSA in 1947 and also received the OBE.

Sir William McTaggart *(1903-1978)*

Born at Loanhead, Midlothian, a great grandson of William McTaggart, the illustrious Victorian painter, he studied at Edinburgh College of Art and travelled widely. He became an RSA in 1948 and was known inter-nationally for his exhibited paintings.

He was knighted in 1962.

Photography

No individual can claim the invention of photography. It was the result of many years of experiment involving men of all nations. But the artistic possibilities of photography were first demonstrated by a group of Scottish artists.

David Octavius Hill *(1802-1870)*
Robert Adamson *(1820-1860)*

Born at Perth, and responsible for the erection of the National Gallery, Hill became interested in the calotype photography of the Englishman Fox Talbot, seeing the great potentialities of this in aiding the artist. In 1843 Hill, as an accomplished portrait painter, was given the formidable commission to make an enormous group painting of all the ministers who had disrupted from the Established Church. They numbered 451. Hill called upon Robert Adamson, a young science student, to help him. They made portraits by calotype of all the ministers and Hill was thus able to achieve the famous painting of the Free Church Assembly.

Hill and Adamson did not stop there. Hill arranged photographs of picturesque interest around Edinburgh, of Newhaven fishwives and other characters and also of the buildings and landscape. Adamson attended to the technical work. Their work was forgotten after they had produced hundreds of amazing works during the forties and fifties of last century. It was only re-discovered in the 1890s.

James Valentine *(1815-1880)*

He was founder of the famous commercial printers of views in Dundee. He travelled through Britain taking photographs of all kinds of scenery, in town and country, from an artist's point of view. These were usually embodied in postcards, but also used in calendars and commercial advertising. Many of his early photographs form important evidence of Victorian Britain as well as of the immense interest taken by the public in beauty spots in their own land.

Charles Piazzi Smyth *(1819-1900)*

Mentioned in our chapter on Astronomy, he was also a remarkable photographer. He was able to take pictures of some of the stars and planets. His stereotype photographs, in his book *Teneriffe, an Astronomer's Experiment*, marked the beginning of an epoch in photography, as early as 1858.

279

Robert MacPherson *(c.1820-1880)*

For health reasons, this surgeon born in Edinburgh exiled himself in Italy for much of his life. His photographs of the magnificent ruins of classical Rome are so artistically presented that each one is itself an affecting masterpiece.

Alexander Gardener *(1821-1882)*

A Paisley native, he was instrumental in securing some remarkable photographs from the battlefields, camps and staff meetings of both Federals and Confederates during the Civil War of 1861-65. He is suspected of having posed some of the scenes, but his records are of great historical value.

George Washington Wilson *(1823-1893)*

Son of a Banffshire crofter, an ex-soldier of the Napoleonic wars, George, one of eleven children, had a hard upbringing, rarely eating meat and being sent to labour in the fields when seven. But like most Scottish children he had a sound education in the local school.

He served as apprentice to a carpenter, but his hobby was drawing and painting. Through this he was noticed by a wealthy local gentleman who introduced him to a friend in Edinburgh. There he painted miniature portraits, a lucrative trade.

In 1848, on his father's death, he moved to Aberdeen, only leaving it for a few months to study art in London and Paris. He set up business in Union Street as a teacher of drawing and painting, and a painter of miniature portraits. In 1852 he offered his clients a choice, water-colour or photograph. These latter were the newly-invented calotypes. He now entered into partnership with John Hay and a prosperous business ensued.

Among many commissions they photographed, at Prince Albert's request, the successive stages of the rebuilding of Balmoral Castle. This led to countless photographs of all the persons and scenes in the district associated with the Royal residence, most of these being made at the Queen's request for private use. Wilson, unofficially, called himself Photographer to the Queen.

Commercially, G.W. Wilson and Co. expanded beyond all expectations, and from their large workshops of St Swithin's they produced artistic photographs in all styles from all over Britain, Europe, Africa and Australia. One of their popular productions was the stereograph, a dual photograph taken by a special camera, which, when viewed in a frame, gave a three-dimensional impression. The fashionable mid-Victorian cartes-de-visite were also produced for many years.

William Notman *(1826-1891)*

Son of a designer of Paisley shawls, he emigrated to Canada where he made numerous portraits of Indians, hunters and backwoodsmen, as well as of local white celebrities. He formed a Company and was a successful studio artist in photography in New York and Boston.

Thomas Keith *(1827-1900?)*

Born at St Cyrus, Kincardineshire, one of seven sons of the minister there, he was educated at Aberdeen Grammar School and at Marischal College. He studied medicine at Edinburgh and was apprenticed in 1845 to J.Y. Simpson, the discoverer of chloroform. Keith was house-surgeon at Edinburgh Royal Infirmary, assistant to Professor Syme. He later was surgeon in Sardinia before returning to Edinburgh where he left the Infirmary in 1853, being succeeded by Lister.

He became interested in photography through his work in chemistry under Syme and took many hundreds of photographs of artistic excellence, his enthusiasm being aroused by a visit to the Great Exhibition at London in 1851, where photographs were on view.

At a great photographic exhibition in 1854 there were works by Keith, Hill, Adamson, Gustave le Gray and G.W. Wilson.

Keith was later appointed Photographer-Royal to Queen Victoria.

John Thomson *(1837-1921)*

He was born in Edinburgh and travelled widely in the Far East, photographing landscape, town and country life and members of the communities. His photographs were used to produce books of scenes in Cambodia and China, published in 1867 and 1873. He also recorded scenes in Cyprus, but the most notable records were made of the streets of London, which, like Annan's work in Glasgow, shock us by their realism.

Thomas Annan *(1829-1887)*
James Craig Annan *(1864-1946)*

Thomas Annan was a copperplate engraver who was so interested in the photographs taken by Hill and Adamson that he took up their study in 1855. His work became famous in the USA and Europe, particularly his portraits, including that of David Livingstone, then at the height of his fame. His street scenes in Old Glasgow bring to reality the horrors of Victorian slums.

James, his son, exhibited his celebrated photographs in New York towards the end of the nineteenth century. Both father and son were distinguished by their simple approach to photography, eliminating the stiffness and formality of pose and background which characterises most Victorian portraiture by camera.

Tom Kent *(1863-1936)*

A native of Firth, in Orkney, he emigrated to the USA when a young man and developed an interest in photography. Returning to Orkney in 1897, he set up as a photographer in Kirkwall. He recorded all aspects of Orcadian life over a period of thirty years, specialising in landscapes, seascapes and group portraits, the latter being a departure from the formal photos of the period.

The bulk of his work is now preserved by the Orkney Library, where it will always be an important visual record of Orkney's heritage.

Film-making

John Grierson *(1898-1972)*

He was born at Kilmarnock, educated at Glasgow and Chicago Universities, taking his MA and LLD at Glasgow.

He helped form the Empire Marketing Board and GPO Film Units and was on many film boards during and after the Second World War.

His first memorable documentary film, on the fishing industry, was entitled *Drifters* and was an epoch-making work, conspicuous for its dramatic scenes of real life at sea.

He also produced *Song of Ceylon* (1934), *Night Mail* (1936), the *World in Action* series and *This Wonderful World*, shown on TV in 1961, in which year he was made a Commander of the British Empire. He has been named 'The Father of Documentary Films'.

Architecture

The earliest native architects were the builders of the Iron Age brochs of which hundreds existed complete during the Roman invasions but most of which have been vandalised by being long used as stone quarries. Only one or two remain to show the amazingly exact stonework, uncemented but jointed. The oldest remaining Anglo-Saxon building is St Margaret's Chapel on Edinburgh Castle Rock. It dates from the eleventh century. Norman influence can be seen in many Scottish churches such as Corstorphine and Dalmeny. The old peel-towers of the Borders and several castles such as Borthwick and Hermitage were built during the Wars of Independence as places of strength, but before these came the abbeys, dating from the High Middle Ages and probably the work of Continental as well as Scottish craftsmen. Many of the castles, however, in the North, are of native workmanship, built for defence.

After the Union of the Crowns in 1603 more ornate and expensive buildings were made, influenced by architects from Europe and England, but many outstanding Scottish buildings were of native architecture. For example, in Edinburgh, George Heriot's Hospital, built from 1628 to 1649 and reputed to have been designed by Inigo Jones, was actually the work of two local architects William Wallace and William Aytoun. Country houses of the great landowners, some of vast proportions such as Hamilton Palace and Hopetoun House, sprang up, many designed by Scottish architects whose work extended far beyond the Borders. The most influential British architect was Robert Adam but his father William had been a well-known architect of the early eighteenth century. A century earlier Scots had designed important buildings both in Scotland and England.

Sir William Bruce *(1630-1710)*

Sir William Bruce of Balcaskie was Royal Architect to Charles II and James II. He had schemed to bring back Charles to the throne in 1660 so was in royal favour. He helped to restore Holyroodhouse, first demolishing the additions made by order of Oliver Cromwell. Bruce was the first to introduce the Classical style into Scotland. He was responsible for the large and elegant Kinross House built in 1685 for the residence of the Duke of York, afterwards James II. He was also the architect of Hopetoun House, West Lothian, which can compare in magnificence with any palace in Britain. Bruce died before it was completed and the building was finished by William Adam, the father of the famous Adam brothers.

Colen Campbell (?-1729)

Little is known of his origins, probably Argyllshire, but he must have been well acquainted with the principles of classical architecture because he published his architectural volume *Vitruvius Britannicus* in 1715, the title being taken from the famous Roman architect and engineer of the reign of Augustus.

Most of his best work was done in England where he was influenced by the famous Italian architect Palladio who relied upon copying the heavy classical style of Roman days. Wanstead House, designed by Campbell, is looked on as the model of an English Palladian country house. He also built Burlington House (1718-19), Mereworth Castle (1722-25), Houghton Hall (an enormous and imposing edifice) and the equally splendid and elegant Compton Place, Eastbourne.

James Gibbs (1682-1754)

Born in Aberdeen, he went to Rome when he was twenty-one, to study under the architect Fortana. He returned to Britain in 1709 and took on work in the Italian Baroque style, modified to a certain extent by the Palladian. The great English exponent of the Baroque at this time was Vanbrugh, but Gibbs was the most influential London church architect of that age. His first church was St Mary le Strand (1714-1717), followed by St Martin-in-the-Fields (1722-26). Shortly after that he published his book on Architecture (1728), which had an enormous influence in Britain and America for a century or more. It seems that the White House in Washington was inspired by one of Gibb's illustrations.

Secular buildings of importance were the Octagon, Twickenham, the Senate House and King's College, Cambridge, and a building unique in all England as exemplifying the Italian Baroque, the Radcliffe Library, Oxford (1737-49). The extravagant mannerisms, adorned to the highest degree of ostentation, which characterised the Baroque and which may be seen at the Louvre and Versailles, passed away with the years, but Gibbs' adaptations of it in England still reflect the glory of the early eighteenth century.

Sir William Chambers (1723-1796)

Son of a Scottish merchant he was born at Gothenburg, Sweden. At sixteen he joined the Swedish East India Company and voyaged to and from the Far East until he was twenty-five. He left the service and studied architecture in Paris under Blondel. He then trained in Italy for five years and returned to London at thirty-two where he became an immediate success. He was made architectural tutor to the Prince of Wales, later to become George III. With Robert Adam, he was appointed architect to the King. Honours flowed upon him. In turn he became Comptroller and Surveyor-General of Architecture and after helping to found the Royal Academy he became its Treasurer, being knighted at that time. His treatise on Civil Architecture became the standard work.

Robert Adam *(1728-1792)*

He was the second son of William Adam of Maryburgh. He was born in Kirkcaldy, Fife, studied at Edinburgh University and was trained by his father, an established architect, amongst whose works was the Old Royal Infirmary of Edinburgh.

Robert spent three years studying in Italy, especially the remains of Roman architecture of which nothing substantial remained but a few public buildings. The private palaces so much esteemed in Imperial Rome had vanished, that is, all except one. This was in far-off Dalmatia at Spoleto. It had been the palace of the Emperor Diocletian (c.AD 300), noted for his persecution of Christians and enlarging the power of the army.

Adam was interested only in the unique palace and took with him to view it the famous French antiquary and architect M. Clérisseau, along with two good draughtsmen. Although arrested as a spy, Adam procured enough plans and measurements to draw restorations of the entire palace. He published his *Ruins of the Palace of Diocletian* in 1764. He regarded this building as the climax of Roman architecture, before its gradual decline.

Adam had been appointed architect to the King (George III) in 1762, an office combined with the Board of Works which he handed over to his brother James, and another, in 1768 when he became MP for Kinross. In that year with his three brothers, James, John and William, he leased the ground fronting the Thames on which the magnificent Adelphi Terrace was built. For many years the Adam brothers designed innumerable public and private buildings and published a fine series of engravings and descriptions of them.

Robert died at the height of his fame and was buried in Westminster Abbey.

The most remarkable feature of Adam's genius was that he created a completely new world of internal decoration quite consistent with his architecture. 'English' furniture is still being manufactured on the same style invented by this Fife native two and a half centuries ago.

Robert Mylne *(1734-1811)*

He was descended from at least six generations of Edinburgh architects, all of whom had added to the famous buildings of Scotland. Robert was trained in Edinburgh by his father. He then studied in Paris for a year (1754), and in Rome from 1755-58. Here he won the first prize in the Academy of St Luke, a remarkable achievement for a young man. But he did not wholly fulfil this promise, although he was sufficiently endowed with genius to build Blackfriars Bridge from 1760-69 and also the Stationers Hall in London. In his time he set up to be a rival of Robert Adam, but Adam had superior organisation and originality.

Charles Cameron *(1740-1812)*

Like many Scots he is better known and honoured in Russia than in his own native land. He studied at Rome in 1768, his interest being Roman baths, a volume of this side of architecture being published in 1772. Shortly after this he was taken notice of by the notorious Catherine the Great, Tsarina of Russia, and invited to work for her and other Russian nobles.

Cameron designed the Great Palace of Pavlovsk for Grand Duke Paul. It took sixteen years to build (1781-96). He also designed the magnificent interiors in Tsarskoe Selo where the Cameron Gallery is one of the show-pieces in this model town which holds many of the artistic treasures of the Soviet Union. It is about fifteen miles south of Leningrad on a healthy site selected over two centuries ago.

Cameron was superseded by his pupil Brenna but he continued to work for private patrons until he was reinstated. In 1805 he designed the naval hospital and barracks at Kronstadt following the plan of Robert Adam.

James Craig *(1740-1795)*

He was born in Edinburgh, son of Robert Craig, merchant. His mother was the sister of James Thomson, poet, author of *The Seasons*. Craig trained as an architect and when in his middle twenties he laid out the plan of the projected New Town of Edinburgh on the ridge and slopes to the North of the old city. The streets and squares were named after the Royal family of that time, or the patron saints. Princes Street was named to commemorate the Prince of Wales, later George IV, and his brother.

Not many were willing to buy feus in the New Town as it was notoriously exposed to wind and rain but at last some bold citizens erected houses. Craig himself laid out the foundations of one hesitant householder. Craig's plan envisaged houses of uniform height and style for Princes Street but luckily these were alleviated by varied styles. He did not see his plan beyond the initial stages and it was left to other architects to erect the palatial houses of North Edinburgh. He died in comparative poverty and for a long time his New Town was subjected to censure by those opposed to rectilinear civic planning.

Robert Mills *(1781-1855)*

Though born in America he was of Scots descent and was to some extent self-trained but his merits were discovered by Jefferson and his first important commission at the age of twenty-nine was to design the State House at Harrisburg. After the war with Britain (1812-14) he was responsible for the Washington Memorial at Baltimore which took fifteen years to complete. Meantime he had many public buildings to design, including the Government Buildings at Washington, the Patent Office and the Post Office. His most famous work was the Washington Monument at Washington itself which he designed in 1836 but which took nearly half a century to complete.

A more utilitarian edifice was the Columbia Lunatic Asylum where he demonstrated his Scottish character by building it in a Greek Doric style and, with a view to the nature of its inhabitants, making it fireproof.

William H. Playfair *(1789-1857)*

He was a member of a gifted Scottish family, his uncle being the famous mathematician John Playfair. Most of the classical buildings which give Edinburgh its claim to be the Athens of the North were designed by Playfair. One of his earliest works, however, was never to be completed. This is the Parthenon on Calton Hill, originally meant as a memorial to the Scots soldiers, mainly Highlanders, who fell in the long Napoleonic Wars. But funds ran out and only twelve pillars were built. But Playfair designed the New Observatory on the Calton Hill, the Dugald Stewart Monument and the monument to his uncle.

His was the notable Royal Institution at the Mound which houses the Royal Scottish Academy and also the adjoining Art Gallery of Scotland. Further up the Mound is his Free Church Assembly Hall.

One of the finest buildings in Scotland, which Queen Victoria would have liked to acquire, is Donaldson's Hospital, designed by Playfair. He also completed the University, designed first by Adam but left unfinished for many years.

William Burn *(1789-1870)*
Born in Edinburgh, son of an architect, he trained in London under Smirke and with him worked on Covent Garden and Lowther Castle. He laid out the architectural plan for the Calton extension of Edinburgh and was beaten by Playfair in a competition for Edinburgh University's rebuilding. He designed hundreds of banks, insurance offices and country and town mansions, including Camperdown House, Dundee, and Falkland House, Fife. His style moved from severe Greek to Jacobean, and finally Scottish Baronial, in which his apprentice Bryce excelled.

George Meikle Kemp *(1794-1844)*
He was born near Eddleston and lived in his youth near Silverburn where his father was a shepherd. A visit to the nearby chapel at Roslin inspired him to be an architect but he was apprenticed to a mill-wright. He wandered freely about the country setting up mills. He made a model for the proposed restoration of Glasgow Cathedral but was unsuccessful. However, in a competition for a monument to commemorate Sir Walter Scott his design won the award in 1838. The foundation stone was laid in 1840 and Kemp took an active part in the building. In 1844, when the work was well in hand, he went to Port Hopetoun to see some stone brought by canal barge, and was accidentally drowned. Kemp's original design was deliberately Gothic, to symbolise Scott's attitude to history and in this respect the Scott monument is unique in Britain, resembling the early Gothic cathedrals such as Chartres.

The most amazing feature of Kemp's work is that it arose from a self-taught humble shepherd's son.

David Bryce *(1803-1876)*
Born in Edinburgh, son of an architect, he early came into Wm. Burn's business and became his partner. Together they designed and executed many exquisite buildings, Bryce being the designer of Free St George's

Church, Edinburgh, of Hamilton Mansion House and Fettes College. The latter is in a magnificent adaptation of Gothic, like his monument to Catherine Sinclair in Edinburgh. His architectural school was the most influential in Britain.

Alexander Thomson *(1817-1875)*

He was born in Glasgow and trained for his profession by studying widely. His style was strongly influenced by Ancient Greek buildings and is noted for its purity of design and proportion. Moray Place, in the New Town of Edinburgh, is a supreme example of this. He had also studied Hindu and Egyptian architecture and this was very apparent in his church buildings. He made a bold use of iron. Probably the most forcefully designed churches of the nineteenth century in Europe are the United Presbyterian churches of Caledonian Road, Vincent Street and Queen's Park in Glasgow. In the Egyptian Halls we have a unique application of exotic architecture to commercial warehouses. His nickname was 'Greek' Thomson, yet he was not just a slavish imitator but one of the most individualistic builders of last century.

Sir James Gowans *(1821-1890)*

Born in West Lothian, son of a working mason, he joined with his father to re-house working people in artistic and efficient dwellings, using stone of matching colours. The first houses were Rosebank Cottages in Edinburgh. His own house, Rockville, in the Merchiston area, was in a highly striking style based on the principles of mediaeval architecture. Many remarkably beautiful buildings in Edinburgh and elsewhere were to his plans. He was honoured by being made chairman of the great 1886 Exhibition in Edinburgh.

Sir Robert Lorimer *(1864-1929)*

Of a well-known Fife family, Lorimer was inspired by the ideals of Ruskin and Morris. He became the driving force behind a revival in craftsmanship associated with architecture, as Macintosh also was. Lorimer employed many artists in ornamental ironwork to make screens for the Thistle Chapel of St Giles Cathedral, the restoration of Dunrobin Castle, the Gothic screen in Carlisle Cathedral and the great entrance gates of Pittencrieff Park, Dunfermline.

His commissions are too numerous to note but his crowning achievement was the National War Memorial in Edinburgh Castle.

Charles Rennie Macintosh *(1866-1928)*

He was born in Glasgow, one of the eleven children of a Police Superintendent. At sixteen he was apprenticed to an architect and when twenty-four he won the 'Greek' Thomson travelling scholarship to France and Italy. For the next twenty years he worked in the Glasgow area, and made excursions to London, Venice and Turin.

Although generally regarded as an architectural genius he was also a very competent artist. His precise flower sketches show his ability as a draughtsman and observer. In 1892, when Beardsley and others were producing their memorable drawings, Macintosh exhibited his *Harvest Moon*, melancholy, macabre and allegorical, yet with an unearthly poetic beauty.

His principle regarding architecture was derived from an architectural writer of that time (W.A.Lethaby), 'Architecture is a combination of all arts, crafts and industries'. Apart from Robert Adam, no other British architect has been honoured as a decorator as well as a builder. Macintosh created a style fully as distinctive as Adam.

He died a disappointed man, never fully appreciated in Scotland and although honoured in Europe never invited to build there. Only now is his original genius being acknowledged.

Sir Basil Urwin Spence *(1907-1976)*

Born in India of Scottish parents, he was educated at London and Edinburgh Universities. He designed many private houses in Scotland, the major influence on his work having been Sir Edwin Luytens. As he had always inclined to monumental work, he entered the competition to rebuild the bombed Coventry Cathedral, winning it with a brilliant plan to use the ruined walls and the mediaeval spire as a foil to the long low mass. His design had much severe criticism. He was the architect of England's 'red-brick' universities, so called because he used red brick and concrete arches to plan Cambridge, Durham, Exeter, Newcastle and Southampton. The British Embassy in Rome, and churches and civic centres in Hampstead and Kensington are to his plans.

Sculpture

In common with other branches of art, sculpture suffered a severe setback from the Reformers. Few of the sculptural ornaments of the churches and abbeys escaped the iconoclasts led on by Knox. But, of the surviving sculptures, such as the famous Prentice Pillar at Rosslyn Chapel and one or two inaccessible parts of the abbeys, it is possible to form an estimate of the beautiful work of the mediaevals, all of whom are anonymous.

Only towards the end of the eighteenth century was sculpture revived and suffered to be seen in public places, though ideal human figures were rarely to be seen in Edinburgh and less so in Glasgow. Even as late as the end of the nineteenth century the gift of the Ross Fountain with its striking nudes was an embarrassment to the Town Council of Edinburgh, and indeed several of the supporting nymphs were never erected, so prurient were the City Fathers a century ago. It is noticeable that in Modern Athens the statues are more than adequately covered, the notable exception being the Gladstone Memorial in Shandwick Place.

Thomas Campbell (1790-1855)

He was the first of many gifted Scottish sculptors whose works were generally admired throughout Britain. He studied and worked in Rome during his formative years and had the best of examples before him there. He specialised in portrait busts of which he exhibited no less that thirty-eight in the Royal Academy, including the Duke of Wellington, the Duke of Buccleuch, Mrs Siddons the celebrated actress and Raeburn. He had a very extensive clientèle.

Lawrence Macdonald (1798-1878)

He was born at Gask, Perthshire, and although he studied and worked for a time in Edinburgh, like Campbell, his artistic home was in Rome where he spent four years (1822-26). Although he returned to Britain and made statues and busts of many people, including Prime Minister Canning and Sir David Baird, the soldier, he spent most of his long life in Rome, where he died. He was one of the few to devote himself to ideal statues. Of these his best works are *Eurydice, Venus* and *Ulysses*.

James Thom (1799-1850)

Born in Ayrshire, he became highly popular for his models of Burns characters Tam o' Shanter and Souter Johnny, which were widely distributed over Scotland and England.

Amelia Hill *(1802-1870)*

She was the wife of the artist and artistic photographer David O. Hill. She was undoubtedly the best of women sculptors and by no means inferior to most of the men. A talented artist, she exhibited consistently for many years at the Royal Academy. Her best works are of Livingstone, Carlyle, Sir David Brewster, Sir Noel Paton and of her husband, the latter in marble, not the most docile of media.

Sir John Steell *(1804-1891)*

Born in Aberdeen, he was trained by the sculptor Graham, and went to Rome to study. His equestrian statues are remarkable for their spirited rendering of movement and power. His *Alexander and Bucephalus*, showing the tension of the warrior subduing his remarkable steed, was cast in bronze and is to be seen at the City Chambers, Edinburgh. A more ingenious equestrian statue is that of the Duke of Wellington on Copenhagen, where the rearing horse is supported by his tail. The only comparable statue is in Leningrad.

Steell also produced Sir Walter Scott's statue for the Scott Monument, Thomas de Quincy for the National Portrait Gallery, and the composite group in Charlotte Square, of which the central figure is Prince Albert on horseback. Steell was knighted by Queen Victoria on the unveiling of this memorial in 1876. His works are to be seen in many countries.

James Fillans *(1808-1852)*

Born at Paisley he trained in Paris and Rome. His works included both the actual and the ideal. Thirty of his sculptures are to be seen in London galleries or in private possession. His *Sir Walter Scott* was much admired, also *Professor Wilson* (Christopher North) a notably handsome subject to which Fillans did justice.

On his grave in Paisley Abbey is the symbolic 'Rachael Weeping', a very poignant memorial to a man of genius who died before he realised his promise.

Patrick Park *(1811-1855)*

Born in Glasgow, he worked for some time in Hamilton Palace where his merits were appreciated by the Duke of Hamilton who sent him to Rome to study sculpture. There he was fortunate enough to be taught by Thorwaldson, a noted artist. At the age of twenty-five, Park exhibited in the Royal Academy. In his relatively short life he was popular and successful, among his works being *Charles Dickens* (taken from life), *Napoleon III* (also from a series of sittings), *Oliver Cromwell* from a portrait, and a colossal statue of *William Wallace*.

William Calder Marshall *(1813-1894)*

Born in Edinburgh and educated at the High School and University there, he studied under Sir Frances Chantrey, the finest sculptor of his age and also under E.H. Baily, the sculptor of the Nelson Column. He then went to Rome

291

and returned to London in 1839.

He is noted for his imaginative work and is one of the most eminent Victorian sculptors, exhibiting more than 150 pieces. His field of interest covers sculpture, classics and poetry as well as actual persons. He made statues of Thomas Campbell and William Cowper for the Poets' Corner in Westminster Abbey, and one of Robert Peel the reforming Premier for Manchester. His Biblical masterpiece is *Ruth* and his poetical success is *Ophelia*.

He was made a Chevalier of the Legion of Honour in 1878. His many works are to be seen in, amongst other places, the Guildhall and in Liverpool and Salford.

William Scoular *(fl. 1815-1846)*

Born in Edinburgh, he went to London where he gained the Gold Medal and a travelling scholarship from the Royal Academy. He studied at Rome from 1825. He returned to Britain where he had an extensive clientèle, contributing eighty-four busts to the London Galleries. These included Albert (Prince Consort), Dr Monro, Dr Gregory and James Watt.

William Brodie *(1815-1881)*

Born at Banff and educated at Aberdeen University, he resided for some years in Edinburgh where he made a very much admired bust of Francis, Lord Jeffrey in 1847. Like most aspiring sculptors he studied at Rome for a time in 1853.

In 1859 he was made a full member of the RSA but, although thirty-one of his works were exhibited at Burlington House he never sought acceptance by the Royal Academy and, sad to say, he was never offered it.

Many of his statues are in Edinburgh. These include *Lord Cockburn, Sir David Brewster* and *Queen Victoria* (seated on top of Playfair's Royal Institution). He made busts of Tennyson, J.Y. Simpson, Henry Irving, Ellen Terry and a model from life of that faithful dog, 'Greyfriars Bobby'. His impressive bust of Carlyle is in the National Portrait Gallery, Edinburgh.

Alexander Munro *(1825-1871)*

The most eminent of all British sculptors of his age, his statues express grandeur and dignity. Perhaps his best-loved is the nymph fountain in Berkeley Square, but of actual persons he made impressive statues of James Watt (for Birmingham, scene of most of Watt's labours), of Sir Robert Peel, of Millais, Gladstone and of Queen Mary I for Parliament.

John Hutchison *(1833-1910)*

Born in Edinburgh he studied in Rome from 1860-1863. His statues are mainly of Scottish interest, being of Robert the Bruce, John Knox (in bronze), and George Buchanan. For the Scott Monument he made a statue of Flora McIvor.

David Watson Stevenson *(1842-1903)*

He exhibited in the Royal Academy the busts of Mrs Siddons and Robert Louis Stevenson and in ideal statues *Scotch Peasant Girl* and *Lady Godiva*, the first being in the National Gallery of Scotland.

William Grant Stevenson *(1849-1919)*

Born at Ratho, Midlothian, he trained in the Royal Scottish Academy. He produced the statue of Burns for Kilmarnock and that of Wallace for Aberdeen. Abroad he made statues of prominent figures in Denver and Chicago. He also exhibited in the Royal Academy.

Thomas S. Burnett *(1853-1888)*

In his short life he exhibited several works in the Royal Academy. He also made a statue of General Charles Gordon for Aberdeen, and one of Rob Roy. His ideal, *Florentine Priest*, is in the National Gallery of Scotland.

George E. Ewing *(fl.1862-1877)*

He was a Glaswegian, the most successful of all Scottish sculptors of his time. He showed fifty pieces in the Royal Academy. He made an excellent bust of Colin Campbell, Lord Clyde, for Glasgow. He had many sitters of distinction including the Prince of Wales, afterwards King Edward VII.

Mary Grant *(fl.1866-1892)*

Born in Perthshire, she exhibited in the Royal Academy for about thirty years, her best works being of Parnell, the Irish statesman, of Queen Victoria and of Lord Tennyson.

Sir William Reid Dick *(1879-1961)*

Born in Glasgow, he studied there and in London. He exhibited at the Royal Academy when he was twenty-nine.

He was a most successful and industrious sculptor, very much in demand. He was made President of the Royal Society of Sculptors and among other honours he was appointed King's Sculptor-in-Ordinary.

His most notable works were of President Roosevelt, Princess Elizabeth (the present Queen), George VI and Queen Elizabeth (the Queen Mother), Winston Churchill and George V.

Of historical people he made statues of the Elder Pitt (Lord Chatham), and David Livingstone (to stand at the Victoria Falls).

His war memorials are numerous, the most impressive being the Lion in the Menin Gate at Ypres.

Drama

In the widest sense drama is any work in verse or prose adapted for presentation on the stage. In modern times this of course extended, first to the cinema, then to radio, television and video.

In mediaeval times Scotland, like all countries, had its public theatre, usually in the open, presenting morality plays such as Lindsay's *Thrie Estaites*. But the Reformation put an end to all such shows associated with the Catholic Church. Although John Knox personally advocated the enjoyment of music and other harmless recreations, it was his successors who imposed a stern ban on such frivolity, which lasted for two centuries.

Allan Ramsay opened a theatre in Edinburgh in 1735 and the magistrates clamped a closing order on it, whereby Ramsay lost a lot of money. When John Home presented his play *Douglas* in Edinburgh in 1756 he was dismissed from his post as a minister by the General Assembly. In Glasgow repression of drama was even more severe.

By the end of the eighteenth century theatre-going began to boom. In Glasgow a theatre in Dublin Street was opened by Mrs Siddons, the famous actress, in 1785. The Queen Street Theatre opened shortly after. In Edinburgh the national opera *Rob Roy* played in the 1820s to full houses.

It would take a volume to note the Scots actors and actresses of the nineteenth century, but the most universally famous of the modern age are these:

James Finlayson *(1877-1953)*

A native of Edinburgh, educated at George Watson's College, he emigrated to Hollywood in the early days when 'silents' conquered the world. He developed a style of his own, with exaggerated grimaces and gestures, playing the comic villain in Laurel and Hardy films. Finlayson's film appearances include *Small Town Idol* (1921), *The Hoosegow* (1929), *Grand Canyon Trail* (1948), as well as the hilarious *Bonnie Scotland* where he plays the diminutive irascible kilted sergeant.

Eric Campbell *(1878-1917)*

He emigrated to California and was enlisted by the director of Charlie Chaplin's first films, the legendary two-reelers, starting in 1916. Campbell, a heavily-built, bearded ogre, made fame in *Easy Street*, *The Cure*, *The Adventurer*, etc.

Finlay Currie *(1878-1968)*

His real name was Finlay Jefferson. He had a long career on music-hall and stage before entering film work. His massive and handsome features and great head of hair made him a natural for character parts. He played in over one hundred films.

Donald Crisp *(1880-1974)*

He was a man of many and varied abilities, actor in many films, and also director of the silent films of the twenties, now recognised as classics. In the film *How Green was my Valley* he was awarded an Oscar (1941) as Best Supporting Actor.

John Laurie *(1897-1980)*

He was born in Dumfries and educated at the Academy there. After serving in the Royal Artillery from 1916 to 1918, he studied at the Central School of Speech Training at the Royal Albert Hall, so he presumably could speak the King's English, but he was most effective in Scots. He made his debut in Dumfries in 1921 in J.M. Barrie's play *What Every Woman Knows* (1908), a satire against male arrogance. Laurie appeared in many plays and films, perhaps his best part being as the village funeral undertaker, Private Fraser, in the TV series *Dad's Army*.

Alastair Sim *(1900-1976)*

Born in Edinburgh, he started work as a tailor in the family firm, but an interest in the theatre developed and he ran a school for poetic drama and taught elocution. He also trained as a teacher and was appointed to the Fulton Lectureship at New College, Edinburgh. His first stage appearance as a professional was in London in 1930 as a walk-on in Paul Robeson's *Othello*. Numerous stage and film appearances followed. Alastair Sim was undoubtedly one of the best comedy actors to emerge from Scotland and receive world-wide acclaim. One of his funniest films is *Laughter in Paradise* (1951).

James Robertson Justice *(1905-1975)*

He was descended from a distinguished Scottish legal family and had a majestic appearance, portly and bearded. His christened name was James Norval Harold Robertson-Justice and he was a public school product, educated at Marlborough. He attended Bonn University to study Natural Science. In later life his merits were acknowledged by the award of an LLD in Edinburgh.

He became a full-time actor in the 1940s and played dignified and often imperious parts in many films. In the 'Doctor' series he was memorable as the surgeon Sir Lancelot Spratt, the terror of the operating theatre, but the admiration of the hospitals.

Duncan MacRae *(1905-1967)*

John Duncan Graham MacRae was born in Glasgow, where he was

educated, trained as a teacher and taught for some years before turning to acting.

His first film was *The Brothers* (1947). He may be said to have reached fame and a wide public in 1949 in Compton MacKenzie's *Whisky Galore*. In 1950 he played in *Women in Question*, in 1952 in *You're Only Young Twice*. *Geordie* (1953) was successful, with *Tunes of Glory* following in 1960. He played a Scottish character of Victorian times in Walt Disney's *Greyfriars Bobby*, a colourful but mythical version of the story.

He was noted for his skill in portraying whimsical characters, full of inimitable humour.

Molly Urquhart *(1906-1977)*

She was born and brought up in Glasgow with an overwhelming ambition to be an actress and to own her own theatre. She was with the Tron Players, the Curtain Theatre, the Sheldone-Brown Group and the Dumbarton People's Theatre. Then she founded her own theatre in Rutherglen, where she put on more than one hundred plays and, in so doing, started many actors on the road to fame. Of these were Gordon Jackson, Eileen Harlie, Andrew Crawford and Nicholas Parsons. She played in Tyrone Guthrie's famous version of *The Thrie Estaites* and in *Dr Finlay's Casebook*. She was an early and much-loved pioneer of the renewed Scottish Theatre.

David Niven *(1909-1983)*

Like James M. Barrie, he was a native of Kirriemuir, being christened James David Niven. He entered the military colleges of Stowe and Sandhurst and enlisted, much against his desire, in that very tough unit, the Highland Light Infantry, recruited mainly from Glasgow. After a short but strenuous spell with the HLI, very vividly described in his autobiographical *The Moon's a Balloon*, he went to Hollywood where he was fortunate to get a part as an extra in *Mutiny on the Bounty*. Ultimately his sang-froid and unusual charm gained him leading parts in many films where he was paradoxically described by the Americans as their ideal of the perfect *Englishman*. His books of reminiscences are quite uninhibited, frank to the point of embarrassment, and, of course, sell enormously.

Roddy McMillan *(1923-1979)*

He was educated at Finnieston Public School, Glasgow, and took up a theatrical career by studying at the Glasgow Unity Theatre. At the age of twenty-one he played a part in the *Song of Tomorrow*, by James Floy, in the Queen's Theatre, Glasgow. He acted for several years in the Citizens' Theatre, Glasgow, and in the Edinburgh Lyceum, taking a leading part in his own play *The Bevellers* (1973). He also took the title-role in the TV series *Daniel Pike*. He appeared in many films, perhaps his most celebrated being as the skipper in the comedy of the Clyde puffers, *The Vital Spark*. He seemed to be almost indispensible in any important Scottish film. His early death was a great loss to the arts.

Mary Ure *(1933-1975)*

She was a native of Glasgow and studied at the Central School of Drama. She was married twice, to men famous in the world of literature and theatre; first to John Osborne, the author of the famous play *Look Back in Anger* (1956), in which she took a part in 1958 in its stage appearance. She later married the actor Robert Shaw.

At the age of twenty-one she played Ophelia in *Hamlet* and in the year of her early death, aged forty-two, she appeared in *The Exorcism*. She appeared in principal parts in the famous films *Storm Over the Nile* (1955), D.H. Lawrence's *Sons and Lovers* (1960), *Where Eagles Dare* (1968) and many others.

Sport

From the earliest times, however pressing were the dangers of war and starvation, Scots were very fond of sports of all kinds. Even repeated Acts of Parliament, with increasing penalties for disobediance, failed to dissuade the Scots from their favourite games of golf and football. In fact, the kings and queens and courtiers were the worst offenders. It is recorded as a scandal of the times that, a few days after the murder of her unlamented husband, Henry Darnley, Mary Queen of Scots was enjoying a game of golf at Seton, only a few miles east of the scene of the crime. When she resided at Falkland Palace in Fife she amused herself with archery and tennis, for a walled tennis court had been built there by James VI and is still to be seen.

Football was not governed by rules until late in the nineteenth century. In olden days it was a sort of warfare between bands of young men, where injuries were part of the fun. A sixteenth century poet ironically describes the *Bewties of the Futeball*, which reads in modern English,

> Bruised muscles and broken bones,
> Strife, discord and ruined homes,
> Bent in old age and lame as well
> These are the beauties of the football.

In winter, when golf and football were stopped by frost and snow, curling was the national sport. It was called the 'Roaring Game', perhaps because the players shouted advice or encouragement, but more likely because the stones made a roaring sound as they slid along the rough ice. As frost was not always prolonged and keen, curling was not a regular sport each year but when a severe winter set in, huge gatherings, numbering thousands of players, assembled on certain large shallow lochs such as Loch Leven, the Lake of Menteith and Carsbreck.

Games of skill, like outdoor quoits, played with horseshoes or iron rings, were very popular. Bowling was also played from antiquity. All the above were frowned on in times of English aggression, as they kept the lieges from practising at the bow-butts which were marked out near every Scottish town and village. Even at Crail, in the tip of Fife, the Bow-butts is still indicated. When gunpowder was introduced the early guns were so inefficient that archers were still much in demand, though the Scots in this respect were inferior to the English, who, though they were loath to admit it, had inherited the deadly long-bow from the Welsh. Shooting at a mark was common in many Scottish towns. In Dumfries the Siller Gun was competed for every year.

In the Highlands among the Gaels, annual games, usually of a local character, had been held from the earliest ages, attended by great ceremony with music and dancing, feasting and drinking, with athletic contests of all sorts. The purpose was to encourage the clan spirit and to be ready for instant uprisings against rivals or national enemies. For this reason all such gatherings were penally suppressed after the '45 Rebellion, along with the wearing of Highland dress, the playing of Highland music and the carrying of weapons. But with the lifting of the proscription in 1782, Highland Games with all their background of tartans, piping, marches and weaponry were rapidly taken up and have now become universal, particularly in America, Australia and New Zealand.

Blood sports are now under a cloud but in the callous days of our ancestors they were widely enjoyed, though latterly the law put paid to the baiting of bears, bulls and badgers, and to cockfighting, which was an annual event in schools.

When Scottish monarchs organised deer-hunts, hundreds of beaters were engaged to drive the prey on to the waiting crossbows, longbows, guns and deer-hounds. The carcases were also numbered by the hundred, just as at present we have the same barbaric system of driving grouse and pheasants over unsuspected shotguns.

It makes dreary reading to enumerate the victims of wanton carnage in such books as St John's *Wild Sport in the Highlands* and hear the authors relate with gusto the toll of beautiful creatures, shot to be stuffed and mounted. Man's shocking record in Scotland is detailed in James Ritchie's *Animal Life in Scotland*.

More innocuous and just as exciting are the various forms of racing, either horse, dog or pigeon. Motor-racing, either against competitors or the clock, has a special appeal to Scots because of their natural bent for mechanics. Cycling, rowing, yachting, flying, gliding, parachuting, water-skiing and motor-boat racing are universal, as are winter sports.

GOLF

Golf has a very long history in Scotland. It was a thoroughly democratic game and, unlike many vigorous outdoor games, it could be enjoyed by individual players. In this way it seemed to suit the Scots character though match-play was equally attractive as it involved a test of nerves and skill. The list of famous golfers is interminable and controversial and is evergrowing.

Allan Robertson *(1815-1859)*

In his relatively short life Robertson became a legend. He was not only one of the greatest of St Andrews players, he was also, as most of these old players were, a professional maker of golf-balls and clubs, both wood and iron. Like many of the golfers in the nineteenth century, he belonged to a family dynasty of players and manufacturers. The generations preceding Allan went back as ball-makers at St Andrews for over a century, Allan being the most famous.

Tom Morris *(1821-1908)*

All are agreed that the Nestor of golfers, that is, the wisest and most experienced of that great army, was Tom Morris. He was born in North Street, St Andrews, Fife, and educated at the Madras College there. As a youth he was apprenticed to the famous Allan Robertson, acknowledged to be not only the finest golfer of his time but also the best maker of clubs and balls. Allan was at the height of his fame, and Tom was in many ways lucky to be working for him and playing with him on the links close to the workshop. He stayed with Robertson for nine years, four of which were as apprentice. Feeling sufficiently independent, Morris left St Andrews and with his young wife went to Prestwick, in Ayrshire, as greenkeeper and ball-maker and club-maker. Here he encouraged the use of the new guttapercha ball, which annoyed Robertson who made featheries, i.e. balls of sheepskin stuffed with feathers.

Tom now became better than his master. He beat Robertson in an open competition after a very hard struggle. Morris was never very good at putting but his driving and approaches balanced this weakness. He now challenged Willie Park of Musselburgh, the champion of that era, but Park and he, in 1854, proved to be about equal. Even when the Open Championship was organised in 1860, Morris and Park monopolised it for seven years, winning it alternately.

Morris had now moved back to St Andrews where he was greenkeeper of the Royal and Ancient for forty years (1863-1903). His advice was sought all over Britain on the planning of courses, as he was recognised as the undisputed Patriarch of Golf, conspicuous by his great beard which whitened as he approached his eighties. He still played well even in old age, attributing his good health to a daily swim in the sea, and to sleeping with open windows.

His death at eighty-seven was prematurely hastened by a fall downstairs. His portrait graces the Royal and Ancient Clubhouse.

Willie Park *(1834-1903)*

A native of Musselburgh, he was the most prominent of three golfing brothers, ball-makers, club-makers and champion players. He won the Open Championship when it was inaugurated in 1860, and again in 1863, 1866 and 1875.

James Anderson *(1842-1905)*

Son of a well-known St Andrews ball-maker and greenkeeper, he was Open Champion in the consecutive years 1877, 1878 and 1879. He made long-headed woods in St Andrews bearing his name. He died in a Poor House at Perth.

Bob Ferguson *(1848-1915)*

He was British Open Champion in 1880, 1881, 1882 and lost the Play-off to Bob Fernie in 1883.

Tom Morris, Jun. *(1852-1875)*

Known as 'Young Tom', he was born at Prestwick, and proved to be the extraordinary player of all time. 'Old Tom' entered him for the Open in 1868 when he was sixteen and was asked what he meant by entering a 'laddie'. But to the shock of everyone the 'laddie' won the Open and went on to win it for three successive years, a feat never repeated. The trophy became his own property. But tragedy unequalled also followed. Young Tom's wife and child died and it is thought that this broke his heart for he was found dead from natural causes on 25 September 1875.

Clubs from all over Britain subscribed to erect a marble tomb to his memory in St Andrews, where there are also memorials to Old Tom and to Allan Robertson.

Andrew Kirkaldy *(1860-1934)*

He was professional at St Andrews for most of his career and published his memoirs, *Fifty Years of Golf*.

Willie Park, Jun. *(1864-1925)*

He learned his father's trade so thoroughly that at sixteen he went to Northumberland (Ryton) as assistant greenkeeper and professional, but returned in 1884 to Musselburgh to assist in the growing demand for clubs. He invented several new designs for clubs and patented the first diamond-meshed ball. He won the Open Championship in 1887 and 1889. He took up manufacturing of golf apparatus on a large scale.

James Braid *(1870-1950)*

Born at Earlsferry, Fife, he was Open Champion in 1901, 1905, 1906, 1908 and 1910. He ran a club-making workshop and was professional at Walton Heath for nearly half a century.

William Auchterlonie *(1873-1963)*

He was professional to the Royal and Ancient and won the Open Championship in 1893. He was Honorary Curator of the Royal and Ancient Museum.

It was at this period that Scots golfers took the game over to the USA and laid out courses there, though the game did not really approach its present popularity until after the First World War.

Golf had been played in America in the late eighteenth century but it was in 1886 that J. Hamilton Gillespie laid out the first golf-course in Florida at Sarasota. He was the son of a Scottish knight who had emigrated from Scotland in 1885.

Robert Lockhart, another emigrant Scot, laid out a course at Yonkers, north of New York City, in the following year. The subsequent club, the first in the USA, was named the St Andrews Golf Club in 1888.

England took up the game with enthusiasm, and champions such as the remarkable J.H. Taylor competed successfully in the Open until the

American contingent arrived and began to dominate the play. This was a good example of Scotland's chickens coming home to roost, and for Scots golfers perhaps this softened the blow.

FOOTBALL

Although traditionally a popular game, equal in attraction to golf, it has in modern times, like golf, attracted many times more spectators than players. This applies equally to soccer and rugby, and it leads to strong partisanship with its subsequent evils. No matter how impartially a list of famous players was presented, and in what order of ability, it would be found fault with. The stronger argument against singling out famous footballers is, that we are dealing with a team game where, in theory, the credit for a win is shared equally by each member. Nevertheless, human nature being inclined to hero-worship or villain-hissing, certain players get more or less credit than is their due. However, all this having been considered, it is generally agreed that a man born early this century deserves much the same position as Morris in golf or Clark in motor-racing.

Alex. James (1902-1953) was born in Mossend, a mining-village at that time, a few miles from Glasgow. After a local schooling he was a clerk in the neighbouring steel-works. He became a close friend of Hugh Gallacher, later to achieve football fame. James played for a season or two in a Glasgow Junior Club named Ashfield. At the age of twenty he was signed on by Raith Rovers, centred in Kirkcaldy. In 1925, like many Scots, he was attracted to an English club because of better pay and prospects. He played for Preston for four seasons before being enrolled by Chapman, manager of Arsenal, in 1929.

James did not like Chapman's imperious ways but he had to acknowledge the wisdom of his manager. In the Cup Final against Huddersfield Town in 1930 he scored a very important first goal and Arsenal won 2-0.

His idiosyncrasy was to wear very long shorts, covering his knees. As he was only 5ft. 6in. this gave him a deceptively clumsy look which his skilful play soon dispelled. He was capped for Scotland eight times, helped Arsenal to win the Cup twice and the English League flag four times between 1929 and 1937 when he retired for a commercial job as a salesman, to everyone's surprise.

His greatest day was 31 March 1928, when at Wembley, with a Scottish international team of brilliant players, including Hugh Gallacher (and named the Wembley Wizards), he scored two of Scotland's five goals against England's one.

To avoid any charge of partisanship we would like to append in alphabetical order the names of outstanding players of the past, all of whom gained recognition outside Scotland as well as within its own borders.

Willie Bald, Jim Baxter, Jimmy Cowan, Hugh Gallacher, Patsy Gallacher, Alan Morton, Gordon Smith, John Thomson (goalkeeper) and Tommy Walker are all entitled to places among the football immortals.

RUGBY

It was in 1823 that a youth at Rugby School picked up a football and ran with it, so inventing the handling game. In Scotland the new game was being played before 1850, and in 1858 Edinburgh Academicals played Merchiston Castle. The game, until twenty years later, was still taking shape and new rules were being argued about. The first International between Scotland and England was played at Raeburn Ground, Edinburgh, with twenty players a side. Scotland won by a goal and a try, to a try. The game rapidly gained in popularity in Scotland, especially in the Borders, and there was not the same schism as in England where most of North England went over to a different style, rather allied to American Football.

The famous Scots Rugby players of the early period, who deserve the title, the 'Immortals', were W.E. MacLagan, A.R. Don Wauchope, C. Reid, the Finlays and the Irvines.

A remarkable hero was Jock Wemyss who was capped in 1914, was severely wounded and blinded in one eye in the First World War, yet came back to gain his cap in 1922.

After that the great names were: full-back, Dan Drysdale of Heriots; the three quarters, G.B. Crole, Eric Liddell (the Olympic Medallist), G.P.S. MacPherson and Ian Smith (the last being capped thirty-two times). The famous forwards were J.M. Bannerman, R.G. MacMillan and H. Leggatt.

In the Centenary Match in 1971 the Scots overwhelmed the 'Auld Enemy' 26-6, and in 1983-4 Scotland won both the Triple Crown and the Grand Slam.

ATHLETICS

In the resurrection of Highland Games after 1782 the heavy events such as putting the weight, throwing the hammer and tossing the caber took the most important place. In these, the outstanding champions were Donald Dinnie and A.A. Cameron, though there were a few who on occasion could beat these Samsons.

Donald Dinnie *(1837-1916)*

Dinnie was born in Aberdeenshire in 1837, son of a stone-mason, an employment he at first followed, before becoming an hotelier and carriage-hirer. He was Champion from 1871 to 1876. He travelled widely as a professional athlete in America, Australia, New Zealand and South Africa, winning thousands of contests in all events of strength and agility.

Alexander Anthony Cameron *(1875-1951)*

Cameron was born in Inverness-shire and became the greatest heavy athlete of his time, dominating the field from 1900 to 1914. He was a farmer, though for a time he was a policeman in Glasgow. He was induced to go as a strong man on the stage but did not like the footlights. He toured Australia, New Zealand and even into Russia. He, like Dinnie, was also very agile and once cleared nearly five feet in a standing high jump.

The following were the most outstanding track athletes of their day:

Robert Barclay-Allardice (Captain Barclay) *(1779-1854)*

Allardice was a farmer, estate owner and army officer from Urie, near Stonehaven, who turned his predilection for long walks—he thought nothing of a thirty-mile spin before breakfast—into profit from 1801, when he successfully covered ninety miles in 21½hrs at his third attempt. He had 'set-up' the bookmakers by waging 100 and 200 guineas on his two previous attempts, before staking 500 guineas on the third.

Anything which was of uncertain result was considered by the officers and gentlemen of the Regency period as the proper subject of a wager. Barclay, though successful over many shorter races, was held in great esteem by his contemporaries for his accomplishment of what was afterwards known as the 'Barclay match': to walk 1000 miles in 1000 hours. For over six weeks in the summer of 1809 Barclay walked one mile in every single hour, up and down a measured half-mile of the turnpike road on Newmarket Heath. Despite lack of sleep and consequent ailments and depressions, Barclay walked on to the applause of up to ten thousand spectators in the latter stages. His winnings amounted to £16,000, which in modern terms approximates to £180,000, probably the largest sum ever won in a single athletic contest.

Barclay recovered quickly and a few days later went off to Holland with his regiment. He remained active into old age, indeed until his sudden death at the age of seventy-five, which was occasioned by a kick in the head from a horse.

William Jeffrey Cummings *(1858-1919)*

Cummings was the outstanding professional track runner, or 'pedestrian', of the 1880s. Pedestrianism at this period was a rough and often dubious sport whose members had long since recognised the financial necessity of a system of inter-dependence which involved practises like staging results or sharing prize-money. Middle-class reaction to this state of affairs resulted in the 'amateur' movement around this time.

After an 'apprenticeship' in his runner's craft, Paisley-born Cummings was invited to compete at Lillie Bridge, London, in 1878. At this Mecca of professional (and amateur) running, the twenty-year old became Champion of England over one mile in 4min. 28sec. On his return to Scotland he ran a sensational 4min. 18¼sec., the fastest mile on record since 1863.

By 1885 Cummings had made himself king of professional distance-running, but his realm was diminishing as football, racing and even amateur athletics usurped the place of pedestrianism in public affection. Cummings was therefore pleased to agree to a three race series (1, 4 and 10 miles) against Walter George, the leading amateur runner who of course had had to abandon his amateur status to challenge the Scot.

Over 30,000 spectators attended the mile race on 31 August 1885, causing enormous traffic jams and breaking down part of the fence to get in. The race was magnificent. George led through 440yds., 880yds. and three-quarters of a mile at world-record pace, and Cummings could not keep up after 2¾ laps. George slowed to win in 4min. 20.2sec.

Cummings won the 4 mile run at Powderhall grounds on 12 September 1885 in drenching rain; George retired at 3½ miles, well beaten. The 10 mile race was again held at Lillie Bridge, on 28 September, and George, who had been ill, offered little challenge. Cummings ran his hardest after a slow first mile to establish a world's best time, by amateur or professional, of 51min. 6.6sec. From the series he earned enough to buy a second public house in Lancashire, where he was living.

Two further series between George and Cummings were held but proved anticlimactic.

Cummings continued to compete until he was sixty-one (in an 880yds. veteran event).

He died in hospital in Glasgow in July 1919, after a serious illness.

Alfred Reynolds Downer *(1873-1912)*

Downer was one of Scotland's great sprinters. He was born in Jamaica but his mother brought him at an early age to Edinburgh, where he was educated at Watson's College, and the Edinburgh Institution (Melville College).

His amateur sprinting career was marked by triple victories in the SAAA 100, 220 and 440yds. championships in three consecutive years, 1893, 1894 and 1895. Along with several of the other top runners of the day, however, Downer accepted too great 'expenses' and demanded 'appearance money'. As a result he and several others were banned by the AAA (the offences had occurred in England) in July 1896.

Downer turned professional and enjoyed great success. His speed over short distances, for example, 12.4sec. for 128½yds. (i.e. 130yds. less 1½yds. handicap) was matched by his strength over 350yds.

Downer was rather an inconstant character, tending to dissoluteness, and his late life was tragic. In the poignant words of the athletic historian David Jamieson: 'in his short life—he died when in his thirty-ninth year—Downer quaffed to its deepest from the goblet of life—and in its dregs he found much bitterness.'

He died on 5 June 1912 and is buried in Morningside Cemetery, Edinburgh.

Wyndham Halswelle *(1882-1915)*

Halswelle, the son of a prominent nineteenth century book-illustrator and water-colour painter, is one of the small number of Scottish Olympic Gold Medallists, and was outstanding as an athlete in his generation.

Gazetted into the 2nd Battalion HLI as a second lieutenant, Halswelle took up running on a South African tour of duty. In 1905 he had progressed to the status of SAAA 440yds. champion (in 51.0sec) and AAA 440yds. champion (51.8sec. in adverse conditions). He was never defeated by a fellow Briton and won the AAA title in 1906 (48.8sec.) and again in 1908 (49.4sec.).

In April 1906 at the Olympic celebrations in Athens he was beaten by an

American, Paul Pilgrim; but he made amends, although in a rather unsatisfactory manner, at the 1908 London Olympic Games at the stadium at Shepherd's Bush. In the 400m. final, Halswelle made a move to pass the leading American coming into the home straight (no lanes in those days), but another American, Carpenter, forced him to the outside edge of the track. Carpenter was disqualified and his fellow-Americans boycotted the re-run, which Halswelle won in 50.0sec. by a 'walk-over', the only gold-medal 'walk-over' in Olympic history.

Halswelle, pressurised by senior officers who thought he was being exploited, retired from athletics shortly after. He was killed at Neuve Chapelle on 30 March 1915.

Halswelle's British 440yds. record of 48.4sec. stood for twenty-six years – he set it in the St John's Men's Catholic Union Sports, at Ibrox Park.

Duncan McLeod Wright *(1896-1976)*

Wright had the rare distinction of competing in three Olympic marathons and was Gold medallist in the Marathon at Hamilton, Ontario, in the inaugural British Empire Games in 1930. His performances in Paris (1924) where he retired at 20 miles, and in Amsterdam (1928) where he finished well down the field (20th), led up to a superb performance in Los Angeles (1932), where he led the field by a minute at 20 miles. Unfortunately a muscle strain slowed him and he finished fourth in 2hrs. 32min. 42sec., less than a lap behind Zabala (Argentina), the winner.

Before he began marathon running, Wright (Dunky) was four times Scottish cross-country champion and ran eleven times in the International Cross-country Championships.

After retiring from competitive athletics at the age of fifty, he devoted himself to administration, particularly to coaching, and held among other offices the position of President of the SAAA in 1959.

Eric Henry Liddell *(1902-1945)*

Liddell won the 400m. in the 1924 Paris Olympic Games, setting an Olympic record of 47.6sec., and his name will always be associated with that race.

Because of his Sabbatarian beliefs, Liddell, the son of a missionary and himself born in China on a mission station, decided in the winter of 1923 to change his prospective Olympic event from 100 to 400m., because the short sprint races were scheduled for a Sunday.

He took up athletics seriously at Edinburgh University and in 1921 won the SAAA 100yds. (10.4sec.) and 220yds. (22.6sec.) titles, and shortly afterwards defeated the AAA champion over 100yds. (10.4sec.). In 1921-22 Liddell won Scottish rugby 'caps', but forsook rugby in 1923-4, to train for the 400m. in Paris. His best sprint season was 1923, when he won the AAA 100yds. in 9.7sec. (British record), and the 220yds. in 21.6sec.

After his Olympic victory, Liddell had a final season in UK athletics in 1925, winning the SAAA 100, 220 and 440yds. titles. Soon afterwards he went to China as a missionary and ran intermittently there until 1930. He was interned by the Japanese in 1941, and suffered a fatal brain haemorrhage on 21 February 1945.

Liddell's Christian beliefs were unquestionably vital to his performances as an athlete, and to his achievements as a man. Of all the Scottish athletes, he was probably the most 'heroic', the only one whose efforts went beyond the confines of sport.

Donald McNab Robertson *(1905-1949)*

He was an athlete conspired against by fate. He won selection for the 1932 Olympic Games in Los Angeles, but, as his family's sole breadwinner (a bachelor, he lived with his mother in Glasgow), he could not afford the necessary time off his work as a coach-painter with Glasgow Corporation.

In 1934 he ran in the British Empire Games marathon in Cardiff. Always a slow starter and fast finisher, he was told by his cyclist attendant as he came through the field that he was leading. In fact it turned out that a Canadian runner was still some distance ahead, but of course Robertson, imagining that the race was his, took it easy.

The Berlin Games (1936) marked Robertson's first experience of Olympic competition, and he finished seventh in 2hrs. 36min., a fine performance but again marred, perhaps, by too slow a start.

After the war, Robertson resumed marathon running and won the first two SAAA Championships, in 1946 and 1947. This great friend and rival of 'Dunky' Wright, who still holds the record number of six wins in AAA Championships, died suddenly in his sleep on 14 June 1949. He was only forty-three.

MOUNTAINEERING

The Scottish Highlanders were all mountaineers and thought nothing of it, any more than the Alpine guides and chamois hunters. But when the attraction of the Alps drew British and other climbers to conquer such unattained summits as the Matterhorn and Mont Blanc in the late eighteenth century, several Scots were prominent in these exploits.

James D. Forbes *(1808-1868)*

We have mentioned Forbes as a geologist, but he was also an experienced Alpinist and accompanied the famous geologist Agassiz on excursions among the glaciers, from which Forbes was able to verify by innumerable measurements that they were fluid. In 1841, Forbes, with Agassiz and four learned men, with six guides, made the ascent of the Jungfrau, conquered only three times earlier. He also crossed the Col du Geant in 1842, guided by the experienced Joseph-Marie Couttet, who had survived a catastrophe in 1820.

The Col du Geant was a terrifying place. In 1860 it was the scene of a disaster when three young Englishmen and a guide fell to their deaths.

Revd George McCorkindale *(1828-1865)*

In September 1865 a long line of climbers, guides and porters left Chamonix to climb Mont Blanc. They were a mixture of enthusiastic amateurs and experienced mountaineers. The raw recruits of the party were two Americans, Mr Randall of Massachussetts, and Dr Bean of Baltimore, and a Scot, the Revd George McCorkindale of Gourock.

The weather, at first stormy, cleared, and the party reached the sunlit snows of Mont Blanc under a cloudless sky. They spent the night in a shelter and set off at dawn under the stars, watched from Chamonix by telescopes.

Suddenly storm clouds began to pour over Mont Blanc. The watchers at Chamonix hoped the party would return. But they pressed on and in a blinding blizzard reached the summit at half-past two in the afternoon. All they could do now was descend, following their tracks. But the snow fell thicker, the cold increased and the track had long since vanished. The party halted. For a moment the clouds broke and they saw Chamonix clearly in the grassy meadows. But a violent squall carrying blinding snow struck them. They could not move so they decided to dig a refuge in the snow to wait for the storm to pass. But the storm raged for a week. Rescue was impossible and eventually five climbers were found frozen to death. The other six were never found. A macabre sequel concerns the Revd George McCorkindale. Owing to a wrong identification, the corpse of Mr Randall lies under the Gourock minister's gravestone, and Mr McCorkindale is still entombed in a glacier.

Reginald J.S. Macdonald *(c.1840-1876)*

He made the first ascent of Pelvoux with Whymper in 1861 and of the Jungfrau in 1864.

Revd Julius M. Elliot *(c.1840-1869)*

He was the first to climb the Matterhorn (1868) after the disaster. He was killed (unroped) on the Schreckhorn in 1869.

Francis, Lord Douglas *(1847-1865)*

He was the son of the Marquis of Queensberry and, at eighteen, was the youngest member of a party which set out to conquer the Matterhorn (14,780ft.). It is a beautiful mountain which has fascinated generations, sometimes, as in this instance, to their terrible death.

Douglas was an Alpine enthusiast. In July 1865 he met Edward Whymper, a kindred spirit, a young Englishman who had for years longed to conquer the Matterhorn. They went to Zermatt and met Croz, a famous guide who was escorting two English climbers, the Revd Charles Hudson and Mr Hadow. With two other guides the party of eight set off, on 13 July. All went well. The ascent was surprisingly easy and at 1.40 p.m. on 14 July they stood on the summit, the first conquerors. They were just in time. As they looked over the precipice on the Italian side of the mountain they saw a rival party, led by a Swiss guide, nearing the summit.

Triumphantly Whymper and his party descended. But the ropes were not carefully chosen. At a rock-wall which had troubled them on the ascent, Hadow slipped and dragged Croz, Hudson and Douglas after him, to be hurled instantly over a 4000ft. precipice. The survivors were motionless with horror, but eventually reached Zermatt to tell of the tragedy. A weak rope had broken, but a false rumour accused the survivors of cutting it.

The body of Lord Francis Douglas was never recovered.

Sir Hugh Munro *(1857-1919)*

Although a Scottish baronet, the fourth in line of the estate of Lindertis, Angus, he was born in London and educated in England and Germany for a business career. But he was appointed Private Secretary to the Governor of Natal in 1880, where he fought in the Basuto War as a cavalryman. In later life he was a King's Messenger, carrying despatches.

He managed the estate of Lindertis for an uncle from whom he later inherited it. This gave him plenty of leisure, especially in winter, to indulge in his hobby of mountaineering. He preferred to travel alone even on dangerous ground and he was often in trouble, but his stocky physique and mental resilience brought him home safely when nobody expected to see him return.

He is chiefly remembered for his exploration, with or without parties from the Scottish Mountaineering Club, of that wild land between Glen Lyon and Wester Ross. He tabulated all the notable peaks and recorded the views from them in his voluminous diary. He established his name for ever by having all the peaks in Scotland over 3000ft. named after him, the 'Munros'. This would not have pleased him, however, because he had a strong objection to mountains being named either after or by persons. He preferred the traditional names.

He travelled much abroad, for business or pleasure and, during the First World War, ran a canteen for French troops in Southern France, where he died prematurely of influenza.

Harold Raeburn *(1865-1926)*

He climbed the Matterhorn in 1906 and in the Caucasus in 1913-14. He reached 21,000ft. in Kangchenjunga in 1920.

He took part in the first Everest Expedition of 1921, under the leadership of Lt-Col Howard-Bury. The party also included Mallory who, with Irvine, was fated to die near the summit in 1924.

The object of the expedition of 1921 was to explore the approaches to Everest by the Rongbuk Valley. They established a camp on the North Col and returned with much information useful in future attempts.

Thomas Graham Brown *(1882-1965)*

A native of Edinburgh, where his father later became President of the Royal College of Surgeons, Graham Brown took a Science degree in 1903 before qualifying in medicine three years later. He was assistant to professors in Glasgow and Liverpool, where his chief interest was in neuro-physiology, carrying out several years of research into muscular reflexes.

He served in the RAMC in the Balkans until 1919 when, on being demobbed, he took the Chair of Physiology in Cardiff. His interest now turned to mountaineering, and of course he approached this in a strictly scientific manner, laying his plans most meticulously.

Every year from 1924 to 1940 he spent climbing on the Alps, where he surpassed any other British climber. He climbed with guides who supplied the techniques for carrying out his plans. His greatest achievement was a series of climbs on the Brenva face of Mont Blanc.

He also climbed on Nanda Devi in the Himalaya, though rather old to venture very high. He persisted in climbing, well into his sixties. He edited the *Alpine Journal* for some years and collaborated in the volume *The First Ascent of Mont Blanc*. His last years were spent encouraging and befriending Edinburgh University Mountaineering Club.

Tom Patey *(1932-1970)*

A son of the manse, he was born and educated in Aberdeen. He took his medical degree, winning the Gold Medal in Physiology, and established a practice in the North-West Highlands, centred on Ullapool. He had two prevailing ambitions; to be a good doctor and an unsurpassed mountaineer.

Patey was a man of iron nerve, yet he could relax on occasion and entertain his friends with song and verse. He entertained a much wider audience with his writings in his book *One Man's Mountains* and in his TV appearances, performing the most hair-raising feats on sheer rock-faces. He was the inspirer of a great company of working lads and lasses from Aberdeenshire and thereabouts who took to the Grampians in the early fifties of this century and named themselves the Kincorth Club, building bothies and shelters for their week-end climbs.

From 1957 to 1961, Patey served in the Navy with the Royal Marine Commandos, practising mountain warfare. Near the end of his career of daring he had hopes of performing such feats as scaling the North Face of the Eiger, solo, at night. Doubtless, had he been spared, he would not have flinched, even at that. He died as a result of a climbing accident when abseiling from a sea-stack on the sequestered North Coast.

Dougal Haston *(1940-1981)*

Born in Edinburgh and educated at Edinburgh University, he early acquired a love of the heights and accomplished some amazing feats of daring and skill. At twenty-three he climbed the North Face of the Eiger. He then climbed the Eiger directly in the winter of 1966, being the first to do this. He climbed several Alpine classical summits in bad conditions. Moving to the Himalayas in 1970, he made the first ascent of the South Face of the Annapurna massif in Nepal, a much glaciated range rising to 26,500ft. His next success was Changabanga in 1974, never before climbed. He climbed the South-west face of Everest in 1975, being the first to do so. The following year he moved to Alaska and climbed Mount McKinlay, the highest point in the Rocky range.

By a cruel irony Haston was killed in the Alps not far from his home by an avalanche when enjoying an apparently peaceful ski-ing excursion.

CANOEING

John MacGregor *(1825-1892)*

The pioneer of canoeing as a sport was undoubtedly John MacGregor. His father was an army officer who had fought in the Napoleonic War in charge of Highland infantry. John was born at Gravesend and sailed with his parents a few weeks later on a transport carrying Highlanders of his father's regiment, bound for India. The ship, the *Kent*, went on fire in the Bay of Biscay and it was only by a miracle that the infant John and his parents were saved.

He early became interested in sailing-boats and designed canoes which he sailed in many parts of the world. He described his adventures in books and articles and gave lectures in London and elsewhere to enthusiastic audiences, seated in his canoe and enlivening his talks with various objects brought from his travels. One of his journeys was along the course of the Jordan where he was captured by desert Arabs. His canoe, the *Rob Roy*, is at present on exhibition in Tel Aviv, and the curators are seeking information on his life and descendants.

ROWING

Steve Fairbairn *(1862-1928)*

He was a Scot whose family had emigrated to Australia. In 1881 he matriculated at Cambridge and not long after, as a member of the rowing club, he developed and introduced a revolutionary rowing stroke which superseded the traditional body-swing with shoulders carried well back at the finish of the stroke. Fairbairn emphasised arm-pull, and leg-drive and smooth blade-work. As a member and coach for Cambridge he won all the races for many years in 'Head of the River' competitions. His monument is the one mile mark on the Oxford and Cambridge Boatrace Course between Putney and Hammersmith Bridges.

YACHTING

In Scotland, the thousands of miles of sea-lochs and sounds on the West and North-west coasts offer a unique territory for the yachtsman. The firths on the East Coast are also suitable, if not so full of good harbourages. The Royal Northern Yacht Club was founded in the Clyde in 1824, closely following the institution of the Thames and Solent Clubs. The Royal Eastern Yacht Club was founded at Granton on the Forth in 1836.

J. Scott Russell *(1808-1892)*

He was an experienced yachtsman and designer of hulls. Over several seasons he pointed out the folly of constructing sailing vessels on the 'cod's head and mackerel tail' design. He clearly enunciated his wave-line theory and arranged to have the builder Ware put it into practise. At Blackwall in 1848 an entirely new vessel was built with long hollow bow and full but short after-body. This was the iron cutter *Mosquito*, weighing 50 tons but, though successfully sailed, there was a strong prejudice against it. Russell was the builder of the *Great Eastern*, and a distinguished engineer.

George L. Watson *(fl. 1860-1880)*

He was a yacht designer of Clydeside who in 1881 designed and built a cutter named the *Madge* for the industrialist James Coats of Paisley. The America Cup, the greatest yachting trophy, had been inaugurated in 1857 and was competed for each year by all nations. Until 1983, when it was won by Australia, it was continuously held by the USA. The reason for this pre-eminence was the arrival in New York in 1881 of George Watson's *Madge*. Its design was so successful that it influenced yacht-design in America for many years. The *Madge* won nearly every race against American 'centre-board' yachts. Only when an American designer copied the principles of Watson's hull and built the *Puritan* did the *Madge* own defeat, though the morality of the method is questionable.

Sir Thomas Lipton *(1850-1931)*

He was the world-famous Glasgow wholesaler who by his original methods of 'cornering' the wholesale markets made a fortune with his multiple stores. He spent much of his wealth, year after year, building and racing his famous *Shamrock* yachts, so named because, although born in Glasgow, he was of Irish parentage. The *Shamrocks* (I to V) were never successful though they challenged the Americans from 1899 until three years after Lipton's death.

HORSE-RACING

This has been described as the 'Sport of Kings', but not many race-goers are aware that the popularity of horse-racing in England was initially due to Scottish kings.

James VI and I *(1566-1625)*

On arrival in London to succeed Queen Elizabeth, he continued to enjoy the chief sport of his previous years as King of the Scots. This was hunting. He maintained no less than seven establishments for stag-hunting and preferred this sport to the court and council-chamber.

The rise of the turf in England was due to him. He sponsored meetings at Croydon and Enfield near London and patronised racing at Epsom and Newmarket. Henry VIII had established racing studs in the previous century but it was James who made them notable. The Duke of Buckingham, James' favourite, was in charge of all the royal horses.

Charles I *(1600-1649)*

He had little interest in racing but maintained a large breeding stock at Tutbury where, on his death by execution in 1649 he was found to own a stud of 139 stallions and 37 brood mares.

Charles II *(1630-1685)*

He earned the title 'Father of the British Turf'. He raised Newmarket to its centuries-old prominence. He personally rode for prizes and plates, often winning. He bought horses and mares from abroad. His purchases are still known in their descendants as royal mares, but authorities say that most of these are English and the famous sires are only three in number, of which the earliest was named Byerley Turk because it was ridden at the Battle of the Boyne (1690) by a Captain Byerley.

Queen Anne *(1665-1714)*

She patronised Ascot and continued the Stuart interest in racing and breeding of blood-horses. Subsequent monarchs of Hanoverian origin kept up the traditions but it was the displaced Scottish dynasty who initiated the sport.

Archibald Primrose, 5th Earl of Rosebery *(1847-1929)*

He was perhaps the most influential Scot in racing circles. He is described in our chapter on politicians. An undergraduate at Oxford, he was financially independent as he had succeeded to his grandfather's estates on the death of his father. He owned a small racing stable. When the proctor found this out he requested Rosebery to give it up as it was inconsistent with the strict morality of Oxford. But the young man refused and was sent down. He did not worry. He purchased 'The Durdans' at Epsom, rebuilt it in a splendid style, and adorned it with the finest turf-portraits. He owned a famous stable and on three occasions he realised every horse-owner's dream, winning the Derby in 1894, 1895 and 1905, as well as many classic races.

MOTOR RACING

The motor car is not yet a century old but motor racing is the only true global sport even surpassing football in its universality. Competitors from all countries criss-cross the world to compete in contests which test man's ingenuity and courage to the limit. Unfortunately, like mountaineering, the road to the top is fraught with tragedies but this has not deterred the Scots from attempting and winning the highest awards.

Ron Flockhart *(1924-1962)*

He was a native of Edinburgh. He was an engineering graduate working in Wolverhampton in 1956 when he joined the team of drivers for Ecurie Ecosse's sixth season. David Murray was impressed by Flockhart's knowledge of cars. He was also a first-rate driver who already had a fine reputation for handling pre-war racing cars and testing for the BRM team.

At Rheims, in the twelve-hour race, Flockhart and Sanderson crewed the Ecurie Ecosse car which was content to finish prophetically fourth behind a formidable trio of works Jaguars. This race was a run-up for the big event, Les Vingt-Quatre Heures du Mans. Motoring history was made on 28 July 1956. Flockhart, co-driving with Sanderson, won the race at an average speed of 104.3 m.p.h., no less than 35 starters of 49 dropping out, which proves that, as a testing ground for men and machines Le Mans has no equal. Nobody expected the result, which was a world sensation and sent Scotland into hysteria. Support for Ecurie Ecosse was massive.

For the Le Mans race of 1957 the Scots entered two Jaguars, the first driven by Flockhart and Bueb, the second by Sanderson and Lawrence. The opposition was provided by the cream of the world's drivers, including Fangio, Hawthorn and Moss. The Jaguars, driven by Ecurie Ecosse, took first and second places, Ron Flockhart and Bueb in a new record speed of nearly 114 m.p.h.

Flockhart went on to win several Grand Prix before he was killed in an air accident when trying to break the solo air speed record from Australia to England in 1962.

Jim Clark *(1936-1968)*

He was born in Kilmany, close to Cupar, in Fife, the son of a farmer. He had four older sisters. He learned very early to drive farm machinery. When he was six the family moved to Berwickshire near Duns and took over the large farm of Edington Mains, two square miles in extent. Jim could drive what and where he liked long before he was eligible for a licence. He drove his father's Austin Seven when he was nine by watching his father working the controls.

His education was at Loretto Public School, Musselburgh, but he preferred the open air and left at sixteen to be shepherd at Edington, not before having had his love of driving kindled by reading from cover to cover the school library's three books on motor racing.

His first competition was in a Berwick and District Motor Club driving test at seventeen. From this his career flourished rapidly and he established an extremely successful rapport with Colin Chapman, the builder of Lotus cars, to gain considerable success in Formula Junior, Formula 2 and Formula 1 racing. He became World Champion in 1963 with Chapman's revolutionary Lotus 25 car, having been beaten in the Championship in 1962 by the narrowest of margins by Graham Hill (after mechanical misfortune at the last race).

His relationship with Champman continued fruitfully. In 1965 Clark again won the World Championship and also broke, once and for all, the American stranglehold on the Indianapolis 500, winning this race convincingly (having been contentiously beaten into second place in 1964).

1966, 1967 and the early part of 1968 continued the successful Clark-Chapman liaison to such effect that Clark amassed a total of 25 Grand Prix wins – a total which has subsequently been beaten only by Jackie Stewart, with 27 wins.

Jim Clark was killed in a works Lotus 48 at Hockenheim on 7 April 1968 in a European Formula 2 Championship race of little consequence.

MOTOR-CYCLE RACING

Jimmy Guthrie *(1897-1937)*

Born in Hawick, his first TT appearance was in 1923, riding a Matchless machine in the Junior race from which he retired. He had earlier been conspicuous at Brooklands in speed trials. For the next eight years he had his ups and downs until he began riding the famous Norton machines. He rode these in fourteen TT races from 1931 to 1937, never being slower than fifth place. He won the TT on the Isle of Man circuit six times, his riding being exceptionally daring and brilliant. Five of these wins were on Nortons and one on an AJS. He had the unusual experience of being declared winner of the 1935 Senior TT then to be told that, owing to a miscalculation, he had been beaten by four seconds.

Guthrie also captured several World Records. These included the One Hour Record on the Montlhery track near Paris in 1935. His speed was over 114 m.p.h. He rode on several continental circuits so very successfully that in 1937 he was Junior and Senior European Champion.

He was killed at the height of his glory, leading the German Grand Prix on the very last corner, about to triumph in that event for the third successive time.

Robert McG. McIntyre *(1928-1962)*

Born in Glasgow and known everywhere as Bob Mac, he learned to drive on a 1931 Norton costing £12. At first he took part in scrambles. His first road race was at Kirkcaldy. In 1954 he entered the Senior Manx Grand Prix for the first time and was second on a Junior machine. In that year he was a works rider for AJS before becoming Gilera team leader in 1957. In that year at Monza he created a new world record of 151 m.p.h. which was not beaten for seven years and then only fractionally.

His successes were in the Senior and Junior TT races of 1957 and in the same events in 1959. He was never to win a World Championship. The first World Championship which eluded Bob Mac was won in 1980 by Jock Taylor. This was the World Sidecar Championship clinched at Silverstone in August of that year. This would have been his at Monza in the 500 c.c. class but he was ill and could not compete. However he was the first TT rider to lap the Isle of Man course at over 100 m.p.h. This was in June 1937 when he won the Senior TT at an average speed of just on 99 m.p.h.

Despite his reputation as a canny Scot, never taking unnecessary risks he was killed like Guthrie at the peak of his career, trying out an experimental Norton in August 1962.

BOXING

The great names of the pugilists of the eighteenth and nineteenth century were Englishmen, Broughton, Cribb, Mendoza, Belcher, and Pearce (the Game Chicken). The fighting was rough, there were no gloves and many 'bruisers' died as a result of a slogging-match. Although no Scots competed, it was a famous Aberdeenshire man who introduced the first training regime for pugilism. He was Captain Robert Barclay-Allardice, already noted as a pedestrian. Seeing the poor condition of many of the fancied boxers, he asked Tom Cribb if he would undergo a period of preparation for the Championship. Cribb accompanied Barclay to his estates at Urie, Aberdeenshire, and was ordered a strict regime. Barclay took him on increasingly long walks over rough country, cut out certain watery vegetables and poorer quality meats, condemned spirits and water-drinking as well as sexual intercourse. After a few months he reduced Cribb's sixteen stone to twelve stone and had little hesitation about wagering large sums on his protégé who became champion, knocking out the loose-living bruisers who knew no discipline. Barclay himself was an accomplished fisticuffs athlete.

Although Broughton used gloves in practice, bare fists and dirty tactics characterised the game for a long time, though Barclay's regime was largely recommended during his lifetime.

Sholto Douglas, Marquis of Queensberry *(1844-1908)*

In 1866 another Scottish landowner, Sholto Douglas, 8th Marquis of Queensberry, in alliance with Mr Chambers (1843-1883), an amateur of the noble art, formulated the Queensberry Rules, and the old prize ring, beloved of the Regency bucks, became illegal.

James (Tancy) Lee *(1882-1941)*

A native of Leith, a clever fighter with a right swing, Lee was first an amateur who trained with Charles Cotter's renowned establishment in Leith Street. He won the Scottish and British Bantamweight (not over 8st. 6lb.) Championships in 1910, as an amateur.

Turning professional, his great feat, in London on 25 January 1915, was beating Jimmy Wilder (the referee stopping the fight in the 17th round) for the British Flyweight Championship. He lost the title to Symonds nine months later.

In 1917 he knocked out Hardcastle in Round 4 to become British Featherweight Champion for two years. At the same weight he won the Lonsdale Belt outright by defeating Joe Conn and Danny Morgan. Lee relinquished the Featherweight title in 1919. He died in a bus accident in Leith in 1941.

Benny Lynch *(1913-1946)*

He was born in Glasgow in a time of industrial depression. He started his career by taking part in contests in fair-grounds for a few shillings a time. He was noted for his very spare figure and remarkable stamina, combined with the clear-headed stratagems which brought him points from the judges. He eventually was able to qualify for the World Title fight as a Featherweight (under nine stone) against Jackie Brown in Manchester in 1935. It was a long hard contest, but it finished when the referee stopped the fight near the end of the match. Lynch's career ended tragically. He drifted about in all sorts of bad company and was found dead of debilitation at an early age.

Jacky Paterson *(1920-1966)*

He was an Ayrshire man, known in boxing circles for having administered the quickest KO in the history of the ring, disposing of an opponent with a punch eight seconds from the start of a championship match. In 1943 in Glasgow he was matched against Peter Kane of England in the Fly-weight Championship of the World (under eight stone). He came up to form and administered a KO to Kane sixty-one seconds from the start. He retired from the ring in 1951 and emigrated to South Africa. Like Lynch, he came to a very miserable end. He was murdered in a bottle-fight in a bar in Johannesburg in 1966.

SWIMMING

William Edward Barnie *(1896-1983)*

He was born at Portobello, near Edinburgh, on the shore of the Firth of Forth. From an early age he gained many distinctions in swimming. In 1909 he won the Stevenson Medal, open to schoolboys. In 1912, in the 100yds. Sprint, he was East of Scotland Junior Champion, then Senior Champion in 1913. At that time a newspaper prophesied that he would never be more than a sprinter.

In the 1914-18 War he won the Military Medal, but could never be persuaded to reveal how. He now studied at Edinburgh University and gained an Honours B.Sc.

Despite prophecies he became East of Scotland Champion in 1921 for the 440yds., in 1922 for the 220 and 440yds., and in 1923 for the 220yds., 440yds. and 880yds. He swam the Forth from Burntisland to Granton in 4hrs. 10min. in 1924, and also established a new Scottish half-mile record, retaining it in 1925.

His career seemed ended in 1926 when, severely blood-poisoned, he was told he would never swim again; but he recovered and won several salt water long distance events, culminating in a double crossing of the Forth in 1935.

His greatest triumphs were yet to come. In 1950, at the age of fifty-four, he swam from France to England in 14¾hrs. being the only Scot and the oldest man to accomplish this feat. In 1951 he crossed the Channel in both directions within about a fortnight.

He was still making regular swims in the sea all the year round until well into his seventies.

Benefaction

As a final rejoinder to the common accusation that Scots are mean, we would like to mention that many of the greatest financial benefactors have been Scots. This is only one aspect of Scottish generosity which, as the many examples in this book show, is concerned with benevolence of word and deed in every field of human life. We give here only a few representative figures to refute this libel.

Devorguila *(d.1290)*

She was the daughter of Alan of Galloway and she married John Baliol, the father of King John Baliol, the puppet King of Scotland. Baliol was one of the wealthiest men in Britain. In 1268 he gave lands for the endowment of the college of Oxford, with large funds to maintain it. On his death in 1269 Devorguila continued the generosity and in her will she substantially increased the endowment. Balliol College commemorates these benefactors.

William Elphinstone *(1431-1514)*

Born at Glasgow and educated to be a teacher, he took his MA in 1452 and became rector of St Michael's, Trongate. He studied law at Paris and Orleans.

At intervals in his distinguished career he set about, at his own and the royal expense, the establishment of the University of Aberdeen and other public works. He introduced printing into Scotland in 1507.

Robert Reid, Bishop of Orkney *(d.1558)*

Son of John Reid, killed at Flodden, he was educated at St Andrews and Paris. He was a historian and was made Abbot of Greyfriars, Edinburgh, in 1528. He acted in many political missions and it was on one of these, to the court of France to arrange the marriage of the princess Mary to the Dauphin, that he died.

His benefactions consist of the erection in Kirkwall, Orkney, of a college, and the bequest of a large sum for a similar college in Edinburgh.

George Heriot *(1563-1624)*

He was born in Edinburgh, son of a goldsmith, a trade which George followed. In 1597 James VI appointed him goldsmith for life to Queen Anne his consort, through which he made £50,000 sterling. When James became King of Great Britain in 1603, Heriot lived in London as His Majesty's Jeweller.

In his will, having no legitimate heirs, he left his vast fortune 'to educate the children of decayed (impoverished) burgesses of Edinburgh'.

Heriot's Hospital, a marvellous building, was opened in 1659 and still flourishes. Heriot's beneficiaries also included many schools built for city children.

George Hutcheson *(1580-1639)*
Thomas Hutcheson *(1589-1641)*

George was a lawyer in Glasgow, his native town. He added much to the wealth inherited from his father, and lived for long in the Trongate. In 1611 he built the house on the Kelvin, known as the Bishop's Castle. By strict honesty he gained a high reputation as well as wealth, and on his death, unmarried, he left all his property to the founding of a hospital for 'poor, aged, decrepit men of honest life'. Thomas left funds for the same purpose, the upkeep of Hutcheson's Hospital, and in addition for the provision of education for sons of burgesses of Glasgow, which developed into the famous school.

George Drummond *(1687-1766)*

A native of Edinburgh, of which he was six times Provost, he was an apt mathematician and also deeply religious. He was chiefly responsible for setting up the Faculty of Medicine and, following this, he established the Royal Infirmary in 1736, being known as 'The Father of the Infirmary', to whom Scotland was indebted forever for all its benefits. His bust stands in the present Royal Infirmary of Edinburgh.

William Hunter *(1718-1783)*

He was the older brother of the equally famous John Hunter, both being noted in our chapter on Medicine. John left his vast collection of specimens to the Royal College of Surgeons in London, but William, who had fallen out with his brother, left his museum entirely to the University of Glasgow, near his native place of East Kilbride. It now forms the Hunterian Museum.

James Gillespie *(1726-1797)*

He was born at Roslin, by religion a Cameronian, a stern Covenanting sept. With his brother John he set up a tobacconist's business in Edinburgh and bought a snuff-mill at Colinton, near Edinburgh. He gradually bought all the estates near the mill.

He left all his wealth to found a school, and a hospital for poor old men and women. His bust is in the Merchant Company's Hall, Edinburgh.

John Anderson *(1726-1796)*

Born at Roseneath, Dunbartonshire, son of the local minister, he studied at Glasgow and became Professor of Oriental Languages and later of Natural Philosophy. He allowed workmen to attend his lectures in their working clothes. He sympathised with the French revolutionaries and also invented a recoiling cannon, which, on its refusal by the British, he offered to the French. This made him unpopular, but he published several erudite works and left all his apparatus, library and money to form the Andersonian Institute in Glasgow, which for long continued to give free lectures to working men.

James McGill *(c.1740-1813)*

A fur trader who emigrated to Canada after Culloden, he became wealthy and left his money to found the McGill College in Ontario. In 1821, it was given a royal charter and became a University, which today has extensive institutions in all faculties.

James Donaldson *(1751-1830)*

Son of an Edinburgh bookseller, he inherited £100,000 from his father and doubled it by wise investment. He published the *Edinburgh Advertiser*. He was very benevolent and gave money every week to many beggars. He left about £220,000 for the maintenance of three hundred poor children, to the annoyance of his relatives who went to law to prove his insanity. W.H. Playfair was the architect of the magnificent hospital in Elizabethan style built for the poor foundationers, one wing of which was devoted to deaf and dumb children.

Thomas Guthrie *(1803-1873)*

Born at Brechin, descended from farming ancestors, but son of a banker, he was educated at Edinburgh University in Arts, Philosophy and Mathematics, and Theology. He also studied in Paris. He was a fine preacher and started savings banks, libraries and Sunday School in his Forfarshire parish.

His great benefaction was in founding the Scottish Ragged Schools in 1847 for street waifs, where his teachers washed, clothed, fed and taught boys and girls. His initiative started hundreds of Ragged Schools throughout British cities.

Andrew Carnegie *(1835-1919)*

Born in Dunfermline, he emigrated with his family to Alleghany City, Pennsylvania in 1848. He worked in a cotton factory, then as a telegraph clerk, becoming a superintendent in 1859. By judicious buying he controlled a steel plant, coalfields, a long railroad and a line of lake steamers. He became immensely rich, but he enunciated this creed in 1900, 'a man who dies rich is disgraced'. He now began to distribute his millions by providing public libraries in Britain and the USA. He set up educational trusts, made gifts of all kinds to his native land and in Europe founded the Carnegie Peace Fund in 1910. He received the freedom of over fifty British cities.

Sir William Alexander Smith *(1854-1914)*

Born in Thurso, Caithness, and educated at Thurso Academy, he joined the Lanarkshire Volunteers in 1874, rising to Colonel in 1908. On the basis of his volunteer experience, he founded the Boys' Brigade in 1883. He visited the Boys' Brigade in Canada in 1895, and in the USA in 1907. He commanded a parade of 10,000 Boys' Brigade members in Glasgow on the semi-Jubilee in 1908 before the Duke of Connaught. His benefactions to countless boys still continue after a century.

Sir William Burrell *(1861-1958)*

He was born in Glasgow and entered his father's shipping firm at the age of fifteen, as a clerk with a clerk's wages. In 1885, on their father's death, William and his brother George took over the firm, William managing the commercial and financial affairs. An astute business man, William was soon elected as councillor and housing convenor in Glasgow. Robert Lorimer, the architect, was one of his closest friends, as also was Alexander Reid, a connoisseur of painting. With such expert friends Burrell never hesitated to buy up masterpieces and collector's items. He spent between £20,000 and £80,000 per annum in this way. Perhaps the most valuable item was the eight ton Warwick Vase, so valuable that Napoleon said he would have invaded Britain for the sole purpose of getting it.

Burrell gifted £450,000 to Glasgow to build a suitable home for his collection, but it was not until many years after his death at ninety-six, that the enormous collection was mounted in the new museum at Pollock Park. By this magnificent gift Burrell became not only Glasgow's but one of Scotland's greatest benefactors.

Index

323

Elphinstone, John, 2nd Lord Balmerino, politician, 162
Elphinstone, Mount Stuart, politician, 173
Elphinstone, William, churchman, politician, benefactor, 62, 158, 318
Erigena, John Scotus, philosopher, 46
Erskine, Henry, lawyer, 196
Erskine, John of Carnock, lawyer, 193
Erskine, Thomas, lawyer, 196
Ewing, George E., sculptor, 293

Fairbairn, Steve, oarsman, 311
Fairbairn, Sir William, inventor, 149
Falconer, Hugh, botanist, 131
Ferguson, Bob, golfer, 300
Ferguson, James, astronomer, 110
Fergusson, Adam, philosopher, 52
Fergusson, Robert, poet, 225
Fergusson, Sir William, doctor, 93
Ferrier, Susan, writer, 244
Fillans, James, sculptor, 291
Finlay brothers, rugby players, 303
Finlayson, James, actor, 294
Fleming, Sir Alexander, doctor, 96
Fleming, Revd John, geologist, 116
Fletcher, Andrew, politician, 163
Flockhart, Ron, motor racer, 313
Forbes, Duncan, politician, 166
Forbes, Edward, oceanographer, 122
Forbes, James D., geologist, mountaineer, 118, 307
Forbes-Mackay, Alastair, explorer, 105
Fordun, John, scholar, 202
Forsyth, Revd Alexander, inventor, 146
Forsyth, Andrew R., mathematician, 60
Fortune, Robert, botanist, 131
Fraser, James B., explorer, 103
Fraser, Simon, Lord Lovat, politician, 164

Gairdner, James, scholar, 214
Gallacher, Hugh, footballer, 302
Gallacher, Patsy, footballer, 302
Galt, John, writer, 244
Garden, Mary, singer, 268
Gardener, Alexander, photographer, 280
Ged, William, inventor, 140
Geddes, Sir Auckland, politician, 184
Geddes, Sir Eric, politician, 183
Geddes, Sir Patrick, zoologist, 134
Geikie, Archibald, geologist, 119
Geikie, James, geologist, 119
Gibbs, James, architect, 284
Gillespie, James, benefactor, 319
Gillespie, J. Hamilton, golfer, 301
Gillies, Sir William G., artist, 278
Gladstone, William E., politician, 175
Glas, John, churchman, 69
Goodsir, H.D.S., zoologist, 133
Goodsir, John, doctor, 94
Gordon, Alexander, scholar, 206
Gordon, George, Lord Byron, poet, 229
Gordon, Sir John W., artist, 275
Gordon, Patrick, warrior, 25
Gordon, Seton, zoologist, 136
Gow, Nathaniel, musician, 259

Gow, Neil, musician, 259
Gowans, Sir James, architect, 288
Graham, James, Marquis of Montrose, warrior, 23
Graham, Sir John de, warrior, 14
Graham, John of Claverhouse, Viscount Dundee, warrior, 27
Graham, Robert, botanist, 128
Graham, Thomas, inventor, 150
Grahame, James, poet, 229
Grahame, Kenneth, writer, 251
Grant, James A. explorer, 101
Grant, Mary, sculptor, 293
Grant, Robert, astronomer, 111
Gray, Sir Alexander, poet, 233
Gregory, James, astronomer, inventor, 110, 140
Gregory, James, doctor, 87
Gregory, John, doctor, 87
Gregory, William, doctor, 88
Greig, Sir Samuel, warrior, 35
Grierson, John, film-maker, 282
Grierson of Lag, persecutor, 27
Grieve, Christopher M., (Hugh MacDiarmid), poet, 233
Gunn, Neil, writer, 255
Guthrie, Jimmy, motor-cycle racer, 314
Guthrie, Thomas, benefactor, 320

Haig, Sir Douglas, Earl, warrior, 43
Hal o' the Wynd, warrior, 19
Haldane, John S., philosopher, 55
Haldane, Richard B., Viscount, philosopher, 54
Hall, Basil, explorer, 103
Hall, Sir James, geologist, 113
Halswelle, Wyndham, athlete, 305
Hamilton, Sir Ian S.M., warrior, 43
Hamilton, John, Lord Belhaven, politician, 163
Hamilton, Patrick, churchman, 63
Hamilton, Sir William, scholar, 208
Hamilton, Sir William, philosopher, 53
Hardie, James Keir, politician, 182
Haston, Dougal, mountaineer, 310
Hay, George Campbell, poet, 235
Hay, J. MacDougal, writer, 254
Hector, Sir James, explorer, 106
Henderson, Thomas, astronomer, 111
Henry the Minstrel, poet, 220
Henryson, Robert, poet, 220
Hepburn, Sir John, warrior, 22
Heriot, George, benefactor, 318
Hill, Amelia, sculptor, 291
Hill, David O., photographer, 279
Hislop, Joseph, singer, 268
Hogarth, George, musician, 260
Hogg, James, poet, 227
Home, Henry, Lord Kames, lawyer, 193
Home, Revd John, writer, 71
Hope, Sir John, botanist, 127
Hume, David, philosopher, scholar, 49, 207
Hume, Joseph, politician, 172
Hunter, John, doctor, 86

325

327